Dressed to Rule

Dressed to Rule

Royal and Court Costume from Louis XIV to Elizabeth II

Philip Mansel (signature)

Philip Mansel

Yale University Press
New Haven and London

For information about this and other Yale University Press
publications, please contact:
U.S. Office: sales.press@yale.edu   yalebooks.com
Europe Office: sales@yaleup.co.uk   www.yalebooks.co.uk

Set in Minion by MATS, Southend-on-Sea, Essex
Printed in Great Britain by T. J. International

Library of Congress Cataloging-in-Publication Data

Mansel, Philip, 1951–
    Dressed to rule: royal and court costume from Louis XIV to Elizabeth II/
Philip Mansel.
        p.   cm.
    Includes bibliographical references and index.
    ISBN 0–300–10697–1 (cl.: alk. paper)
    1. Courts and courtiers—Clothing. 2.   Courts and courtiers—Europe—
Clothing. 3.   Great Britain—Courts and courtiers—Clothing. 4. France—
Courts and coutiers—Clothing. I.   Title.

GT1754.M36 2005
391'.0094—dc22

                                                                2004029806

A catalogue record for this book is available from the British Library

10 9 8 7 6 5 4 3 2 1

whatever we might do to conciliate opinion . . . is nothing beside the effect that the lapel of an uniform will produce . . . you win the French people with ribbons, with remarks, with smiles.

Barnave to Marie Antoinette, December 1791[1]

Clothes called to clothes, cutting out words and greetings.

Richard Cobb, on the evening train from
London to Tunbridge Wells, *c.* 1930[2]

Contents

Illustrations

Acknowledgements

The author would like to thank all those who have helped with this book. In particular: Aouni Abdul Rahim, Anwar al-Ali, Christopher Allan of Ede and Ravenscroft, Kambiz Atabay, Sabine Baels, Tom Barczay, Mark Blackett-Ord, Lesley Blanch, Michael Bloch, James Buchan, Miguel Carriedo, Edward Chaney, Elizabeth Crofton, Simon Cundey of Henry Poole, Nilufer Dobra, Jaroslaw Dumanowski, Ossama el-Kaoukgi, Sue el-Kaoukgi, Fayza el-Khazen, Suraiya Faroqhi, Caroline Finkel, Roy Foster, C. Foster-Hickling of Meyer and Mortimer, Flora Fraser, Robert Frost, Carne Griffiths of Hand and Lock, Yahya Hakim, Russell Harris, Nancy Hatch Dupree, Bruce Ingham, Amin Jaafer, Brigid Keenan, Laurence Kelly, Linda Kelly, Martin Kohlrausch, Ziad Ali Labban, Robert Lacey, Thomas Luettenberg, Shireen Mahdavi, Nur Majdalany, Joanna Marschner, Giles McDonogh, Jane Mulvagh, Fouad Nahas, Paulo Nello, André Nieuwazsny, Antoine de Noailles, Celestria Noel, Curt Noel, Jacques Perot, Lena Rangström, Samir Rebes, Nick Robinson, John G. Röhl, Kenneth Rose, Sir Malcolm Ross, Alan de Lacy Rush, Samia Saab, Saleh al-Said, Ian Scott, Bassam al-Suri, Adam Thorpe, Mathieu da Vinha, Michael Voggenauer, Lord Weatherill, Mme Zeyneb Younes, Adam Zamoyski. Thanks to all at Yale University Press, particularly to Emily Lees for her help with the illustrations; and to the staffs of the Bibliothèque Nationale, the British Library and the London Library. Special thanks to Didier Girard who chose the title.

Introduction: The Power of Clothes

From Paris to Peking, monarchs' preoccupation with dress and appearances is one of the common threads linking them across time and space. Monarchy was a system relying on emotions and senses, as well as political and military might: the right dress was, for many monarchs, indispensable to the functioning of their monarchy. In 1870, when the Emperor of Japan was beginning to impose western dress on his subjects, his doctor urged him to let the ladies of his court retain kimonos: they were healthier than the corseted garments which tortured western women. The Emperor replied: 'Doctor, about matters of health you may know a great deal. About politics you know nothing.'[1]

Dressed to Rule is an enquiry into the reasons why monarchs have imposed rules of dress, and the political, economic and social effects of those rules. Dress was a political instrument. It was believed to transform behaviour. Since it was both personal and visible, more than any other material artefacts, it touched a nerve. As Balzac wrote: 'Dress is therefore the most immense modification experienced by man in society, it weighs on his entire existence . . . it dominates opinions, it determines them, it reigns!'[2] In fairy stories like 'Cinderella', dress was a central metaphor for transformation from poor to rich and back again.[3] Dress also transformed the status of real princesses. Before their formal introduction to court society, daughters of George III could go to court functions provided they did not wear lappets (a form of veil, obligatory for women who had been presented at court). The absence of one small element in court dress was enough to make them, in theory, invisible.[4] Before 1914 servants at Welbeck Abbey, principal residence of the Duke of Portland, felt transformed into new people, with 'a new kind of individuality', when, once a year, they were allowed to hold a party and wear ball dress like their masters.[5]

This belief in the transforming power of dress, shared by many contemporaries,[6] is a key to the royal insistence on dress rules, from Louis XIV to Elizabeth II. The right dress – court dress, national dress, military or civil uniform, or something simpler – was believed to encourage loyalty, satisfy vanity, impress the outside world, and help local industries. To rulers and ruled alike it gave status reassurance – or its opposite.[7] Charles James Fox, for example, considered that 'the neglect of dress in people of fashion' had 'contributed much to remove the barriers between them and the vulgar and to propagate levelling and equalising notions'.[8] Radicals such as Peter the Great, the Ottoman Sultan Mahmud II and Reza Shah of Iran regarded dress as an essential element in their programme of modernisation. Dress reform both signalled the ruler's determination to change, and transformed his subjects, at least in outward appearance, into equals of citizens of stronger states.

Whether dress was an effective instrument of transformation is impossible to prove, since it is impossible to prove that dress was a stronger factor motivating private or public behaviour than emotions such as fear, greed, hate or love. Yet no society has modernised itself successfully without a dress revolution. The dictators of the twentieth century, Stalin, Hitler and Mao, valued dress as a political instrument even more than the monarchs of previous centuries. Military uniform would not have been adopted by armies between 1650 and 1750 if it had not been known to transform behaviour.

The importance of dress is shown by the fact that, at times, it inspired greater respect than the regime which created it. Worn and respected in all monarchies of the nineteenth century, military uniform had been particularly idolised in the German Empire – the only monarchy in which civilian chief ministers wore military uniform. In November 1918, in the trauma of defeat, Hindenburg and other German generals encouraged the Kaiser to abdicate and depart into exile: the monarchy had become an embarrassment. A month later a proposal by a congress of soldiers' councils that officers abandon their uniforms and rank insignia drove Hindenburg apoplectic with rage: 'What do these people dare to ask? That I should tear off my insignia I have worn since my youth? . . . Tell Herr Ebert that I do not recognise the decisions of the Congress . . . I will fight it to the last ditch.'[9] A change in regime was accepted. A change in uniform was not.

Dress was not only a political instrument but a personal signal. Queen Victoria reflected the views of other monarchs when she wrote in 1858 to the Prince of Wales: 'Dress is a trifling matter . . . But it gives also the one outward sign from which people in general can and often do judge upon the *inward* state of mind and feeling of a person; for this they all see, while the other they cannot see. On that account it is of some importance particularly in persons of high rank.'[10] Palaces, pictures or jewels might reflect the choices of a monarch's predecessors, advisers or artists. Clothes signalled the preferences and policies of the monarchs themselves. No one was more convinced of the importance of dress than the future Edward VII. However restricted his authority in other spheres, over matters of dress he tried to exercise autocratic powers.

The importance of dress as a signal is shown by the fact that many observers of court life described coats, dresses or embroidery at greater length than people or palaces – as quotations in this book will show.[11] Dress, for example, dominated Pepys's impressions of Charles II's procession from the Tower on 22 April 1661, his coronation day: 'it is impossible to relate the glory of that this day – expressed in the clothes of them that rid – and their horses and horse cloths. Among others, my Lord Sandwich. Imbroidery and diamonds were common among them . . . The King, in a most rich imbrodered suit and cloak, looked most nobly.'[12] On 6 February 1713 such an independent observer as Swift wrote: 'This is the Queen's birth-day and I never saw it celebrated with so much luxury and fine clothes. I went to court to see them and I dined with Lord-Keeper where the ladies were fine to admiration.' He did not write about the architecture, the decoration or the individuals attending court.[13]

Dress also signalled the nature of court society. Courts were not isolated systems. They were at the heart of national life, serving the needs of monarchs' subjects as much as those of monarchs themselves. Constantly demanding rich and fashionable new clothes, Versailles was an insatiable system of conspicuous consumption, on which thousands of livelihoods depended, like the annual fashion shows in Paris and Milan today. Under Queen Anne, despite the unsurpassed commercial wealth of London, court entertainments, requiring new court costumes for several hundred people, were described, by London weavers, mercers and silk merchants petitioning for more of them, as 'certainly the greatest support to ours and almost all other trades'.[14] During periods of court mourning, the dress of entire nations followed the example of the court. In 1695, two years' general mourning for Mary II in England, Scotland and Ireland, according to John Evelyn, put 'all people in Mourning'.[15]

Dressed to Rule starts in the year 1660, since it marked the beginning of an age of particular magnificence in court dress, announced by the ceremonial entries into their capitals of two young kings: the recently restored Charles II into London on 29 May, the newly married Louis XIV into Paris on 26 August. The courts studied are the principal courts of Europe: Paris/Versailles,

London, Madrid, Vienna, Berlin, Stockholm, St Petersburg, Constantinople, and the courts they influenced.

In 1660 splendid dress was considered so important that, with name, wealth and manners, it helped define the boundaries of court society. Court dress alone – helped by a shilling pressed into a gentleman usher's hand – could transform its wearers into 'courtiers for a day' and admit them to receptions in the state apartments of St James's Palace.[16] Thus on 1 August 1715, anniversary of the accession of George I, a future Lord Chief Justice Dudley Ryder wrote: 'I came home, dressed myself in best clothes and lace ruffles and went to St James's at 9 o'clock . . . When came to Court got an easy passage through the bar by following another that went before me. The Drawing Room was full of company dressed very fine, scarce any without gold or silver trimmings to their clothes.'[17] If courtiers did not consider their clothes 'fine enough', they did not go to court.[18] Not to wear expensive and fashionable clothes would be demeaning for the courtier, insulting for the monarch.[19]

By household ordinances only 'Persons of good Fashion and good Appearance that have a desire to see Us' had been admitted to see Charles II dine in public.[20] In 1716 it was an act of exceptional condescension, conceivable only in the circumstances of a new dynasty's need to win popularity, when people 'of the lowest sort and rank in their common habits' were admitted to watch the new Prince and Princess of Wales dine in public.[21]

Before 1789 court dress and a sword were also enough to admit their wearers to the state apartments of Versailles. In May 1770 the duc de Croÿ described the wedding procession of the future Louis XVI and Marie Antoinette through the state apartments of Versailles, watched by 'all the men and women of the Court, or who called themselves so, by favour of the fine clothes they had had made in order to push their way in'.[22] In 1793 at St Petersburg, a visitor found: 'On admet à la cour . . . tout homme bien mis et ayant l'épée au côté.'[23]

Splendour was the basis of court dress. Monarchs considered lace, velvet, silk and embroidery to be as necessary and agreeable at court as noble names and large, lavishly decorated palaces. They often complimented courtiers on the beauty of their clothes.[24] Yet, contrary to a widely held opinion,[25] out of personal taste, reverse ostentation or policy, some monarchs, especially those with unusual self-confidence, preferred sobriety to splendour. This preference had an illustrious pedigree. In the Roman Senate the Emperor Augustus, in keeping with his pretence of republicanism, boasted that his togas were made not of silk or linen, like the senators', but of simple cloth woven by his own wife. Modesty in dress also had the blessing of religion. In the Sermon on the

Mount, familiar to all Europe, Jesus Christ himself denounced splendour in dress: 'why take ye thought for raiment? Consider the lilies of the field, how they grow; they toil not, neither do they spin: and yet I say unto you, that even Solomon in all his glory was not arrayed like one of these.'[26]

Six centuries later the Prophet Muhammad also condemned splendid dress. Men and women should dress with simplicity and modesty. White, which he himself generally wore, he called the 'cleanest and most agreeable' colour for Muslims. He forbade men to wear silk or any gold or silver ornaments other than a silver signet ring. Among his Hadith is the remark 'Whoever wears a silken garment in this world will not wear it in the next.'[27]

One of the most powerful monarchs of the fifteenth century, Louis XI of France, had been famous for dressing *si mal que pis ne povait,* in the words of the first great French memoir-writer, Philippe de Commynes.[28] In *The Book of the Courtier* (1528), one of the bibles of the Renaissance, Baldassare Castiglione, who believed that clothes revealed their wearer's inner qualities, considered that a courtier should rather be grave than garish: 'black is more suitable for garments than any other colour; and if it is not black let it at least be somewhat dark'.[29] Raphael's portrait of Castiglione himself, now in the Louvre, and many other pictures, such as the portraits in the National Maritime Museum of the Spanish and English negotiators of the Treaty of London in 1604, and in the National Gallery of the ratification of the Treaty of Münster in 1648, confirm that many statesmen and courtiers preferred black. Black was an expensive and striking dye, often associated with power and wealth. Yet its choice also indicates a preference for sobriety. The battle for the courts of Europe, between splendour and sobriety, is one of the themes of this book.

1 *Splendour*

On 9 June 1660, at Saint-Jean-de-Luz on the Franco-Spanish frontier, Louis XIV married the Infanta Maria Teresa, daughter of Philip IV of Spain. After twenty-four years of war from 1635 to 1659, the marriage was designed to strengthen the peace recently signed between the two kings. As observers noted, it was a meeting of rival styles as well as rival monarchs. As a sign of mourning, since the assassination of Jean sans Peur, Duke of Burgundy, in 1419, the Dukes of Burgundy and their heirs the Kings of Spain had favoured black clothes.[1] Old and broken, Philip IV wore a sober grey coat embroidered with silver: his courtiers wore black, without jewels, as most had done since the introduction of a law in 1623 to protect the Spanish dress trade from foreign, especially French, competition.[2]

In contrast, young and handsome, Louis XIV, like his courtiers, wore a many-coloured coat of silk and satin, glittering with gold embroidery. There was a fashion for ribbons in France: the French wore them on hats, sleeves, petticoat breeches, canes, swords and high-heeled shoes.[3] On one side simplicity, economy. On the other splendour, expense.[4] On 26 August 1660, at Louis XIV's entry into Paris with his new Queen, surrounded by the household troops known as the Maison militaire, dress renewed the message of royal splendour, helping to raise the King and his court, in some eyes, far above the rest of humanity. According to Madame de Motteville, one of his mother's *femmes de chambre*, he looked 'like the men whom the poets represent to us as transformed into gods. His coat was embroidered with gold and silver, as fine as it should be, given the dignity of the person wearing it . . . the grandeur which he showed in his person made him admired by all.'[5] Such dress appeared all the more startling since most Parisians wore clothes that were shabby, torn and dirty.[6]

Contemporaries agree that his 'grand and majestic air', his height and his *prestance* made Louis XIV look 'every inch' a king.[7] Louis XIV also enjoyed the prestige of royal blood, ritual coronation, a deferential court, palaces, guards, wealth and victory. However, more than most kings', his dress reflected a craving for splendour. In France more than in most countries, perhaps because royal authority had been so frequently attacked during the Wars of Religion and the Fronde, dress was a political issue. It was a common belief that, as Nicolas Delamare wrote, 'splendour is necesary to maintain the rank of birth, to teach respect to the Peoples and to uphold commerce and the Arts.' Luxury in dress was by definition both virtuous and beneficial, since it encouraged the circulation of wealth.[8]

Louis XIV can be seen, unmistakable in blue and red, in pictures of his military triumphs in the north and east of France by Van der Meulen.[9] At a review of the Gardes français, Gardes suisses and Maison militaire on 6 April 1665, the King in a flame-coloured hat wore a coat and waistcoat so lavishly covered in embroidery that it hid the material beneath. There were diamonds even on the gold buckles which fastened Louis XIV's enamelled violet spurs.[10] At a court where men's and women's clothes, particularly at weddings, were smothered in jewels, the King's brother Monsieur, duc d'Orléans, with his *yeux de lynx,* was unsurpassed in the art of arranging jewellery, both on men and women: he went into battle dressed as for a ball, beribboned, made-up, and in such high-heeled shoes that it seemed impossible that he could remain upright.[11]

The King's love of finery was imposed on his courtiers, male and female alike. In Louis XIV's presence at Versailles and Fontainebleau, men had to wear the elaborate silk or velvet coat known as the *habit habillé* which was often covered in jewellery and embroidery. In the presence of the King and Madame, women wore the even more elaborate *grand habit de cour,* a bare-shouldered embroidered dress with boned bodice, puffed sleeves, a heavily trimmed skirt worn over a hoop, and a long train. The train's length depended on the wearer's rank, and it needed considerable practice to manage.[12] The hoop, bodice and stays helped give that erect posture particularly prized at court.[13] At Fontainebleau in 1704 the King was angered when ladies neglected to wear the *grand habit* to the theatre. 'A few words he said on the matter,' according to the duc de Saint-Simon, 'and the account he demanded of the execution of his orders, ensured that all the ladies of the court were very assiduous in their attendance.'[14] The *grand habit* asserted femininity as well as wealth and status: it had to be worn bare-shouldered, showing a lady's naked flesh, whatever the weather. Dress advertised the court's role as the one public arena where men and women of the nobility mingled freely.[15]

The King used dress, like architecture, to send out a signal of his court's wealth and splendour. A court costume was a group 'installation' to which cloth and silk merchants, weavers, tailors, cutters, hosiers, embroiderers, lace-makers, ribbon-makers, featherers, jewellers, manufacturers and decorators of buttons and shoe buckles, shoe-makers, glove-makers, wig-makers and many other tradesmen, contributed many days' work (in the case of a woman's court dress the tailor made the bodice and the train, the *couturière* the petticoat and the *marchand de modes* the ornaments and trimmings).[16] Court dress was far more expensive than ordinary clothes: in 1700 most nobles in Paris invested no more than 3 per cent of their wealth in clothes, while princes and courtiers spent astronomically larger sums. The *grand habit* of a minister's wife in 1787 cost 2,049 livres, the equivalent of 2,000 days' wages for a worker.[17]

Some contemporaries believed that the King's insistence on splendid dress was a way to keep courtiers in debt.[18] However, since Louis XIV, more than any of his fellow-monarchs, paid a massive array of pensions and salaries to members of his court nobility, and sometimes their debts too, this is implausible. Magnificence in dress was the essence of Versailles, under Louis XV as well as Louis XIV. To ensure the splendour of courtiers' clothes was one of the priorities of the King and Madame de Pompadour when planning entertainments at court. Sometimes Louis XV helped pay for them himself.[19]

In his desire to place the monarchy on an Olympian height, Louis XIV also ensured that the act of dressing, as well as clothes themselves, continued to play a greater role at the court of France than at others. The King of France was an anointed monarch. Dressing him had a semi-religious aspect, like the robing and unrobing of priests before and after a service. Except on certain state occasions, other monarchs, even the Holy Roman Emperor, were dressed and undressed in private, by servants, or junior court officials.[20] George I of Great Britain, for example, was dressed by his Turkish servant Mehmet.[21] Since at least the sixteenth century, however, both the King and Queen of France had been dressed and undressed, before the court, by some of their highest court officials, the *grand chambellan,* the *maître de la garde-robe* and the *premier gentilhomme de la chambre.* As Catherine de' Medici informed her son Charles IX, referring to the reign of François I: 'When he took his shirt and the clothes entered, all the princes, lords, captains, knights of the order, gentlemen of the chamber, *maîtres d'hôtel* and *gentilshommes servans* then entered and he spoke to them and they saw him, which greatly contented them.' If a prince of the royal family, or even a foreign sovereign like the Duke of Savoy, was present, he replaced the court officials and handed the King his shirt.[22]

The King's dressing (*lever*) and undressing (*coucher*) were not only physical processes, but also critical moments of contact, when the King's most favoured relations, courtiers and officials could talk or listen to him.[23] Under Louis XIV, antechambers were crowded with courtiers waiting to enter the King's state bedroom for the *lever*. While he rose, was dressed and shaved, only those with the *grandes entrées* were admitted. They included court officials with the most personal duties such as the *premiers gentilshommes de la chambre, premier valet de chambre, premier médecin* and *grand maître de la garde-robe*, and ministers with important news. Princes of the blood received the *entrées* by favour rather than by right: under Louis XIV even the Grand Condé failed to obtain them.

At a later moment in the *lever*, as the King's shirt was presented to him the *entrées de la chambre* – marshals, lieutenant-generals, cardinals, bishops, ambassadors, ministers, governors of provinces, *premiers présidents de parlement* and others – were admitted. Sometimes there were as many as a hundred in the room. All were eager to obtain or hear a word from the King. The same process, which lasted about an hour and a half even when the King was on campaign, was repeated in reverse during his *coucher*, with the difference that at the end the King gave a password to the heads of the different units of the Maison militaire.[24] Even during what was called his *petit coucher*, after he had undressed and, wearing no more than his *manteau de chambre*, sat on his *chaise percée, par cérémonie bien plus que par nécessité*, the King received a few favoured courtiers, honoured recipients of what was called the *brevet d'affaires*, after his *chaise d'affaires*.[25]

Many nobles also combined dressing with talking and doing business with visitors. Hogarth painted a nobleman's *lever* in *Marriage à la mode*. *La grande toilette*, that is being dressed in formal clothes by servants, is one of the eight moments of the duc de Choiseul's ministerial routine, illustrated by Van Blarenberghe in a miniature of 1770–71.[26] In the first third of the nineteenth century, deliberately following the examples of Choiseul and the great eighteenth-century Austrian Foreign Minister Prince Kaunitz, the Prince de Talleyrand, the most famous Foreign Minister of his day, was also, during an hour or more every morning, washed, dressed, shaved and powdered by valets, while talking with relations, confidants and diplomats.[27] Only at the court of France, however, did the *lever* and *coucher* become formal daily ceremonies performed before a large audience.

Louis XIV's elevation of dress and dressing into acts of state received further confirmation in 1669, when he established the post of *grand maître de la garde-robe du roi* – the only new office which he created in his own household. The first holder was M. de Guitry, who was killed during the crossing of the Rhine by the French army in 1672.[28] The *grand maître* was head of a separate department of the Maison du roi, entirely devoted to the King's clothes. It included two *maîtres de la garde-robe* (the previous heads of the department); four *premiers valets de garde-robe* who served in rotation every three months; sixteen *valets de garde-robe* and many more servants and tradesmen. They helped dress and undress the King and order and look after his clothes.[29] The clothes themselves were kept in three rooms on the ground floor of the central block of the château of Versailles.[30]

The court of France functioned as a double agent, exalting the King in its acts, criticising him in its words. In their memoirs both Madame de Motteville and the King's cousin the duchesse de Montpensier praised the King's clothes. Other courtiers, however, considered that Louis XIV was dressing like a *nouveau riche*. When the duc de Roquelaure was asked by the King his opinion of the dazzling display of embroidery and jewellery at the King's marriage, he replied in his Gascon accent, referring to a financier called Moncrot who had recently made a fortune out of war supplies: 'Parbleu, sire, il me semble que Moncrot se marie.'[31]

Another disrespectful noble was the duc de La Rochefoucauld, one of the few *frondeurs* whom the King never forgave. At the time of the King's marriage, he expressed the moralist's traditional scorn for splendid dress: 'People speak only of the magnificence of the costumes of our court; it seems to me to be a bad sign for those who wear them, and that they should wish to be talked about also.'[32] For some courtiers, however, talk of their dress, far from being a 'bad sign', was the best of all. Dress was one of the principal ways by which they sent the public, each other, the King himself, and themselves, a reassuring message of status and wealth. In 1713 Lady Strafford wrote of an English peer: 'Lord Bathurst was here this morning to show us his person before he went to court, his cloths ware both extremly fine and very handsome and [he was] . . . very well pleased with his own person.'[33]

Dress appealed to La Rochefoucauld's own family. His son, a particular favourite of Louis XIV, who often paid the courtier's debts, served as the King's second *grand maître de la garde-robe* from 1672 until his death in 1714.[34] Louis XIV wrote to him on his appointment: 'I rejoice as your friend for the present I have given you as your master.'[35] Saint-Simon denounced the Duke's determination to assert the prerogatives of his new court office at the expense, and to the rage, of other court officials, in contrast to his indifference to his prerogatives as a duke. At least twice, at Saint-Cyr in 1688, and Marly in 1706, La Rochefoucauld quarrelled with the *premier gentilhomme* in waiting over who had the right to present a particular garment to the King. On neither occasion would the King decide.[36] Thus dress reveals the King's dependence on his court officials as well as theirs on him. Both master and prisoner of court etiquette, the King was too polite to wish to offend a court official.

La Rochefoucauld clearly liked the post: he was said never to miss a royal *lever* or *coucher*, and, in ten years, never to have slept in a different building from the King. He knew the King so well that he sometimes accompanied him on secret visits to his mistresses.[37] In keeping with the hereditary system favoured at the court of France, the La Rochefoucauld family remained *grands maîtres de la garde-robe*, with a large apartment in the palace, until the fall of the monarchy in 1792.

Louis XIV's desire for splendour in dress at court survived even when, in old age, he himself had begun to prefer simple clothes: it was primarily a matter of policy, not personal taste. For the marriage of his grandson the duc de Bourgogne at Fontainebleau on 7 December 1697, Louis XIV insisted on magnificence. He wished to elevate this dynastic occasion and to counteract the effect of the Treaty of Ryswick, signed in the same year, by which France had lost territory. Saint-Simon recorded:

> He had explained that he would be very pleased if the court was magnificent on this occasion and he himself who for a long time had worn only very simple coats wanted the most superb ones. That was enough for there to be no more question of consulting one's purse nor almost one's status for everyone who was neither an ecclesiastic nor *de robe*. Everyone competed to surpass each other in richness and invention ... the most unbridled luxury dominated the court and the city.

Courtiers stole embroiderers and tailors from each other in order to have their costumes ready for the wedding. Such was the magnetism of the occasion, and the importance of dress as a status symbol, that simply to watch the processions, non-courtiers dressed almost as lavishly as courtiers.[38] The King, his son and his grandsons were covered in gold embroidery; Monsieur wore his large diamonds.[39]

Saint-Simon's reference to those who were *de robe* reflected a custom of the court of France, which lasted until 1789. The English government had given up trying to regulate dress by legislation by 1604.[40] Until 1724, however, the French government continued to issue traditional sumptuary *ordonnances* which since the fourteenth century had tried to regulate luxury in dress, stop subjects and their servants from wearing clothes 'beyond their quality' decorated with gold or silver embroidery, and force them to dress 'according to their station'. These regulations, which no longer reflected economic realities, were rarely enforced. In reality, as *Le Bourgeois Gentilhomme* of Molière showed, ambitious financiers had long been indistinguishable in dress, though not manners, from *les gens de qualité.*[41]

However, men serving in the semi-independent law courts known as *parlements,* or born into *parlementaire* families, were still obliged to wear black clothes at court, rather than the multicoloured *habit habillé* of silk or satin worn by courtiers – or the red robes they wore at their formal sittings. This black dress can be seen in, for example, the portraits of the great finance minister Colbert by Claude Lefebvre in 1666 at Versailles, and of a later finance minister, Calonne, by Madame Vigée-Lebrun in 1784 at Windsor Castle. The dress of Colbert's rival Fouquet, in contrast, had been as imprudently opulent as the decoration of his château of Vaux-le-Vicomte. A picture of Louis XIV, during the few weeks he himself held the 'seals of justice', at a meeting of the *conseil d'état* in 1672 shows him, in brightly coloured clothes, surrounded by men in black – the *conseillers d'état.*[42] The Ottoman ambassador to France in 1669, Suleiman Aga, was accustomed to the splendid dress of French ambassadors in Constantinople. When he saw a man wearing

1 French school, Louis XIV holding the seals of France, 1672.
The councillors of state wear the formal black dress of members of the *noblesse de robe.* The King wears cloth of gold. Only the most favoured *nobles de robe* with ministerial or household office might, occasionally, obtain a dispensation from the obligation to wear black dress at court.

a black *parlementaire* costume, he asked if he was a Jesuit.[43] Thus, while asserting nobles' splendour and wealth, French court dress also emphasised divisions among them.

Under the energetic direction of Colbert, the French government used the court as a showcase for the French cloth and dress industry. The cloth and clothing industry employed about a third of wage-earners in Paris – and in the whole of France, as late as 1847, it employed 969,863 individuals compared to only 38,000 in the iron and steel industry.[44] On the orders of Colbert, foreign lace, cloth and trimmings were banned in France. After a lace war in the 1660s, French lace, made in factories Colbert had founded, replaced Venetian lace as the most fashionable in Europe.[45] Thus on one occasion at court Madame de Montespan, in her public role as 'a triumphant beauty to display to all the ambassadors', wore a dress entirely covered in *point de France* lace.[46] French cloth of *serge de Berry* was substituted for light grey English cloth as the dress of the French infantry, and high tariffs were put on English cloth. In his determination to encourage use of French cloth to the exclusion of all others, Louis XIV even ordered one of his son's coats to be burned, because it 'was not made of our cloth'.[47] No branch of French life was more dependent on the court than the silk industry. Founded in the sixteenth century, the Lyon silk industry had subsequently been the object of constant royal interest.[48] The number of silk looms at Lyon rose from 3,296 in 1660 to 5,067 in 1720.[49] At times, in deciding the level of expenditure, the court obeyed Lyon, not Lyon the court.

Court dress reveals not only the political and psychological needs and economic impact of monarchy but also the predominance of France. France was the largest and most powerful state in western Europe, with a population of twenty-three million in 1700, compared to six million in Great Britain and Ireland, the same in Spain, and sixteen million in the Holy Roman Empire. From the reign of Louis XIV, for the first time since the Valois, France also had the grandest court in Europe. Its court dress, known as *habit à la française*, as well as *habit habillé*, was in effect the national dress of France (although frontier provinces such as Brittany, Alsace and Provence retained their own dress into the twentieth century).

French dress was more widely imitated than French architecture or etiquette. Paris tailors were considered the best in Europe. Until the late eighteenth century – when they were replaced by fashion plates – dolls wearing the latest style extended French fashions further than Louis XIV's soldiers extended French conquests. They were welcome even in hostile capitals, such as London and Vienna. Soon a Paris fashion doll was going to London once a month; a doll 'dressed in the court dress' was sent from Paris to Queen Caroline of

Ansbach, on her husband's accession in 1727.[50] In 1731 a Lyon silk merchant called Barnier wrote a long report requesting further orders for the looms of Lyon from the court of Versailles, and more *fêtes* at court because 'The same spirit which reigns at the court influences all the other orders of the Kingdom and even all foreign courts.'[51] By the 1780s the journalist Louis Sebastien Mercier wrote that Paris fashion dolls had even reached Constantinople and St Petersburg: 'The twist given by a French hand is repeated by every nation, humble observers of the taste of the rue Saint Honoré.'[52]

The French dress empire had begun before the court's move to Versailles in 1682. Sumptuous costumes, saddles, canopies and coaches, smothered in embroidery, had been ordered from France for the coronations of Queen Christina of Sweden in 1650, of her successors Charles X in 1654 and Charles XI in 1675, and for the latter's wedding in 1680.[53] They can be seen today on display in one of the finest collections of royal dress in Europe, at the Livrustkammaren Museum in the Royal Palace of Stockholm. By a decision taken by the Swedish Privy Council in 1633, after the death of the hero King Gustavus Adolphus II, dead monarchs' clothes were to be kept together as a perpetual memorial to the Swedish monarchy. There are now 1,000 such costumes in the museum.[54]

French dress conquered one of the last bastions of resistance after Louis XIV's grandson succeeded the last Habsburg King of Spain in 1700. Philip V made a gesture to the traditional black dress of the Spanish court, by being painted in it, wearing a *golilla* or stiff collar, at Versailles by his grandfather's court painter Hyacinthe Rigaud in December 1700, during the few days between his proclamation as King of Spain and his departure for his new kingdom. (However, Versailles did not get the details right: Philip V is, incorrectly, shown wearing a wig and, in French style, gesturing to a crown on the table beside him.)[55] On Louis XIV's advice, to satisfy national pride *par cette complaisance*, Philip V continued to wear Spanish dress in Spain. According to the comte d'Ayen, it was 'une galanterie très agréable à la nation'.

However, while the King remained in Spanish dress, grandees of Spain eager to please him were beginning to adopt French dress: his French servants in Madrid also pushed him to wear French dress even, on one occasion, telling him no Spanish clothes were *en estat*. In 1707 the victory of Almanza had heralded his triumph over his Habsburg rival, the Archduke Charles. Thereafter all Spaniards except judges, wrote the French adviser M. Amelot to Louis XIV, 'have renounced *l'habit à l'espagnole* absolutely without anyone having been told the slightest thing on behalf of the King your grandson, to procure this change'.[56] So in this domain at least, the Bourbon method – to effect change by agreement, rather than by commands from above – had worked. From the court French dress spread across

2 Hyacinthe Rigaud, Philip V, 1700.
Dress as signal: to help win hearts in
Spain, Philip V at first wore the traditional
black court dress of Spain, with a golilla or
stiff collar (but with a French wig and the
French Order of the Holy Spirit). Black
was an expensive colour, which suggested
both status and sobriety.

Spain. In 1766, fearing that they were used to disguise thieves, the government
banned the Spanish long cloak and broad-brimmed hat. The resulting riots made
King Charles III tremble for his throne, but failed to get the ban lifted in Madrid.
In 1774 Major William Dalrymple wrote: 'The people in general here have
adopted the French dress; none but the lower sort wear the cloak.'[57]

French dress was also adopted in Naples by the 1680s, in Tuscany in 1723.[58]
The future King Augustus II of Poland had been impressed by the dress of
Louis XIV on a visit in 1687–8. In 1717, in preparation for the wedding of his
son and heir to the Archduchess Maria Josefa, he wrote to his agent in Paris
that he wanted 'a coat such as the deceased King of France wore at great
ceremonies, such as his marriage, *en marteau pourpoint et rhingrave*. It will not
be enough to send a drawing of this costume; but he must have a doll exactly
dressed in this kind of coat.'[59] Only in Vienna, capital of France's enemy the
Habsburg monarchy, and in cities without a court, like Genoa, Lucca,
Amsterdam, Hamburg and Frankfurt, did men not wear the *habit habillé*.[60]

After 1660 French dress had also conquered England. From 1653 to 1658
Oliver Cromwell the Lord Protector, 'no friend of fashions', had been famous,

like most of his followers, for generally wearing suits in a dark colour known as 'the Protector's colour'.[61] The royalist Sir John Reresby remembered that, during the interregnum, 'The citizens and common people of London . . . should scarce endure the sight of gentlemen so that the common salutation of a man well dressed was "French dog" or the like.'[62]

The restoration of Charles II meant a change of dress as well as regime. Even before the return of the King, Pepys records in his diary the purchase by himself and his cousin and patron, Edward Montagu, and others, of 'fine clothes . . . very rich as gold and silver [and, in Pepys's case, silk and velvet] can make them . . . in expectation to wait upon the King.' On 3 February 1661 he recorded: 'This day I first begun to go forth in my coate and sword, as the manner now among gentlemen is.'[63]

Charles II, who owed his life to the disguise he had adopted while fleeing England in 1651 after the Battle of Worcester, knew the transforming power of clothes. He was generally well and neatly dressed.[64] When he wore 'a plain common riding suit', however, Pepys found that 'he seemed a very ordinary man to one that had not known him'.[65] Under Charles II, London like Paris was a capital where, in Pepys's words, many felt 'a great happiness' in 'being in the fashion and in variety of fashions in scorn of others that are not so, as citizens wifes and country gentlewomen'.[66] But many contemporaries found

3 Coat worn by James Duke of York, the future James II, on 21 November 1673 at the ceremony in Dover Castle to confirm his marriage to Mary of Modena: English wool smothered in silver and silver-gilt embroidery, lined with red silk. After the ceremony, the Duke gave this suit as a token of favour to Sir Edward Carteret, one of the few courtiers who had dared attend this Catholic service. It was kept by descendants of Carteret's sister-in-law, until sold to the Victoria and Albert Museum in 1995.

that, though 'neat and gay in their apparell', in their personal habits Charles II's courtiers were 'very nasty and beastly'.[67]

Charles II retained a French tailor, Claude Sourceau, whom he had used in exile. Sourceau started the King's clothes, even his coronation robes, in Paris; the King's tailors John Allen and William Watts finished them in London.[68] As in the French court, the King's clothes were looked after by a separate department of the royal household: the Wardrobe of Robes, under the Master of the Robes. There was a staff of yeomen and grooms of the wardrobe, supplied by an army of royal milliners, drapers and embroiderers (the department called the Great Wardrobe looked after the furnishings of the royal palaces). Charles II's masters of the robes included such important politicians as Laurence Hyde and Sydney Godolphin.[69]

Even a monarch with a reputation for austerity like William III, whose clothes have recently been studied by Patricia Wardle, maintained a magnificent wardrobe. Protestantism had no effect on a king's need for splendour – although his French tailor M. Darquet made considerably grander clothes than his English tailor Mr Graham. The King had a liking for scarlet suits, adorned with Venetian (in preference to French) lace and gold buttons and heavily embroidered with silver-gilt thread. His first Master of the Robes from 1689 to 1695 was his cousin Nassau, Earl of Rochford; his second, from 1695 to 1701, was his handsome, lavishly rewarded, young favourite, Arnoud van Keppel, Earl of Albemarle.[70]

After the destruction of the palace of Whitehall in 1698 the English court was based at St James's Palace, a brick warren at the bottom of St James's Street described by one French visitor as 'the most miserable hovel ever inhabited by a great king'.[71] An Englishman called it 'an object of reproach to the kingdom in general . . . universally condemned'.[72] Yet the magnificence of courtiers' dress at Saint James's compensated for, and was more often recorded than, the ignominy of its architecture. Thus on 6 February 1705 it was noted that Queen Anne's birthday was observed at St James's 'with Great Solemnity. There was an extraordinary Appearance at Court of the Nobility and Gentry, as well for their number as the Magnificence of their Habits.'[73]

Such was the primacy of dress that the female head of the Queen's household was called the Mistress of the Robes, although she also held the two other important court offices of Groom of the Stole and First Lady of the Bedchamber.[74] Under Queen Anne, the office was occupied by her favourite, Sarah, Duchess of Marlborough, who had been one of her ladies of the bedchamber since 1683. Like Louis XIV's insistence on splendour in dress, the Duchess of Marlborough's years as Mistress of the Robes confirmed and symbolised the link between power and dress. The Queen had long asserted her dependence on, and abandoned formality with, her favourite. After 1702, however, the Duchess of Marlborough put her political preferences before her court duties. She tried to push or bully the Queen towards Whig politicians and policies – in particular favouring the war with France which was making the Duke of Marlborough the greatest commander of the age. When she could not dissuade the Queen from what she called her 'infatuation' with Tories, the Duchess preferred to spend long periods in the country.[75] As Mistress of the Robes, however, she continued to arrange the Queen's clothes for state occasions – and to keep for herself and other members of the bedchamber staff, many of whom were her relations and protégés, discarded items of the royal wardrobe. When the Queen did not wear the jewels the Duchess had selected for her to the thanksgiving service on 19 August 1708 for the victory of Oudenarde (possibly because they were too heavy for comfort), the latter upbraided her mistress from St James's to St Paul's, finally bidding the Queen be silent. Nor was this the only quarrel between the former friends.[76] The Duchess had become a hindrance, rather than a help, to her husband's career.

Dress helped ensure her fall from favour by 1708, and the fall of the Whigs from power in 1711. Her first cousin Abigail Hill had been 'raised from a broom' – she had been a servant in a private household – by the Duchess to become one of the women or dressers of the bedchamber.[77] Abigail Hill's menial and intimate body service for the Queen included helping her to dress, pouring water on her hands when she washed, pulling on her gloves when she could not do so herself and, as the Queen's health deteriorated, nursing. This physical intimacy became a political force when used by Abigail's other cousin, the Tory leader Robert Harley. Both before and after Harley replaced the Marlboroughs in power, Abigail Hill enabled him to see and correspond with the Queen directly and discreetly – despite the Duchess of Marlborough's spy network in the royal household. In ciphered letters carried by her brother, Hill kept Harley informed of the Queen's feelings and policies. Thus, despite the Queen's reserve, a dresser could influence, or be thought by the public to influence, a change of ministry.[78] In reality the Whigs' insistence on continuing the war, even to the point of obliging Louis XIV to remove his grandson Philip V from the throne of Spain, had destroyed their own popularity with both Queen and country.

Despite the fall of the Whigs in January 1711, the Duchess of Marlborough was succeeded as Mistress of the Robes by another royal favourite with Whig sympathies, the Duchess of Somerset. Again dress influenced politics. The Duchess of Somerset's Whig politics and scandalous past – her second husband Thomas Thynne was said to have been assassinated in her presence by her lover Count Königsmarck – led Swift, a friend of Lady Masham (as Abigail Hill had now become), to publish, in December 1711, *The Windsor Prophecy*. Like many pamphlets and diplomatic dispatches of the time, it sees English politics in terms of relations within the royal household.

> And dear England, if ought I understand,
> Beware of Carrots from Northumberland
> [the red-haired Duchess of Somerset, daughter of the
>   Earl of Northumberland].
> Carrots sown Thyn a deep root may get,
> If so be they are in Sommer set:
> Their conyngs mark thou, for I have been told,
> They assassine when young and poison when old.
> Root out these Carrots, O thou whose Name
> is backwards and forewords always the same [Anna];
> And keep close to Thee always that Name,
> Which backwards and forwards is allmost the same [Masham].
> And England wouldst thou be happy still,
> bury those Carrots under a Hill.

Like the Tory ministers, he was frightened of her influence – her 'poison' – as Mistress of the Robes on the Queen. Despite pressure from the Tory ministers, the Queen, appreciating the Duchess's calm and 'breeding', would not be parted from her. In constant attendance on the dying Queen in 1714, the Duchess of Somerset was able to alert her Whig husband to come to the Queen's bedroom in Kensington Palace and attend the crucial council meeting, when the Queen was guided to hand the white wand of the Lord Treasurer from Masham's friend Lord St John to the moderate Duke of Shrewsbury.[79]

Despite wars and attempts to boost English manufactures, France remained the model of fashion and magnificence for the court of England. Recounting the richness and expense of the embroidered brocades worn by Louis XV and his courtiers at his wedding at Fontainebleau in 1725, the British ambassador wrote: 'by universal consent they are acknowledged to outdo all the world'.[80] In 1741 when Horace Walpole ordered his 'birthday suit' from Paris – a suit to wear to court to celebrate the King's birthday with suitable magnificence – nineteen other suits from Paris arrived at the same time.[81] In *Joseph Andrews* (1742), Henry Fielding mocked the love of French fashion of a fickle noble called Bellarmine, who wore a coat of cinnamon velvet lined with pink satin and covered in gold embroidery: 'Yes Madam this Coat was made at Paris and I defy the best English Taylor even to imitate it. There is not one of them can cut, Madam, they can't cut . . . I never trust anything more than a Great Coat to an Englishman.'[82]

One aspect of French court dress survives today. Red heels had been introduced by Louis XIV by 1673,[83] probably to confirm the elevation of his court above the rest of humanity. Red heels, which were restricted to nobles with the right genealogical qualifications to be presented at court, demonstrated that the nobles did not dirty their shoes (although, in *Le Costume français* of 1776, a more heroic explanation was advanced: red heels are described as 'the mark of their nobility and [show] that they are always ready to crush the enemies of the state at their feet'). Louis XIV displays red heels in a marked manner both in his portrait in coronation robes by Hyacinthe Rigaud at Versailles and in the famous group portrait of four generations of the French royal family, painted in 1710 by Nicolas de Largillière, now in the Wallace Collection. *Talons rouges* became a synonym for French courtiers' futile insolence. Hence pamphlets with titles like *Portefeuille d'un talon rouge* (*c.* 1780, an attack on Marie Antoinette), and the phrase is still occasionally heard today: *il est très talon rouge.*

Red heels remained part of formal wear at the French court, for members of the royal family and the *noblesse présentée.*[84] The red heels of Louis XVI in his portrait in coronation robes by Callet at Versailles are noticeably lower than those of Louis XIV in the Rigaud portrait; in that by J. S. Duplessis in the Musée Ingres, Montauban, Louis XVI has no red heels at all. From Versailles red heels spread across Europe. They were worn by Louis XIV's greatest enemy, William III, and can be seen in the coronation portraits of George II, George III and George IV, by Shackleton, Allan Ramsay and Thomas Lawrence respectively, hanging in Buckingham Palace; and in state portraits of Scottish and English peers, such as the Earl of Melfort in Thistle robes of 1687 (in the Scottish National Portrait Gallery) and Marquess Wellesley by Sir M. Archer Shee (in Buckingham Palace). They are also worn by the Austrian Chancellor Prince von Kaunitz; by the princes of Bavaria and Saxony in a group portrait of 1761; and by some of the dwarfs offered by colonial governors to the Queen of Portugal in the 1780s.[85] Today red heels are still worn every year, at the state opening of parliament in Westminster and the Garter Ceremony at Windsor, by the pages of Elizabeth II.[86]

After 1660 the growing economic and psychological impact of court society and court dress was also shown by the spread of court mourning. Traditionally court mourning had been restricted, by law, to members of the nobility and the royal household. The English royal household had issued 18,000 yards of black fabric or 'blacks' to its members, and to peers, ambassadors and other mourners, attending the funeral of Elizabeth I in 1603.[87] From the early seventeenth century, however, officially regulated periods of court mourning imposed black, grey and white clothes, not only on court officials and peers, but also on all 'persons of quality'.[88]

In September 1660, for example, Pepys, a junior naval official, and his wife wore mourning for Henry, Duke of Gloucester, youngest brother of Charles II.[89] Soon, often to the disgust of peers and heralds, observation of court and private mourning extended beyond 'persons of quality' to the general public. Vanity was a motive as powerful as loyalty: people wanted to prove that they, and their servants, could afford the elaborate and expensive black clothes worn during periods of mourning. On the death of Charles II in 1685 the Earl Marshal instructed 'all persons concerned' to 'put themselves into the deepest mourning that is possible'.[90] The court transformed the visual appearance of the entire capital.

Court mourning not only imposed black, white and grey clothes – and black or blackened buttons, shoe buckles, fans, jewels, swords and nails – but also suspended court and many private entertainments. Therefore no new clothes were ordered by the thousands of guests who would have attended them. In France and England periods of court mourning were so long, and so widely followed outside the court, that they crippled the dress industry – as its representatives loudly complained.[91] In 1711 a petition from Lyon asked Louis XIV why, if the Dauphin died of illness, they should die of hunger: 'Sire, du travail ou du pain!'[92]

Court mourning's effect on the economy was magnified by its adoption, from the mid-seventeenth century or earlier, on the deaths of foreign as well as local monarchs, princes and princesses: visible proof of the existence of a European 'family of kings'.[93] In 1665 both France and England observed court mourning for the death of Philip IV of Spain.[94] In 1715 it was said that mourning for the death of Louis XIV was more strictly observed in Vienna than in Versailles. In 1716 in France (on account of the distress caused by the previous year's mourning), and in 1768 in England (because 'people in trade . . . are . . . deprived in a great measure of the means of getting bread'), the duration of court mourning was reduced by a half: the latter decision prompted a procession of 500 manufacturers to St James's Palace to thank the King.[95] To satisfy the Chamber of Commerce of Lyon, in 1730 court mourning in France had been further reduced.[96] Nevertheless the six months' mourning in France in 1747 for the Queen of Poland, mother of Queen Marie Lezsczynska, following the six months' mourning for the Dauphine in 1746, was said to ruin the French silk trade.[97] In France before 1789, court mourning was so universally observed that it had a proto-revolutionary effect. Dress normally advertised differences of wealth and rank; putting all men in black, court mourning made all men appear equal.[98]

2   *Service*

Louis XIV projected an image of royalty as the embodiment of luxury and splendour. In the last two decades of his reign, however, a younger but equally celebrated monarch, Charles XII of Sweden, projected a rival image. Military service was its basis. Charles XII, a professional soldier almost always on campaign between 1699 and his death in 1719, generally wore, with his own hair rather than a wig, a simple military uniform with no embroidery: usually the long blue coat, yellow waistcoat, black cravat and elkskin breeches of his élite guard unit the Drabants, whom he had led to victory over Peter I of

4 J. D. Swartz, Charles XII of Sweden, *c.* 1705.
Dress as self-advertisement: Charles XII's many victories and reluctance to wear anything but this simple blue and yellow uniform helped to establish a fashion for military monarchy in Europe.

Russia at Narva in 1700.[1] Charles XII was proud of his simple, soldierly image, which he had disseminated in many realistic portraits. When, looking like a rough peasant soldier, he met the courtly and sophisticated Augustus II of Saxony and Poland at Gunthersdorf, after the peace of Altranstadt in 1707, he boasted that he had not taken off his boots for six years.[2]

This use of uniform and disregard for finery reflected two changes. First, the spread of uniform in European armies between 1650 and 1720. Uniform had been adopted for many reasons: to inculcate discipline, courage and *esprit de corps*; to distinguish soldiers from civilians; to impress spectators; to shape bodies for combat; to inspire fear in the enemy; and, as innumerable recruiting posters show, to attract young men to enlist. As one sergeant in the Gardes français wrote, uniforms made young men envious. By 1720, in most armies, military uniforms had become at once standardised and obligatory.[3]

Making uniforms became an industry even more important and profitable than making court costumes. Possibly as much as £252,950 a year was spent on clothing the soldiers of the British army in the 1690s, Beverley Lemire has written. Every soldier received a full new set of clothing every two years.[4]

At the same time that armies were adopting uniform, they were becoming larger, better organised and more important: the French army under Louis XIV could be 400,000 in number, those of Sweden or Brandenburg 30,000. As each ruler's household, and couriers and postilions throughout their dominions, wore his livery colours,[5] so each army adopted one basic colour, usually from the ruler's livery, for military uniforms: grey-white or dark blue in France (*bleu de roi*); dark blue in Prussia ('Prussian blue'); red in England ('England's cruel red', to an Irish poet); blue and yellow in Sweden; white in Austria; green in Russia.[6] Thus in 1684 Louis XIV had decided to clothe his regiment of foreign-born Gardes suisses in red, but the Gardes français (previously in grey) in blue.[7]

Like Charles XII, Peter the Great also wore military uniform, and like Louis XIV used dress as a political weapon, in his case to enforce westernisation. Already in the second half of the seventeenth century a few Russian nobles had begun to adopt western dress, and some Russian regiments had begun to wear western-style uniforms.[8] However, in 1675 and 1680 there had been a reaction: edicts had been issued to oblige Russians to wear, instead of 'outlandish' western dress, 'traditional' – in reality semi-Ottoman – Russian dress, which, like Russians' beards, had become a symbol of Russian Orthodoxy and xenophobia: kaftans, richly embroidered long coats with long sleeves, often of brocade or velvet from Italy or the Ottoman Empire, and often loaned to boyars by the Tsar. Those who failed to wear Russian dress were threatened with the Tsar's displeasure, and with reduction in rank.[9]

After 1690, however, Peter the Great abandoned traditional Russian kaftans and generally wore western dress, ordered from German tailors already established in Moscow.[10] On 26 August 1698, the day after his return to Moscow from his 'grand embassy' around western Europe, he launched an attack on Russian dress. Despite their reluctance, he encouraged nobles to shave their beards: sometimes he shaved them himself. In 1700 and 1701 he went further, placing 'fashion dolls' wearing the prescribed new dress at the gates of Moscow and issuing orders obliging men and women, except 'ploughing peasantry' and clergy, to replace traditional kaftans with 'German or "French" dress': coats, waistcoats, breeches and shoes.[11] Believing in the transforming power of clothes, he considered a dress revolution indispensable to his modernisation of Russia.

Although some Russians complained that the Tsar was 'ungodly', the new fashions were soon adopted – under pressure from Peter's troops. The Tsar's orders were reinforced by a decree of 28 February 1702, which ordered courtiers to appear in clothes 'made after the English fashion, and to appear with Gold and Silver Trimming, those that could afford it'. From 1705 men of all ranks were ordered to shave their traditional beards or pay fines.[12] Russian noblewomen endured an even more traumatic transformation. Hitherto concealed from the public eye by high-necked, many-layered garments and veils, they were suddenly obliged to bare part of themselves in western dress.[13] In five years, between 1700 and 1705, the outward appearance of urban Russians had been transformed. By 1722 a foreigner entering a gathering in St Petersburg, if he relied on outward appearances, could believe himself in Paris or London. Only Old Believers and some merchants continued to wear traditional Russian dress.[14]

The Tsar himself, however, like his rival Charles XII, preferred to wear military uniform. As a young prince between 1683 and 1695 he had trained his own troops in a children's regiment, which developed into the Preobrazhensky Guard regiment, in which he himself served, wearing the appropriate uniform, in every rank from drummer-boy to colonel. After 1695, he sometimes led the Preobrazhensky Guard on the battlefield. In 1698 the regiment helped him crush and kill his enemies, the traditional élite troops the Streltsi. At the Epiphany procession on 15 January 1700, the Tsar did not sit on a throne beside the Patriarch of Moscow, but, for the first time, marched past as their colonel at the head of his Preobrazhensky guards: all, like the Tsar himself, were dressed in 'handsome new green uniforms'.[15] The Tsar continued to wear this dark green uniform, as well as civilian costumes made in Berlin, and was married in it. The Tsar's attitude was completely alien to the court of France. A French courtier sent to receive him on his visit to France in 1717 changed his coat every day in order to show his 'extreme magnificence'.[16] The Tsar's sole comment was to express pity for M. de Nesle, who had such a bad tailor that he did not own a coat which fitted. Peter the Great's wardrobe was much simpler than that of his favourite the first governor of St Petersburg, Prince Menshikov.[17]

One of his Preobrazhensky uniforms is in the 270-piece collection of clothes known as the Wardrobe of Peter the Great which, after his death in 1725, like the clothes of Swedish kings, was preserved as a public memorial. Since 1848 the Wardrobe of Peter the Great has been in the Hermitage museum.[18]

Peter's reorganisation of the Russian monarchy as a state with a hierarchy based on official and military service, with appropriate uniforms for each rank, was codified in the Table of Ranks of 24 January 1722, which remained the base of the monarchy until its overthrow in February 1917. Stating 'We nevertheless do not grant any rank to anyone until he performs a useful service to Us or the state', it gave military and naval officers precedence over civilian officials of the same status. But there was a link between rank and splendour. Only men in the Table of Ranks had the right to wear velvet and only those in the top five ranks could wear lace.[19]

Although Russia was a service state, the French *habit habillé* also remained popular, perhaps because it suited the national passion for jewels. After the death of Peter I's grandson Peter II in 1730, Russia was ruled by the Tsarinas Anne and Elizabeth who, although they owed their power to their guards, wore uniform only on exceptional occasions. At the birthday celebrations of the Tsarina Anne in 1733, 'there was a great appearance of Russian nobility and persons of distinction in the richest clothes that could be got from France and Germany'.[20] In 1778 Archdeacon Coxe noted of Russian courtiers: 'The costliness and glare of their apparel, and a profusion of precious stones, created a splendour, of which the magnificence of other courts can give us only a faint idea. The court-dress of the men is in the French fashion . . . Many of the nobility were almost covered in diamonds; their buttons, buckles, hilts of swords, and epaulets, were composed of this valuable material . . . their hats were frequently embroidered, if I may use the expression, with several rows of them.'[21] No one dressed more splendidly, often in jewel-strewn clothes ordered from France, than the Empress's secret consort and principal adviser, Prince Potemkin.[22]

More than Sweden or Russia, the principal model of military monarchy in Europe was Brandenburg-Prussia. No dynasty loved its soldiers as much as the

Hohenzollerns. In 1684 the Brandenburg troops were described by a French diplomat as the finest in Germany, comparable to the best regiments in the French army. King Frederick William I (1713–40) believed that the power of the sword was the only source of respect in the world.[23] Imposing a new style of military monarchy, he gave court offices to army officers. In 1718 Johann Michael von Loen recorded the change: 'I see a court that has nothing more splendid than its soldiers. It is possible to be a great sovereign without having to demonstrate one's majesty in outward pomp . . . when speaking of the court in Berlin one speaks of the warriors; they alone constitute the court.'[24] From 1719 Frederick William I rarely wore anything but uniform. When a pastor read out the biblical text, 'naked shall I, too, appear before Thy stern countenance', it is said that he cried out that it was not true, he would be buried in his uniform.[25] In 1728, when the courts of Saxony and Prussia met in Berlin, the superb *habits habillés* of the former contrasted with the uniforms of the latter: the Prussians' jackets were so short and tight, recalled the King's daughter Princess Wilhelmina, that they hardly dared move for fear of tearing them.[26]

5 Louis de Silvestre, The meeting of Augustus II King of Poland (left) and Frederick William I King in Prussia in 1728.
The King of Poland maintained a lavish, civilian court; the King in Prussia, to whom he sold a regiment of giants in exchange for a room of porcelain, militarised both the dress and the composition of his court.

In keeping with Prussia's military ethos, Frederick William I's son the future Frederick II was educated as a professional officer. Hating military life, he sometimes secretly removed his uniform and put on the French clothes which, to his father's fury, he had begun to buy.[27] Indeed on 27 August 1730 the Crown Prince's appearance in the latter, instead of in uniform, alerted a valet to his intention to flee his father's court.[28] As punishment he was forced to wear uniform, arrested, imprisoned, made to watch the execution of his best friend and to serve in a regiment. Both in his dress, and soon in the man within, the ethos of the Prussian army triumphed over that of the French court.

After he became king in 1740, Frederick at first, on special occasions, wore suits so lavishly embroidered, sometimes by his own sisters, that the embroidery cost eight times more than the fabric. Generally, however, he wore the uniform of the first battalion of his celebrated Foot Guard regiment, which later called itself the first regiment in Christendom: by the time of his death his wardrobe contained only cloaks, shirts and blue Prussian uniforms.[29] In Frederick's opinion the King of Prussia 'must of necessity be a soldier and the head of the army'. Military uniform was part of his creed: 'without uniforms', he stated, 'there can be no discipline'.[30]

Like the Emperor Augustus and Louis XI, Frederick II used reverse ostentation to proclaim that he was above normal standards. The more victories he won in the War of the Austrian Succession and the Seven Years War, the shabbier his uniforms became. Some were stained with snuff, torn, darned and patched at the elbows. He wanted to look as he had appeared on the battlefield.[31] Perhaps also what a former Prussian officer, Rudolph Wilhelm von Kaltenborn, called his 'carefully studied coquetry' of shabbiness was a further repudiation of the French court dress which, in his youth, he had loved.[32]

Prussia's repeated victories confirmed that its rise to great power status was due to its army, rather than to its size or location, or its monarchs' abilities. The influential French military reformer the comte de Guibert considered the Prussian army 'the finest and the best disciplined in Europe'.[33] Mirabeau remarked that Prussia was not a state which possessed an army, but an army which possessed a state. The Danish minister Count Bernstorff said that Frederick II 'had made his State into an armed camp and his people into an army'.[34] Indeed for most of the century about a quarter of Berlin's inhabitants were soldiers or members of soldiers' families.[35] The success of this military state helped make uniforms fashionable throughout Europe.

One of Frederick's most fervent admirers was the Duke of Holstein, a grandson of Peter the Great. After he ascended the Russian throne as Peter III

6 After E. F. Cunningham, The return of Frederick the Great from manoeuvres, 1785. By the last year of Frederick's reign the Prussian monarchy was a model for Europe, as is shown by the presence on this occasion of the Duke of York (fourth to the right of the King) and the marquis de La Fayette (sixth from right), as well as (in the centre) the King's heir: his nephew, the future Frederick Wilhelm II.

on 5 January 1762, he introduced Prussian-style uniforms into the Russian army. However, on 28 June 1762 his wife Catherine II seized power by armed force, going from Guards barracks to Guards barracks in St Petersburg in search of support. Dress was one of her weapons – although it is impossible to judge its importance compared to the Empress's personality, her collaborators' efficiency and her husband's cowardice. On the day of the coup she wore the traditional green and gold coat and trousers of a Life Guards officer of the Semyonovsky regiment (as opposed to a new uniform introduced by her husband). In her accession manifesto, one charge made against Peter III, after hostility to Orthodoxy, was his introduction of Prussian-style uniforms and drill, and alleged hatred of – in reality desire to improve discipline in – the Russian Guards regiments, to which he had preferred his own Holstein Guards regiment.[36]

The Empress demonstrated her pride in her coup and her guards – and the importance of wearing the right uniform at the right time – by shortly thereafter commissioning an equestrian portrait of herself, by Vigilius Eriksen. A visible expression of the dictum 'Might is right', it still hangs above the throne in the throne room of the palace of Peterhof. It shows the Empress,

7 Vigilius Eriksen, Catherine II, *c*. 1764. Dress as weapon: Catherine II's traditional green Semyonovsky guards uniform, worn on the day of her *coup d'état* against her husband Peter III on 28 June 1762, helped win the hearts of Russian soldiers alienated by Peter III's introduction of Prussian-style uniforms. Revealing the military basis of the Russian monarchy, this portrait – commissioned by the Empress shortly after the coup – hung above the throne in the throne room of Peterhof Palace.

sword in hand, in the Semyonovsky uniform which she had worn on the day of the coup, on her horse Brillante. In the background soldiers of the regiment march towards St Petersburg.[37]

Further affirming the military character of the Russian monarchy, Catherine II institutionalised the tradition, on the anniversary of the foundation of each Russian Guards regiment, of entertaining its officers to dinner in the Winter Palace, after a parade and a religious service. The Empress herself would help officers to bowls of soup and glasses of wine (as, on exceptional occasions, her predecessors Catherine I and Anne had done).[38] On these occasions she used dress to advertise the connection between the monarchy and the regiment. She took great pride – like a peahen, as she wrote to Prince Potemkin[39] – in wearing the appropriate 'regimental gown' (a voluminous female version of regimental uniform, with 'old Russian' elements such as long hanging sleeves). In the desire to celebrate the memory of Russian monarchs, some of her regimental gowns, like the Wardrobe of Peter I, were preserved in the arsenal of the Winter Palace and are now in the Hermitage museum.[40] In general in her reign, Russian uniforms, in accordance with the instructions of Prince Potemkin, were 'free of foppish fetters' such as narrow

8 Jean-Etienne Liotard, Corfiz-Anton Count Uhlfeld in court dress, 1740/41. Known as 'Spanish dress' (but quite different from traditional Spanish court dress), Austrian court dress consisted of a lace-covered cloak, jacket and breeches. Count Uhlfeld is here shown wearing it in Constantinople when about to be presented to Sultan Mahmud I as imperial ambassador. As Obersthofmeister in Vienna, however, he failed to prevent its abolition by Joseph II in 1766.

boots, tight undergarments, pigtails and powdered hair – in other words they were unlike the Prussian uniforms favoured by Peter III.[41]

Fifty years after Sweden, Prussia and Russia, the Habsburg monarchy also became a military monarchy. Before his death in 1740 the Holy Roman Emperor Charles VI, who had spent the years 1703–7 fighting for the throne of Spain, had maintained as formal court dress the elaborate *Mantelkleid*, a black suit and cloak covered in piped and gathered gold lace, with feathered hat, ribbons and hose, and red stockings, which had been worn by rulers and court officials in Vienna since the seventeenth century. It was known as 'Spanish dress'.[42]

His daughter Maria Theresa, however, was a military monarch. She attended manoeuvres on horseback, and wrote that the army was the only section of the administration 'for which I harboured a real personal interest'.[43] During the War of the Austrian Succession from 1740 to 1748, when Prussia conquered Silesia, she attributed the survival of her monarchy, as contemporaries attributed the rise of Prussia, not to hereditary right, nor to the love of the people, nor to geographical or administrative cohesion, but to the army.

In 1751 she issued a decree which established military service as one basis of court society and, like the Russian Table of Ranks, remained in force until the fall of the monarchy. It stated: 'To give the military men new proof of my special affection, I have at my pleasure resolved that any officer of my armed forces wearing his uniform may attend court.' The monarchy needed the army more than ever. Because the victory of Kolin in 1757 proved that the Austrian army could defeat the Prussian, she called it 'the Birthday of the Monarchy'.[44] From 1757 all Austrian officers with thirty years' unblemished service were granted automatic right to nobility.[45]

In 1766, one year after his assumption of the co-regency on his father's death, the Empress's son Joseph II, who detested the *Mantelkleid*, decided to abolish it. The Obersthofmeister Count Uhlfeld was in opposition. In accordance with Austrian tradition, distrustful of the army since the great General Wallenstein's threatened takeover of the monarchy in 1634, Uhlfeld believed that officers 'do not belong at court but on the field . . . like bishops in their dioceses': if an officer was also a chamberlain, 'always the court character should take precedence'.[46] Another critic of military monarchy was the Austrian Chancellor Prince Kaunitz, who detested 'Prussian slavery' – and liked the *habit habillé*. He lamented 'the misfortune of exclusively military governments and the revolution with which this mania threatened Europe'.[47]

On 8 November 1766, however, with imperial brevity, Joseph II wrote to Count Uhlfeld: 'This note ends the wearing of the Spanish *Mantelkleid*.'[48] Whereas many courtiers adopted the *habit habillé*, Joseph II wore nothing but military uniform, generally the green uniform of his light cavalry regiment 'Number 1 Kaiser', of which he was *Oberst Inhaber*, sometimes the white and gold uniform of an Austrian Field Marshal.[49] The sole concession to visual splendour, on special occasions, came from the diamonds in the stars of his orders, his sword hilt and his shoe buckles. His brothers followed suit. In 1774, before the Archduke Maximilian came to Versailles to visit his sister the Queen, the Imperial ambassador to France, the comte de Mercy-Argenteau, had to buy him two *habits habillés*:[50] the Archduke possessed nothing but uniforms.

Thus by 1770 military service had joined birth, loyalty and wealth as one of the defining elements in court society. Most monarchs and nobles had abandoned traditional, often bejewelled, costumes projecting a message of grandeur and wealth, for military uniforms projecting a rival philosophy of service and simplicity. Kings were beginning to look like serving officers, and to derive part of their legitimacy from association with their army. The individual nature of the *habit habillé* – no two of which were the same – was beginning to appear less appealing than a uniform advertising service in the largest institution in the country: the army.

As those who have worn one relate, the wearing of uniform has a 'mass-psychological effect'.[51] Uniform defined and advertised the wearer's status in the armed forces, masking his status in the social hierarchy.[52] 'The anonymity of uniform', both on and off duty, according to Anthony Powell, is 'something that has to be experienced to be believed'.[53] The spread of uniforms – often called *der Kaisers Rock*, or 'the King's coat' – across Europe helped spread law and order, government authority and deference, and increased soldiers' sense of belonging to a separate world from civilian society. For many, their uniform became their dearest possession. If a soldier stopped wearing uniform, often, like the Free French pilot Romain Gary after 1945, he felt 'disconcerted, dispossessed, as if he had had a limb amputated'.[54]

A hundred years earlier contemporaries had been impressed by the splendid coats of Louis XIV. Now they preferred the simple uniforms of Joseph II. When the Emperor visited Versailles in 1778, unlike the Archduke Maximilian in 1775 he continued to wear uniform. A French courtier, the duc de Croÿ wrote: 'moreover it could only be a good example for our Court and likely to give it an idea of true grandeur'.[55] Meeting Joseph II in 1784, a Swedish courtier, Axel von Fersen, had a similar reaction: 'the great simplicity of his manners, his speeches and his clothes made a great contrast with the elegance and frivolity of ours; he had a solid air and we light . . . I do not believe that our red heels, our fine *coiffure*, our diamonds, our watch-chains and our satin suits were superior to a good uniform of clean cloth.'[56]

Uniforms conquered the courts of Europe. By 1778 or earlier, military uniforms could be worn to the court of St James's: by 1796, when Great Britain was again at war with France, uniform was being worn by more than half the men attending it, including the King's sons.[57] By 1789 all Spanish army officers below the rank of *maréchal de camp* were obliged to go to court in military uniform,[58] while a civil uniform, 'of black velvet with scarlet satin lining and sleeves and waistcoat embroidered in gold flowers', had been created for senior officials and ambassadors.[59] By 1790 in St Petersburg, according to two French travellers, 'almost all the men appear there [at court] in uniform'.[60]

Men without uniforms frequently created their own, simply in order to have a uniform to wear when going to court, or when having their portrait painted. In Dresden in 1764, for example, James Boswell called his red coat the uniform of a British officer, when he wore it to attend the court of the Elector of Saxony.[61] In Turin, capital of a military monarchy which at times spent half its budget on its army,[62] where the royal family and most nobles always wore uniform to court, special decrees were issued to try to prevent nobles from attending court wearing uniforms to which they had no right.[63] Many

9 Francesco Liani, Ferdinand IV of Naples, *c.* 1773.
Such was the popularity of military monarchy that even the King of Naples, not a natural soldier, had himself painted as a grenadier on sentry duty and manoeuvred troops for the benefit of visiting sovereigns – although he also remarked that, whatever uniform they wore, they would still run away.

Englishmen applied for commissions in the militia, or the post of Deputy Lieutenant, as many Irishmen joined the Volunteer movement in the 1780s, for the sake of the uniform.[64] The future George IV was obsessed with dress. In 1779 at the age of seventeen, he had sent Mary Hamilton, a reader to his sisters, a plan for a new *habit habillé*: 'I send you a Pattern of it, I intend to make it up for New Year's day with a white Ermine lining with a White Sattin Waistcoat embroidered with Cheneal . . . [to be] very full dress.'[65] Like many contemporaries, however, he was soon dissatisfied by the *habit habillé*. 'Military-mad' since he was a boy, he yearned for military uniform.[66]

Deprived of military rank by a jealous and contemptuous father, in 1782 he commissioned a portrait of himself by Gainsborough, wearing a self-designed red uniform.[67] When finally appointed colonel of the 10th Light Dragoons in 1793, his head was '*almost turned*' and he felt 'boundless joy'. He made it one of the smartest regiments in the army, with the most elaborate uniforms.[68] His lack of further military promotion infuriated him, but did not stop him, as surviving tailors' accounts reveal, ordering uniforms to which he was not yet entitled, for his private enjoyment. One of his first acts on becoming Regent in 1811 was to promote himself Field Marshal: he had owned uniforms of that

10 Girolamo Prepiani, Lord Byron, 1813.
Byron wore, and had himself painted in, a self-invented scarlet military uniform for two reasons. When he was travelling in Spain during the Peninsular War, or being presented to Ottoman authorities during his grand tour, it inspired greater respect. In addition, uniform reflected his desire to play a military role, which was realised when on 5 January 1824, wearing another self-invented uniform, he landed in Greece to lead the struggle for independence against the Ottoman Empire.

rank since 1800.[69] Thus Great Britain and Ireland, as well as Russia, Prussia and Austria, contained the elements necessary for a military monarchy.

The principal exception to the fashion for military monarchy and uniforms was France. In 1762, during the Seven Years War, uniforms in the French army had been minutely regulated by an ordonnance of the duc de Choiseul, as they would be by further ordonnances in 1767, 1775, 1776 and 1786.[70] However, at court, at the King's personal wish, courtiers continued to wear magnificent *habits habillés*.[71] There is no trace of uniforms in the accounts of the *grand maître de la garde-robe du roi*, the duc de Liancourt: they consist of bills from the King's *plumassier*, *brodeur*, lace-maker and other tradesmen.[72]

Whereas the spread of uniform cut the costs of clothes for nobles in other monarchies, at the French court dress remained a major item of expense. For the celebrations of the marriage of the duc de Chartres in 1769, the duc de Villars wore a fortune in diamonds on his sable-lined cloth-of-gold coat.[73] The duc de Croÿ wrote in 1770 of people ruining themselves by buying embroidery to be worn at the wedding of the Dauphin and Marie Antoinette.[74] The coats made for the weddings of the Dauphin (the future Louis XVI) and the comtes de Provence and d'Artois, in 1770, 1771 and 1773, sparkling with jewellery, cost 64,347, 55,726 and 31,695 livres respectively: they were as spectacular as those made for the weddings of their father the Dauphin in 1746 and their grandfather Louis XV in 1725.[75]

Versailles was not isolated from the army. The Ministry of War was beside the palace. All princes of the royal family and of the blood were nominal commanders of at least one regiment, and often, in addition, colonel-general of a branch of the army: thus the duc d'Orléans was Colonel-General of the Hussars. Louis XV and Louis XVI wore a scarlet uniform coat with gold embroidery at the few military reviews they held, such as the annual review of the Gardes français and Gardes suisses, and the review of the guards and the entire Maison militaire every four years, on the Plaine des Sablons near Paris.[76] On such occasions contemporaries commented on the King's 'majestic air'. Louis XVI and princes of his family also wore the uniform of the regiment of which they were colonel, when they reviewed or drilled it: for example, the King that of Roi-infanterie, Monsieur that of his Carabiniers.[77]

Trying to justify themselves after the revolution, many courtiers of Versailles claimed that they had been primarily officers. The duc d'Escars wrote in his memoirs that he had felt a *joie excessive* when made a colonel in 1773: the court had been for him 'as for the greater part of the French nobility less an end than a means to facilitate a military career.'[78] Although he held the great court office of *capitaine des gardes*, and was a Noailles, a member of the best-connected of all French court families, the prince de Poix considered the army, not the court, his vocation. He too wrote in his autobiography that when he had been made colonel of a regiment, 'the joy which I felt as a result was at its height. I thought I was commanding an army.'[79]

However, the dress worn at Versailles sent out a signal contradicting its military ethos: it advertised the splendour of a class, not the service of the state. Serving officers were allowed to wear uniform only on the day they arrived from, or departed for, their regiment, or if they were officers of the Maison militaire or the Guards regiments *de service*. Even foreigners (if not of royal rank) were not allowed to appear at Versailles in uniform. The main reason why military uniform was otherwise forbidden was economic: the need, as a diplomat the marquis de Bombelles wrote in 1783, 'to favour the manufactures of the country'.[80] The King put trade before war, the economic needs of the silk industry of Lyon before the prestige of the French army.

In 1782, during the War of American Independence, Captain Sheldon, an Irishman in the French service, had driven straight from the port of Brest to bring the King news of the fall of the British colony of Grenada. However,

11 Jean-Michel Moreau *le jeune*, *La grande toilette*, 1777.
Servants finish the toilette of a *grand seigneur*, while he receives a lady, a writer and
soldiers. Dressing was such a lengthy process that it was often combined, in private
houses as well as at court, with receiving people. As *dessinateur des menus-plaisirs du roi*,
Moreau *le jeune* was well aware of the importance of dress at court.

because he wore his captain's uniform, he was forbidden to enter the
apartments of Louis XVI until he changed out of uniform into an *habit habillé*.
His cousin Madame de La Tour du Pin commented sixty years later in her
memoirs: 'and people are surprised that the Revolution overthrew a Court
where such childishnesses occurred . . . The costume which had conquered the
flags was not worthy to present them.'[81]

Indeed both Louis XVI and Marie Antoinette publicly encouraged the
French textile industry. For the Sunday reception at court, and at other
ceremonies, Louis XVI remained *très magnifique dans ses habits*, wearing the
Order of the Holy Spirit in diamonds.[82] His coats, too, often sparkled with
diamonds.[83] He personally ensured that actors in the royal theatre companies
wore magnificent costumes;[84] and in 1784 he sent his trusted *premier valet de
chambre* and *intendant du garde-meuble*, Thierry de Ville d'Avray, to Lyon to
place new orders with the silk industry: for example, a new *tenture d'été* for the
Queen's bedroom at Versailles in 1786; new hangings for the *Salon des jeux du
roi* at Fontainebleau and the *Grand cabinet de la reine* at Rambouillet.[85] In 1785
Provence was still buying, at considerable expense, jewelled shoe buckles
and hat and coat ornaments, while the duc de Saulx-Tavannes, *chevalier*

d'honneur de la Reine, spent about a quarter of his income on dress and other adornments.[86]

Illustrated fashion magazines had begun with the prints of French nobles and courtiers published in the *Mercure galant* founded in Paris in 1672.[87] After 1750 the growth of the Paris fashion industry, and of new fashion magazines such as *Le Cabinet des modes* and *Le Journal des dames*, further increased the publicity for, and economic impact of, French court dress.[88] Marie Antoinette was the first Queen to link court society and the fashion industry. Dress had defined her role in France from the moment of her entry into the kingdom in May 1770. She had been obliged, at the frontier, to change out of Austrian into French clothes, as a way of demonstrating that she was henceforth French. In reality her clothes were a deceptive façade. Frenchmen felt – it was the main reason for her loss of popularity – she remained loyal to Austria.[89]

Soon after her husband's accession to the throne, the Queen started a fashion for wigs piled so high with models of ships, mountains or forests that ladies had to kneel in their carriages: some said the Queen would ruin all the ladies of France.[90] In 1775, referring to the Queen's influence on French fashion, a journalist wrote: 'The toilette of a woman becomes in this country a political matter by its influence on commerce and manufactures.'[91] That year she launched a fashion for wearing white ostrich feathers in the hair, which aroused the especial wrath of her mother the Empress Maria Theresa; from Versailles, however, it spread to Paris. Ostrich feathers are worn by women in the prints of Jean-Michel Moreau's *Monuments du costume* (1776–7), such as *Le Rendez-vous pour Marly*, *Le Rencontre au bois de Boulogne* and *La Dame du palais de la reine*.[92] With Marie Antoinette's encouragement, her friend the Duchess of Devonshire helped make ostrich feathers fashionable in England – a fashion which lasted, at court, until 1939.[93]

Dress-making, like court life, was one of the few public arenas open to female enterprise. Since 1675 Frenchwomen had been allowed to go into business on their own as *couturières* and from 1776 they formed a separate female guild of *faiseuses de modes*.[94] The most successful was the Queen's favourite *marchande de modes*, Mlle Rose Bertin. Treating princesses as her equals, she soon acquired a reputation for insolence.[95] Against precedent, as *marchande de modes de Sa Majesté* she was allowed into the Queen's private apartments. She became so famous that, at the royal couple's state entry into Paris on 8 February 1779 to celebrate the birth of their first child, the King publicly rose to applaud Mlle Bertin, who was standing with thirty workers on the balcony of her house in the rue du Faubourg Saint-Honoré. Thus, in the streets of Paris, the court of Versailles advertised its extravagance and

12 Jean-Michel Moreau *le jeune*, The *Festin Royal* at the Hôtel de Ville, given to the King and Queen to celebrate the birth of the Dauphin on 21 January 1782 (detail).
Louis XVI, Marie Antoinette and their courtiers are wearing full court dress, as they continued to do on ceremonial occasions until the fall of the monarchy ten years later.

frivolity.[96] Indeed the Queen's collection of magnificent dresses, displayed in three large rooms at Versailles, could be visited by members of the public.[97] Rose Bertin also created the dress for the wax model of the Queen displayed with the rest of the royal family 'exactly as at Versailles', in the salon of waxwork figures opened by Curtius in the Palais Royal in 1783.[98] Before 1789, its popularity reflected that of the royal family.

The King and Queen continued the formal etiquettes of the French court. The *lever* and *coucher du roi* continued much as in the reign of Louis XIV and the *salon de l'œil de bœuf* was often too small to contain all the courtiers come for the ceremony.[99] The morning *toilette de la reine*, when her *dame d'honneur* and *dame d'atours*, and princesses of the royal family if present, helped the Queen in the physical process of dressing, was one of the main occasions used to pay her court.[100] As was expected of a queen of France, she ordered an impressive number of dresses every winter: twelve *grands habits*, twelve *robes parées* and twelve *petites robes*.[101] In 1780, in the middle of the War of American Independence, the Queen instituted a new presentation costume, the *robe parée*, with a monstrous hoop, to replace the *grand habit*. Again the purpose was economic: 'to revive the old form with more magnificence and splendour and that, it is said, on the representations of commerce on behalf of our velvet and gold embroidery factories, which will collapse if the Court does not come to their help'.[102] For her presentation to Marie Antoinette, Madame de La Tour du Pin wore rows of diamonds in her hair, around her neck, and lacing the front of the special corset made for presentation costumes. Her skirt was 'entirely embroidered in pearls and in silver'.[103]

Despite frequent attempts by officials in the Maison du roi to control the expenses of the Maison de la reine, they rose by over 400 per cent, from 1.056 million livres in 1771 to 4.7 million in 1788. At times the efforts of *fournisseurs* to persuade or trap the Queen into buying their products were so audacious that her *dame d'atours* the comtesse d'Ossun considered forbidding them to meet her.[104] The Queen's apartments were so public and accessible, however, that it was impossible to do so. Gradually the *robe parée* replaced the *grand habit de cour* except on the most formal occasions. By 1787 an even simpler *robe ordinaire de cour* was being worn.[105] Away from the court, *robes de grande parure* were being worn only for the most formal balls and dinners.[106] However, there were limits to the fashion for simplicity. In 1783 a portrait by Madame Vigée-Lebrun of the Queen wearing a simple muslin dress had caused an outcry.[107]

Male courtiers also began to find their traditional court costume, the *habit habillé*, too expensive. Even an elaborate temporary uniform was cheaper. At the celebrations of the marriage of the granddaughter of the baron de Breteuil, *ministre de la maison du roi* to the baron de Montmorency in 1788, 'to diminish the expenses of the guests . . . a uniform for the men was created, which consisted of *un habit de canele de soie prune de Monsieur claire*, embroidered in white silk and *pierre d'argent* with a white waistcoat'.[108] If such a coat was an economy, normal courtier's dress must indeed have been expensive.

The reason for the French monarchy's loss of respect after 1750 was not only its perceived extravagance, immorality and protection of the court nobility, but also its anachronistic civilian character. Unlike in other monarchies, military rank gave automatic access neither to the court nor to the nobility. After 1750 criticism of the recivilianisation of the French monarchy became louder. In 1756 in *La Noblesse militaire*, the chevalier d'Arc wrote: 'let soldiers appear at your court only in the uniform which distinguishes them from the rest of Your subjects . . . the uniform of glory and honour'.[109] Viewing Versailles as an Austrian officer, the prince de Ligne wrote: 'What is needed is a military king in order not to be obliged to be a soldier king; let him [Louis XVI], his brothers and his cousins no longer blush to wear military uniform several times a year.'[110]

French courtiers such as the prince de Poix and the marquis de La Fayette showed their taste for military monarchy by travelling as far as Potsdam to attend the reviews and manoeuvres of Frederick the Great. The King of Prussia was shocked when some French officers were presented to him in *habit habillé*, rather than the uniform of their regiment.[111] In 1783, a young French officer, Alexandre Berthier, watched manoeuvres at Potsdam and inspected Silesian battlefields. After his audience with the King, Napoleon's future chief of staff wrote that despite his old blue uniform, 'personne n'a jamais eu plus l'air d'un grand roi'.[112] Potsdam was the future. Years later, Louis XVI's cousin Louis-Philippe, duc d'Orléans, who was neither a militarist nor a reactionary, nevertheless wrote that it was the lack of martial spirit and glory which had destroyed the French monarchy.[113]

3   *Identity*

In 1741 Prince Charles Edward Stuart, grandson of James II, astonished the company at a ball given by the Cardinal de Rohan in Rome by appearing in Scottish Highland dress. It was a dramatic example of another element in royal and court dress: national identity. Like dress based on splendour or service, national dress had a political message. The Prince's dress, which had been supplied from Scotland by the Jacobite Duke of Perth, proclaimed his intention to use Scotland to restore his dynasty to the thrones of its ancestors.[1]

Before the twentieth century most countries and regions had developed their own dress, which was a means for inhabitants to assert their identity and loyalty to a particular location, as well as to clothe their persons.[2] What Soraya Antonius claims, of Palestine in the 1930s, was also true of most of Europe a hundred years earlier: 'you knew at a glance where people were from, which particular village as well as the region, and often you could see what they did in life. Their place in life socially and geographically, was signalled very clearly because they liked others to know, it was a confirmation, an affirmation of a sense of security, of a meaning to their lives.'[3]

In general the stronger the challenge to national identity, the greater the importance of national dress. Hence its popularity among Poles and Swedes; and Scots, Hungarians and Albanians. The former felt threatened by expansionist neighbours like Prussia and Russia, the latter by powerful majorities inside Great Britain, the Habsburg monarchy and the Ottoman Empire, respectively.[4] By the outbreak of the anti-British rising of 1936, the black and white head-dress worn by the rural population in Palestine had also been adopted by city-dwellers, to indicate support for Palestinian nationalism. Among Arab neighbours, as well as in Palestine, it sells better during times of conflict with Israel.[5]

Indeed in the Ottoman Empire, particularly heterogeneous in religions and nationalities – it was said to contain seventy-six and a half (including gypsies) – dress was especially important as an identity indicator, and as a means to help the government control and regulate life in the cosmopolitan imperial capital.[6] An elaborate dress code regulating the colour, shape and material of the headgear and costumes assigned to different ranks and religions had been formalised in the Ottoman Empire under Suleiman the Magnificent. It is discussed here since its provisions continued to be applied, with relatively few changes, until the Ottoman dress revolution of 1826–9.

The bases of the Ottoman dress code were religious and racial identity and official rank. As in the West, the dress code was not only imposed from above. Authorities of religious and racial minorities often asked for dress rules as a sign of official protection and a means of controlling their group.[7] In accordance with Muslim tradition since the conquests of the seventh century, in order to teach the minorities humility and distinguish them from Muslims, Christians and Jews were ordered to wear sombre colours and sometimes further badges of identification, such as caps or kalpaks. Imperial orders stated: 'Jews and Christians . . . are required by *shariah* and the judgement of reason to have the lot of common people and [exhibit] a thoroughly abased, dispirited demeanour'; 'they are firmly and vehemently forbidden to wear garments equal to or resembling Muslims'.[8] The turban, which left the forehead free for Muslims' prostration during prayer and according to a saying of the Prophet Muhammad conferred blessings on the wearer, was restricted to Muslims.[9] Muslims wore yellow slippers, Armenians red, Greeks black and Jews blue.

This was a fixed dress code, completely different, as western visitors noted, from those of the West. Religious identity replaced the demands of class and fashion.[10] Recording the costumes of the different offices, races, religions and regions of the Ottoman Empire was a favourite occupation of western travellers and painters in Constantinople, from Du Fresne-Canaye in the sixteenth century to Jean-Baptiste Vanmour in the eighteenth.[11] Contravention of the dress code, by Muslims imitating non-Muslims as well as the other way round, could lead to death or confiscation of property. Even making insulting remarks about another man's headgear could result in a court case.[12] The frequent repetition of such orders, however, shows that they were equally frequently disobeyed.

Dress was also used to convey the grandeur of the Ottoman Empire. The oldest dynastic costume collection in Europe, of 2,500 items including 1,000 kaftans, is in Topkapi Palace. Owing to reverence for the Ottoman dynasty, from the early sixteenth century it became customary to put a dead sultan's or prince's belongings in wrappers, sealing them with his name and storing them in the palace treasury (in a few cases they were kept in a mosque, inside or above his tomb).[13] The basic unit of imperial costume was the kaftan. Kaftans were single robes, cut straight from the neck to the feet, often with a flare at the waist, and long sleeves. Contrary to the teachings of the Koran and the Hadith, they could be made of velvet, satin, brocaded silk or cloth of gold, and, from the eighteenth century, lined with sable or black fox fur. In theory the last was reserved for the Sultan alone, and the Sultan alone had the right to two heron plumes in his turban.[14]

The Sultan and his viziers would sometimes wear three kaftans, so that their contrasting fabrics and colours could be admired. In such costumes, Ottoman writers noted with pride, the Ottoman Sultan and his servants resembled a garden of tulips. The *ulama* (teachers of religious law) wore purple, viziers green, palace officials and servants scarlet.[15] Thanks to its *brillants, resplendissants et éclatants* costumes, the Ottoman court, as diplomats and travellers constantly remarked, provided the finest spectacle in Europe. Ottomans laughed at Franks as 'people of a thousand colours', whose clothes, and sword protruding like a tail, made them look like monkeys.[16]

As in France and England, textiles were one of the capital's principal industries. By 1577 there were 268 looms in Constantinople, of which eighty-eight were 'attached to the palace', with the privilege of making 'cloth of gold'. At times the Mint threatened to run out of gold and silver, since so much was used for making thread. In vain the Sultan issued edicts forbidding their use in clothes: these were rarely obeyed.[17] Embroidery was one of the principal occupations of Ottoman women: they were more likely to go to school to learn embroidery than to learn to read and write.

Worn mainly on ceremonial occasions, Ottoman kaftans also functioned as political weapons. In the West courtiers, officials and officers generally had to buy their own clothes. In the East, however, in accordance with the customs of both the Byzantine and Abbasid empires, robes of honour known as *khilats*, *kaftans* or *tiraz*, made in government workshops, were awarded by the Sultan – as they still are by some Middle Eastern rulers[18] – as symbolic expressions of patronage, protection and sovereignty, to honour, and assert control over, the recipient. The process was often linked to investiture in office, as if a robe, as a personal object linking (and often worn by) ruler and ruled, transmitted authority. Power came through the wardrobe.[19] The first Ottoman sultan was said to have been given a robe of honour by a Seljuk sultan of Rum, as a symbol of his investiture with lands at Soğut – a tradition invented to give legitimacy to the Ottomans.[20] At the Sultan's inauguration, when he sat on his throne in Topkapi Palace, senior officials paid him homage by kissing the hem of his kaftan.[21] After a victory a successful pasha might be rewarded by the Sultan with a robe of honour in gold-encrusted sable.[22] Provincial governors, generals and officers were given fur cloaks or kaftans of lesser value.[23] The most important object in the ceremonial of investiture, by the Sultan or Grand Vizier, of a new Oecumenical Patriarch, or Prince of Wallachia or Prince of Moldavia, was a kaftan.[24]

The wardrobe could also impart blessing. The *abaya* or cloak of the Prophet was considered particularly sacred, since he had used an *abaya* to carry a stone to help rebuild the Ka'aba in Mecca.[25] One of the relics of the Prophet sent to Constantinople from Mecca after the acknowledgement of Ottoman suzerainty by the Hejaz in 1517, until the end of the empire it was revered by the Sultan and his family with other relics at an annual ceremony in the special chamber in Topkapi Palace, where it was housed and where it can still be seen today. In the inauguration rites of the Ottoman sultans it became an important symbol of sovereignty.[26] Possession of the Prophet's relics increased the Ottoman dynasty's aura of sanctity, as possession of the 'holy shroud', housed in a chapel in the royal palace in Turin, increased the prestige of the House of Savoy.

In the Ottoman Empire most European merchants and travellers dressed in local dress, *à la longue*, since it suited the climate, and local manners and customs. Away from Constantinople, especially in Egypt and inland Syria, where Muslim prejudice was strongest, physical survival was a further reason: local dress protected them from the insult, assault or murder to which European dress might expose them.[27] Even in Constantinople, a cosmopolitan capital used to western Europeans, in order to avoid insult French officers instructing the Ottoman navy often had to wear grey clothes rather than their own uniforms.[28]

Out of respect for their diplomatic functions, however, all European ambassadors and consuls – even if they relaxed in Ottoman dress at home – wore European dress in public.[29] (Dubrovnik ambassadors' use of long robes, rather than European dress, in Constantinople was a sign that they were Ottoman tributaries, rather than representatives of an independent state.[30]) The ceremony of 'kaftaning the ambassador', before he entered the Sultan's presence at the start of his mission, incorporated him in the dress code of the empire – and signalled that he and his suite were guests under the Sultan's protection.

Ambassadors in Constantinople judged their status and success by the number and magnificence of the kaftans they were given. Such was the importance attributed to this signal that ambassadors refused to proceed to the throne room in the imperial palace from the imperial divan or council chamber, where they had breakfasted with the Grand Vizier, until servants sent to an adjoining vestibule had reported how many kaftans awaited them. Only when they had put on kaftans over their European dress were they admitted to the Sultan's throne room. Ambassadors thus became living symbols of their country's conjunction of interests with the Ottoman Empire. In the presence of the Sultan they retained, as a mark of their identity and religion, their hats – hence the Ottoman use of the word 'hats' as a description for west Europeans.[31]

In the seventeenth century ambassadors generally received about forty kaftans; from 1644 exceptionally important ambassadors, such as an Ambassador Extraordinary of the Holy Roman Emperor, also obtained a cloak of sable.[32] In 1724 the French ambassador received forty-two kaftans for members of his embassy, in addition to his own, which the dragoman assured him was of richer material than those usually distributed to ambassadors, and similar to that worn by the Grand Vizier himself.[33] The catastrophic defeat of the Ottoman Empire in its war of 1768–74 against Russia was reflected in its treatment of ambassadors. From 1772 every ambassador began to receive a sable cloak.[34] In 1775 the new Russian ambassador Prince Repnin returned in triumph to Constantinople, where he had been imprisoned by the Ottoman government during the war. For himself he received a sable coat covered in brocade; for senior members of his embassy, four sable coats; for ten cavaliers accompanying his embassy, ermine coats; and for lesser officials one hundred kaftans.[35]

A comparable dress system existed in the Mogul Empire. The basic unit was a wider version of the kaftan called the *chakdar jama* or *khilat*. In contrast to the strict religious demarcations of the Ottoman Empire, the Emperor Akbar and his descendants succeeded in amalgamating Muslim and Hindu dress, while at the same time revealing and respecting religious identities, by having Hindus' robes tied under the left arm, and Muslims' under the right.[36] From the reign of the Emperor Akbar, as one of his officials recorded, a thousand complete suits were made every season in government workshops. They were stored in bundles according to colour, 'ready at all times for bestowal'.[37] Although often, like some of his successors, himself preferring simple dress with few jewels, the Emperor 'acquired in a short time a theoretical and practical knowledge of the whole [textile] trade'. Iranian, Mongolian and European materials were used as well as Indian.[38]

On occasion, as a special sign of honour the Emperor would take off his own *khilat* and bestow it on a subject.[39] In 1666 the great Hindu leader Shivaji, still a national hero in India today, used dress to show his detestation of the Muslim Mogul Empire and rejection of its service. He threw his *khilat* on the ground in front of the Emperor Aurangzeb (1658–1707) and cried: 'Kill me, imprison me if you like, but I will not wear the *khilat*.'[40] Then he fled the imperial presence. Later he led the first great Maratha rebellion against the Mogul Empire.

At a time when other European monarchies had abandoned sumptuary laws, Ottoman sultans continued to enforce them in person. This was especially frequent from the mid-eighteenth century, as if strict enforcement of dress rules could counteract economic and military decline.[41] Osman III (1754–7) 'prowled the streets of Constantinople in disguise haranguing men and women for their clothing improprieties. In the same breath he condemned women for clothing that was too tight and men for using gold thread on their horses and saddle-cloths in a manner inappropriate to their rank.' Mustafa III (1757–74) sent criers through the streets to announce the renewal of the dress regulations. He was especially concerned to enforce distinctions between Muslims and minorities.[42]

In 1758 the Sultan, in disguise, followed at a distance by executioners (presumably also disguised), visited Jewish and Christian quarters to conduct a personal dress check. The French ambassador, the comte de Vergennes, claimed that both the Grand Vizier and the Mufti of Constantinople tried to restrain the Sultan, assuring him that such behaviour lacked dignity. The Sultan ignored them. An Armenian found wearing the wrong clothes was executed. An unfortunate Christian beggar who wore an old pair of yellow slippers just given him by a Turk in charity was stopped by the Sultan; and this excuse could not save his life.

Mustafa III also banned western dress among minorities, since 'this abominable situation disturbed the order among the subjects'.[43] A later sultan, Selim III (1789–1807), also roamed the streets in disguise, handing over violators of the dress code to officials for punishment. He was particularly concerned by shameless women in light-hued coats.[44] As an innovation he stressed that clothes should be made of local products: 'I always wear Istanbul-made and Ankara-made cloth. But my statesmen wear Indian-made and Iran-made cloth. If they would wear the clothes of our country local goods would be in demand.'[45]

By then, however, the Ottoman dress system was winding down. The palace itself was buying silks and brocades from Lyon.[46] If they were in the service of a foreign embassy, or had bought a diploma from a foreign ambassador saying that they were, rich Greeks, Armenians and Jews obtained the envied distinction of wearing the yellow slippers of the Muslims.[47] Writing in 1809, John Cam Hobhouse noticed Greeks' desire to wear a hat 'instead of a cap or turban, to look Frankish' – and to gain freedom from Ottoman taxes and oppression.[48]

The Ottoman Empire exercised an influence on foreign dress rivalling that of France. Foreign traders and travellers, even the French ambassador the comte de Vergennes, were painted in Ottoman dress.[49] From the sixteenth century until the dress revolution of Peter the Great, Ottoman textiles were used in Moscow in secular and religious costumes. In the early seventeenth century, threatened on all sides by Russia, Sweden and western Europe, Poland also turned to the Ottoman Empire as a model for national dress. The new Polish national dress consisted of yellow boots, such as those reserved for the Ottoman élite; a long robe like a kaftan called the *kontush*, with a long fur-lined cloak; a shirt or *zupan*, a Magyar cap, and a brightly coloured 'Persian' sash. At first the sashes were manufactured by Armenians in Constantinople; later they were made in Poland, and even as far away as Lyon.[50] Polish national dress was worn with a shaved head, in the manner of the Ottomans and the Tartars of Crimea, but without accompanying turbans.[51]

The choice of an Ottoman model was intended to assert Poland's differences from western Europe – perhaps in order to mark Polish rejection of the monarchical absolutism associated with France and Austria.[52] Ottoman dress may have been introduced in Poland by Stephen Bathory, Prince of Transylvania since 1571 (and as such an Ottoman vassal who, like the princes of Moldavia and Wallachia, wore Ottoman dress). He was elected King of Poland in 1575, and reigned there until his death in 1586.[53] In their Polish dress, Wladislaw IV (1632–48) and many Polish magnates look more Ottoman than western.[54] In 1683 at the siege of Vienna some Polish soldiers looked so Turkish that they had to wear straw hats to distinguish themselves from the Turkish troops they were attacking.[55]

In the eighteenth century, as surviving inventories show, Polish country gentlemen still wore traditional dress. In contrast King Stanislas Augustus Poniatowski, who reigned from 1764 to 1795, considered this a sign of backwardness, and always wore French dress. In his case personal vanity was stronger than national feeling. He was so proud of his luxuriant hair that for his coronation he obtained a doctor's certificate that his health would suffer if he cut it off. Without a shaved head in Polish style, he could not wear Polish national dress.[56]

After the first partition of Poland in 1772, however, Polish dress became a symbol of the threatened motherland, surrounded by the expanding, military

13 Louis de Silvestre, King Augustus III of Poland in the Polish dress he had worn at his coronation, with the Order of the White Eagle, 1737.
Augustus III wore traditional Polish dress to try to prove that, although also Elector of Saxony, he was as Polish in feeling as his Polish-born rival King Stanislas Leszczynzki. After his coronation, Augustus III never wore Polish dress again.

and uniform-wearing monarchies of Russia, Austria and Prussia. In 1776 the shock of partition led to the introduction of a law imposing uniforms on nobles, deputies and government officials. They were to be made of Polish materials, in different colours for each palatinate or county, and often resembled military uniforms. This dress reform had four aims: to heighten national and provincial loyalty; to emphasise nobles' role in the defence of the country; to encourage national industries; and to eliminate differences in dress between rich and poor nobles.[57] In 1788, as part of his programme for Polish revival, the Prince de Ligne, who had received Polish *indigénat* (a form of naturalisation), and dreamt of becoming King of Poland, advised making Polish national dress compulsory, except in the army: 'they would be allowed to take off the tunic only to go riding and while on military service: but they must keep the large breeches, the very Polish bonnet and the most oriental air. Perhaps I would not insist on the shaven head.'[58] That year patriotic deputies changed into Polish dress for meetings of the 'Great Sejm' which challenged the hegemony of Russia. The national leader Kosciusko wore Polish dress to read the Act of Insurrection in the market square in Cracow on 24 March 1794. From 1830 Poles wore national dress in Austria, especially on public occasions such as weddings and court entertainments, and even at meetings of the Reichsrat, as a symbol of identity, of defiance of the partitioning powers and of belief in Poland's 'resurrection'.[59] In 1866, after the failure of the Polish insurrection of 1864, the Tsarist government banned not only Polish dress but also Polish horse trappings in Lithuania and Ukraine; even the Tsarist government, however, could not ban them in Poland itself.[60]

Instead of imposing one court dress like the Ottomans or Moguls, the Habsburgs practised a more supple policy. They had little choice: they ruled a great number of nationalities, each with its own dress.[61] Until 1900 the streets of the imperial *Haupt und Residenzstadt* Vienna were brightened with the 'peculiar costumes' of their different provinces, and of travelling Serbs, Armenians, Greeks and Turks.[62]

Despite many periods of antagonism between Hungary and the Habsburgs, Hungarian dress was welcome at the court of Vienna. Like Polish dress, Hungarian dress reflected Ottoman influence: in its gala form for nobles, it consisted of tight-fitting trousers; a tunic or dolman, often embroidered with gold and silver braid, gold sequins and tinsel; a fur-lined cloak; a velvet or fur cap and yellow boots like those of the Ottomans and Poles. Women wore tight-fitting dresses, small embroidered and bejewelled caps, and richly embroidered veils and aprons.[63]

From the seventeenth century Habsburgs themselves wore Hungarian dress, when crowned as King of Hungary or serving as Palatine of the kingdom.[64] The Empress Maria Theresa wore Hungarian dress and frequently dressed her son and heir Joseph in it – although this would not prevent him, in the 1780s, from attacking Hungarian particularism.[65] The most splendid uniform in Europe, red with silver embroidery, a fur cap, a white egret aigrette, a leopard skin slung over the shoulder, and yellow boots, was that of the Hungarian Noble Life Guard founded in 1760 by Maria Theresa: only someone who had seen them, recalled Prince Clary, the last surviving chamberlain of the last Emperor of Austria, 'can even begin to picture the splendour of their uniform'.[66]

In Scotland national dress could arouse even fiercer loyalty than in Hungary or Poland. Although different tartans had not yet been formally assigned to different clans, the brightly striped tartan wool plaid or cloak, with stockings but often without breeches or trousers, had been worn by Highlanders since the Middle Ages. After the Act of Union with England in 1707, and the loss of an independent Scottish parliament, tartan became a symbol of identity for

14 Anon., The 'Young Pretender' in
Scottish dress, *c.* 1745.
The 'Young Pretender' wore Scottish dress
during the 1745 campaign, in England as
well as Scotland.

Scots hostile to the Union, from the Stuarts in Rome to Edinburgh Tories –
though it was also worn by Highlanders serving in the British army.[67] The kilt
or short skirt was invented soon after, and began to replace more traditional
plaid trews.[68]

The Jacobite poet Alexander Macdonald wrote:

> Better for me is the proud plaid
> Around my shoulder and put under my arm,
> Better than though I would get a coat
> Of the best cloth that comes from England.[69]

When the English MP Sir John Hynde Cotton visited Edinburgh in 1744, to
demonstrate his Jacobite loyalties he ordered a tartan suit (on show in the
National Museum of Scotland today).[70] At the beginning of the last serious
Stuart bid for the throne, Prince Charles Edward Stuart arrived from France
in August 1745 in a plain black suit.[71] However, he soon adopted tartan for
himself, his Highland and his Lowland troops, and wore it to enter English
towns as well as Edinburgh.[72] Thus on 29 November 1745 'the Highland

laddie', as he was now known, entered Manchester wearing 'a light tartan plaid belted with a blue sash, a gray wig and a blue velvet bonnet, topped by a rose of white ribbons the badge of his house'.[73] The Battle of Culloden in 1746 was depicted for the victorious general the Duke of Cumberland by David Morier as a victory for red-uniformed British troops over tartaned Scots. Thereafter the Prince fled through the Highlands disguised in tartan, and was frequently so depicted in Jacobite portraits. In London Flora Macdonald, who had helped the Prince escape to France, was painted wearing a tartan dress covered in Stuart white roses, by Richard Wilson in 1747 and by Allan Ramsay in 1749.[74]

Never a Jacobite monopoly, tartan was also worn by Hanoverians. The son of George II, Frederick, Prince of Wales, wore it occasionally, to annoy his father's Whig government.[75] In 1747 the Earl of Loudoun, Governor of Stirling Castle, commander of Highland forces opposed to the Jacobites and an ADC to George II, was painted by Allan Ramsay in red army jacket and tartan kilt and stockings.[76] Nevertheless, such was the terror inspired by the 1745 rebellion in London that on 1 August 1746, as part of the government's measures to destroy the Highland way of life, men and boys in Scotland were by law forbidden to wear 'the clothes commonly called Highland clothes, that is to say the Plaid, Philabeg or little Kilt, Trowse, Shoulder-belts or any part whatever of what peculiarly belongs to the Highland Garb'. The penalty was six months' imprisonment and, on a second offence, seven years' trans-portation overseas.[77] On the recommendation of the Duke of Cumberland, the victor of Culloden, the sole exceptions to the proscription were Scottish Highland regiments in the British army, which continued to wear tartan. Hence when two Highland officers entered Covent Garden theatre one night in 1763, they were instantly identified. A mob in the upper gallery yelled: 'No Scots! No Scots! Out with them!'[78] In Scotland, however, one reason for Scottish regiments' popularity, and the principal feature of their recruiting posters until the late twentieth century, was the abundance of tartan, kilts, caps, sporrans and other Scottish symbols in their uniforms.[79]

Despite or because of the ban, some Highland chiefs continued to wear, or be painted in, tartan.[80] New wars, however, killed old fears. In 1782, to reward the performance of Scottish regiments in the British army during the War of American Independence, the ban on tartan in Scotland, never systematically applied, was rescinded. Particularly after the extinction of Stuart hopes on the death of Charles Edward Stuart in Florence in 1788, tartan became increas-ingly popular, both in and outside Scotland. Like the Habsburgs with Hungarian dress, the Hanoverians used Scottish dress as a weapon to assert their claims over, and to calm the irredentism of, a potentially rebellious

15 David Wilkie, George IV in Scottish dress, 1829.
In 1821 George IV wore this costume, with flesh coloured pantaloons, at a levee in Holyrood House. More than most monarchs, George IV considered dress an essential element in the construction of his public image.

kingdom. The Prince of Wales wore the tartan of a Highland chief at masquerades in London in 1788 and 1806. As King, he encouraged Scots to wear it to court – 'I will always be happy to see you in that dress,' he told Clanranald.

In the early nineteenth century, partly through the efforts of the English clothes manufacturers Wilson and Son of Bannockburn, tartans of specific colours and patterns – 'tailors' tartans' – were, for the first time, systematically assigned to different clans, or even estates. Under the presidency of George IV's friend Walter Scott, a Celtic Society 'to promote the general use of the ancient highland dress in the Highlands' was formed in Edinburgh in 1815.[81] In August 1822, during the first visit to Scotland by a reigning monarch since 1651, it received the royal seal of approval.

On most formal occasions, in keeping with his 'military madness', George IV wore a Field Marshal's uniform. At a levee in Holyrood House on 17 August, however, in a celebrated gesture to Scottish feeling, the King wore a kilt in Royal Stewart tartan, lined with green silk, with sporran, belts of black Moroccan leather, brooches, pistols, a feathered bonnet, a jewelled badge, an emerald-hilted dirk and flesh-coloured pantaloons.[82] Among the 1,200 gentlemen who attended, some complained: 'Sir Walter had ridiculously made us appear a nation of Highlanders'. Others found the King 'a verra pretty man'.[83] From the 1830s, as Scotland suffered the double trauma of the industrial revolution and the 'Highland clearances', dress provided a symbol of identity and tradition, both real and spurious. To this day tartan remains a profitable industry in Scotland.

In other countries national dress was less popular. German dynasties had a custom, for exceptional entertainments, of dressing up in the peasant and regional costumes worn by their subjects: the Saxon court often wore the dress of local miners.[84] Attempts to create a German national dress, however, as advocated in 1775 by Justus Moser in his book *Patriotische Phantasien*, and in 1813–15, at the height of German national exaltation against Napoleon I, in order 'to escape the dangerous influence of French fashions', failed.[85] A revival of Spanish traditional dress and mantillas in the 1790s, and legislation against novelty in dress, in reaction against the 'godless' French revolution, was more sucessful. In their portraits by Goya painted around 1800, in contrast to those painted ten years earlier, the Queen, the Duchess of Alba and other ladies wear not the latest Paris fashions but Spanish dress and mantillas.[86]

In Ireland, perhaps due to the lack of enthusiasm of the Anglo-Irish élites for Celtic traditions, and the abundance of English legislation against them, the traditional national dress of cap, mantle and trews, widely worn before 1600 (visible in the 1680 portrait of Sir Neil O'Neill by J. M. Wright in Tate Britain), was thereafter abandoned in favour of English dress. St Patrick's Day on 17 March, however, was still celebrated with the wearing of shamrock, and of the 'national' colour green, in opposition to 'England's cruel red';[87] from the mid-seventeenth century most educated Irish dressed English.[88] Dress patriotism was limited to repeated requests, or orders, by Lord-Lieutenants of Ireland for guests to wear items of local manufacture such as Irish silks, lace, linen and poplin, at the court balls, drawing-rooms and levees which they held in Dublin Castle, partly to encourage the local dress trade. One eighteenth-century Lord-Lieutenant, Lord Chesterfield, was so successful in his task that he was escorted to the boat taking him back to England by a phalanx of grateful Irish weavers.[89]

In England dress nationalism was similarly limited. Perhaps because England felt secure in its identity, and had been a unified kingdom since 1087, there was only one attempt to create an English national dress. It took place in October 1666, after French aid to the Dutch during the second Anglo-Dutch War. Determined 'to leave the French mode', Charles II started a fashion for

English dress, using English materials and long black cloth or wool vests, or plainer coats cut close to the body, in accordance with denunciations of 'the French mode', and 'the Monsieurs Vanitys' by John Evelyn and Samuel Butler – and, the King said, 'to teach the nobility thrift'.[90] John Evelyn called it 'a comely Vest after the Persian mode ... a comely and manly habit', and claimed the King 'had brought the whole Court to it'.[91] According to Hardy Amies, this was the first example of wool being worn to court.[92]

On 17 October Pepys reported, 'the Court is all full of Vests'. Between 1670 and 1672, however, as Charles II reverted to a pro-French policy, 'vests' went out of fashion. Lord Halifax suggested that part of the mission of the King's sister the duchesse d'Orléans, at the time of the secret Treaty of Dover with Louis XIV in 1670, had been to laugh the English out of their vests.[93] A few years later, in response to petitions from the Weavers' Company of London in 1673 and 1675, Charles II proclaimed that he would 'henceforth wear none but English manufactures except linen and calico', and that none of his subjects wearing foreign lace 'should be allowed to appear in His Majesty's presence'. These words were, however, no more than pious promises never intended to be kept.[94]

After their expulsion from France in 1685, the arrival of French Protestant silk manufacturers, some of whom settled in Spitalfields in east London, helped the English silk trade.[95] Under every subsequent reign, down to and including the present day, as part of its patriotic duty, in response to relentless pressure from the dress trade, the royal family has tried to help British (and until 1922 Irish) silk-weavers, linen manufacturers, tailors and dress-makers, by wearing clothes of British or Irish manufacture and encouraging others to do so.[96] In 1765, for example, Queen Charlotte asked courtiers to wear nothing but English silks manufactured at Spitalfields. The *Ipswich Journal* reported that 'the rich dresses in which the Nobility appeared yesterday at Court and which were fabricated at Spital-fields evidently showed that no Nation on Earth can vie with them'. In 1769 the weavers of Spitalfields rioted against imports of foreign silk. In the 1790s the Spitalfields silks worn by the Queen and her daughters were known as 'Queen's silks'.[97] Nationalism extended even to shoe buckles. The Prince of Wales wore British buckles in response to their makers' despairing pleas: 'We make no doubt but your ROYAL HIGHNESS will prefer the blessings of the starving Manufacturers to the encomiums of the drawing room.'[98]

The 'Vandyke dress' fashionable in England from 1740 to 1780 (George III and his family were portrayed in it by Zoffany in 1770), and the *costume à la Henri IV* which the future Louis XVI and his brother the comte de Provence wore at balls in Versailles in 1774, were in part English and French attempts to create a national dress.[99] In 1775 a group of princes and courtiers, including Provence, Artois, the prince de Poix, the marquis de La Fayette and the comte de Ségur, petitioned the Queen to impose Henri IV dress at court. 'If this costume suceeds it will be made the costume of the court and little by little it will become the costume of the nation,' wrote the Swedish ambassador.[100] Employees of the department of *menus-plaisirs* stayed up all night making a mangificent Henri IV costume *garni de dentelles* for the King himself to wear to one of the Queen's balls.[101] This fashion soon passed, possibly on account of the cost: however, its temporary popularity suggests the extent of dissatisfaction, even among the highest in the land, with the traditional *habit habillé*.

The most dramatic attempt by a monarch to create and impose a national dress for political purposes occurred in Sweden. In a bloodless coup on 19 August 1772, three months after his coronation, Gustavus III used his guard to seize power from what he called 'an unbearable aristocratic despotism', government by nobles in the pay of France, Britain or Russia. The uniform he wore on the day of the coup was self-designed, inspired by the plain blue uniform worn by Charles XII when he had set off for war in 1718: the heroic – and anti-Russian – autocrat of the past was emulated by his successor. The white armband which Gustavus III wore that day, later known as a *suédoise*, was adopted as a rallying sign by his supporters and worn by Swedish soldiers for the rest of the reign.[102] Before the King's coup, Sweden had seemed as divided and vulnerable as Poland: Frederick the Great sneered that foreign corruption had perverted its national spirit.[103] Gustavus III responded by trying to nationalise every aspect of Swedish life: dress, as well as the army, the navy and the arts.

The King's clothes proclaimed his anti-Russian intentions. On his visit to his aunt Catherine II in St Petersburg in June 1777, Gustavus III wanted to wear the anti-Russian uniform he had worn on the day of the coup. However, this gesture was seen as so provocative that her ministers obliged him, when he saw the Empress, to wear a green French coat.[104]

Both policy and personal taste made it impossible for Gustavus III to remain content with a French coat. In February 1778 he instituted a competition to decide whether it would be advantageous to introduce a Swedish national costume. In his own essay *Réflexions sur les moyens de détruire entièrement le luxe dans l'habillement*, he wrote that his motives were to cut the expense of, and eliminate luxury from, court dress; to encourage Swedish industry; above all to assert Swedish national identity.[105] He did not mention his love of dressing up, which led some of his subjects to call him the Theatre King, nor his need to compensate, as a prince of the House of Holstein, for his lack of Swedish blood, nor the possibility of influence by the Polish dress reform of 1776.

On the day of his introduction of national dress, 28 April, the annual feast day for Sweden's orders of chivalry, he said: 'Let all of you adopt a national spirit and I dare say that a national dress contributes to it more than one thinks.' The day was proclaimed a holiday and – perhaps the only time in history – a medal was struck to commemorate a change in dress: *Providentiae Augusti Re Vestiaria Stabilita*: 'By the providence of the monarch, the matter of dress has been stabilised'.[106]

The new dress combined elements of early seventeenth-century dress; of theatrical costume; and of the costume of the Order of the Seraphim founded by Gustavus III's father in 1748. There were two versions: black with red lining for everyday use, light blue and silver for gala occasions. On his own suits the King sometimes wore extra embroidery. Gustavus III had been impressed by his visit to the French court in 1770–71 and, as at Versailles, men's shoes had red heels. At the same time the King imposed new uniforms on legal, government and military officials.[107] A similar national dress in similar colours was imposed on women and was worn in modified form, until 1952 for presentation at court, until 1974 by princesses, ladies-in-waiting and ministers' wives, at the state opening of Parliament.[108] Court society was visibly demarcated from the rest of Sweden. Men who had not been presented at court were not allowed to wear red lining and ornaments on their national dress and were 'dressed almost entirely in black'; women who had not been presented were forbidden white gauze sleeves.[109]

In December 1778, six months after the dress revolution in Stockholm, the arrival at Versailles of a handsome young officer of the Royal Suédois regiment in the French army, wearing the new national dress, caused a sensation. One Swede wrote: 'all Versailles is speaking only of a Count Fersen who came to court wearing the Swedish national dress which the Queen, according to what I have been told, examined very carefully' – in her private apartments.[110] This was one of the first signs of the love affair which in 1791–2 was to affect the fate of the French monarchy.

Further reaction was equally enthusiastic. According to a Swede called C. F. Ristell,

> The Swedish dress gives an appearance of magnificence to the Court without being half so expensive as the ordinary custom of Europe; with three or four suits of clothes you may appear at every Drawing-Room for as many

years . . . The colour and form being once fixed there is no room for variation . . . This uniformity of dress has a very good effect in the Drawing-Room and strangers generally allow that that it gives an air of grandeur more striking than all the party coloured magnificence of other Courts.[111]

However for many, including Fersen himself, military uniform retained more prestige than national dress. In August 1783, on Gustavus III's second visit to Catherine II, at Fredrikshamm on the Russo-Swedish frontier, he insisted that, like himself, his courtiers wore national dress. The Empress, who wore one of her regimental gowns and was surrounded by courtiers in uniform, considered Swedish national dress ridiculous. Like Frederick the Great, she was particularly shocked that serving officers were not allowed to wear the uniform of their regiment, 'since according to me there is no form of dress more honourable or lovable than a uniform'.[112]

Catherine herself, however, equally eager to assert her Russian identity and to hide her increasing size, also began to wear a form of national dress. From 1777 or earlier, she was increasingly seen, and painted in, a 'Russian dress, namely a robe with a short train and a vest with sleeves reaching to the waist, like a Polonaise'.[113] Another sign of her desire to promote Russian identity was her introduction in 1783, perhaps more influenced by Polish and Swedish national dress than she liked to admit, of uniforms for the nobles of each province of her empire, in the colours of that province.[114]

In his desire to assert the Swedish monarchy against its internal and external enemies, Gustavus III was also one of the very few monarchs to create a special ceremonial costume for himself, in addition to coronation robes: it was purple silk, trimmed with ermine and gold lace, worn on special occasions like the passing of the Act of Union and Security in 1789 by the Riksdag, which further strengthened the monarchy and weakened the nobility.[115] Gustavus III was the most dress-conscious monarch of the age. He even made a collection of ninety of his most important costumes: the elaborate wedding suit ordered in 1766 from Paris and his coronation, mourning, theatrical, chivalric, ceremonial, national and military costumes. The collection was used to help engravers make the series of medals by which the King commemorated the events of his reign. It is preserved, with other Swedish royal costumes, in the Livrust-kammaren and is described in chronological order, revealing much about the King's personality, ambitions and court, in *Kläder för tid och evighet* by Lena Rangström.[116]

In addition to national dress, Gustavus III introduced 'Burgundian-style' medieval dress, and often wore gilded armour at the tournaments he organised in the summers of 1776, 1777, 1779 and 1785.[117] The King also wore carousel costumes when he acted on the stage. Theatre and reality were becoming indistinguishable. On 17 March 1792, at a masked ball during the carnival, held on the stage of the opera house he had founded, the King was betrayed by his dress. Three nobles planning his assassination recognised him among the other masked guests, because his tunic showed the insignia of the Orders of the Sword and the Seraphim. They then shot and stabbed him.[118] Dress also betrayed the complicity in the conspiracy of his brother the Duke of Sudermania. The night of Gustavus III's assassination, he put on his uniform as Grand Admiral and waited in his palace for a signal to act.[119]

Against expectations, the King took two weeks to die. After his death, the Swedish national dress, which had never been compulsory, became less popular – particularly because of the difference it made in appearance between those who had been presented at court and those who had not.[120] On New Year's Day 1804 a reception was held at the Stockholm bourse. Nostalgic for Versailles, Fersen wrote: 'There were fewer people than usual for the burghers are offended by the difference in dress and do not go and others stay away so as not to have to take the trouble to dress, which nowadays is considered a nuisance. Now they only like to go in uniform and one cannot tell the difference between a nobleman and a shoemaker.'[121] In 1818, on the accession of the new French king, Carl XIV Johan (the former Marshal Bernadotte), Swedish national dress was abolished. It is impossible to prove whether the adoption of national dress in Sweden from 1778 to 1818 was a successful instrument of government. What is certain is that it signalled the monarchy's determination to assert national independence against Russia, and that Gustavus III's contemporary, Stanislas Augustus of Poland, was much criticised for not pursuing a similar dress policy.[122] In other countries at other periods, moreover, national dress would continue to play a dramatic role in asserting national, and regional, identity.

4 Revolutions

Pleasure was the basis of another style of royal and court dress. Royal hunts and residences, like other activities and localities, had long acquired special costumes.[1] A favourite costume of Kings of France was the blue coat, with red collar and cuffs and silver embroidery, worn, since a decree of Louis XIV in 1661, by followers of the King's deer hunt.[2] Most such costumes were

16 After J. B. Oudry, Louis XV hunting in the forest of Fontainebleau, 1738.
Like the accompanying courtiers and hunt sevants, the King is wearing the coat of his deer hunt, in his livery colours of blue, silver and red.

destroyed in the hecatombs of royal objects organised during the Reign of Terror. However, examples survive in the Danish and Swedish royal collections since, on their visits to Versailles in 1768 and 1771 respectively, Christian VII of Denmark and the future Gustavus III had been given such costumes by Louis XV, to wear when following his hunt.[3]

Another French court costume, the *justaucorps à brevet*, of blue lined with scarlet, with scarlet facings and waistcoat, heavily embroidered with gold and silver thread in a particular pattern, was a distinction created by Louis XIV in 1664. Signalling the right to follow the King on his hunt whenever the wearer wanted, it showed that the King both deliberately used dress to foster competition among courtiers and regarded dress as an affair of state: each *brevet* was signed by the King and countersigned by a secretary of state such as Colbert. Between 1664 and 1750, it was granted to no more than fifty favoured individuals at a time. Even among princes of the blood, every new vacancy aroused fevered competition.[4] The Grand Dauphin gave similar costumes, *gris brun brodés d'argent*, to the twenty or thirty courtiers who hunted deer with him; green with gold braid for those who followed his wolf hunt.[5]

Special uniforms were also worn by courtiers who accompanied the King to particular residences: green for Compiègne, green and gold for Choisy.[6] When the duc de Guiche, one of Louis XVI's four *capitaines des gardes du corps*, emigrated from France in late 1789, he took his military uniforms with him, correctly anticipating military action. Equally correctly, he left his uniforms of pleasure behind, assuming that they were no longer needed. Confiscated and listed by revolutionary officials, they included the coats of the King's deer hunt (blue, silver and red) and boar hunt (blue and crimson, with broad gold and silver lace); of the prince de Condé's deer hunt (yellow *ventre de biche* coat and crimson collar) and boar hunt; of the comte d'Artois's boar hunt (green, crimson and gold, like Artois's livery); and of the residences of Trianon (scarlet and white, like the Queen's livery) and Choisy.[7]

These hunting and palace uniforms were symbols of sovereignty as well as badges of pleasure. Blue, silver and red were the colours of the livery worn by the servants of the King of France and of the uniforms of his Gardes du corps and Gardes français:[8] courtiers following his hunts were therefore wearing a form of livery. Indeed in pictures by Jean Baptiste Oudry of the King's deer hunts in the 1730s in the forests of the Île de France, Louis XV and his courtiers are almost indistinguishable, except by the blue ribbon of the Order of the Saint Esprit, from the hunt servants. Princes of the blood such as the duc d'Orléans at Saint-Cloud and Villers-Cotteret, and the prince de Condé at Chantilly could also create their own coats for their courtiers.[9] Only occasionally were similar uniforms created for private châteaux. Many guests would have considered them demeaning.[10]

Indeed there was a correlation between uniforms of pleasure and assertions of royal sovereignty, as if royal hunts symbolised royal mastery over – or contempt for – humans, as well as animals. Both Louis XIV in 1655 and 1673, and Louis XV in 1766, wore hunting costume and boots when, escorted by Gardes du corps, the Maison militaire and the Gardes français and Gardes suisses, they entered the Paris Parlement on the Île de la Cité to deliver speeches making extreme assertions of their sovereignty.[11]

The clearest case of a hunting uniform being adopted as a badge of royal power occurred in England. George II had been sufficiently interested in dress to be called 'dapper George', and, within a few months of his accession, to help redesign the red and gold uniforms of his British and Hanoverian forces. The new uniforms are shown in portraits in the Royal Collection, commissioned in 1751 by his son the Duke of Cumberland from David Morier; however, the King created no court uniforms.[12] George III, in contrast, was known for his preference for a frugal life. Stories and caricatures abounded of the King being dressed so 'very plain' that his subjects did not recognise him.

These stories describe the King outside his palaces. In his 'royal character', remarked Robert Huish, he 'was partial to show and pageantry'. In 1779, for example, the *Ladies' Magazine* recorded, of the *habit habillé* he wore at court of 'sea-green chained silk richly ornamented with foil and spangles', that it created 'an agreeable sensation in the heart of every loyal subject: they behold in their sovereign an amiable person, at the same time they have the pleasing sensation not only to see him look, but be indeed a King'.[13] The implication is that, as Pepys had felt 120 years earlier, a simply dressed king was not 'indeed' a king. It was intended as an affront when, in 1782, the Whig MP Thomas Coke 'of Norfolk' wore 'country clothes' (in which he was subsequently painted by Gainsborough) to court, when he presented George III with a petition against continuation of the war in America.[14]

George III's interest in his own image led him to create a new court costume. Sasha Llewellyn has shown that George III took this decision in July 1777, at the time that he decided to make Windsor Castle his principal country residence: the previous royal retreat at Kew, where the royal family had lived as 'the simplest country gentlefolk', was considered too small for his expanding family and perhaps – at the beginning of the War of American Independence – too difficult to defend. The colours of the new 'Windsor Uniform' were dark blue and gold, with red collar and cuffs. They probably reflect the colours of the hunt coat created by his father Frederick, Prince of

Wales in 1729, soon after his arrival in England, which can be seen in John Wootton's painting of that year, showing the Prince hunting with courtiers (in contrast, followers of the King's buckhounds, such as the Prime Minister Robert Walpole, wore green and gold). The origins of the Windsor uniform are shown by references to it, long after its creation, as 'the King's Hunt'.

From October 1777 the King began to order between three and fourteen new Windsor uniform coats a year. There were two versions: what the Master of the Robes' accounts call 'plain Windsor Uniform frocks', and 'dress Windsor Uniform coats'. The latter had gold lace on the front of the coat, the collar and cuffs, and buttons engraved with the royal monogram.[15] At birthday celebrations for the Prince of Wales at Windsor Castle in 1781, 'those belonging to the King's family' (i.e. his household) wore undress Windsor uniform in the morning, full dress for the ball in the evening. In the same year Gainsborough painted portraits of the King and his sons in Windsor uniform.[16] From about 1787 Windsor uniform began to be worn away from Windsor: the conflict between the King and the Whigs, the King's madness, and the Regency crisis of 1788–9 raised political feelings to such a pitch that men and women wanted to use dress, as well as words and deeds, to show their political loyalties. The use of what had originally been a hunt costume as a badge of loyalty may also reflect the rise of fox-hunting, hitherto slightly despised compared to the traditional royal pastime of deer-hunting, as a popular sport in the second half of the eighteenth century.[17]

Windsor uniform became the dress in which the King and his chief minister Pitt the Younger were most often painted or caricatured.[18] In opposition to the blue and red of the Windsor uniform, the Whigs adopted as their colours buff and blue – to show support for the Americans fighting since 1776 for independence from Britain. American uniforms, as innumerable portraits of George Washington show, were buff and blue.[19] For contemporaries, portraits and caricatures of Whigs like Charles James Fox, Lord Holland, the Prince of Wales and many others, in blue coats and buff trousers and waistcoat had a clear, and for some a treasonable, political message.[20] After Fox stood for Parliament in Westminster in 1784, and again in 1788, triumphal processions through the streets of London from St Paul's past the Prince of Wales's residence at Carlton House to the Whig headquarters at Devonshire House proclaimed a strident Whig message: men, women, footmen, carriages, horses were dressed or draped in buff and blue.[21] In 1784 the Prince of Wales himself, one of Fox's greatest admirers, put his household into an 'extremely costly and elegant' uniform of buff and blue.[22]

The toast at Whig dinners, referring to a Whig beauty and friend of Fox, was:

Here's buff and blue and Mrs Crewe!

To which Mrs Crewe would reply:

Here's buff and blue and all of you![23]

In the early months of 1789, as George III recovered from madness, London was in a state of dress war, between buff and blue and red and blue. Female as well as male dress was affected. Already, during the War of American Independence, fashionable ladies such as Mrs Fitzherbert, the Duchess of Devonshire and Lady Worsley had, on occasion, dressed *en militaire*, in costumes based on their lover's or husband's uniform.[24] In early 1789 the Prince of Wales requested ladies to wear three large white feathers and a band with his motto *Ich Dien* in front of their caps.[25] Most, however, refused.[26] From the Queen down, they preferred to wear caps decorated with purple satin ribbons, with mottoes worked in purple and gold, proclaiming 'God save the King', 'Vive le roi, Dieu nous l'a rendu'.[27]

Even more than Marie Antoinette, Queen Charlotte became an active agent in dress politics. Like Frederick the Great's sisters, she sometimes embroidered the King's coat herself: until her death in 1818, she insisted that ladies came to court in hoops, although since the 1770s they had ceased to be part of fashionable dress.[28] By the physical space they occupied at court, women were able to proclaim a sense of self-importance which, in public affairs, they had to mask.

Between 1786 and 1791 the Queen's attitudes to dress were observed by the novelist Fanny Burney, who served as one of the two keepers of her robes, at a salary of £200 a year. As in the days of Queen Anne, the Queen's clothes were still the domain of 'gentlewomen'.[29] Fanny Burney's duties were to assist the wardrobe woman to dress the Queen at around seven in the morning; to assist around 1 p.m. when the Queen generally changed into full dress; and again at night when she undressed. Although Burney liked the Queen, she frequently complained in her diaries and letters about 'the irksome and quick returning duties of the toilette', and disputes with the other, overbearing, German-born keeper of the robes Madame Schwellenberg. Some days were 'all dressing'.[30]

In her diaries Burney recorded the Queen's submission to the rules of court dress, despite a personal preference for simplicity. The Queen 'equips herself for the drawing room with all the attention in her power . . . sensibly conscious that her high station makes her attire in public a matter of business'. Both for her own and the King's birthday each attendant was expected to have two new 'attires', one half and one full dress. Nevertheless, after a drawing room, 'she can never refuse herself the satisfaction of expressing her contentment to put on a quiet undress'. As she often told Fanny Burney, dress and jewels had few attractions for her: they were just 'fatigue and trouble'.[31] The same was true of Fanny Burney who resigned in July 1791, after only five years at court, 'worn with want of rest and fatigued with laborious watchfulness and attendance'.[32]

Like Marie Antoinette, Queen Charlotte was trapped in the court system. Against Queen Charlotte's wishes, feathers were adopted by women going to formal court occasions.[33] In 1792 the Queen explained to her treasurer Lord Ailesbury that she had to order more clothes than she could wear, with more lace than was necessary, as they were perquisites for her servants: if she were to order less, she feared 'the noise it [economy] would make amongst the Bedchamber women'.[34] At the courts of England and France, used royal clothes were passed on to or inherited by court officials and servants (as were masters' and mistresses' used clothes in private houses).[35] They were then often resold or reused in ecclesiastical vestments or adornments.[36] Hence the absence, in both countries, of collections of royal clothes as old as those in Sweden, Russia and Turkey.

At the 'Grand Restoration Drawing-room' held on 26 March 1789 to congratulate the King on his recovery, the Queen and all her daughters and ladies wore blue and orange (the colours adopted by Pitt and his followers in the Constitution Club). The King told the Duke of York: 'that as he and his brother had divided up the world into blue and buff, and orange and blue, the old blue and red must stick together, or they would be quite forgotten'.[37] For the next celebration, a ball held by the Tory club White's on 31 March, ladies wore a uniform of white with gold fringes, white feathers and ribbons with the words 'God save the King! Long live the King!'[38] At the ball held at Windsor Castle on 3 April, Lady Louisa Stuart reported: 'everybody is to appear in a uniform, the men in the King's Hunt, which you have often seen, and the ladies in deep blue trimmed with scarlet and gold, the same colours . . . Loyalty is a most expensive virtue at present. This dress which by the Queen's directions is to be from Mrs Beauvais only, comes to thirty pounds; the uniform for the White's ball to about three or four and twenty'.

After the ball at Windsor, Lady Louisa Stuart expressed the epoch's growing fondness for dressing as a group, rather than according to individual taste, shown also in C. F. Ristell's praise of 'the very good effect' of 'conformity of dress' in Sweden: 'it really was the finest sight I ever saw and answered one's idea of Royal magnificence. The vast size of the room all so well lighted up, and

17 Anon., *Dressing for a Drawing-Room*, 1789.
In the political crisis of 1788–9, women advertised their Whig or Tory loyalties through their dress and the ribbons in their hair.

the number of persons dressed alike, had a splendour not easily to be described.'[39] She also described the procession to the next celebration, a thanksgiving service at St Paul's on 23 April, St George's Day, as 'the finest sight I ever saw'. The King and all his sons, including the Prince of Wales, were in full dress Windsor uniform; the Queen, the princesses and their ladies wore purple silk dresses, edged and finished with gold fringe.[40]

The Prince of Wales, however, disliked Windsor uniform, the symbol of his father's triumph. On 23 May, before the French ambassador's congratulatory ball, for which the Queen had again given orders that men should wear Windsor uniform, he told the Duke and Duchess of Devonshire 'in very bad humour', 'he would not wear the uniform nor his brothers nor the [King's brother the] Duke of Cumberland, neither would they be [set] up with the Queen . . . [However, the King's other brother] The Duke of Gloucester stood within the railed place with his son Prince William and in the Windsor uniform.'[41]

Thereafter the Windsor uniform became increasingly popular – visible proof, like the 1789 celebrations for George III's recovery, that the English, Scottish and Irish ruling classes contained the elements of a court society. Windsor uniform's use continued to be personal and haphazard, by request

18 Edward Dayes, Thanksgiving in Saint Paul's Cathedral on 23 April 1789.
To assert their loyalty to George III, whose recovery is being celebrated, his Whig son the
Prince of Wales, as well as his other sons and his ministers, are wearing Windsor uniform.

from below, as well as imposed by royal policy from above. On 21 April 1789
Queen Charlotte wrote to a junior diplomat: 'I think Lord Robert Fitzgerald
may safely make up the Windsor uniform without my mentioning it to the
King.'[42] In 1793 the King wrote to his Foreign Secretary: 'Lord Grenville is to
acquaint Sir Watkin Williams Wynn [Lord Grenville's nephew, a rich Welsh
landowner with political ambitions] that I should be very glad to see him in
my uniform as also to confer on Wednesday the lieutenancy of Merioneth-
shire on him.'[43] In 1794 Lord Dorchester wrote directly to the King to request
'Your Majesty's permisssion to wear Your Majesty's uniform when he pays his
duty to Your Majesty at Weymouth' – the King's summer residence in Dorset,
where most of his courtiers wore the uniform of his castle in Berkshire.[44]

The desire to wear 'His Majesty's uniform' extended outside the British
Isles. In 1793 Ninian Home, Governor of Grenada, ordered a Windsor
uniform in especially thin cloth for the tropics.[45] A portrait of Lord
Wellesley, Governor-General of India, wearing Windsor uniform hangs in
the dining-room at Stratfield Saye. British ambassadors wore Windsor
uniform in Paris in 1797, in Constantinople in 1806, in Vienna in 1814, in
Tabriz in 1817.[46]

Nevertheless, despite the popularity of the Windsor uniform, on court occasions inside St James's, such as drawing-rooms and royal marriages, the King, the Prince of Wales and many courtiers continued to wear the *habit habillé*, until 1811 or later.[47] It was still considered a status symbol of such importance that, at a time when Dr Johnson believed that an ordinary man need spend only £10 a year on clothes and linen, one *habit habillé* could cost £500 or more – as much as a substantial house.[48] In 1791 the *St James's Chronicle* described the Prince's dress for the King's birthday:

> bottle-green and claret-coloured striped silk coat and breeches, and silver tissue waistcoat, very richly embroidered in silver and stones, and coloured silks in curious devices and bouquets of flowers. The coat and waistcoat embroidered down the seams and spangled all over the body. The coat cuffs the same as the waistcoat. Diamond buttons to the coat, waistcoat and breeches, which with his diamond epaulette and sword made the whole dress form a most magnificent appearance.[49]

Outside the court, a dress revolution had occurred. Since the 1740s there had been a change in attitude, for two principal reasons: the growing demands of parliamentary, military and financial business; and the growing fashion for simplicity. This can also be seen in, for example, a relaxation in attitudes to children or inferiors; decreased use of state rooms; a growing love of nature and informal gardens; and increased use of horses rather than carriages.[50] In *Émile*, Jean-Jacques Rousseau, one of the most famous writers of the day, advocated clothes which freed the body from 'Gothic shackles' and put health and freedom before luxury and formality.[51]

Instead of the *habit habillé*, what John Harvey called 'the great masculine renunciation' began to impose simple dark frock coats, generally black or blue.[52] The frock coat or *frac* cost about four or six pounds, a tenth of the *habit habillé*, and took much less time to put on. The *frac* revolution began in England. As early as 1725 a Swiss visitor called César de Saussure wrote that, while looking magnificent when going to court, elsewhere 'Englishmen are usually very plainly dressed, they scarcely ever wear gold [embroidery] on their clothes; they wear little coats called "frocks" without facings and without pleats, with a short cape above . . . You will see rich merchants and gentlemen thus dressed, and sometimes even noblemen of high rank, especially in the morning, walking through the filthy and muddy streets.'[53] By the 1750s the plain coat or frock was the most common dress.[54] Even Lord Chesterfield, Lord of the Bedchamber of George II and former Lord-Lieutenant of Ireland,

19 Francisco Goya, Charles III of Spain
in hunting dress, 1786.
The King's passion for hunting
encouraged him to dress simply, even on
occasion wearing hunting breeches under
court costume in order to be able to leave
his palace for the hunting field as quickly
as possible.

felt the need for simplicity. In 1749 he complained that men were constrained by their clothes: they seemed 'rather their prisoner than their proprietor'.[55]

In London the *frac* triumphed in the 1770s. By 1778 most peers and gentlemen could be seen in the House of Lords, at receptions or the opera, in *frac* and boots: the *habit habillé* was worn, even by the King and his courtiers, only on formal occasions at court.[56]

Europe also embraced the fashion for simplicity. Indeed the first king since Louis XI to spurn court dress was not English but a great-grandson of Louis XIV: King Charles VII of Naples, younger son of Philip V of Spain. In 1739, while receiving homage on his birthday in the royal palace of Naples from magnificently dressed nobles, he wore, as the Président de Brosses noted, 'un vieil habit de droguet brun à boutons jaunes'. After he ascended the throne of Spain in 1759 as Charles III, his habitual dress was a 'plain grey Segovia frock'.[57] A passion for hunting increased his love of the *frac*. On gala days at court he wore an embroidered coat with hunting breeches, in order to be able to escape more quickly to the hunting field once the reception finished.[58]

In Paris in 1763 Smollett noted that, although newly arrived Englishmen still immediately sent for a tailor and started to wear embroidered coats,

20 Jacob Philipp Hackert, The Royal Family of Naples harvesting, 1791.
Despite their peasant dress, worn as a mark of identification with their subjects,
Ferdinand IV and Queen Maria Carolina can easily be identified on the right.

'When I was last in France no person of any condition, male or female,
appeared but in full dress, even when obliged to come out early in the morning
. . . but at present I see a number of frocks and scratches in the morning. The
French begin to imitate the English.'[59] By 1785 this was common; it was
known as being *en chenille*, in cocoon; in the evening they would burst out in
the full glory of *habit habillé*.[60]

In 1786 the marquis de Conflans, who had been to Potsdam, was the first
man to attend the Paris opera in 'un frac simple et des cheveux coupés à la
jockey sans poudre ni pommade'.[61] That year the *Cabinet des modes* noted that
it was increasingly rare to see women 'en robes de Grande Parure' or men in
'Habits à la Française, avec le chapeau sous le bras et l'épée au côté'.[62] Thus
several years before 1789 differences of social rank had stopped being expressed
in daily dress. This indicated a different attitude to dress and manners, not to
the political and social order. Although committed to absolute monarchy and
a *société d'ordres*, on days when there was no reception at court, and he did not
wear a *habit habillé*, Louis XVI himself was famous, among his subjects, for his
simplicity of dress and manners.[63] On his visit to the *Hôtel-Dieu* in Paris in
1786, for example, he wore the *frac*.[64] In 1789 *fracs* were noticed at the suppers

21 Charles Monnet, Mirabeau refuses to obey the order of the marquis de Dreux-Brézé, Grand Master of Ceremonies, to sit separately from the deputies of the Church and the nobility on 23 June 1789 (detail).
The political conflict between the court and Mirabeau, leader of the Third Estate, is reflected in the contrast between Dreux-Brézé's court dress and Order of the Holy Spirit, and the black Third Estate deputy's costume of Mirabeau. Mirabeau liked his costume enough to commission himself in it.

of the comtesse de Brionne where 'tout ce que Paris renferme de plus élégant' gathered to hear obscene songs against the King and the royal family.[65]

In the middle of the '*frac* revolution', however, at the opening of the Estates General in 1789, old dress rules were suddenly reimposed – one of the four occasions in this period (with others in 1790, 1792 and 1814) when, in Paris, dress became a political issue. In traditional French royal style, at the opening of the Estates General, Louis XVI blazed with diamonds on his Order of the Holy Spirit, his embroidered *habit habillé*, sword, buttonholes, epaulettes and shoe buckles.[66] Regulations for members of the three orders re-imposed the same dress worn at the last meeting of the Estates General, in 1614. Deputies of the First Estate wore the costume of their ecclesiastical rank. Nobles wore black silk or cloth trimmed with gold braid, a lace cravat, white stockings, a feathered hat and swords. The Third Estate wore black cloth, including black short-back cloaks, a black toque and black stockings 'as the *gens de robe* are in the habit of wearing at Court'. Although merchants had been given the right to wear swords in 1767, Third Estate deputies were not.[67]

This was a humiliation, affirming almost obsolete differences between the nobility and the Third Estate: by 1776, or earlier, as *Le Costume français* stated, 'as the bourgeois is a half-noble, sometimes he wears black clothes like the magistrate, sometimes clothes in embroidered velvet the same as nobles'.[68] Fury at what one deputy called 'une loi ridicule et bizarre', creating 'une inégalité inadmissible, destructive de l'essence même de l'Assemblée' was widespread. However, on 30 April the costume was changed to meet most objections: a *tricorne* hat was substituted for the black toque. Contrary to the received view, many Third Estate deputies came to appreciate their costume: it gave them *esprit de corps* and helped inspire respect in the people. Bailly, the first revolutionary mayor of Paris, called it *très convenable*.[69]

The revolution in the Estates General had been preceded by a revolution in the *garde-robe du roi*. In contrast to his courtier ancestors, Louis XVI's *grand maître de la garde-robe*, the duc de La Rochefoucauld-Liancourt, was a philanthropist, interested in improving agriculture and the condition of the poor. His account of the death of Louis XV in 1774 expresses revulsion for that King's 'inconceivable' fears, his 'cowardly and revolting weakness', his Catholicism, his mistress, his daughters and his ministers (Liancourt was a supporter of the disgraced minister Choiseul). Louis XV was 'the most null, the most vile, the most cowardly' of kings: 'we take revenge for their [kings'] authority by the deepest contempt'. Fifteen years before 1789, this court official was ready for revolution.[70]

Of the King's two *maîtres de la garde-robe*, the marquis de Boisgelin was dismissed in 1788 for his support of aristocratic opposition to the ministry; the marquis de Chauvelin resigned in 1792 because of his support for the revolution.[71] Between those extremes Liancourt, attached to Louis XVI, and himself a progressive deputy in the National Assembly, supported a strong constitutional monarchy. On the morning of 15 July, the King's ministers dared not tell him that the Bastille had been stormed by Parisians, led by Gardes français whose fine uniforms in the King's livery colours had not prevented them from joining the revolution. By virtue of Liancourt's *grandes entrées* as *grand maître de la garde-robe*, he entered the King's bedroom. After listening to his account of Paris, the King exclaimed:

C'est une grande révolte!

To which Liancourt made the celebrated reply:

Non, Sire, c'est une grande révolution![72]

In the next few days, between the flight of the old ministers and the arrival of new ones led by the popular hero Necker, Liancourt, briefly President of the National Assembly, may have had a certain influence in advising Louis XVI to avoid civil war, visit the National Assembly in Versailles, then on 17 July, wearing the new revolutionary symbol of the tricolour cockade (blue for France and justice, white for royalty, red for courage or for the blood patriots were ready to shed),[73] sanctify the revolution by going to the *hôtel de ville* of Paris. This court official acted as a link, rather than a barrier, between the King and his subjects. His office outlived the monarchy itself. Throughout the revolution and emigration Liancourt continued to regard himself as *grand maître de la garde-robe*, refusing Louis XVIII's request to resign the office in 1797, and hoping to resume it in 1814. However, a new favourite from Provence, the comte de Blacas, had been appointed *grand maître* in 1809; he would be both the last and, as the King's chief adviser until 1815, the most important holder of this office.[74]

The next stage in the destruction of the court took place on the morning of 6 October 1789. Already in 1725 a French police official called Pierre Narbonne had noted the cruel contrast between the golden splendour of courtiers' clothes at the wedding of Louis XV and the hunger and misery of the people in the surrounding countryside.[75] Now the hungry and miserable had their revenge. A mob of Parisians, incensed by rumours of counter-revolution, including alleged insults to the tricolour cockade by *gardes du corps du roi*, stormed into the château of Versailles. The King's cousin Philippe Egalité, duc d'Orléans, was suspected of being its secret leader. The main physical evidence was his dress: he was seen by witnesses entering the palace at the same time as the crowd (some of whom cried 'Vive le roi d'Orléans' or 'Vive M. le duc d'Orléans!'), *en frac gris, en frac rayé* or *petit habit gris du matin*, although this was his normal costume, not an attempt at disguise. Only one witness claimed that he was seen showing the crowd the way to the Queen's apartment, which they subsequently attacked, screaming for her head and her liver.[76]

The royal family was taken by force by the Paris National Guard to Paris on 6 October 1789; on 15 October the formal dress of deputies was abolished. Thereafter the tricolour cockade became an indispensable outward symbol of support of the revolution and the new social order – hence the mob's fury when it had been allegedly trampled underfoot by *gardes du corps* at Versailles. Not to wear the tricolour cockade in a public place, after July 1789, led to insults from 'the populace' and, after July 1792, to the possibility of arrest or execution. All other cockades were banned.[77]

The year 1789 witnessed not only a 'democratic' revolution, but also the militarisation which the French monarchy and nobility had hitherto avoided.

After 6 October 1789, the *gardes du corps* were dismissed. The Paris National Guard, which included many former *gardes français*, became the main force guarding both the exterior and the interior of the royal palaces. Its commander the marquis de La Fayette was master of Paris, and the King. Its uniforms became a critical legitimising factor, and for revolutionaries a 'rallying cry against the enemies of liberty'.[78] They cost 80 livres and were paid for by the guards themselves.[79]

Members of the new National Guard were determined to look as military as soldiers of the regular army. A visitor to Paris from the Île Bourbon in 1790 noted, when the National Guards of France arrived for the *fête de la fédération*: 'One sees nothing in Paris but uniforms and epaulettes . . . Almost the whole Nation is in the national guard. The variations in the uniforms present a fine appearance . . . Paris seems like a *place de guerre.*'[80]

In 1790 both La Fayette and his cousin the prince de Poix, one of the *capitaines des gardes du corps du roi*, were convinced that it was 'very important' – underlined by La Fayette in a letter to the King – for Louis XVI to review the Paris National Guard, wearing either its own uniform or the red and gold uniform which, before 1789, the King had worn on the few occasions he had reviewed his troops. An age addicted to uniforms required a uniform connecting the King to the Paris National Guard: the red and gold uniform would signal that the King respected his new guard as much as his old army.[81]

Most of the time, like some of his remaining courtiers and his secret visitors, Louis XVI wore the *frac.*[82] At reviews of the National Guard in 1790, the King refused to wear uniform, preferring to continue to wear a plain grey *frac* – thereby appearing to snub the National Guard. Although his motives are unknown, it was a considered decision. He wrote a furious letter to Poix on the subject saying, about La Fayette's views, 'whatever confidence I have in him I can very well not think the same on several points'.[83] Poix, equally furious, offered his resignation, telling the King what so many knew: 'Sire, Your Majesty is impossible to serve.'[84] Finally the quarrel was resolved and the resignation refused.

The King soon had other plans. In his memoirs the duc de Choiseul, one of the officers charged with arranging his flight from Paris on 20 June 1791, claimed that Louis XVI sent on ahead, packed by his own hands, the red and gold uniform which he had refused to wear at reviews of the National Guard in 1790 and 1791 – proof of his intention, when he was surrounded by loyal troops in the east of France under the marquis de Bouillé, to be a military king in his own fashion. Choiseul says he took the uniform in a parcel from the Tuileries on 18 June. The King's explanation to his servants, for removing the

22 M. Maurin, The comte de Provence on
21 June 1791, 1822.
Dress as self-preservation: to escape from
revolutionary Paris, the future Louis XVIII
disguised himself 'as an Englishman' in a
simple *frac* without orders.

uniform from a cupboard, was the need to prepare it for a review of the
National Guard.[85]

The flight to Varennes on 20 June 1791 shows the importance of dress, and
wardrobe officials, in matters of personal, identity and physical safety. The
comte de Provence successfully escaped from the Luxembourg Palace in Paris
'disguised as an Englishman' – that is to say, wearing a *frac* and speaking
English: like Charles II in 1651, Provence owed his safety to his wardrobe. His
companion and the organiser of the flight was his *maître de la garde-robe en
survivance* and subsequent principal favourite, the comte d'Avaray.[86] The King
could not leave the Tuileries Palace until after the *coucher* – one of the few
court ceremonies which continued until the fall of the monarchy. He left the
palace wearing a green *redingote* or coat, and a brown *habit* with no *marques
extérieures de distinction*, accompanied by three *gardes du corps* disguised, on
his orders, as couriers: they wore couriers' *vestes*, under brown *redingotes*.[87]

As early as 4 April the man Louis XVI had selected to organise his journey
from Paris to Montmédy, Axel von Fersen, by then colonel of the Royal
Suédois regiment, had wondered which uniform he should wear when
escorting the King. Revealing his vanity, he wrote to Count von Taube, First

Gentleman of the Chamber of Gustavus III: 'To accompany the King of France, it will be decent for me to be sometimes in Swedish uniform; ask the King if, independently of the uniform of the *gardes du corps* [of Sweden, whom Fersen commanded], he will permit that I sometimes wear that of the dragoons, as it is very attractive; that would give a fine idea of our troops and of their dress.'[88] Thus, instead of wearing his French uniform, Fersen wanted to advertise, through Swedish uniforms, that alliance with foreign counter-revolutionary monarchs which would help destroy Louis XVI and Marie Antoinette.

The end of court entertainments, and the widespread adoption of the *frac* in Paris, dismayed the silk merchants of Lyon: they were more loyal than many nobles and ecclesiastics. Before 1789 the industry was already in difficulties. In 1786 there were 12,000 looms for working textiles in Lyon; in 1788 9,335; in 1789 7,500. Between 1782 and 1791 the number employed in the embroidery industry fell by half.[89] An appeal for the starving workers of Lyon, headed by a contribution of 30,000 livres from the King, had been launched in 1787.[90] A new *habit* and a new *robe* were made for the King and Queen and dispatched to Paris with this *cri de coeur*: 'if the royal family decided to wear these materials and restore the etiquette of the court relating to dress to the point where it was when, for the happiness of France, Louis XVI was called to the throne, who doubts that the habit would soon become general?'[91] However, the industry continued to decline, at the same time as the court on which it had depended. In 1791 a petition to the National Assembly stated that embroiderers were going bankrupt, fashion shops closing, dress-makers sacking three-quarters of their workers.[92]

The Queen's expenditure on dress had declined from 217,187 livres in 1787 to 190,721 in 1788. Noble titles, formal presentations at court, and the use of liveries and coats of arms, were abolished in June 1790. The last formal presentation dress made by Rose Bertin, for the vicomtesse de Preissac, was delivered on 5 July 1790.[93] Thereafter, freed from social constraints, most women enjoyed a greater variety and informality of dress.[94] The Queen and ladies already presented, however, continued on occasion – for example Madame de La Tour du Pin visiting the Queen to announce the birth of a child – to wear formal court dress.[95] On formal occasions Louis XVI also continued to wear the *habit habillé*: for example at the *fête de la fédération* on 14 July 1790; at his acceptance of the constitution in the National Assembly on 14 September 1791, when most deputies were *en frac*; and at the celebrations of 14 July 1792, in contrast to the National Guard uniforms of Parisians around him, including his own son.[96]

In contrast, in emigration his brothers had joined the world of European military monarchies. The comte d'Espinchal recorded the day, 27 September 1789, when Artois, Condé and their followers, arriving at the court of Piedmont, began to wear uniform: 'the ordinary costume [in Turin] is uniform. The King [of Sardinia] and the princes often wear it. Our princes have conformed to this usage and will wear nothing else.' Artois generally wore his red uniform as colonel of the Gardes suisses.[97] Former *parlementaires* and financiers, for the first time in their lives, began to wear military uniform.[98] At Koblenz in May 1792, Madame de Falaiseau wrote in her diary, again showing contemporaries' love of uniform: 'the princes and all their court are in uniform which truly gives the air of a martial and imposing court.'[99]

Since uniform was a badge of loyalty, the continued use of the *frac* and the *habit habillé* in the Tuileries aroused fear and hostility. The use of black *fracs* was encouraged by two six-month periods of court mourning, for the Queen's brothers the Emperors Joseph II and Leopold II, after their deaths in February 1790 and March 1792 respectively. Court mourning now affected the court and royalists alone, not the entire country. Dislike of *les habits noirs*, as royalist courtiers were therefore called, appears in accounts of the revolutionary *journées* of 20 June and 9/10 August 1792.

A revolutionary counter-culture, a conscious challenge to the dress and values of the rich and powerful, had emerged. The tensions between rich and poor which had led to so many riots and uprisings since 1789 finally expressed themselves in dress.[100] In 1792 Parisian revolutionaries began to be called *sans-culottes*, since they wore trousers rather than breeches; a short jacket known as a *carmagnole*; and, during demonstrations, red 'caps of liberty' or *bonnets rouges*. For some it was a term of admiration, for others of abuse.[101] A younger son of the duc de Liancourt, François de La Rochefoucauld hated the *sans-culottes* as 'people without stockings, without shoes and without coats [who] shamelessly insulted all those who were not dressed like themselves'.[102] On 20 June, a mob of *sans-culottes* invaded the Tuileries Palace, and made the King put on a *bonnet rouge*, and drink to the health of the Nation.[103] In contrast, 'people in black coats, mostly decorated with the cross of Saint Louis' – courtiers and royalists who had rushed to defend the King – were expelled from the palace by national guards in tricolour uniforms.[104]

There was a last attempt to persuade the King to wear National Guard uniform. When he reviewed sections of it on 24 June, some national guards told him of 'the desire which the citizens of Paris had that he adopt the national uniform'. Resolute only in irresolution, the King replied that he had

23 Pierre Gabriel Berthault, Louis XVI drinking to the health of the nation on 20 June 1792.

When a mob invaded the Tuileries Palace for four hours on 20 June 1792 demanding that the King recall the 'Girondin' ministers, one *sans-culotte* thrust a revolutionary 'Phrygian cap' on the end of a pike in front of the King. He put it on and later drank a toast to the nation, while members of the mob, for the first time that day, cried *Vive le roi!* He did not, however, recall his ministers.

desired his courtiers, and ordered his son, to wear the uniform. He himself, however, told the national guards that 'since a long time he had desired it but that he did not precisely know if certain articles of the Constitution were not opposed to it'.[105] George III and Gustavus III had used dress to increase support for their monarchy. Louis XVI used dress to cut away support from the French monarchy.

The monarchy's final hours were marked by a dress war between the uniforms of the national guards and the *fracs* of the royalists. One pamphlet asked the question: 'What difference could exist between them and the National Guard? None except that of the coat.' That difference, however, touched a nerve. On 9/10 August 1792, when the monarchy needed every defender it could find, as they were not in the uniform of the Garde nationale de Paris, many courtiers or *noirs* were refused access to the palace by the national guards on duty.[106] Years later Madame de Staël complained that courtiers had not admitted constitutional royalists such as her lover the comte de Narbonne to the Tuileries to defend the King.[107] However, she attributed to courtiers' distaste for his politics what was probably national guards' rejection of his costume.

The Paris National Guard tried to expel all courtiers inside the palace not wearing uniform, specifically the uniform of the National Guard. They were told 'that it was not the time to present yourself in the palace without wearing a uniform'; 'that it was not the moment to pay court to the King and that no one entered except in the coat of the National Guard and to give reinforcement to that guard'.[108]

Even at this date, on the eve of a popular uprising, some royalists still wore the *habit habillé*, as François de La Rochefoucauld, who himself wore a *frac* and a sword, noted in his memoirs.[109] His valet reported that the baron de Vioménil, an officer from Lorraine who had often travelled abroad on missions from the Queen to the King's brothers, went to the Tuileries on the morning of 10 August wearing a dress coat of reddish silk. He was one of the nobles in charge of the defence of the palace. With François de La Rochefoucauld he helped escort the King – who, as usual, wore a grey *frac* – from the palace to the Legislative Assembly. He died from his wounds two and a half months later.[110]

Later that day revolutionaries stormed the palace and slaughtered Gardes suisses and courtiers defending a cause abandoned by the King. Already before 10 August insulted in the street if they wore their red uniforms in public,[111] Gardes suisses now fled through Paris, discarding their uniforms to save their lives.[112] Since national guards were also suspected of royalism, fear also led many of them to shed their uniforms.[113]

The fall of the monarchy led to the triumph of the *sans-culottes* and of simplicity in France. In the summer of 1792 an English traveller found: 'There is hardly any possibility of distinguishing the rank of either man or woman by their dress at present, or rather, there are no ranks to be distinguished . . . The nation in general is much improved in cleanliness and politeness. The French no longer look on every Englishman as a lord but as their equal.'[114] All ecclesiastical costumes were banned.[115]

In prison in the Temple, the royal family wore the simplest clothes, fragments of which were later transformed into royalist relics.[116] The Queen changed her clothes once a day and had to mend them herself.[117] The clothes she left behind in the Tuileries were sold, for very low prices, at public auction.[118] Women who, in Paris, had dressed in the latest fashion, as *émigrées* in London found themselves on the other side of the shop counter. They lived by selling muslin dresses, straw hats and embroidery made by themselves.[119] The French fashion industry collapsed. Between 1793 and 1797 there were no fashion magazines in Paris.[120]

The few orders for the silk merchants of Lyon in these years came from abroad: for example for silk hangings for palaces in Madrid,[121] and for clothes for the King of Spain and his family. Orders were kept secret for fear of complaints from the merchants of Madrid.[122] Lyon lost 20,000 inhabitants; only 5,000 looms were left in operation.[123] Perhaps discontent with the revolution in dress contributed to Lyon's support for federalism and counter-revolution in 1793.

In 1793–4 government regulation of dress increased with the rising demands of war and totalitarianism. The wearing of a tricolour cockade with an expanded white element could lead to arrest. Even checked clothes or tight breeches were regarded as signs of subversion.[124] The Republican government considered the idea of a French national dress: 'a true republican costume', suitable 'to republican habits and the character of the revolution'. David produced sketches based on military uniform and ancient Rome.[125] Robespierre suggested that, to accustom children to the idea of equality, they should wear a uniform from the age of five.[126]

The *frac* reigned supreme. *Habits habillés* were thrown away, or stored in cupboards and attics to be removed and sold, two hundred years later, when a market in eighteenth-century dress had been re-established thanks to the creation of museums of costume.[127] The triumph of the *frac* was a visual revolution. It became commonplace to say that, since all men wore black *fracs*, society resembled a funeral: indeed in pictures of evening parties, against ladies' white or coloured dresses, men do look like undertakers.[128] In contrast to the period before 1789, court mourning now made no difference to men's appearance, apart from the imposition of a black armband.[129]

By 1795, except on formal occasions, all monarchs, including the Kings of Spain and Naples and the Emperor of Austria, dressed in ordinary brown or grey frock coats.[130] Nothing in their dress distinguished them from other members of the élite, or as one French émigré noted of the Elector of Bavaria, from his own farmers.[131] Thus, if it was a visual revolution, the triumph of the *frac* was not a social or political one, despite the complaints of an aged courtier like the prince de Ligne.[132] The frac was adopted as enthusiastically by absolute monarchs and counter-revolutionary nobles as by revolutionary politicians. At the same time as political changes were making nobles one among several elements in a larger ruling class,[133] the *frac* also helped homogenise the new élite by removing remaining visual differences between nobles and non-nobles. Only Paul I of Russia, who also had a passion for Prussian-style uniforms, was sufficiently mad, in 1796–7, to ban the *frac* as Jacobin and reimpose the *habit habillé*.[134]

The novelty of the new simplicity and uniformity, in a hierarchical society which revered titles and birth, encouraged the phenomenon of dandyism. The supreme dandy was George 'Beau' Brummell. Between 1793, when he became an officer in the Prince of Wales's regiment the 10th Hussars and a favourite of the Prince, and 1816 when he fled to Calais to escape his creditors, the cut of his coat, the twist of his cravat set the fashion in London. 'No perfumes but very fine linen, plenty of it and country washing', and 'To be well dressed you should not be noticed' were among Brummell's sayings.[135] Dandyism was the attempt to reconquer, by simplicity, cleanliness and cut, the social distance lost by the adoption of a common male dress.[136] Baudelaire, who himself deplored the *frac* as the 'universal livery of desolation which reveals equality', called dandyism a heroic attempt to found a new aristocracy, in protest against the rising tide of democracy.[137]

Dandyism also demonstrated that London had replaced Paris as the capital of men's tailoring. From the 1790s the shops of London men's tailors in Savile Row and its surrounding streets north of Piccadilly had become, as they remain, a separate world of cloth and wealth, with its own language and traditions.[138] On occasion one London tailor, John Meyer of Mortimer and Meyer (a firm still operating in Savile Row and making uniforms for the Household Division today), wearing a page's livery, would help dress the Prince Regent himself.[139] London men's fashions began to be imitated, and discussed in fashion magazines, throughout Europe: 'he dresses like an Englishman!' was now a term of the highest praise.[140] Even as far as Sicily, London tailors' pronouncements on cloth and cut were treated as the Word of God.[141]

Simplicity was so fashionable that for some even uniforms were distasteful. Barras, one of the five directors of the Republic in 1795–9, wrote: 'I do not think that the respect for a republican authority should lie in the elaboration and richness of its costume. I believe on the contrary that the day has come when officials' simplicity should be the first of their distinctions.'[142] Indeed under the First Republic the negligence of French ministers' dress had shocked foreign diplomats.[143]

The cult of simplicity in dress was practised in the new republic of the United States. Both before and after the War of Independence, a cult of 'homespun' clothes flourished in opposition to the corruption and luxury represented by British clothes.[144] Echoing earlier moralists, George Washington told his nephew Bushrod Washington that fine clothes do not make fine men, any more than fine feathers make fine birds.[145] As American ambassador in Paris, Thomas Jefferson had worn fashionable French clothes. In the United States, even for his inauguration as President in 1801, he wore a plain suit.[146]

5   *The Age of Gold*

In France, however, President Jefferson had few imitators. In contrast to the United States, after 1800 France and Europe shared a passion for gold-embroidered uniforms, civil as well as military. Criticisms of civil uniforms in the eighteenth century help explain their attractions in the nineteenth.

Until the seventeenth century liveries had been worn by followers of a monarch or great noble, whether gentlemen or not.[1] By the eighteenth century liveries had acquired an aura of subordination. They were given to lower menservants, by their master, in the colours of the 'field' of the master's coat of arms: hence red and gold for the liveries of the King or Queen of England, still visible today on royal footmen and Royal Mail vans. Upper servants such as butlers dressed as gentlemen.[2]

In 1783, although 'extremely costly and elegant', since it recalled a servant's livery, the Prince of Wales's new household uniform was considered 'another innovation upon the attendants as gentlemen.'[3] In the 1790s Lord March, the Whig son of the Duke of Richmond, called the Windsor uniform 'the most humiliating fashion I can think of . . . like a livery servant'.[4] The ministers of George IV at first refused to wear the blue and gold civil uniform he had designed.[5] In the 1820s the young Cavour loathed his lobster red uniform as a page of the Prince of Carignano;[6] a few years later, Pushkin detested his green and gold uniform as Gentleman of the Chamber of Nicholas I.[7]

Yet these were minority reactions, by exceptionally independent individuals. Faced with the trauma of the French revolution and the execution of Louis XVI, nobles throughout Europe closed ranks with monarchs. In their formal dress they were happy to proclaim loyalty to the monarch and subordination in his service, rather than individual wealth and rank. For their part, monarchs appreciated the sight of men wearing uniforms advertising rank in their service. Group solidarity triumphed over individual self-assertion. Perhaps also the visual and sexual attractions of uniform, in an age of black *fracs*, increased the popularity of government and military service. Dickens wrote in *The Pickwick Papers* (1837), 'A good uniform must work its way with the women sooner or later.'[8] In *The Leopard* (1960) Giuseppe di Lampedusa claimed that the 'silver and gold stars, twirls and sashes and endless loops' of uniforms were 'a delight for girls used only to severe frock-coats and funereal tail-coats'.[9] Cavour was later portrayed wearing the uniform of a minister of King Victor Emanuel II of Italy.[10]

Another factor in popularising uniforms was practical: officials' desire to facilitate the performance of their duties. In the eyes of the public, uniforms proclaiming official or military rank inspired greater respect and obedience than the *frac*.[11] Uniforms also had the advantage of indicating in a second the rank and function of the wearer – which explains their persistence on nurses and doctors in hospitals to this day. In Prussia before 1804 civil servants wanted uniforms because, especially in districts where they were unknown, uniforms would help them perform their functions.[12] Under Napoleon I a *payeur du trésor de la couronne* called Guillaume Peyrusse insisted on acquiring an uniform, even though it cost 800 francs and absorbed all his capital. He called it 'this costume indispensable in the army and without which one seems to have right to no respect, no regard'.[13] In 1818 the officers of the *chambre* and *garde-robe du roi* wrote to the duc de Duras to ask for a uniform: 'The consideration which the *Chambre du roi* should enjoy necessitates, to restore it to the rank which it used to occupy, that the officers who compose it wear the most honourable coat.'[14]

Even the Directory that had ruled the French Republic from 1795 to 1799 had, despite Barras's opposition, adopted civil uniforms for all legislators and officials. Like Louis XIV or Gustavus III, it believed in the impact of the 'language of signs' on the imagination.[15] Moreover, elegance was beginning to return to the streets of Paris: the dress of the *sans-culottes* had become a relic of a hated past.[16] An elaborate uniform of a red silk *habit manteau* (blue on formal occasions), with gold embroidery fringes, a blue silk sash with gold tassels worn over a white tunic and pantaloons, with a tricolour feathered hat, had been devised for the five directors and the ministers by a decree of 25 October 1795. They were ordered to wear the uniform during the exercise of their functions – as they can be seen doing in prints of the directors giving audience to petitioners in the Luxembourg Palace.[17]

So great was the fascination inspired by these republican uniforms that a book of prints, which praised them as 'at once worthy of republican pride and

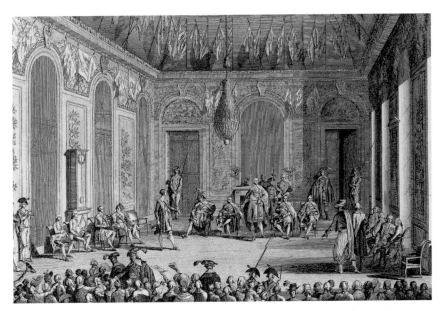

24 Jean Duplessis-Bertaux, An audience with the Directory on 30 Brumaire 1796.
In their official residence in the Luxembourg Palace, the directors who governed the
French Republic between 1795 and 1799 are holding an audience wearing the official
costume that they had invented for themselves – gold-embroidered blue silk coat, white
tunic and plumed hat.

of the wealth of an opulent nation', soon appeared in German, Italian and
English editions.[18] Within a year official uniforms, both *grand* and *petit
costume*, had also been designed for judges and deputies.[19] Other revolutionaries also found uniforms useful. Since green was the national colour of
Ireland, in 1798, as an indispensable prelude to his planned revolution, the
Directory's ally Lord Edward Fitzgerald ordered a green jacket with scarlet
braiding, a green cape and scarlet and green caps of liberty.[20]

After Bonaparte's military coup overthrew the Directory on 18 brumaire (8
November) 1799, France finally became the military monarchy which so
many Frenchmen had desired. Uniforms at once increased in splendour.
Created the day after the *coup d'état*, by 3 January 1800 the Garde des consuls
numbered 2,089 – more than Louis XVI's Garde Constitutionelle of 1792.
From the beginning it was an élitist unit with taller men, more splendid
uniforms, and privileges of pay and rank over line units.[21]

Dress revealed Bonaparte's monarchical ambitions before the proclamation
of the Empire in May 1804. Among the early decrees of the consulate was one
creating, on 9 December 1799, heavily embroidered official uniforms for the
consuls and ministers, followed later that month by members of the legislature

and the Conseil d'État, in May 1800 by prefects and senators, and in May 1801 by members of the Institut and most remaining public officials. The uniforms of members of the Académie française and students of the École polytechnique are the sole survivors today of the uniform frenzy of the first months of the consulate.[22]

By 1801 the First Consul was holding official receptions in the Tuileries after his review of the Garde consulaire every ten days or, after the re-introduction of the old calendar, every Sunday. While officers and officials wore uniform, the *habit habillé* was required for men without official positions. Thus only twelve years after the fall of the *ancien régime*, citizens of the French Republic were happy to wear its dress again (some ministers of Napoleon, and Duroc, *grand maréchal du palais*, his most intimate and important courtier, would even wear red heels).[23] The Foreign Minister himself, M. de Talleyrand, often wore, and was painted in, an embroidered *habit habillé* rather than the uniform of a minister.[24]

In March 1801 the English traveller J. G. Lemaistre admired at the First Consul's reception his 'grand costume of scarlet velvet richly embroidered with gold' and 'the handsome uniforms and commanding figures of the soldiery'. He also wrote: 'everyone not in uniform is in the full dress of the old court'.[25] In April 1802 an Irish visitor noted that 'the etiquette of a court and court dress are strictly observed and everyone agrees that the splendour of the court of the Tuileries is much greater than ever was the old Court of France'.[26] The *habits habillés* foreigners wore to the Tuileries were often specially made for them in Paris, since elsewhere on the continent they had been abandoned: under the consulate the French court was already more old-fashioned than other courts.[27]

Saying that he wanted to be dressed like a simple officer of his guard, Bonaparte himself generally wore the blue and white uniform of colonel of the *Grenadiers à pied* of the guard on Sundays, the green and white uniform of colonel of the *Chasseurs à cheval* of the guard on weekdays.[28] On campaign he also wore the famous grey *redingote* or overcoat, which inspired a cult among his soldiers.[29] However, the court system's need for splendour soon reimposed itself. Bonaparte was surrounded by courtier-advisers, such as Berthier and Talleyrand, whose families had served at Versailles. They were not the only people who wanted a revival of court life. In 1800, in a gesture revealing a desire at once for peace, trade and splendour, the city of Lyon presented the *Citoyen premier consul* with an 'habit à la française en velours cerise brodé de rameaux d'olivier en fils de soie d'or et d'argent et doublé de faille rose'.[30] On 18 April 1802 Bonaparte wore his present from Lyon, rather than his official

First Consul's uniform, at the Te Deum for the concordat restoring the Catholic Church. On this occasion he also, for the first time, dressed his footmen in his new livery of green and gold. According to an English witness, the watching crowds exclaimed (as no doubt Bonaparte had hoped): 'Ah voilà encore la bourse et la livrée! oh comme c'est beau! Comme ça fait plaisir, voilà qui commence véritablement un peu à prendre couleur! . . . Ah c'est bien . . . c'est comme autrefois – enfin nous reconnaissons notre pays.'[31]

In January 1803 Bonaparte imposed mourning for his brother-in-law General Leclerc on all his 'court' and on foreign ambassadors.[32] Later that year, when some men dared visit the Second Consul Cambacérès dressed in black *fracs* rather than uniforms, he asked: 'Are you in mourning? I feel sympathy for the loss you have suffered.'[33] The consuls had no doubt of the political importance of dress.

Napoleon's rival in generalship and popularity was General Moreau. Moreau deliberately attended a reception of the Minister of War – he did not go to the First Consul's – in a simple black coat, 'which stood out in such a definite manner from the brilliant uniforms and costumes of gold and silk which could be seen on all sides'. Dress was a way of proclaiming public opposition, at a time when words and deeds were watched by the police.[34] Royalist agents reported to Louis XVIII that Moreau also attended a ball of the Minister of the Marine in a simple grey coat: it was said that he did not possess a general's uniform.[35]

Dress at Napoleon's court became increasingly monarchical. Throughout the army he introduced elaborate new uniforms, using embroidery, lace, plumes, breastplates, dolmans, towering helmets, bear and tiger skins, more lavishly than the royal army ever had.[36] On 18 July 1804 (29 messidor, an XII), two months after the proclamation of the Empire, a decree regulated the official costumes of princes, marshals, *grands officiers* and court officials, for which a credit of 650,000 francs was opened. Velvet in winter and taffeta in summer, the costumes were designed by Jean-Baptiste Isabey, *dessinateur ordinaire du cabinet et des fêtes et spectacles de la cour* for the Emperor. The guiding principle was that, as the Intendant of the Grande Armée M. Daru wrote to his master, 'It is not enough for the pomp that surrounds Your Majesty to be magnificent, it must be inimitable.'[37]

These costumes were a major innovation. Isabey received advice from the comte de Ségur, *grand maître des cérémonies*; the comte de Rémusat *premier chambellan maître de la garde-robe* (in charge of the Emperor's clothes under the *grand chambellan*, M. de Talleyrand); and Vivant Denon, *directeur du Musée Napoléon* and the Emperor's chief artistic adviser. Each service in the

25 Jacques-Louis David, The Empress Josephine with her ladies (detail from *Le Sacre*, 1807).
The Empress's train is held, at the moment of her coronation by the Emperor, by her two principal ladies, her *dame d'honneur* Madame de La Rochefoucauld (left) and Madame de Lavallette, who as *dame d'atours* was officially in charge of her wardrobe.

Emperor's household was assigned a different colour: scarlet for the *grand maréchal du palais*; crimson for the *grand chambellan*; light blue for the *grand écuyer*; green for the hunt; violet for the *grand maître des cérémonies*.[38] In the months preceding the Emperor's coronation on 2 December 1804, so many tailors, embroiderers, shoe-makers and dress-makers were working on these costumes in Paris that wages rocketed and Paris embroiderers were forced to import workmen from Lyon.[39]

The Emperor himself regulated some details with Ségur; not only the costume and location of each official, but also the requirement that princes bore the train of the Emperor, princesses that of the Empress.[40] As at the royal *lever* and *coucher*, the handling of clothes, as well as clothes themselves, emphasised hierarchy. The new imperial highnesses were furious. At one point the Emperor's sisters dropped the portions of the Empress's train which they were holding, so that she almost fell down. Some witnesses were impressed by the majesty and magnificence of the costumes at the ceremony; others were reminded of a masquerade.[41]

Henceforth, in full costume, and in some military uniforms, coats and sleeves vanished beneath their gold and silver embroidery – as can be seen in

26 Jean-Baptiste Isabey, *The Emperor in petit costume, c.* 1805.
The Emperor wore this heavily embroidered red and gold official costume, diamond-studded sword and lavishly plumed hat for ceremonies such as his coronation and his second marriage. He wore more feathers in his hair than Marie Antoinette.

portraits of Napoleon's marshals and ministers. The higher the rank, the wider the embroidery. Contemporaries wrote that the Emperor, or the sky itself, could not be seen in the blaze of embroideries and uniforms around him. Napoleon had given the French élite what it wanted: glittering uniforms which proclaimed their rank and satisfied their vanity.[42] When he wore his uniform as *auditeur du conseil d'état*, Stendhal wrote: 'I found this costume *fort bien* and exactly as elaborate as is appropriate for a young man.'[43] Later in the century the glorious literary careers of Stendhal's successors Victor Hugo, Eugène Sue and Alfred de Musset were, in some ways, attempts to compete with their fathers' glamorous uniforms under the Empire. The sons could not forget, wrote de Musset in *La Confession d'un enfant du siècle* (1836), their fathers' *poitrines chamarrées d'or.*[44]

For the Emperor himself Isabey designed, in addition to the coronation costume, a special *petit costume*. It consisted of a white satin tunic; a coat and knee-length cloak of purple velvet, heavily embroidered in gold and silver thread, with bees, oak leaves, ears of wheat and the letter N; a plumed hat; and a sword with the Regent diamond in the hilt. By 1811 Napoleon had three velvet and two silk *petits costumes*. It was called the *grand costume de France* (he also had another version in green as King of Italy), and was worn at banquets, receptions and weddings.[45] If, as Balzac claimed, the revolution had been a debate between silk and cloth, silk had won.[46]

With the Emperor's encouragement,[47] the *Costume Napoléon* spread as far as the *Code Napoléon*, and was discussed more often in contemporaries' memoirs. All the satellite courts (Lucca, Italy, Holland, Naples, Spain, Westphalia) adopted lavish costumes.[48] After Louis Bonaparte became King of Holland in January 1806, he created his own court on the model of his brother's, with its own costumes, in a previously semi-republican society. Some of his French courtiers mocked the 'good robust Dutch who decked out in court coats had such an embarrassed air that one could not look at them without appearing to laugh at them'. A Paris actor called Morcutier was hired to teach them how to wear court costumes and swords.[49] By May 1807, however, Stanislas de Girardin could write: 'the court presents an excessively brilliant appearance: the coats of the public officials, of civil officers are magnificently embroidered. People seem to want to compensate for never having worn embroidery in this country.'[50]

In Naples the arrival of a Napoleonic regime also led to a return to splendour. Before 1806, like his father Charles III of Spain, the Bourbon king, Ferdinand IV had generally worn a grey frock coat.[51] He had even been painted by his court artist Hackert in peasant dress with his family, surrounded by the wheat harvest. Life in his great country palace of Caserta was simpler than in most country houses in England, noted an English visitor called John Morritt: 'we are always invited in our morning dress [*frac*] with or without boots' – although the King had founded and personally supervised a silk factory nearby at San Leucio.[52] When Neapolitan soldiers had been dressed in new uniforms, Ferdinand IV had remarked with prophetic indifference that, whatever uniforms they were put in, they would still run away.[53]

When Marshal Murat reigned in Naples as King Joachim-Napoleon from 1808 to 1815, however, the Neapolitan army became a serious fighting force. Even during lessons, his sons always wore their uniforms as colonels of the lancers of the Royal Guard and the Gardes du corps. Their tutors wore the only *fracs* seen in the palace. Murat himself was never seen in a *frac* by his daughter Louise, except for a few hours on two or three occasions; he always wore military uniform, except on days of 'grand gala' when he wore a coat in crimson velvet embroidered with silver, like the *petit costume* of Napoleon, a Spanish cloak and a velvet toque with white feathers. Every civilian official had to wear a similar uniform: 'Nothing was finer than the sight of this crowd sparkling with embroideries, with an appearance as rich as it was varied and picturesque.'[54] She was not alone in this opinion.

Comte Hippolyte d'Espinchal wrote of the New Year reception in Naples in 1811:

> the brilliant court costumes of the ladies of the household of the Queen, the richness of the uniforms of the aides de camp, the *officiers d'ordonnance*, the dignitaries composing the civil and military household of the King, of the officers of the guard, many of whom wore the striking blue dolman, trousers of white cashmere embroidered in gold, red boots with golden buttons, the uniforms of the higher officials of the different civil administrations, *enfin* this rich mixture of uniforms, costumes enhanced by gold and silver, by stars, grand cordons and decorations, everything gave this fête a distinctive splendour, animation and physiognomy.[55]

The splendour of the uniforms was such that they became a financial resource, as well as an instrument of government. After the defeat of her husband's bid for Italian independence by Austrian troops in June 1815, Caroline Murat, ex-Queen of Naples, was at first reduced to selling the braid on her husband's uniforms, and the gold embroideries from her dresses, in order to raise money on which to live.[56]

The Napoleonic court reproduced a pattern of consumption and expenditure as lavish as that of Versailles – proof that a court system in France was as much an expression of national needs as of monarchs' desires. Taking into account all bills from all tradesmen, the great Napoleonic court historian Frédéric Masson estimated that the Empress Josephine spent about 1.1 million francs a year on clothes – more than Marie Antoinette, and enough, it was said, for many Paris dress-makers to survive by working for the Empress alone.[57] The Emperor tried to forbid them access to her private apartments but, in this domain, was as powerless as Louis XVI. An exasperated *dame du palais* of the Empress, Madame de Rémusat, herself a pioneer of female education, remembered: 'the *petits appartements* were full of them as well as of every kind of artist . . . she was endlessly brought diamonds, jewels, shawls, materials, every kind of trinket. She bought everything, without ever demanding the price and most of the time forgot what she had bought . . . Everything was arranged between her and her *femmes de chambre* [i.e. Madame de Rémusat was not responsible]. She changed her linen three times a day and only wore new stockings.' She owned three to four hundred cashmere shawls. 'She was always dressed with extreme elegance; we rarely saw the same dress or the same flowers reappear.' By the time of her divorce in 1809, excluding the many items already given away to her household, she owned 210 *robes d'été* and 676 *robes d'étoffe*. In one year she had bought seven *grands habits*, 136 dresses, 71 pairs of silk stockings and 980 pairs of gloves. Even on her deathbed on 30 May 1814 the Empress put on a new bed gown, in hope of a visit from Alexander I of Russia.[58]

Two of her *dames du palais*, the duchesses de Rovigo and de Bassano, were each said to spend 50,000 francs a year on clothes, and this is confirmed by tailors' registers: one *grand habit* for a New Year reception at the Tuileries cost 1,300 francs.[59] Some dresses worn at court were embroidered in gold or silver, covered in diamonds and garnished with mother-of-pearl.[60] Hunting costumes for the households of the different members of the imperial family were also created: green and gold for the Emperor (his livery colours), crimson for the Empress, blue and silver for Queen Hortense, pink and silver for Queen Caroline, lilac and silver for Princess Pauline.[61]

Equally indicative of the strength of the court system, in addition to the return of *grands habits*, the Empress's expenditure, and the creation of civil uniforms, was the continued requirement for men without office to wear the *habit habillé*. Under the Empire the *habit habillé* was often more elaborate and expensive than under the old regime. Embroidery spread down sleeves, and over the backs and tails of coats: courtiers looked like silken flowerbeds. A young officer like Hippolyte d'Espinchal, appalled that he once had to wear the *habit habillé* for presentation to the Emperor, devoted four pages of his memoirs to his ordeal.[62] However, in 1806, sending the French consul in Constantinople an *habit habillé* for gala evenings, an elderly diplomat showed a different attitude: 'Try to remember our dress in 1787 and 1788. Today it is absolutely the same . . . how beautiful it is and how sweet at present to be French. You will be a little astonished to find yourself dressed as we were at Versailles. The sleeves, the bag, everything has returned and I am charmed by it.'[63]

Napoleon I was so charmed by this traditional status symbol that he was one of the last monarchs to wear the *habit habillé*. At his wedding to Marie-Louise in 1810, he wore not military uniform or *petit costume* but an *habit habillé* of crimson velvet with gold embroidery.[64] That year the Emperor dictated a note which shows the French court's renewed symbiosis with the Lyon silk industry. Already in 1807 he had placed orders for new fabrics for the palaces of Versailles and Compiègne specifically to help Lyon factories.[65] At *bals parés* and theatres, Napoleon wrote in 1810, men should wear only *habits de soie*. There were similar exceptions to before 1789: 'officiers de service près de l'empereur et près de l'impératrice' and, in addition, officers of the Imperial Guard and the Paris garrison on duty.[66] 'To get the looms which make *étoffes unies* working, His Majesty is disposed to make orders of objects foreign to the needs of his palaces. The deputies from Lyon must first say how much these orders should amount to . . . It is necessary to examine what could be done for the Lyon factories by the regulations of the court. One can say that during winter and every occasion that *grand costume* is worn, the velvet coat will be obligatory and that on other days . . . everyone except the officers on duty will appear at court not in uniforms but wearing Lyon materials . . . the example of the court will influence rich private people who will adopt its usage.'[67] (Another motive was to help the lace industry of Alençon, which claimed to be totally dependent on orders from the court, since lace was no longer worn anywhere else.)[68] Thus veterans of the Republican army, such as Marshals Augereau, Ney, Junot and Lannes, were seen at court entertainments in *habits habillés* in pink, green and *gorge de pigeon*.[69]

On 18 January 1811 Madame de Souza, mother of one of Napoleon's favourite officers, the comte de Flahaut, wrote from Paris that no one could talk of anything else: she herself regretted the uniforms.[70] The *fête* of the Empress Marie-Louise was celebrated on 25 August 1811 by festivities at Trianon where all men wore the *habit habillé*. 'Quelles singulières tournures il y avait, bonté divine', the duchesse d'Abrantès remembered years later.[71] The Emperor wore a brown velvet *habit habillé* with a gold and diamond embroidered waistcoat.[72]

Such dress anachronism is part of a pattern: the Emperor's use of his *lever* and *coucher* as occasions to show favour or test candidates for office; the role of his brother Joseph as his lieutenant 1800–06 and in 1814–15; the effacement of the legislature; the development of the court as a parallel government; the Emperor's plans, as early as 1806, to restore and live in Versailles. Although careers remained open to the talents, Talleyrand was right to call Napoleon 'le dernier roi de l'ancien régime'.[73]

Rabelais's claim in *Gargantua* – 'L'habit ne fait pas le moine'[74] – had less validity, under the Empire, than the rival proverbs 'L'habit fait l'homme' or 'L'habit fait tout'. Clothes became so important that it was commonplace to say, and believe: 'In Paris more than elsewhere one is duped by costumes and deceived by appearances.'[75] Balzac wrote: 'the question of costume is anyway enormously important for those who want to appear to have what they do not have, for it is often the best way of possessing it later'.[76] This could have been applied to many of his contemporaries, as well as to his young hero, Lucien de Rubempré.

Paris was a city built on clothes. One of the first sounds the traveller heard on entering Paris was street sellers shouting 'Habits et galons à vendre ou à acheter'.[77] Access to the garden, the chapel and the state apartments of the Tuileries was decided not by wealth or allegiance but by dress.[78] The crowd streamed up the staircase of the Tuileries on Sunday, eyes fixed in the inspection of chests and shoulders (that is to say, embroidery, orders and epaulettes).[79] According to the final lines of *Les Étrennes forcées, ou Ah! mon habit que je vous remercie!* (1814), a play about an impoverished valet who obtained a loan thanks to his *habit*:

> Le luxe est partout accueilli;
> on l'aime, on le renomme,
> Et, dans le monde comme ici,
> c'est l'habit qui fait l'homme.[80]

L'habit could also make events. For a few hours on 23 October 1812 General Malet was able to seize control of part of the centre of Paris thanks in part, the Minister of War wrote to the Empress Marie-Louise, to the prestige of his 'habit d'officier général'.[81] Partly as a consequence of the Malet conspiracy, Napoleon I sped back from Russia as fast as he could. As they approached the Arc de Triomphe du Carrousel in front of the Tuileries Palace, just before midnight on 18 December, his companion and Grand Écuyer Caulaincourt, duc de Vicence, 'unbuttoned my overcoat in order for the embroidery of my uniform to be seen'. The embroidery alone was enough to make the sentry let the carriage drive through the arch.[82]

In 1814–15 the changes of dynasty from Bonaparte to Bourbon, back to Bonaparte, then back to Bourbon again, like the Regency crisis in England in 1788 to 1789, heightened dress consciousness. In addition to the repeated changes of cockade, between Bonaparte tricolour and Bourbon white, poems and caricatures used dress as a metaphor for power: for example Béranger's poem, *Vieux habits vieux galons, réflexions morales et politiques d'un marchand d'habits de la capitale*, with its refrain 'L'habit fait tout'. The caricatures, *Les habits retournés*, and *Allons, retournons encore nos habits*, showed officials, led by the former Archichancelier Cambacérès, literally turning coat, turning their green and gold Bonaparte livery coat inside out to become a blue and silver Bourbon coat.

Dress showed that many Parisians considered the allies liberators, not conquerors. The *Journal des dames et des modes*, a Paris fashion magazine published between 1797 and 1839, reported on 10 July 1814: 'the *guirlandes à*

27 Anon., *Les habits retournés*, 1814.
Dress as treason: in April 1814, after the replacement of Napoleon I by Louis XVIII,
Cambacérès (right) and three of his cronies are shown as traitors, turning their coats in
green and gold Napoleonic livery colours inside out, in order to display blue and silver
Bourbon livery colours.

la Wellington have been replaced by the lily of the Bourbons. People also wear
bonnets *à la Blücher* and shakos *à la Platow*, referring to the names of famous
Prussian and Russian commanders.[83]

Dress not only reflected but affected political events. The Restoration did
not design civil uniforms. Once Napoleon's patronage was removed, the *habit
habillé* was 'feared like a poisoned cup'.[84] It was as 'strange, outmoded,
ridiculous' at the Tuileries, according to the baron de Frénilly, as uniform had
once been at Versailles.[85] Therefore royalist court officials and *émigrés* needed
military uniforms. As the marquis de Mondenard wrote: 'therefore in order
not to be confused with the *huissiers de la chambre*, I am forced to ask
permission to wear epaulettes in order to present myself at the palace'.[86]
Among the royalists promoted in the French army, partly in order to gain a
suitable military uniform, were former *émigrés* who had fought against it, like
Chateaubriand, the ducs d'Aumont and de Duras. As a tribute to the nature of
the kingdom over which he was about to reign, before he returned to France,
Louis XVIII himself added epaulettes to the dark blue *fracs* he had been
wearing as an exile in England.[87] The comte d'Artois – in this respect more
flexible than Louis XVI – usually wore the uniform of the Garde nationale of

which he was colonel-in-chief.[88] By March 1815 'almost all the civil household of the King presents itself in uniform at the palace'.[89]

The promotions of royalists and *émigrés* helped alienate the French army. One Napoleonic officer, the comte de Castellane, wrote that he wanted to put on an *habit habillé* instead of his uniform.[90] Memories were so partisan that the *habit habillé* was associated with the returned Bourbons, who had not worn it since 1791, rather than with Napoleon I, who had been wearing it since 1802. Some, however, did not forget: the Emperor's patronage of the Lyon silk industry may explain why that city supported his return from Elba so enthusiastically in March 1815.

In this age of rapid regime change, it was prudent to retain uniforms of past regimes in case they returned to power. One caricature of March 1815 showed a former *émigré* putting his royalist clothes back in a trunk, and a former revolutionary trying on his cap of liberty and *sans-culotte* dress, with the legend: 'Il ne faut pas se défaire de ses vieux habits . . . on ne sait ce qui peut arriver'.[91] In 1814 some old servants greeted their returned masters wearing the liveries they had been storing in secret since their prohibition in June 1790.[92] In the afternoon of 20 March 1815, Napoleon's former ministers, councillors of state, *maîtres d'hôtel* and valets, and the ladies of his court, streamed back to the Tuileries wearing the liveries, uniforms and court dresses which they had stored, as many of his soldiers had hidden eagles and tricolour cockades, since the fall of the Empire in 1814. Thus the Emperor was greeted by his household as if he had returned from a visit to one of his palaces in the Île de France rather than from eleven months' exile in Elba.[93]

During the Hundred Days, although Napoleon I was trying to present himself as the people's choice, dress revealed the imperial autocrat. The Emperor insisted that he and his brothers wear their elaborate *petits costumes*, rather than the uniform of the Paris National Guard, during the proclamation of the revised constitution on the Champ de Mars on 1 June 1815.[94] An English Whig admirer, John Cam Hobhouse, described the ceremony. Not only were court officials in full dress, 'Spanish mantles and feathered bonnets': the Emperor wore 'his Spanish black bonnet, shaded with plumes, and looped with a large diamond in front. His mantle was of purple velvet edged with broad embroidery of gold on the outside, and lined with white ermine, scarce descending to his ankles, and tied round his throat without any arm-holes. He looked very ungainly and squat.' His brothers 'caparisoned in fancy dresses of white taffety from head to foot [their *petits costumes*] . . . excepting the house of Austria looked as ill as the princes of any legitimate house in Christendom', though they were 'later lost to our sight in the blaze of uniforms'.[95]

28 French school, Comte Carnot, 1815. Dress as transformation: a former regicide, 'the organiser of victory' for the French Republic in 1794 is painted here during the Hundred Days in his official costume as Napoleon's Minister of the Interior. His dress is depicted with greater care than his features.

Following his second abdication after Waterloo, among his followers on St Helena Napoleon maintained the rules of court dress, more rigidly than had Louis XVIII in exile in England or Russia. Servants continued to wear his green and gold livery. Six weeks after his arrival he abandoned military uniform for his green hunting uniform, which continued to be his standard dress, no doubt because his valets had packed many of them, and because he refused to order new coats of English cloth.[96] He was buried in the green uniform of a colonel of the *Chasseurs de la garde.*[97]

Bourbons' costumes had been court officials' perquisites; Napoleon's were dynastic talismans. By the terms of his will, relations not in the line of succession received a carpet, a candlestick or a *nécessaire*. However, he instructed Marchand, 'mon premier valet de chambre', who had followed him to Elba and St Helena, to give 'mon nécessaire de toilette. Un de chacun de mes uniformes, une douzaine de chemises et un objet complet de chacun de mes habillements, et généralement de tout ce qui sert à ma toilette' to his son, the former King of Rome.

His *premier chambellan, maître de la garde-robe* the comte de Turenne, who had custody in France of the Emperor's ceremonial costumes, was instructed to give his swords, orders, toque and *chapeau à la Henri IV* to his son; and a *manteau brodé, veste et culottes* each to his brothers Joseph and Louis – the two dynastic heirs after his son.[98] Some of Napoleon's brothers and sisters also kept their own court costumes, which are now on display in the Museo Napoleonico in Rome. In the portrait of the former King Louis-Napoleon with his elder son standing in front of St Peter's, Rome, which he commissioned in 1816 from J. B. Wicar, both wear uniforms of the Dutch Royal Guard, although it had been abolished, with the kingdom itself, in 1810.[99] Dress reveals the persistence, in exile, of the dynastic ambitions which would be realised by the accession of the King's younger son as Napoleon III in 1852.

The Restoration finally devised its own civil costumes. In 1815 a special *ordonnance* gave deputies a formal costume, which even members of the liberal opposition generally wore for ceremonies, portraits and making a speech. It confirmed dynastic power – by placing *fleurs-de-lys* on collars, cuffs and buttons – but was less humiliating than the black costume they had been given in 1789.[100] In 1825 an English lady visiting Paris called it 'a sort of livery with gold or silver lace at the collar and cuffs which were sometimes also of yellow cloth or I think of white or red. M. de Villèle very grand with his gold lace seemed more like a livery servant than minister of finance.'[101]

In 1820, as part of the only reorganisation of the Maison du roi in its history, all court officials received a civil uniform, which they were obliged to wear when in waiting. These uniforms were modelled directly on those of the Maison de l'empereur, with almost the same colours for each department: red for the Gouvernements; dark blue for the Chambre; light blue for the Écuries; green for the Hunt; violet for the Cérémonies. *Grande tenue* was velvet, *petite tenue* cloth: both were lined with silk. After 5 p.m. all had to wear breeches and silk stockings. In *grande tenue*, *grands officiers* had embroidery on collars, cuffs, pockets and edges of the coat, 140 millimetres wide; *premiers officiers* 122 millimetres; *officiers* 95 millimetres, *officiers du service* 70 millimetres.[102] *Gentilshommes de la chambre* wore their uniforms, which cost them around 6,000 francs each, at the Sunday receptions of the King and the royal family, and then in the Salle des Maréchaux, the great public room of the Tuileries Palace, 'before the good people who admired their fine bearing and the richness of their costumes'.[103]

In the 1820 reorganisation, the separate *garde-robe du roi* was abolished, as an unnecessary anachronism. Four *premiers chambellans, maîtres de la garde-robe,* replaced the last *grand maître de la garde-robe,* the comte de Blacas, in control of the King's clothes. There was no *lever* or *coucher:* every morning they merely handed the King his Order of the Holy Spirit, sword and hat. Like other wealthy

RÈGLEMENT

ARRÊTÉ PAR LE ROI,

Concernant l'Habillement des Grands Officiers de la Couronne, Grands Officiers , Premiers Officiers et Officiers de la Maison de Sa Majesté , et autres Personnes y occupant des places et emplois.

Le ROI, voulant pourvoir à l'exécution de l'article 4, titre 1er de son Ordonnance du 1er novembre 1820 concernant les costumes que doivent porter , dans l'exercice de leurs fonctions, ceux qui remplissent les charges ou emplois de sa Maison civile, a arrêté les dispositions suivantes :

ARTICLE PREMIER.

Il est affecté une couleur distinctive à chacun des services de la Maison du ROI.

Les couleurs sont :
Pour le service du Grand Maître. . . . . l'amarante.
Pour celui du Grand Chambellan. . . . . le bleu barbot.
Pour celui du Grand Écuyer. . . . . le bleu de roi.
Pour celui du Grand Veneur. . . . . le vert.
Et pour celui du Grand Maître des cérémonies. . . le violet.

ART. 2.

L'habillement des Grands Officiers de la Couronne , Grands Officiers , Premiers Officiers et Officiers de la Maison, se divise en grande et petite tenue.

La grande tenue est de rigueur dans les circonstances d'apparat et jours de cérémonies extraordinaires; la petite tenue sera portée habituellement.

29 *Règlement arrêté par le Roi,* 10 December 1820.
Showing the attention paid to the details of colour, embroidery and formality of the uniforms worn to court, such regulations were frequently issued in Europe in the nineteenth century, and in England until 1939.

men, he was dressed by *garçons de toilette* and *valets de chambre ordinaires,* menial positions which had not existed before 1792, instead of the *valets de chambre* and *valets de garde-robe du roi,* who had been men of wealth and education.[104]

Restoration civil uniforms were so popular that they were one reason for the rapid expansion of the court in the decade 1820–30, until by 1830 there were 306 *gentilshommes honoraires de la chambre du roi.* The comte de Jumilhac, for example, wrote: 'I solicit a place of *gentilhomme de la chambre* in order to have a uniform to have the honour to make my court to H. M.'[105]

The costumes of the Restoration court reached an apex of magnificence in the reign of Charles X. The King, who saw himself as a military monarch, habitually wore the uniform of the 26,000-strong Garde royale formed in 1815, which was considered, as the duc de Richelieu had put it, 'the safeguard of our existence . . . the pupil of our eyes'.[106] In contrast to previous Bourbon heirs, from a very early age Charles X's grandson the duc de Bordeaux wore uniform at court receptions, drilled his own regiment of children, 'all wonderfully dressed and disciplined', and reviewed troops.[107]

From 1824, for the first time since 1789, Charles X wore diamonds in his Order of the Holy Spirit, his epaulettes, his shoe buckles and his sword at evening receptions at court. His cousin the duchesse d'Orléans wrote: 'He had a fine appearance. The King was wearing a wig which suited him very well. He had a coat embroidered in every corner, a violet waistcoat, trousers and

30 François-Joseph Heim, Charles X distributing prizes in the Louvre on 15 January 1825 (detail).
The King, wearing his uniform as Colonel-General of the Garde Royale, is presenting the order of Saint Michel to the sculptor Cartellier. Behind is his *aide de camp*, charged with his artistic patronage, Vicomte Sosthènes de La Rochefoucauld. On the left is the comte de Forbin, director of the Louvre, in the gold-embroidered costume of a senior household official. Since the King is present, most artists wear the *habit habillé*.

stockings and he had put on a lot of diamonds.'[108] The duc de Lévis wrote that he looked no more than forty.[109]

Women's dress also reached a peak of luxury. The same Paris couturiers as under the Empire, like Louis Hippolyte LeRoy in the rue de Richelieu, supplied the court and much of Europe with *grands habits*. Before 1814 LeRoy was *Marchand de modes de S.M. l'Impératrice et Reine;* after 1814, *Marchand de modes et robes de la cour, de Madame et des cours étrangères.*[110] The court dress of the Restoration, first worn by the duchesse d'Angoulême on 30 May 1814, was 'a dress of white silk with a long train and a lace bonnet with hanging lappets'.[111] Madame de Boigne, who claimed that the duchesse d'Angoulême had at first wanted to reimpose hoops as at Versailles, found the costume ridiculous, but gradually, as the lappets assumed the form of a veil, not without grace.[112] In June 1825 at the different *fêtes* in honour of the coronation of Charles X, held at court, in ministries and at the *hôtel de ville*, the *Journal des dames et des modes* wrote: 'The quantity and richness of the *parures*, both in gold and in stones, was hard to imagine . . . they say that at the last soirée which took place in the *grands appartements du roi* there were only three dresses which were not gleaming, sparkling or sewn with gold or silver.'[113]

The duchesse d'Angoulême's chief personal contribution to court fashion was her reintroduction of the style for wearing ostrich feathers in the hair, popularised by her mother: she always wore them, with day dress as well as court dress, wherever she was in France. In a famous picture by Baron Gros, now in the Musée des Beaux-Arts of Bordeaux, she is shown distributing her feathers like religious relics among royalists, when fleeing France at the beginning of the Hundred Days.[114]

From 1821 to 1830, however, the chief animator of court entertainments and Paris fashions, who played a role as important as Marie Antoinette from 1774 to 1789, or the Empress Josephine from 1802 to 1809, was the King's niece by marriage, the duchesse de Berri. Unlike the duchesse d'Angoulême, she was young and graceful, with a natural Neapolitan manner.[115] Parisians watching the *Fête-Dieu* procession in June 1821 could be heard saying: 'how young she is, how beautiful she is, and how well dressed!'[116] The least detail of her toilette was noted in fashion magazines; she organised costume balls in her apartments on Turkish, Persian, Peruvian and Scottish themes. In 1829 she encouraged the foundation by Émile de Girardin, an ambitious young journalist, of the famous review *La Mode*. It published some of the finest writers and illustrators of the age, including Balzac and George Sand, and proclaimed: 'La mode est la reine du monde'. The Empress Josephine had helped launch a fashion for cashmere shawls; the duchesse de Berri encouraged a vogue for turbans.[117]

Despite the creation of elegant civil uniforms, many French court officials revealed their 'core values' by wearing military uniform while performing court duties. The first regulation of 1820 stated that all officials were *rigoureusement tenus* to wear their civil uniform 'during the performance of their duties'. However, repeated ordonnances from 1820 to 1830 allowed court officials who were also ministers, generals, *maréchaux de camp* or *conseillers d'état* to wear their military or official uniforms at court, when not performing their court duties.[118] In February 1830, however, just before the July revolution, it was decreed that lieutenant-generals, *maréchaux de camp*, *maîtres des requêtes* and *conseillers d'état* must wear the costume of their court office both during the performance of the duties of their court office *and* when they wanted to enjoy the *entrées* attached to that office.[119] In its final months, the monarchy was trying to raise the personal service of the King above that of the state.

In 1830 one author complained of the 'taste of the age for livery', and feared that the nation would soon be 'entirely in uniform, from the lowest *conseiller de préfecture* to the Secretary of State ... from the student and the simple

31 Horace Vernet, General Foy, *c.* 1826. Despite his defence of liberal principles in the Chamber of Deputies, General Foy is shown in the fleur-de-lys-embroidered official costume of a deputy during the Restoration.

32 M. Dupont, A *grand officier* of Charles X, 1829.
Engraved for the never-completed *Livre du sacre*, the *grand officier* wears the *grande tenue* of a Restoration court official. He is probably the duc de Mortemart, *capitaine-colonel* of the *gardes à pied* and the last Prime Minister of Charles X, appointed during the Revolution of July 1830 in a vain attempt to save the Bourbon throne.

professor to the profound academician'.[120] The marquis de Custine claimed that, in France, 'the taste for uniform seems to have become one of the dominant traits of the national character'.[121] If the outcome of the July revolution had been different, Paris might have remained a city of uniforms, like Vienna, Berlin and St Petersburg.

Such indeed was Charles X's miscalculation: that most Frenchmen preferred a strong monarchy, and the rewards of government and military service, to liberal principles. The struggle between the two traditions, royal and revolutionary, for the heart of Paris was visible and audible at the ball given in the Palais Royal by the duc d'Orléans on 29 May 1830, in honour of the Kings of France and the Two Sicilies. On the Place du Palais Royal the windows of neighbouring houses were lined with spectators so well dressed that they looked like guests: by an instinctive reflex action, they were repeating the behaviour patterns of spectators at the weddings of the duc de Bourgogne in 1697 and the Dauphin in 1770. Down in the garden of the Palais Royal, however, poor Parisians yelled up at the dancers on the first floor: 'À bas les habits galonnés! À bas les aristocrates!'[122] If many in the middle class wanted to join court society, many poorer Parisians detested it.

The spread of civil uniforms was not limited to France. In the early nineteenth century all European states were turning to uniform, to advertise and heighten the appeal of state service, and strengthen the bonds between monarchies and their élites. In Prussia the government was at first more reluctant than its employees to introduce civil uniforms, fearing their cost and the reaction of the public when it saw the number of men in government service. The army was also suspicious of civil uniforms. In the end regulations were issued on 14 February 1804: civil servants were told to wear their new uniforms at official ceremonies and in the King's presence. Soon they became so popular that they were worn off duty; feeling excluded, even university professors petitioned for uniforms of their own.[123]

In Austria, between 1802 and 1808 civil uniforms were created for officials of the war and police departments and, at their request, as a reward for their loyalty during the recent wars, for members of the Estates of Upper and Lower Austria, Moravia, Tyrol, Styria and Carinthia.[124] The government began to debate introducing uniforms in other ministries and the court in 1810. It was a gradual process. At the end of 1810 diplomats and Chancellery officials were allowed to wear uniforms, although they were not compulsory.[125]

The minutes of a conference on dress held in Vienna on 12 March 1812 explain the different motives animating senior officials. Metternich, who had admired the Napoleonic court during three years in Paris as Austrian ambassador in 1806–9 and during a further six-month stay as Minister of Foreign Affairs after the marriage of Napoleon and Marie-Louise in 1810, advocated the extension of uniforms for reasons of economy: 'Wearing a uniform is certainly an economy for officials. One always needs a costume in conformity with one's rank in often unavoidable functions; the difference in luxury disappears and the uniform covers the wealthy and the less prosperous official' – although, like Prussian officials in 1804, he feared the reaction of the people of Vienna, when they saw with their own eyes the number of government officials living in their city. Austria's greatest general, the Archduke Charles, agreed: 'it is generally known how much more economical a uniform is than civil dress. It is subject to no overwhelming luxury, nor to expensive reigning fashion; it remains the same in summer and winter and looks very decent.'[126] The Emperor was concerned to raise the status of his officials. If there had to be official uniforms, he added with customary prudence, they should be black, to cover ink stains: but he hesitated.[127]

Finally in January 1814 Obersthofmeister Prince Trauttmansdorf petitioned the Emperor for uniforms for all court officials, on monarchical grounds: uniforms put service and loyalty before class. The officials themselves also petitioned the Emperor on these grounds. As in France, the spread of civil uniforms reflected the needs of the élites as much as monarchs' wishes. Metternich drafted regulations in Paris, the stronghold of court splendour, where they were approved by the Emperor on 25 April 1814. All court and government officials were given dark green uniforms, with different-coloured facings, depending on the department to which they belonged.[128] As at other courts, rank was indicated by the width of embroidery. The embroidery on the uniforms of ministers and ambassadors cost 300 gulden, on those of officials of the eleventh class 13 gulden.[129] On 19 October 1814 Madame Eynard noted, during the Congress of Vienna: 'the men who were not in elegant military uniform wore court costumes charged with gold and silver . . . everything was so brilliant that your eyes ached'.[130]

However, in Austria as in France, for most members of the élite, even for monarchs themselves, the army had become the basis of status and self-esteem. Even some of the most senior court officials preferred to perform court duties in military uniform: rather than wear their chamberlain's uniform, some chamberlains had their chamberlain's key sewn on to their military uniform.[131]

Civil uniform was also adopted in other monarchies. The day after he assumed the title of King of the Netherlands in 1815, William I issued regulations for new civil uniforms, as did the King of Sweden in 1823, and the King of Sardinia in 1824.[132] After the arrival of the Portuguese court in Brazil in 1808 that country also became a bastion of court dress. At official ceremonies ministers wore the uniform of a court chamberlain.[133]

Civil uniforms were also adopted in the United Kingdom, probably reflecting the Prince Regent's desire to rival the uniforms of Prussia, France and Austria. He may also have compensated for the growing power of his ministers by asserting his authority in matters of dress.[134] A few months after he became Regent in June 1811, it was reported that 'his whole soul is wrapped up in Hussar saddles, caps, cuirasses and sword belts'. The changes he instituted in cavalry uniforms caused considerable expense to the officers.[135] In 1816 his daughter Princess Charlotte wrote that a great mark of '*the most perfect good*

33 Jean-Baptiste Isabey, *The Congress of Vienna*, 1815.
By 1815 the principal statesmen of Europe wear either military uniform – like Wellington
(far left) and the Prussian Chancellor Prince Hardenberg sitting in front of him – or civil
uniform, like Metternich (standing centre left), Castlereagh (sitting, centre in Windsor
uniform) and Talleyrand (sitting on the right).

humour' in her father was for him to talk, for hours at a time, 'upon the merits
and demerits of such and such a uniform, the cut of such a coat, cape, sleeve,
small clothes etc.'[136] In 1829 he was described by Greville as 'occupied in
changing the uniforms of his Guards and has pattern coats with various collars
submitted to him every day . . . this is his principal occupation; he sees much
more of his Tailors than of his Ministers'.[137]

When in June 1811, contrary to expectations, the Regent retained his
father's Tory ministers, his 'very handsome uniforme de cour' was still in 'the
old Fox colours', blue and buff. His clothes and his politics were sending out
conflicting signals. In March 1812 he desired his servants to stop wearing their
household uniform.[138] That June a Whig, Lord Forbes, an ADC of the Prince,
dined with M. A. Taylor 'with the yellow lining and the Prince's buttons taken
away from his coat. He said never again would he carry about him so
degrading a badge of servitude to such a master.'[139] It is possible the Regent
then created a new coat, to which Lord Conyngham referred in 1814, when he
wrote to the Regent's secretary: 'I feel extremely anxious to be permitted to
have the honour of making up the Prince Regent's Coat and wearing it as a
mark of my respectful attachment.'[140]

Valerie Cumming has found the origin of British civil uniforms, still occasionally worn by British ambassadors and court officials today, in a decree of 1817. Its ostensible motive was 'to relieve the distresses of the manufacturing classes, by affording them employment': 'In further pursuance of this plan His Royal Highness ordered all his state and household officers to wear costly dresses of home fabrication and those dresses were directed to be made in three classes of uniforms, according to the respective ranks of these officers . . . The coats are of dark purple [blue] with crimson velvet collars, richly ornamented all over with gold.'[141]

On 19 July 1821 the new civil uniforms could be admired at the most lavish coronation in English history, intended to outshine the coronation of Napoleon I in Paris in 1804. Some of the costumes had been designed by the King himself.[142] The transience of sartorial glory was emphasised, after the King's death, by the sale on his executors' orders, on 15–17 December 1830, of 438 lots of the King's clothes, whips, sticks, stockings, 'beautiful plumes of ostrich and other feathers and miscellanies, expensive military and other dresses etc.', at public auction by Messrs Phillips in Bond Street. The clothes went at knock-down prices (£7 5s. for a robe of rose satin with a Garter star worn at his coronation, 50 shillings for undress Windsor uniform coats). In accordance with custom, the proceeds went as perquisites to his household.[143] His red velvet coronation robe, partly modelled on that of Napoleon I, ended on display at Madame Tussaud's.[144]

However, if his own clothes were dispersed, the uniforms George IV had created survived. Thanks to his influence, in accordance with the European trend to military magnificence, the Household Cavalry received breastplates in 1821, the Foot Guards bearskins in 1830.[145] George IV's civil uniforms became equally popular with Whigs and Tories. In 1831 the Whig Prime Minister Lord Grey told Creevey that he must go to court: therefore he had to buy his blue and gold civil uniform as Treasurer of the Ordonnance and wear it to court – though Creevey grumbled about the £40 he had to pay.[146] The David Wilkie picture in the Royal Collection of the Accession Council of Queen Victoria on 20 June 1837 shows two other Whigs, Lord Holland, Chancellor of the Duchy of Lancaster, and Lord Melbourne, the Prime Minister, in gleaming civil uniform. In 1840 Melbourne had a new full dress uniform made for the Queen's marriage to Prince Albert of Saxe-Coburg – although he complained to the Queen of the time and trouble wasted on fittings: 'like building a 74-gun ship'.[147]

While Britain was embracing uniforms, the July revolution in France, provoked by Charles X's bid for absolutism by the ordonnances of 26 July

1830, rejected not only uniforms but the court itself. Crying 'Vive la liberté! Vive la nation!' and, particularly among *le bas peuple,* 'Vive Napoléon II!',[148] Parisians defeated the Garde royale. A crowd invaded the Tuileries. From a palace window a man wearing a ball dress of the duchesse de Berri, with feathers and flowers in his hair, mimicked her bows and curtsies, and screamed: 'Je reçois, je reçois!'[149]

Even before the duc d'Orléans had been proclaimed king as Louis-Philippe I on 9 August, French deputies had abandoned their uniforms. The comte de Flahaut wrote: 'He is to go without any state and both chambers without any uniform, the fleurs-de-lys on the collars and cuffs of their coats being too detestable to be worn'.[150] All wore tricolour cockades again.

As a prince of the blood Louis-Philippe had been as determined as his ancestors to use dress to signal his rank.[151] An angry letter of 1824 to the *Président du conseil,* the comte de Villèle, demanded that the members of the Cour de cassation visit him on New Year's Day *en grand costume,* as they had his father before 1789.[152] In the post-revolutionary society of the July Monarchy, however, he thought it politic to use dress to present himself, falsely, as *le roi citoyen.*

For a time he abolished liveries in his household, dressing his footmen, like himself, in the *frac.* Since they thereby became indistinguishable from parliamentary deputies, occasionally he would mistake one of his own footmen for a deputy and ask him which department he represented in the Chamber of Deputies. In 1832 when Louis-Philippe was almost run down outside the Palais Royal by an infuriated legitimist, called Albert Anne Jules de Bertier de Sauvigny, the latter's defence was that he could not recognise as the King a person *en frac bourgeois,* wearing a large tricolour cockade and walking in the street, with a lady on his arm.[153]

Newspapers began to reproach the King for his excessive simplicity, compared to foreign courts, and to criticise deputies' dirty costumes.[154] The embroidery industry was said to be paralysed by the suppression of court costumes. *La Mode* wrote: 'luxury in France is a necessity; only it can bring commerce back into action.'[155] As in 1800–04 under Bonaparte, the treble pressure of the court tradition, the clothing industry and fear of public mockery brought a return of liveries and uniforms.

In August 1830 at a reception in the Palais Royal Baron Gérard had been one of the few people who wore his civil uniform (as a member of the Institut) – thereby winning a smile of gratitude from the Queen. In January 1831 Louis-Philippe began to wear military uniform, instead of the *frac,* to receive visitors. Castellane commented: 'cela commence plus à prendre un air de Cour'. By the time of the King's New Year reception at the Tuileries in 1835, men in *fracs* were 'isolated among the great majority of uniforms'.[156]

That year at balls given by his son the duc d'Orléans, valets wore livery and *valets de chambre habits habillés*. The duke had asked the duchesse de Dino whether male guests should wear their uniforms with boots, or with breeches and silk stockings. With the authority of a former *dame du palais de l'Impératrice*, she replied: 'The Emperor Napoleon, who won a few battles, wore silk stockings and shoes with buckles every evening when he dined alone with the Empress.'[157] The July Monarchy used dress to distance itself from its revolutionary roots. At Orléans's wedding at Fontainebleau in 1837, the radical banker Jacques Laffitte, who had helped put Louis-Philippe on the throne in 1830, was the only man not in uniform.[158] That year Louis-Philippe began to impose the *habit habillé* – so feared under the Restoration – on men without uniforms invited to formal court entertainments.[159] At the opening of the *galeries historiques* in Versailles on 10 June 1837, men without official positions were asked to wear *habit habillé* (even Delacroix did so). A hundred deputies were the sole, deliberately disobedient, guests *en frac*. To Madame de Boigne it seemed as if the bourgeoisie had taken the palace of Louis XIV by storm.[160]

As at the ball at the Palais Royal on 30 May 1830, Parisians continued to be torn between two rival traditions, royal and revolutionary. The quintessential Orléanist minister, deputy and writer Adolphe Thiers voiced the anti-court tradition in 1838 when, during discussion over whether to restore an official costume for deputies, he said: 'The coat that everyone wears every day is the one which suits us best.'[161] During the rising of April 1834 in Paris, however, he had worn his embroidered uniform as Minister of the Interior, while riding through the streets to organise repression.[162]

Even under Louis-Philippe court dress could have an impact on political events. In 1847–8 court mourning for Louis-Philippe's sister Madame Adelaide caused a diminution in orders for new clothes, because of the cancellation of the court balls held every carnival, for which they were always ordered. This led to lay-offs in the clothes trade. Therefore – like court mourning at the same time in Vienna, for the Archdukes Charles, Joseph and Frederick – court mourning in Paris added to the economic distress which in February 1848 precipitated revolution. A change in dress at court could help lead to revolution on the streets.[163]

The passion for uniforms in this period affected not only France, Austria and Britain, but also the Ottoman Empire. Until 1826 the traditional Ottoman dress code, and Constantinople's fashion empire, had remained in force. The prince de Ligne wrote: 'Constantinople sets the fashion for Jassy as Paris does for the provinces, and the fashions arrive even quicker. Yellow was the sultana's favourite colour. In Jassy it became every woman's.'[164] Rebellious Serbs temporarily adopted Ottoman Muslim dress after 1804 to show that they had become the equals of their former overlords. When Wallachia and Moldavia had been occupied by Russia in 1806–12, the hospodars had worn western dress. When those provinces reverted to Ottoman rule, the hospodars were obliged by the Ottoman government to revert to Ottoman dress. Between 1818 and 1821 one of them, Alexander Mavrocordato, even wore Ottoman dress and a Muslim turban in western Europe, while planning an insurrection against the Ottoman government.[165]

After the destruction in 1826 of the chief obstacle to reform, the Janissaries, however, Mahmud II embarked on a policy of modernisation in order to reinforce state power. A dress revolution was part of the programme. Mahmud II was encouraged by the example of his vassal and rival the Pasha of Egypt, Mohammed Ali, who since 1819 had been imposing semi-western uniforms on his troops and officials.[166]

The beginning of the revolution in the dress of Ottoman men (not yet of Ottoman women) is described in a dispatch of the British ambassador Sir Stratford Canning of 20 June 1826. Two thousand Turkish soldiers appeared in the outer courtyard of Topkapi Palace 'in various dresses, but armed with muskets and bayonets, arranged in European order and going through the new form of exercise . . . The Sultan, who was at first stationed at the window within sight, descended after a time and passed the men in review. His Highness was dressed in the *Egyptian* fashion [i.e. in a modern uniform] armed with pistols and saber and on his head, in place of the Imperial turban was a sort of Egyptian bonnet' – a change in the monarch's appearance more revolutionary than Mustafa Kemal's adoption of suit and hat a hundred years later.[167]

Henceforth, a common sight in parade grounds around the city, day after day, whatever the weather, was the Sultan, simply dressed in a plain dark blue mantle, 'cossack trowsers' and boots, drilling his troops with 'an expression of firmness and self confidence and of haughtiness not unmixed with a degree of ferocity'.[168] By 1828, although many of the soldiers in new uniforms seemed 'slovenly' to a British eye, among officers there were 'a few really elegant young fellows who wore their uniform of good materials and set off with superior embroidery and a diamond crescent on the breast'.[169] Mahmud II spread news of his dress revolution by touring provinces and commissioning portraits of

34 Henri-Guillaume Schlésinger, The Ottoman Sultan Mahmud II, 1839.
Dress as modernisation: between 1826 and 1829 Mahmud II had replaced the traditional costumes and headgear of Ottoman officials and soldiers by modern uniforms and the fez. Portraits of himself in modern uniform and fez were hung in army barracks, to be saluted by soldiers like the Sultan himself.

himself wearing his new uniform. The portraits were hung in army barracks and were saluted as if he was present. In effect he was saying: 'I even have the power to make you adopt the dress of the infidels'; and 'we must modernise or perish'. Some soldiers were reported to complain: 'The Franks are turning the head of the Sultan and he will soon be as they are.'[170]

The new bonnet worn by Mahmud II and his troops was the crimson wool cap or fez, which left the forehead free for prostration during prayer. Red skull-caps, made in the south of France, in Tunis, or by Tunisians living in Constantinople, had long been worn in the Mediterranean and North Africa, by Christians and Muslims alike: the latter often wrapped them in muslin to form a turban.[171] At the siege of Candia in 1669 Ottoman troops had worn the red fez.[172] In 1804–7 some of the new troops organised by Selim III had worn western-style uniforms and, instead of a traditional turban, a small red skull-cap. Disgust at their foreign appearance had been one reason for the Sultan's deposition by janissaries in 1807. In 1827, after some hesitation, 50,000 such red caps, in a high cylindrical form, were ordered from Tunis for the Sultan's troops. On 3 March 1829 a new law regulated clothing and headgear for seventeen different ranks of civil and religious officials, introducing the fez and modern jackets for all government employees. Only religious officials were allowed to keep the turban.[173] At the same time the traditional etiquette of 'kaftaning' foreign diplomats and distributing furs, described for the last time in 1821 by the British ambassador's chaplain Robert Walsh,[174] was abolished: henceforth diplomats were admitted to the Sultan's presence wearing their own uniforms, and were presented to him by name 'as in Europe'.[175]

On 28 June 1829 another British diplomat R. C. Mellish reported:

> What engrosses everybody here is the extraordinary change which is daily taking place in the manners of this people . . . Very few years more, and not a turban will exist. Grand Vezir, Reis Efendi, Ulema, employees of every description, now wear the red cap, cossack trowsers, black boots and a plain red or blue cloak buttoned under the chin. No gold embroidery, no jewels, no pelisses. The Sultan wears a blue jacket, cossack trowsers, black boots and the red cap like the others.[176]

In 1832 an imperial fez factory was founded in Eyup, employing first Tunisian, then Turkish and Armenian workers to make the fez – a complicated process involving dyeing and stiffening wool and repeated pressing. From the crown of the fez hung a tassel of blue silk or wool, so long and intricate that tasselcomber became a Constantinople profession. In 1845 'the tasselled curse', as it was called, was exchanged for a short black tassel.[177]

Until the fall of the Empire, both in Constantinople and in the provinces, pashas and other officials wore embroidered uniforms on formal occasions, such as the Sultan's visit to a mosque, the opening of a railway station or celebrations for the feast of Bairam.[178] The Sultans themselves were generally more simply dressed.[179] On ordinary occasions after about 1850, most of the educated élite wore the *frac* or its special Ottoman version, with a low collar, known as the *stambouline*.[180] From the 1870s their wives began to wear western dress at home.[181] Janissary and other traditional uniforms were banned. Showing both the importance attached to dress, and these uniforms' relegation to history, the first museum in Constantinople, on the Atmeidan, was opened to display them.[182]

At the same time dress modernisation continued in Egypt. In 1846 the chronicler of Cairo customs and language, Edward Lane, who himself generally wore the Turkish dress of the urban élite, wrote: 'The officers of the Government . . . following the example of Constantinople have begun to put themselves into the complete Frank dress: frock-coat, waistcoats and trousers, the last as narrow as any of ours . . . The sheykhs are very angry at all this which

35 King Fouad of Egypt with princes (left) and pashas (right).
The princes wear the special *habit de cour*, a coat with a black velvet collar, two large
lapels of green silk, and buttons with crowns and the King's name. The pashas wear gold-
embroidered civil uniform.

they justly regard as indicating more important changes.' Egypt soon
developed a hierarchy of embroidered uniforms for ministers and senior
officials, like those in the Ottoman Empire, of which until 1914 it remained
legally a province. The Egyptian court dress code, including special white veils
for women covering neck and hair but not the face, continued until the
military coup overthrowing King Farouk in July 1952.[183]

After the 1840s western merchants and travellers in the Ottoman Empire
began to abandon the habit of wearing local dress, since it was no longer
necessary for their protection.[184] Dress restrictions on religious minorities
such as the Copts were also finally dropped, as, to the dismay of Egyptian
Muslims, they had been during the French occupation from 1798 to 1801
(when even some Muslim women had begun to adopt western dress).[185] Later
cases of westerners adopting Arab dress, such as T. E. Lawrence during the
'Arab Revolt' in World War I, or Harold and Doreen Ingrams in southern
Arabia in the 1930s, were not intended as disguise. They were usually
transformations of another kind: isolated examples of men and women trying
for political reasons, in the words of an official manual, 'to adopt their
[Arabs'] trust and intimacy to a degree impossible in uniform'.[186]

The dress revolution of 1826–9 helped redefine Ottoman identity. After the removal of the last small badges of distinction in the 1840s, it ended differences of dress between Muslims and Christians.[187] In contrast to previous headgear such as the turban, the fez symbolised service of the state rather than religious identity. It was at first rejected by many Muslim notables, workers and soldiers: some believed the Sultan had gone mad. Christians on the other hand adopted it with enthusiasm.[188] Less grandiose than the turban, the fez symbolised the Ottoman way of modernisation. It was adapted to Islam, since it was adopted on the initiative of the Sultan and had no brim interfering with prostration during prayer; but it was modern and not exclusively Muslim. Showing its imperial origin and significance, each sultan gave his name to his own version of the fez – the low, squat *aziziye* under Abdulaziz (1861–76), the high, round *hamidiye* under Abdulhamid (1876–1909)'.[189]

The fez became, in the words of the Turkish nationalist writer Falih Rifki Atay, 'part of the Turkish soul – and of many Arabs'.[190] The way it was worn (sideways, over the forehead, on the back of the head) could indicate wealth or morals. Local Christians and Jews, and foreigners working in the region like Rimbaud or Loti, wore the fez when they wanted to show respect for, or deflect the hostility of, the Muslim population.[191]

The spread of the fez beyond the frontiers of the empire showed the extent of its influence. Anyone who wore a fez in the Dutch East Indies was suspected of being pro-Ottoman and pan-Islamist.[192] It was worn by zouaves in the French and papal armies; by Bosnian troops in the Austrian army;[193] by Kenyan troops in the British army (the King's African Rifles); and, until 1953, by the Egyptian army.

Outside the élite of the fez and *stambouline*, however, the people of the Ottoman Empire continued to wear costumes indicating religion, gender, locality and – through the lavish use of jewellery and embroidery – wealth: thus there were distinct costumes for a Muslim bride of Edirne, a Greek bride of Monastir, or a Muslim of Konya. The Ottoman government remained sufficiently proud of this variety of dress to transport the costumes for display at the 1873 Vienna Universal Exhibition, and to publish a commemorative book, *Les Costumes populaires de la Turquie en 1873*, still the finest illustrated record of the traditional costumes of the region.[194] Differences between Christians and Muslims went so deep that, even today, in the streets of Aleppo (and to a lesser extent Beirut and Damascus), experts believe that they can tell the religion of men of the same class, by Muslims' preference for brighter colours and slower movements, Christians' preference for dark clothes.[195]

In the nineteenth century the spread of embroidered uniforms showed the appeal of military monarchy and state service. Yet not all succumbed, as the early years of the July Monarchy in Paris had demonstrated. Many German cities such as Hamburg, Cologne and Frankfurt retained a consciously civilian and anti-military tradition, no less German or popular than Prussian militarism: the carnival prince's soldiers in the Cologne carnival were caricatures of Prussian officers and their uniforms.[196]

In Austria the costume of the Emperor Franz's liberal brother the Archduke Johann expressed desire for simplicity and rejection of military monarchy. A prince with one foot in the Age of Reason, the other in the industrial revolution, he wanted the Habsburgs to be leaders of constitutional monarchy throughout Germany. Discontented with his brother's conservatism, in 1817 he retreated to the province of Styria in the foothills of the Alps. There he founded factories, museums and learned societies. He fell in love with, and after a wait of many years received permission from the Emperor to marry, a postmaster's daughter called Anna Plöchl.

A sign of his love for Styria was his adoption of the hunting costume of upper Styria – a grey jacket with green collar and cuffs. This liberal prince's commissions of pictures of himself in Styrian dress, contemplating the Alps, hunting, cooking potatoes in a workman's cottage, were a deliberate rejection of military monarchy.[197] His Styrian dress was an Austrian equivalent of the red shirt and Argentinian poncho that Garibaldi habitually wore instead of a uniform after 1848, when fighting to unite Italy (even when visiting King Victor Emmanuel II in 1875), and which aroused such enthusiasm because they also symbolised a rejection of militarism and absolutism.[198]

To his young wife 'Nani', the Archduke Johann wrote on 24 November 1824, criticising her coachman's elaborate livery and the unnecessary luxury and magnificence of Vienna. This Archduke could stand outside his own epoch:

> When I introduced the grey coat into Styria, it was done to set an example of simplicity in manners; my household grew to resemble my grey coat, and so did my speech and my actions. The example took effect and the grey coat, disdained by some, recognized by the more virtuous, became a coat of honour and I will never put it off again; just as little will I give up my simplicity, I would rather give up my life . . . If I had travelled about the country with the pomp that (I believe) is not necessary here, I should have had banquets etc. given for me; I should never have learned the truth, never opened any man's heart, never have won the friendship of

36 Peter Krafft, The Archduke Johann in Styrian dress, 1817.
The Archduke's adoption of Styrian dress was a deliberate challenge to the military autocracy of his brother the Emperor Franz I of Austria, as well as a means of identifying himself with his favourite province, birthplace of his wife Anna Plöchl.

37 Crown Princess Marie of Romania in Romanian dress, *c.* 1897.
Like her aunt the Queen of Romania and many other royal figures, in order to win popularity and identify with the rural population, the Crown Princess encouraged the manufacture of traditional dress, and in the countryside often wore it herself.

the virtuous. It is a serious matter that bears no trifling and that you should understand.[199]

To the horror of his brother this Styrian costume was soon adopted by local officials and village headmen. Although even in Vienna, like Louis-Philippe in Paris, the Emperor habitually wore a plan dark *frac* with no outward signs of rank, he launched a dress war against the Archduke Johann. As the following order shows, officials were threatened with dismissal if they continued to wear the Styrian coat: 'His Majesty has viewed with great displeasure that provincial officials and even local village headmen are wearing peasant dress. As it is the duty of the servants of the state to observe the outward dignity of their office, they should avoid any behaviour which might lower their standing in the eyes of the local population and also lead to pejorative remarks and even jokes. It is Our Highest Wish that state civil servants should wear appropriate clothing.' A further handwritten note from the Emperor stated that Styrian clothing should be worn only by country people. This order was enforced and spies were stationed around the Archduke.[200]

Archduke Johann's popularity, however, stretched throughout the German Confederation. The cult of the Archduke and his grey coat shows a longing for another future than that planned for their subjects by Europe's military monarchs. After the democratic revolutions of 1848, he was named Regent in both Germany and Austria. His Styrian hat was shown as outweighing all the Emperor of Austria's crowns in a cartoon of 1848 with the caption *Es wiegt mehr, als sie alle!*[201] At the liberal Frankfurt parliament in 1848–9 deputies wore civilian clothes: it was above all 'a lawyers' parliament'.[202] Much of liberal Europe rejected uniforms as well as autocrats.

1 Antoine Mathieu, Interview between Louis XIV and Philip IV on 7 June 1660.
In dress, as in power, the King of France outshines his future father-in-law. Louis XIV's love of clothes led him to be called *le marquis de filigrane*, after the filigranes, or metal threads dipped in gold or silver, which covered his clothes. Clothes were so important as status symbols that they were often, as here, depicted with more care than faces and buildings.

2 Jean-Baptise Vanmour, Farewell audience of the marquis de Bonnac with Sultan Ahmed III in 1724.
Dress as transformation: as a sign of respect for the Sultan, in the throne room an ambassador and his suite were obliged to wear Ottoman kaftans over their western dress. An interpreter is in the foreground, the Grand Vizier to the left. A present from Louis XV to Bonnac, this picture commemorates the success of the Franco-Ottoman alliance and in particular of Bonnac's embassy.

3 Pehr Hilleström, New Year's Eve dinner in the Royal Palace, Stockholm, in 1779.
Dress as patriotism: King Gustavus III is shown here dining in state with his wife, brothers and sister-in-law, watched by courtiers wearing the national dress he had created one year earlier in order to encourage Swedish patriotism.

4 Cornelius Hoyer, Meeting of Gustavus III and Catherine II in August 1783 at Fredrikshamm on the Russo-Swedish frontier.
The Empress was shocked that the King of Sweden and his officers wore national dress rather than military uniform. The Empress, in contrast, had chosen one of the voluminous 'regimental gowns' that she wore on certain public occasions, both to show esteem for her army and to try to hide her growing size.

5 Charles Thévenin, The Fête de la Fédération, 14 July 1790 (detail).

Assembling national guards from every corner of France, this ceremony was intended to show united national support for the revolution and the new constitution. Even on this occasion, however, despite the pleas of La Fayette, commander of the Paris National Guard (left), to wear its tricolour uniform, Louis XVI continued to wear traditional court dress.

6 Ignace Goubaud, A deputation from the Roman Senate presenting its homage to Napoleon I in the throne room of the Tuileries Palace on 16 November 1809.

On the left are the Arch-Chancellor Cambacérès; Marshal Bessières, Colonel-General of the Imperial Guard in waiting; and the Grand Almoner Cardinal Fesch. The Emperor wears his *petit costume*. The Arch-Treasurer Lebrun, the Vice-Grand Elector Talleyrand, the Grand Veneur Marshal Berthier and the King of Westphalia Jerome-Napoleon stand on the right. As Grand Master of Ceremonies, the comte de Ségur, holding his baton of office, is introducing the deputation. The Empire, having recently defeated Austria and annexed the Papal States, was at the height of its power. Nevertheless, it had been hard to find Romans willing to join the deputation; the French government had to pay for their travel and their court dress.

7 M. Antranik, Bayram reception of Abdulhamid II in Yildiz Palace, *c.* 1900.
The Sultan is receiving the chief religious dignitary of the empire, the Sheikh al-Islam. On the left, wearing military uniform, are Ottoman princes in order of succession; on the right, senior officials and pashas wear gold-embroidered civil uniforms.

8 I. E. Repin, Ceremonial meeting of the State Council, 1901–3.
The Emperor Nicholas II, in military uniform, is surrounded by officials and senators in full ceremonial dress.

9 Adolph von Menzel, *The Ballsouper*, 1878.
After a ball in the Berlin Schloss, guests are eating supper: men wear military or, more rarely, civil
uniform. Even before the accession of Wilhelm II, dress at the Berlin court was as lavish as at the
other courts of Europe.

10 Anton von Werner, Acclamation of Wilhelm I King of Prussia as German Emperor at Versailles on 18 January 1871, 1885.

Dress as militarism: all the monarchs, princes and officers present wear uniform; many have drawn their swords. In the centre of the picture is Prince Bismarck, wearing the white uniform and black jackboots of the Magdeburg cuirassiers. In reality he had infuriated Wilhelm I by attending in the blue uniform of the rank of lieutenant-general, to which he had just been promoted. Wilhelm I, who with his wife, son (on the left behind his father) and daughter-in-law presented this picture to Bismarck on 1 April 1885, insisted that as principal architect of German unification, Bismarck be painted in a white uniform, in order to stand out against the others. A reactionary director of the Institute of Fine Arts in Berlin, Werner dominated the official art world in Germany for thirty years.

11 Anton von Werner, The signature of the Treaty of Berlin on 13 July 1878, 1881.
Even on this purely diplomatic occasion, Bismarck wears military uniform. Other figures include (on
the right) the Ottoman representatives Alexander Karatheodory Pasha and Sadik Bey in Ottoman
civil uniforms. Standing beside Bismarck is Count Andrassy, the Austrian Foreign Minister, in a
Hungarian military uniform; Count Aloys Karolyi (far left) is in Hungarian gala dress. Prince
Gorchakov, the Russian Foreign Minister (seated), is in Russian civil uniform whilst the British
Prime Minister Disraeli wears Privy Councillor's levee dress.

12 Anton von Werner, The opening of the Reichstag by Wilhelm II in the White Hall of the Berlin
Schloss on 25 June 1888, 1893. On the left are deputies in dark tailcoats; on the right, in blue- and
gold-embroidered civil uniforms, Prussian court officials and ministers. Bismarck, standing near the
throne, as in 1871 wears the white uniform and black boots of his Cuirassier regiment. Like the
princes present, the Kaiser is draped in his newly designed red mantle of the Order of the Black Eagle
– a symbol of his theatrical cult of the Prussian monarchy. Bismarck had refused to wear it on the
grounds that it was 'uncontemporary, unpopular and politically detrimental'. Military uniform, in
his view, was not.

13 Théodore Leblanc, Presentation of ladies to Queen Adelaide in 1834.
Throughout the nineteenth century ladies' dress at the British court remained an elaborate symbol of status, wealth and femininity.

14 The Queen and the Duke of Edinburgh arriving by carriage at Ascot on 'Ladies' Day', 19 June 2003.
The race meeting that the Queen attends every summer at Ascot is the last large-scale court occasion with strictly enforced dress rules, leading to increased profits for the dress trade.

6   *Empires*

The Archduke Johann's regency was an illusory interlude. By the end of 1848, in Paris, Vienna and Berlin, armies had defeated revolutions.[1] The Austrian Parliament was closed in March 1849, the Frankfurt Parliament in May. Prince Schwarzenberg, the Prime Minister most respected by the Emperor Franz Josef, and the restorer of autocracy in Austria, believed: 'one can do anything with bayonets except sit on them'.[2] The nineteenth century would be the century of military monarchy. The red-shirted Garibaldini of 1848 and 1860 would turn into blue-uniformed soldiers of King Victor Emmanuel II, who fired on their former leader Garibaldi and his 'rabble' at Aspromonte on 29 August 1862 and proclaimed: 'With these uniforms we are now respected in quite another way'.[3]

In Austria after 1848, the dynasty bound itself more closely to the army, henceforth run by the Military Chancellery of the Emperor as well as the War Ministry.[4] After the compromise with Hungary in 1867 and the creation of the Dual Monarchy, the unitary army, as the Emperor often proclaimed, remained the monarchy's most effective common institution.[5]

Until the fall of the monarchy, Austrian officers in uniform had the right to attend the annual *Hofball* and request an audience of the Emperor. From 1849 uniform had to be worn by serving army officers even when off duty, and by government officials on public occasions.[6] Thus, as old photographs show, Austrian officers went to the races, or played music *en famille*, in uniform.[7] As the authorities intended, cut off from civilian life, for many Austrian officers and soldiers the army was their only homeland.[8] They defended with ferocity the honour of the *Kaisers Rock* – the Emperor's coat – 'a quasi-sacred symbol of their calling that must never be disgraced by word or deed'. A disrespectful remark or gesture by a civilian could lead to a fatal duel.[9]

In the course of the last quarter of the century, Austrian civil uniforms became more sumptuous. From 1889 there was a new gala uniform for high

38 Wilhelm Gause, *The Court Ball, c.* 1900.
The Emperor Franz Josef, in Field Marshal's uniform, is surrounded by ladies wearing court trains and men in uniform or national dress. Particularly splendid is Sektionschef von Szent-Gyorgy, a *Geheimer Rat* in Hungarian magnate's dress, with heron plume and black leather boots.

officials of the court and the government, in addition to a uniform for lesser functions and a uniform *à la campagne,* each of which was distinguished by the width and elaboration of its embroidery.[10] The dress trade remained one of the most important in Vienna, employing, in 1909, 98,000 of its two million inhabitants.[11]

The Emperor used uniform to signal the mutual dependence of the army and the dynasty, and the army's pre-eminence in society. Like many nineteenth-century princes, including the future Nicholas I of Russia,[12] Queen Victoria's favourite son the Duke of Connaught,[13] and his own son the Crown Prince Rudolf, Franz Josef had worn military uniform at the age of four,[14] and subsequently served as a professional army officer. In 1844, when he received promotion, his mother wrote: 'Never will I forget the look of unutterable happiness when he appeared later before me to show himself in his colonel's uniform.'[15] As Emperor, unlike his two predecessors, he wore uniform, even at council meetings where his ministers wore the *frac.* In old age, he generally wore the service tunic of an infantry lieutenant.[16]

Two incidents confirm the importance of the *Kaisers Rock* to the Emperor himself. At the beginning of the new constitutional era, after the empire's

defeats in the wars of 1859 with France and Piedmont, and of 1866 with
Prussia and Italy, the Vienna bourgeoisie felt growing self-confidence. On
Franz Josef's return from the universal exhibition in Paris in 1867, the city
council of Vienna asked the Prime Minister Count Beust to request the
Emperor to enter Vienna 'in civilian dress'. The Emperor did not. A year later
at the annual *Bürgerball* (the ball of the burghers of Vienna in their *Rathaus*),
'it was hoped that his Majesty would not appear in uniform; his portrait on the
programme showed him in civilian dress'. Beust relates: 'I was urged to induce
his Majesty to give way and I attempted to do so by alluding to the loyal feeling
with which the Viennese still spoke of the Emperor Francis I and his dress coat.
The Emperor, however, answered smilingly but in a very firm tone that I need
not trouble myself about such matters.'[17] The 'very firm tone' suggests that
Franz Josef's insistence on uniform was a political decision as well as a
personal preference.

Baron von Margutti, who served in the office of the Emperor's aides-de-
camp from 1900 to 1917, wrote: 'The Emperor attached the greatest importance to the most punctilious observance of the military dress regulations by
all who appeared before him. No one was more particular in this respect than
himself. In this matter he was inexorable. Discussion with him was quite
useless.' His valet Eugen Ketterl confirms in his memoirs: 'nothing escaped the
Emperor's sharp eye'. He wore the *frac* only outside his empire, when on
holiday on the Riviera or visiting his daughter in Munich.[18] The Emperor's
cult of uniforms was an extreme example of a general phenomenon: on public
occasions after 1848 almost all European monarchs and princes, except in the
United Kingdom, wore uniforms. This was an indispensable psychological
factor, affirming that service in the armed forces legitimised their role in
public life. In 1909 the sons of King George I of the Hellenes, due to local
political turbulence, were obliged to resign their military and naval commands: until their reinstatement in 1911, because they could no longer wear
uniform, they refused to attend public ceremonies.[19]

The Emperor Franz Josef's love of uniforms extended to those of other
countries. The habit of monarchs receiving honorary commands in each
other's armies and navies had probably begun during the many meetings
between monarchs in Paris, London and Vienna in 1814–15, after the fall of
Napoleon, and continued through their desire to prolong the spirit of the anti-
Napoleonic alliance. Thus two Prussian Guards regiments, Kaiser Alexander
and Kaiser Franz had, as honorary colonels, the reigning Emperors of Russia
and Austria. The Duke of Wellington, as a visit to the Wellington Museum in
Apsley House makes clear, became a Field Marshal in almost every army in

Europe (Austria, Russia, Prussia, Spain, Portugal, the Netherlands, the United Kingdom, Hanover), except the French.[20]

Denounced by Queen Victoria as 'fishing for uniforms',[21] the fashion persisted even among monarchs who had fought each other. When Franz Josef put on the uniform of his Prussian regiment to receive Wilhelm I in Vienna, six years after his defeat by that monarch, he wrote that he felt 'like an enemy to myself'.[22] When many different monarchs came to Vienna at the same time, for the universal exhibition in 1873, he had to change uniforms so often that he expressed sympathy with actors in plays with frequent costume changes.[23] Only in Germany were such uniform exchanges taken seriously. After his promotion to the rank of Admiral of the Fleet in the Royal Navy in 1889, Wilhelm II wrote that to wear the same uniform as St Vincent and Nelson made him feel 'quite giddy'.[24]

In counterpoint to the prevalence of uniforms in Austria, national dress flourished in Hungary after the compromise of 1867. The Hungarian magnate's costume was worn at weddings, funerals, sessions of Parliament, court balls and such grandiose affirmations of national pride as the coronation of King Franz Josef in 1868, and the millennium celebrations of the foundation of Hungary in 1896.[25] During the latter Franz Josef took pains to appear at all public functions in *ungarische Adjustierung*, the Hungarianised version of military uniform with a gold-embroidered cloak. The numerous arch-duchesses present also invariably wore Hungarian gala dress. Portraits of the King in Hungarian uniform decorated schools, homes and postcards: if he had not adopted it, his image would not have been so popular.[26] Showing their acceptance of Hungarian nationalism, German and Jewish inhabitants of Hungary also began to wear Hungarian gala dress, as could be seen on 8 June 1898, at a lavish procession to the royal palace of Buda of 995 horsemen, in honour of the thirtieth anniversary of Franz Josef's coronation: some of the costumes dated from the seventeenth century; some of the buttons alone were worth a fortune. 'The ostentation of these historic costumes, with their surfeit of lace, brocade, fur and plumage, occasionally verged on the ridiculous,' writes Tom Barczay.[27]

The costumes worn at the coronation of King Karl in Buda in the middle of World War I in 1916 appeared to one observer like a gallery of family portraits come alive; it was 'the last parade of Hungary's thousand year old history'. The ladies-in-waiting with 'fantastic diamond tiaras and diadems on their heads and their pearl and jewel embroidered capes glittered like a cascade of rippling light'.[28] After the fall of the Habsburg monarchy in 1918, Hungarian mag-nates' dress remained a link with the country's royal past. It was worn on

39 Anon., *Viribus Unitis, c.* 1849.
The young Emperor Franz Josef, in military uniform, is shown as a symbolic figure whose rule unites, and is acclaimed by, the different nationalities of the Empire, represented by men in Dalmatian, Hungarian, Croatian, Bohemian, Tyrolean and, in the middle, urban dress.

occasions such as weddings, religious processions and the presentation of Hungarian ambassadors to foreign heads of state, until the formal abolition of the kingdom of Hungary in 1944.[29]

If the Emperor wore Hungarian dress in Hungary, in Galicia he wore Polish dress. When hunting from his villa in Bad Ischl, he and many of his family and entourage wore a simple rustic coat of rough cloth in the local Salzkammergut style, with a Tyrolean hat, lederhosen and knee-length stockings.[30] In Vienna, of whose loyalty, after the revolution of 1848, he was occasionally suspicious,[31] he insisted on uniform. In contrast he wore Salzkammergut dress for practical reasons and perhaps to lessen barriers between him and his rural subjects.[32] Perhaps because of the examples of the Archduke Johann and the Emperor Franz Josef (and of the Tyrolean national hero, Andreas Hofer), rural dress became popular in the multinational monarchy. Particularly after the 1880s, citizens of Vienna began to wear it – which no citizens of St Petersburg or Berlin would have contemplated. Even the founder of Zionism, Theodor Herzl (a dandy with a keen dress sense) and his children wore Austrian peasant dress on occasion, 'as a mark of conformity with general bourgeois habits'. Many urban Austrians still wear it on formal occasions, in the country or at taverns in the suburbs of Vienna.[33] The sight of national dress on the streets of Vienna, however, could heighten national tensions. The kaftans and fur bonnets (aspects of Polish national dress long adopted by Polish Jews) worn by Jews recently arrived from Galicia appeared so outlandish – particularly since other minorities had stopped wearing national dress in Vienna – that they exacerbated Viennese anti-semitism.[34]

In the other great military empire, Russia, military uniform was even more dominant. When wearing Preobrazhensky or *chevaliers gardes* uniforms, Nicholas I wrote, 'I can always feel at peace with myself'.[35] Unlike Franz Josef, Nicholas I took his uniform mania on visits abroad. When he visited England in 1844, Queen Victoria wrote that she had to hold 'the last two evenings in uniform as the Emperor disliked so being en frac and was quite embarrassed in it'.[36] He spent hours drawing and engraving Guards uniforms, on occasion painting figures of soldiers into Old Master pictures.[37] Brother-in-law of King Frederick William IV of Prussia, Nicholas I expressed his theory of military monarchy, of which uniforms were the visible embodiment, in his eulogy of the Prussian army:

> Here there is order, there is a strict unconditional legality, no impertinent claims to know all the answers, no contradiction, all things flow logically from one to the other. No one commands before he has first learnt to obey. No one steps in front of anyone else without lawful reason. Everything is ordained to one definite goal; everything has its definite purpose. That is why I feel so well among these people and why I shall always hold in honour my calling as a soldier. I consider the whole of human life to be merely service, everyone serves.[38]

The Tsar's love of uniforms extended beyond the grave. At balls in St Petersburg in the 1830s Pushkin was the only man in a civilian tail coat. Partly in order to give him a uniform, Tsar Nicholas I appointed him a gentleman of the chamber.[39] He was dismayed to be informed, by the agent dispatched specially to that effect to Pushkin's funeral, that the poet's corpse had been dressed in a black tail coat rather than a green and gold court uniform.[40]

In keeping with the Tsar's ethos, 'in Petersburg', it was said, 'everyone serves, everyone wears uniform.'[41] An English visitor in 1867 noted that at receptions in the palace 'the number of persons in plain evening dress might have been counted on the fingers of one hand'.[42] Government officials often worked at their desk in uniform, wearing sword and orders – as did the

Emperors of Russia and Austria, and the King of Prussia.[43] Although the marshals of the nobility were the representatives of the provincial nobility, they wore the uniform of officials of the Ministry of the Interior. Even students went to university in uniform.[44] Until 1917 in St Petersburg officers attended private balls, and schoolboys the Imperial Law College or the Tsarskoe Seloe Lyceum, in uniform: officers wore uniform even when staying in country houses, far from the parade grounds of the capital.[45]

Banned for nobles by Peter the Great, Russian national dress began to revive under his successors in the nineteenth century. Already in 1834, female court dress had been reorganised and based on Russian peasant dress. It consisted of a velvet robe with long open hanging sleeves, a white embroidered skirt and a long, richly embroidered train hanging from the waist, worn with a circular pearl-embroidered velvet head-dress called the *kokoshnik*. Photographs, and the film *The Russian Ark* (2003), show they were even more splendid, and occupied considerably more space, than men's uniforms, or the dresses and trains worn at other courts.[46] Like uniforms, they did not change with fashions, and 'The colour of the velvet and the type of embroidery decoration in gold and silver thread, and the length of the train, indicated the wearer's rank'. Ladies-in-waiting and maids of the chamber wore green velvet embroidered with gold; maids of honour wore crimson velvet.[47] In the 1850s some educated Slavophiles began to wear their own versions of traditional Russian dress, to stress their rejection of western Europe. It was so 'Russian' that people in the streets mistook them for Persians.[48]

From the accession of Alexander III in 1881, in keeping with his policy of Russification in order to encourage national feeling and challenge western norms, certain regiments also began to adopt Russian features such as kaftans and baggy breeches. From 1883, under both Alexander III and Nicholas II, at court or grand ducal balls, and later at some Duma meetings, some men began to wear forms of Russian national dress, with baggy trousers. In dress at least resembling his critic Tolstoy, Nicholas II sometimes wore a mujik's blouse at home, and put the regiment of Fusiliers of the Imperial Guard in a militarised version.[49]

Like Franz Josef, Nicholas II was a military monarch who, before his accession, had served as a professional officer. After the army saved his throne in the 1905 revolution, he increasingly regarded himself as a war leader,[50] and was called in official circles, without admiration, 'the Colonel'.[51] During his reign most uniforms had versions in full dress, gala dress, ordinary dress and travelling dress. On gala occasions inside the palace, *chevaliers gardes* on duty were lowered by soldiers into elkskin breeches smeared with soap, so that

40 I. M. Ponomaryov, The Empress Maria Feodorovna in her full-dress white uniform with scarlet collar and cuffs, as commander of the Chevaliers-Gardes regiment, with the Order of Saint Andrew. Since Catherine the Great, consorts and princesses had worn female versions of the uniform of the regiment of which they were honorary commander. Before parades with the Empress, the Chevaliers-Gardes were told:
Chevaliers-Gardes, en garde!
La dame blanche vous regarde.

there would be no creases: to heighten the effect they wore no underwear.[52] A special form of uniform, with pockets for tennis balls, was created for serving officers playing the popular new game of tennis. In 1909 more splendid uniforms (black for soldiers, blue-green for officers), with different forms of embroidery for each regiment and traditional 'shako' headgear, were given to the infantry of the Guard.[53] That November in the Crimea, on three separate occasions the Tsar himself tested the NCO's uniform of the infantry of the Guard, by marching in it for sixteen kilometres.[54]

Indeed, Nicholas II almost always wore uniform: when reading newspapers, playing tennis, rowing, going on a picnic or taking communion.[55] In a time of revolution, uniformed soldiers, saluting, bowing, keeping assassins and protesters at bay, provided the Tsar with visual reassurance as well as physical safety. When the great reforming minister Stolypin was assassinated in the Tsar's presence in the Kiev opera house on 1 September 1911, people cried 'Hold the civilian!' Every man in the opera house was in uniform; the murderer, a former police agent called Dimitri Bogrov, was the only man wearing civilian dress – proof, for some, of police complicity in the assassination. No other explanation for the admission of a man in civilian dress to an

41 Nicholas II sawing wood with his son, Tobolsk, 1918. Even in prison after the overthrow of the dynasty the Tsar and his son wear uniform.

opera performance in the presence of the Tsar seemed possible.[56] The last official dress regulations, governing correct dress for men in state service on different occasions and seasons, were issued in 1915.[57]

Nicholas II's wardrobe outlived his empire. In a reflex survival of dynastic tradition, after the revolution of 1917 the wardrobes of the last Tsar and his family were preserved intact, by museum curators rather than court servants, in the Hermitage and the Alexander Palace at Tsarskoe Seloe. Hence the comprehensive exhibitions of the clothes of the last Tsar, his wife, mother and children, which Russian museums have recently been able to organise.[58]

France had witnessed a revival of uniforms and court dress after the proclamation of the Second Empire, and the vote of a sum of three million francs for official uniforms, in 1852.[59] Like his fellow-monarchs, Napoleon III used dress as a weapon: as President of the Second Republic, he had insisted on reviewing the Paris National Guard wearing the uniform of its colonel, like a sovereign, rather than wearing the *frac*, as the Council of Ministers advised.[60] As Emperor he revived not only civil uniforms for court and government officials, and trains for ladies, but also a special dark green hunting costume,

42 Victor Joseph Chavet, *Ball in the Galerie des Glaces at Versailles on 25 August 1855.* On Saint Napoleon's day, during the state visit undertaken to strengthen the Franco-British alliance against the Russian Empire, the Prince Consort (centre) opens the ball with Napoleon III's cousin Princess Mathilde. To the right is the Prince of Wales in Scottish dress, the Empress Eugénie (seated owing to pregnancy), Napoleon III and Queen Victoria. The gentlemen wear military or civil uniform.

worn with a red waistcoat and braid, for favoured guests and officials.[61] The court resumed its role as a centre of consumption and advertisement for Lyon silk and Paris dress-making. Again the silk trade of Lyon presented costumes to monarchs in the Tuileries, to encourage them to order more.[62] Although herself fond of simple clothes, according to her reader Mme Carette, the Empress wore elaborate dresses on public occasions, made of *de grosses étoffes de Lyon*, often in startling new colours such as 'aldehyde green'. She called them her *toilettes politiques* – and complained that they made her look like a curtain.[63]

Like Marie Antoinette and the duchesse de Berri before her, the Empress Eugénie became a leader of fashion. From the beginning of the regime, opposition circles criticised the extravagance of her dress. The Empress was said, both by example and by personal comments, to encourage women never to appear at court receptions and balls twice in the same dress. A married woman needed 10,000 francs a year to dress suitably.[64] For a week's residence with the court at Compiègne, some women took eighteen dresses.[65]

As Marie Antoinette had made the name of Rose Bertin, so the Empress Eugénie helped make that of Charles Frederick Worth. In 1845 he had left

London for Paris, first working for the silk mercer Gagelin, one of whose *modistes* he married. Soon his dress firm at 7 rue de la Paix was famous for its range of textiles, and for Worth's 'obsession with exact fit'. The rise of Worth was recounted by the woman who presented him to the Empress, the Austrian ambassadress Princess Metternich. The conversations recorded in her memoirs, long after the event, are necessarily inaccurate. Nevertheless their spirit, and the fact that an entire chapter is devoted to Worth, reveal the importance attached to dress.[66]

In 1860, trying on two Worth dresses recommended by her *femme de chambre*, Princess Metternich realised they were 'masterpieces'. She wore a white Worth dress sprinkled with silver and diamonds at one of the Empress's Monday balls in the Salle des Maréchaux in the Tuileries. The Empress at once asked who had made it.

> – An Englishman, Madame, a rising star in the firmament of
>   fashion!
> – And what is his name?
> – Worth.
> – Well let the star have some satellites, I beg you to have him
>   told to come to see me tomorrow morning at ten o'clock.
>   Worth was launched and I was ruined as from that moment
>   the dresses at three hundred francs were never seen again.

Princess Metternich ends the chapter with Worth's boast, seven years later, after she had given a brilliant ball at the Austrian embassy:

> And to say that it is I who invented you!

She comments:

> It is perhaps true.[67]

In 1865 this English Parisian became the Empress's official dress-maker. Among the fashions Worth launched were those for a court train hung from the shoulders rather than the waist.[68] It was said of Paris: 'The men believe in the Bourse and the women in Worth.'[69] The fashion industry and the Bourse complemented each other, through vicarious ostentation. By advertising a businessman's wealth, a well-dressed wife or mistress was said to raise his value on the Bourse.[70] The court of Napoleon III helped raise Paris fashion to an apogee of fame and profit: it was said that half the female population lived off fashion, while the other half lived for it. Jealous of the Empress Eugénie, the Emperor's cousin, Princess Mathilde, complained that, compared to her youth, women's lives were now filled with the details of dress and visits to dress shops. By the end of the century, fashionable women changed clothes five or six times a day – more often than at the beginning.[71] Footmen in grand households also spent much of their time dressing, undressing, changing liveries and powdering their hair.[72] Dress was one of the forms of conspicuous consumption on which the wealth of the industrial revolution was spent.

By 1870 Worth was employing 1,200 seamstresses and his premises on the rue de la Paix were compared, for their size and grandeur, to an embassy.[73] His empire stretched wider, and lasted longer, than that of Napoleon III. He made coronation dresses for two empresses, the Empress Elisabeth of Austria when she was crowned Queen of Hungary in Buda in 1868 and Marie Feodorovna, Empress of Russia in 1882. Rose Bertin had dressed the Queens of Spain and Sweden; Charles Worth dressed the Queens of Spain, Italy, Prussia and the Netherlands, and the Princess of Wales.[74] The range of Worth's foreign clients, and the wealth of Paris, help explain why the firm survived the end of the Second Empire and the official court system. On 15 January 1872, a year after the Prussian siege of Paris and less than a year after the bloodbath at the end of the Commune, Edmond de Goncourt noticed a crowd of carriages blocking the rue de la Paix outside Worth's premises, as if it was the Comédie-Française on a first night.[75] Worth was called the King of Dress, the only absolute monarch left in Europe.[76] The firm did not close until 1954.[77]

After the fall of the Second Empire, its conqueror the German Empire replaced it as the leading military monarchy, and stronghold of uniforms. The triumph of uniforms in Germany can be traced through the career of the architect of its unity, Prince Bismarck. He had never done more than a year's military service (obligatory for Prussian civil servants), from March 1838 to March 1839 in the Garde Jaeger regiment.[78] From 1851 to 1859, as Prussian envoy to the German Confederation in Frankfurt – a city state without a court – he had worn the *frac*.[79] When he had been Prussian ambassador at the courts of Alexander II and Napoleon III in 1859–62, he had worn civil uniform.[80]

Prussian victory in the war of 1866 against the German Confederation and Austria, however, transformed both Germany and Bismarck himself. As a reward for his contribution to victory, since he had invariably behaved with 'the heart and spirit of a soldier', on the eve of the victory parade the King appointed Bismarck honorary *Chef* of the 7 Schwieren Landwehr-Reiter regiment, with the rank of major-general, and in 1868 officer *à la suite* of the Kurassier regiment von Seydlitz (Magdeburgisches) number 7. On 24 February 1867 at the opening of the first Reichstag of the new North German Confederation, Bismarck wore not his civil uniform as Prussian Minister-President and Chancellor of the North German Confederation but the white uniform of his Kurassier regiment.[81]

Bismarck's dress advertised King Wilhelm I's power over the army, and commitment to army expansion and modernisation, to defend which he had, in 1862, first been selected by the King as Minister-President. From the point of view of dress, Bismarck shows the truth of the claim that Germany in the nineteenth century took a different path from other countries. He was the first civilian chief minister in European history who on public occasions regularly wore military uniform. Although he knew the dangers of army influence in politics, he chose to look like an army officer rather than the politician and diplomat he was. Signalling the Prussian monarchy's determination to command a large, modern and independent army, Bismarck's dress was an omen of wars to come.

During the Franco-Prussian War, Bismarck wore the undress uniform of his Landwehr cavalry regiment.[82] The Prussian Foreign Office, which followed him on campaign, including junior clerks, wore dark blue civil uniform and swords – or, in some cases, military uniform.[83] On 18 January 1871 (anniversary of the coronation of the first king in Prussia in Königsberg in 1701), King Wilhelm I was acclaimed as German Emperor by other German monarchs and officers, including Bismarck himself, in the Galerie des Glaces in Versailles. One ceremony confirmed three events: the German defeat of France; the unification of Germany; and the triumph of military monarchy in Germany. No civilians or parliamentary deputies were present.

Bismarck's preference for military over civil uniform reflected not only the nature of Prussia, but also personal experience. In St Petersburg in 1860 his ambassador's uniform had been so covered in gold braid and *Kantillenstickerei*, a particularly complicated technique of raised embroidery, that it had provoked mocking remarks from the Tsar and Tsarina. While always ready to mock others, Bismarck disliked being mocked himself. In 1871 he personally intervened to simplify and reduce the quantity of embroidery on ambassadors' coats.[84]

Bismarck continued to wear military uniform on all public occasions: when adressing the Reichstag, or breakfasting with its deputies;[85] when spending the evening with the *Bürgermeister* in Hamburg, as well as in the Chancellery in Berlin.[86] To English visitors he explained, defensively, that he wore uniform to avoid changing into it each time he was summoned to see the Emperor: both he and Wilhelm I wear military uniform in a portrait by Konrad Siemenroth (1887) of them working together in Wilhelm I's corner study, from which he used to watch the changing of the guard on Unter den Linden.[87] Yet if a summons to the palace had been the decisive factor, Bismarck could have worn a minister's civil uniform.[88] Bismarck wanted to associate himself with the strongest element in the state – the army.

After 1866 uniform became a German passion, shared by subsequent civilian chancellors and imposed on foreign diplomats posted to Berlin. One Romanian attaché remembered: 'the Germans insisted that diplomats, who were also reserve officers should wear military or naval rather than diplomatic uniforms.'[89] Austria imposed similar priorities. As a retired Indian army officer, Richard Burton could be presented in his military uniform at court to the Emperor; as British consul in Trieste, he could not.[90]

After the accession of Wilhelm II in 1888, uniform became an even more conspicuous outward sign of what he had called, in a letter to his grandfather, 'the *furor militaris* which with us is traditional in the family and is taken for granted'.[91] As a young prince, like Franz Josef and Nicholas II before their accession, he had served in different regiments, including the first regiment of Foot Guards. Whereas Wilhelm I had not been especially interested in dress, in the opinion of one of Wilhelm II's court officials he was 'obsessed with this question of clothes and externals'.[92] Wilhelm II's cult of uniforms showed a sense of parade and occasion, in keeping both with the spirit of the age and with the Emperor's personal desire to reassert the supremacy of the monarchy over ministers, Reichstag and socialists.[93]

Like his great-great-uncle, George IV, he designed and altered military uniforms so frequently that he put German officers (except Bavarians, whose army escaped Prussian authority in peacetime) to serious expense. Some of his sketches for uniforms were published at the time in laudatory biographies of himself.[94] Caprivi resigned as head of the Admiralty in 1888, in part because of the Kaiser's determination to change naval uniforms.[95] At a lunch in the Neues Palais in Potsdam, when he saw two American diplomats wearing dark tail coats, he told them that they looked like a couple of crows, like two undertakers at a feast, and spoiled the picture.[96] His passion for uniforms led him on occasion, like a fashionable Paris lady, to change five times a day: he was particularly fond of Jaeger and Hussar uniforms. As in Russia, there was a multiplication of versions of uniform for different occasions. In addition to gala, guard gala, guard, society, dancing gala, service and light service uniforms, there was a special *Hofgarten Anzug*, for officers going to court garden parties, to which they wore uniform without decorations, swords or sword belt.[97]

In 1890 the Kaiser introduced a special court costume for civilians 'mit weissern Unterkleidern' – with white trousers.[98] The Kaiser also designed a special dark green hunting costume with feathered hat, ornate leather belt and high black boots, for himself and his courtiers, which caused amused consternation on the Kaiser's visits to other European courts.[99] The Kaiser's interest in dress crossed the gender barrier: every year, on his wife's birthday, he gave her twelve expensive and elaborate new hats. It is also said that he helped design some of her gowns which, Nicholas II wrote to his mother, made her look 'very ugly in rich clothes chosen without taste'.[100] As at other courts, ladies' trains were fifteen feet long.[101]

Factories devoted to making braid, gold and silver thread and uniforms, such as Tuchfabrik Müller near Cologne, entered a literally golden age. There were six workshops for gold embroidery in Berlin in 1804, 31 in 1840, 50 in 1900.[102] The clothes trade in Berlin was so important that two annual festivals celebrated it: the 'fly festival' of spinners and yarn-makers; and the 'moth festival' of cloth-makers and weavers.[103] Old films show the coexistence in Berlin of three parallel worlds: the bourgeois in *fracs* and top hats; the poor in cheap clothes and cloth caps; and soldiers in glittering uniforms and helmets. The new industrial metropolis occupied the same space as, and supplied and paid for, the guard and army of a monarch who believed in divine right.[104]

Whereas today the Prussian army is associated with the evils of militarism, before 1914 its soldiers were considered by many to add life and colour to Berlin, like the Foot Guards and Household Cavalry in London today. 'In those days the military show and splendour in Berlin were really wonderful . . . the streets were always full of officers very well dressed in military uniform and they certainly added greatly to the brightness of the capital,' remembered a British diplomat.[105] The sight of the Kaiser in the 'white tunic, dazzling breastplate and silver helmet surmounted by the Prussian eagle' of the Garde du corps, or in other uniforms, impressed most observers, including Winston Churchill, who twice (in 1906 and 1909) attended German army manoeuvres.[106] The American painter Marsden Hartley found that the gorgeous public spectacle of soldiers in Berlin contributed to 'a sense of perpetual gaiety here' and was inspired, in his painting, by 'those huge cuirassiers of the Kaiser's special guard, all in white – white leather breeches, skin tight high enamel boots – those gleaming blinding medieval breast plates of silver and brass – making the eye go black when the sun glanced like a spear when the bodies moved.'[107] The 'peacock army', created by the Kaiser, has dominated the subsequent public image of the Prussian army, replacing its simpler image before 1866.[108]

The power of uniforms in the German Empire was confirmed by an incident in October 1906. By virtue of stealing and wearing the uniform of a captain in the First Foot Guards, a convicted criminal called Wilhelm Voigt was able to go to a barracks, summon two squads of soldiers and lead them to occupy the city hall, and arrest the Bürgermeister and treasurer, of the Berlin suburb of Köpenick. He then disappeared with the available cash. His uniform had spared him all questions, although he was later denounced by an acquaintance and arrested.[109] In *The Captain from Köpenick*, the play he wrote on the subject twenty years later, Carl Zuckmayer makes one character explain his love of uniform: 'in ordinary street clothes I feel like a half portion without mustard'.[110]

The Eulenburg scandal of 1908 revealed that uniforms could also exert power of another kind. Tight trousers and jackboots had become a speciality of the Prussian army. The Kaiser's cousin Prince Friedrich Leopold of Prussia, commander of the First Foot Guard regiment, once fainted because the breeches into which he had been sewn were so tight.[111] After the revelations, during the trial of Prince Eulenburg, of the electrifying effect of guards' uniforms on some Berlin homosexuals, such uniforms were banned for soldiers 'walking out'.[112]

More than in other monarchies, the Prussian cult of uniforms was adopted by the civilian bourgeoisie, many of whom served, at their own expense, as *Einjähriger*, or one-year reserve officers. Thereby they obtained a military rank which gave them the right to go to court, and a suitable uniform to wear when doing so and on public occasions such as the Emperor's birthday.[113] The position of reserve officer was called by Theodore Fontane 'the great god of the Prussian cult'.[114] A character in *The Captain from Köpenick* says: 'so you have managed to become a reserve lieutenant – that is the chief thing – that is the thing you must be these days – socially, professionally, in every connection! The doctorate is the visiting card, but the reserve commission is the open door – that's the essential thing these days!'[115]

Despite their civilian functions, Bethmann Hollweg (who was promoted to the rank of general) and other German chancellors continued the Bismarckian tradition of wearing military uniform on formal occasions, as did all German monarchs except the Prince of Schwarzburg Rudolstadt.[116] Like Bismarck they wanted to associate themselves with the strongest element in the state. In *Simplicissimus* and other satirical journals, caricatures attacked Germans' blind trust in uniforms. In one, uniformed officials and students, in a Berlin street,

43 Lyonel Feininger, *A civilian, a civilian!*, 1899.
The passion for uniforms: men and boys, wearing the military, civil or postal uniforms that were so visible in German towns under the 'Second Reich', are mocking an elderly man in civilian dress.

shout 'A civilian, a civilian!' at the sight of an elderly bearded man in English-looking civilian clothes – possibly intended to symbolise the lost liberal generation of 1848.[117] Others attack 'the holy tunic or the power of uniform', and 'the saint lieutenant'.[118] Possibly, however, they attack the abuse of uniforms, by incompetent and arrogant officers, more than uniform itself.[119] At the same time, statues of Bismarck in Prussian uniform (such as the one, formerly opposite the Reichstag, now in the Tiergarten in Berlin) were being erected by public subscription throughout Germany, except in Hanover and Bavaria.[120]

Uniforms imposed obligations as well as privileges. In 1908 Prince Joachim Albert of Prussia was retired from the army without the right to wear uniform. The reason was an act of adultery – and the Kaiser's desire to warn his sons, then reaching maturity, to refrain from following their cousin's example.[121]

As Kaunitz and the Archduke Johann had feared, the practice of military monarchy led to the destruction of the monarchies themselves. If the Bourbon monarchy had perished from a lack of militarism, its rivals perished from an excess of it. Putting expansion before self-preservation, in 1914 the Austrian, German and Russian empires were sufficiently ambitious, and confident of their popularity and stability, to go to war. Two military monarchs, Nicholas II and Wilhelm II, and some of their crack Guards regiments, were away fighting at the front when revolution broke out in the capital.

The army was the arbiter of power. In February 1917 all senior Russian commanders at the front advised Nicholas II to abdicate: they considered that a Provisional government would pursue the war against the Central Powers, and control revolution in the capital, more effectively than the Tsar. In the words of his biographer Dominic Lieven, 'Abandoned by his generals, Nicholas II had no alternative but to abdicate.'[122]

In the German Empire, by November 1918, the pressures of hunger, shortages, including clothes shortages,[123] disease and, above all, defeat had weakened traditional feelings of loyalty to the monarchy, even in Guards regiments. Backed by polls of generals, Hindenburg, Ludendorff and General Gröner the War Minister told Wilhelm II that the army could no longer be trusted to keep its oaths of loyalty, and advised him to go into exile in the Netherlands. They too believed that a republic was in the best interests of both army and country.[124] Generals dismissed monarchs, like the unsatisfactory subordinate officers they had become. To the Kaiser's questions about his soldiers' oaths of loyalty, they replied: 'Sire, today oaths are but words.'[125]

In Berlin, during the revolution of 9 November 1918, when the city filled with soldiers, sailors and strikers supporting a republic, many Prussian officers and soldiers suffered the trauma of having their epaulettes, medals and buttons torn from their uniforms, even by their own soldiers: sometimes they were forced to wrench them off themselves, and put on red cockades. Princess Blücher saw 'youths in field grey uniform or in civil clothes, carrying loaded rifles adorned with a tiny red flag, constantly springing off their seats and forcing the soldiers and officers to tear off their insignia, or doing it for them if they refused. They were mostly boys of from 16 to 18 years of age, who looked as if they were enjoying their sudden power immensely.' They were cheering and shouting and grinning 'like schoolboys on an escapade'. By the time the returning German troops paraded through the Brandenburg gate on 10 December, however, the majority of officers and soldiers were wearing epaulettes and medals again.[126]

On 20 December the arrest of sailors who had insulted officers wearing the imperial uniform signalled that the German revolution was losing impetus.[127] Thereafter, both soldiers in the right-wing Freikorps trying to reverse the revolution, and participants in the failed Nazi putsch of 1923 in Munich such as General Ludendorff, wore imperial uniforms.[128] Indeed on many public occasions, both under the Weimar Republic, of which he became President, and the Third Reich, which he helped establish, Hindenburg would wear his old imperial uniform. Dress confirmed the persistent power, under the new regime, of the old officer class.

In Austria too the Emperor was forced into exile, and the monarchy abolished. After 1918, under a republic, many Austrians continued wearing their court uniforms or liveries, as they were too poor to buy new clothes. Surviving court uniforms are now in the Monturdepot of the Kunsthistorisches Museum or the Hungarian National Museum: Russian court uniforms are in the Hermitage Museum; Prussian uniforms and liveries can be seen in the Kaiser's place of exile in Doorn in the Netherlands.[129]

The revolutions of 1917–18 showed the unpopularity of uniforms in times of hunger, revolution and defeat. As in the days of *Simplicissimus*, however, this revulsion was caused by defeat as much as militarism itself. The next twenty years, indeed, would witness a resurgence of uniforms. More than ever, they touched a popular nerve. If they had not done so, they would not have been adopted by the Fascist and Nazi parties, against the wishes of the Italian and German governments, even before they took control of the state. No regimes showed greater belief in the transforming power of clothes than the megalomaniac regimes of the twentieth century. Combining traditional militarism with revolutionary totalitarianism, they would go even further than military monarchies and extend uniforms to entire populations, female as well as male – moves previously considered only in France during the Reign of Terror.

In Italy violence by Mussolini's Fascist militias created the conditions which led him to be appointed Prime Minister by the King in 1922. Fascists were known, from the colour of their uniforms, as 'Black Shirts'. The origin of the uniform lies in the 'Arditi' shock troops of the Italian army in World War I, who wore black shirts and supplied Fascism with some of its early leaders.[130] The uniform of fez, shirt, tie, trousers and belt, worn by Fascists and all members of the Milizia sports clubs, even children, was entirely black. In summer youths were allowed to remove their black ties, but forbidden to roll up their black shirt sleeves.[131]

In 1928 Fascists even attempted to introduce Fascist hats for students, 'to be manufactured, of Italian straw, by the Italian Straw Federation': 'the new standard straw hat to be worn by all men will be sober, elegant and typically Italian headgear'. Different ribbons would indicate which universities and schools the wearer had attended.[132] From the mid-1930s the 'Fascist Saturday' obliged both men and women to buy Fascist uniforms and wear them on Saturday (a move which led to the remark that soon, to eat ice-cream, you would have to wear Arctic explorer's clothes). The Fascist Saturday showed the totalitarian nature of the regime: the adoption of Fascist dress was intended 'to further the spiritual mobilization of the Nation', eliminate 'bourgeois habits', and help transform Italians into 'new' beings who followed the Fascist creed 'Believe, obey, fight'. Mussolini may have hoped that the entire nation would wear uniform. Further laws, in 1934 and 1938 respectively, obliged all schoolteachers to wear black shirts, and all civil employees of the state to wear uniform at work.[133] The King and the army, however, kept their traditional uniforms: Crown Prince Umberto showed his opposition by not being seen in a black shirt. Mussolini still wore civilian clothes for his audiences with the King, as he had at the first, in 1922. After the King's dismissal of Mussolini in July 1943 and the dismantling of the regime, Fascist uniforms were banned.[134]

If Fascists chose black, Nazis preferred brown. Both colours were relics of World War I: in the early 1920s the Nazi Party had bought cheap army surplus shirts of a light brown colour, once intended for German colonial troops.[135] Later the mud colour would be said to reflect the Party's love of the soil. Soon it was especially associated with the SA militia, known as the 'Brown Shirts'.

Nazi uniforms' appeal was strengthened by Germany's sudden, disorienting deficit in militarism, pageantry and servility after 1918, with the disappearance of all German monarchies and of military conscription. Before 1933, in addition to the 400,000 men of the SA, there were 300,000 members of the right-wing but anti-Nazi ex-servicemen's 'black, white, red' Stahlhelm (whose 'field grey' uniforms were considerably smarter than those of the SA), and a smaller number of Socialists enrolled in the Reichsbanner militia.[136] In the years of mass unemployment and insecurity after the economic slump in 1929, a uniform could restore self-esteem to impoverished, humiliated, bewildered German men. They were prepared to pay 16 marks for an SA uniform.[137] The other mass working-class party, the Communists, also adopted uniforms.[138]

In April 1932, hoping to halt the drift to violence, the Ministry of the Interior of Prussia, and some other German states, banned the SA and SS, the wearing of uniforms by all political groups, and outdoor public demonstrations. The Nazi brown shirt was considered both to embolden its wearer and to provoke his opponents. On 16 June 1932 the new right-wing Chancellor von Papen reversed the ban on the SA and SS and on wearing political uniforms. The number of Nazis' murders of, and street clashes with, political opponents immediately increased. The Bavarian and Baden governments, however, continued to impose the ban: a meeting of the

Bavarian Landtag was suspended until Nazi deputies returned wearing civilian dress, rather than Nazi uniforms.[139] German governments did not doubt the importance of dress as a political weapon.

From the Nazi seizure of power in March 1933, wrote a young liberal called Sebastian Haffner, Berlin was filled with red, white and black flags in the old imperial colours and 'columns of brown uniforms . . . brown uniforms that one could not get away from: not in buses, cafés, in the streets or even in the Tiergarten park. They were everywhere like an army of occupation', engulfing Berlin and other cities in the never-ending sounds of march music and beating drums.[140] Rival forces, like the Stahlhelm, Reichsbanner and Communist militias were amalgamated or dissolved. Bismarck had said that moral courage deserts a German (and more nationalities than he suspected) once he puts on a uniform. The self-destruction of Germany had begun.[141]

The uniforms of the Second and the Third Reichs can be seen in revealing proximity in films of Hindenburg, the ex-Crown Prince and the new Chancellor Hitler, with soldiers of the army and the SA, attending the grandiose service in the garrison church at Potsdam on 21 March 1933 which consecrated Hitler as heir to the Prussian military tradition.[142] The swastika

44 Hitler, Hindenburg and Goering at the commemoration of the Battle of Tannenberg, 18 August 1933.
The proximity of Hindenburg's traditional Prussian uniform and Goering's Nazi uniform, and those on the storm-troopers behind, symbolises the alliance between the old officer corps and the Nazi Party that had helped bring the latter to power. Still only chancellor, Hitler wears formal civilian dress.

had always used the old imperial colours of black, red and white, in opposition to the black, red and gold colours used by radicals since 1817, which had been adopted at Frankfurt in 1848 and under the Weimar Republic.[143] Imperial army accoutrements were reintroduced to German army uniforms in 1936.[144] Howard Smith noticed that in Germany, by 1936, 'towns looked like garrisons, with every third or fourth man in uniform . . . a mass of armed uniformed men'.[145] Uniform became the essence of the regime, and synonymous with terror, persecution and state control. From 1934 the SS acquired an all-black uniform with a particularly elaborate hierarchy of badges and embroidery distinctions.[146] When he became Foreign Minister in 1938, one of Ribbentrop's first acts was to introduce a special blue and black diplomatic uniform, with jackboots.[147]

Other Fascist movements also used uniforms as political weapons. In Spain dark blue was the colour that its founder Antonio Primo de Rivera had chosen for the shirts of the fascist 'Falange' militia, on the grounds that it was 'serious, straightforward, sincere and proletarian': hence the name 'Blue Division' for the troops Franco sent to fight against the Soviet Union in 1941. After the German defeat in 1945, however, the Falange rapidly lost influence and popularity.[148] Under Salazar Portugal also had its 'blue shirts'. In Lebanon the Maronite Phalange party members wore – in some cases still wear – green shirts, since green is the colour of the national symbol, the Cedar of Lebanon.

In the United Kingdom in 1932 Sir Oswald Mosley, leader of the British Union of Fascists, introduced black uniforms for his followers, particularly for 'stewards', in order, he explained, to emphasise action, discipline and authority and to break down class barriers. Black was chosen because it was the opposite to Communist red and because it was not then widely worn in England. In reality Mosley's choice of black showed his ideological allegiance to (and secret financial dependence on) Mussolini. By the Public Order Act in 1936 the British government banned such uniforms – in order to lessen the possibility of provoking disorder.[149]

The defeat of Nazism and Fascism has ended, perhaps for ever, the appeal of uniforms in Europe. The last mass uniform culture was fostered by another totalitarian regime, in China. After the revolution overthrowing the Manchu dynasty in 1911, the first President of the Republic Dr Sun Yat-sen opted for simplicity. He adopted a tunic suit with four pockets, four buttons and a turn-down collar, based on the casual dress of the province of Guandong. In 1929 a new regulation stipulated that the Sun Yat-sen suit was to be worn as official dress by civil servants. Chairman Mao also adopted this suit. The Communist takeover in 1948 led to an extreme case of government control of dress. All

Chinese had to dress like artisans, with no distinction of rank and sex, in a similar tunic, peaked cap and trousers; city workers wore dark blue; the army yellow green; the administration grey. It was pronounced unpatriotic to be smart or individual. After a break in the 1950s when some denied that it was patriotic to be drab, the cultural revolution of 1966–76 reimposed the 'Mao suit' on the entire population.[150]

The principal surving military monarchy in Europe in the twenty-first century is the British monarchy. In the nineteenth century the British Empire had adopted uniforms as enthusiastically as the Russian and Austrian empires – proof that they could have as much appeal in a parliamentary as in an autocratic monarchy. Civil uniform was extended further down the official hierarchy: in 1847 a fifth rank was added for junior officials such as chief clerks.[151] As in Austria and France, the higher the rank, the wider the embroidery: cabinet ministers had the right to five inches of embroidery; fifth class officials to three-eighths of an inch. As personal representatives of the monarch, therefore of higher status than ministers or court officials, ambassadors had embroidery on sleeves and seams as well as coat edges. Members of the royal household were distinguished by scarlet collars and cuffs.[152] Many peers preferred to be painted or photographed in civil uniform rather than in parliamentary robes. Lord Curzon, for example, was photographed wearing civil uniform under the robes of the Order of the Star of India.[153]

In comparison Windsor uniform, having served its purpose from 1787 to 1830 as a British civil uniform and loyalty indicator, was gradually dropped.[154] After 1837 it was worn only at Windsor Castle (where, probably the last surviving palace uniform, it is still worn today by male members of the royal family, favoured relations and courtiers, and male members of the household at state banquets).[155]

As in the reign of Queen Anne, in the early years of Queen Victoria the royal household, and physical functions such as accompanying the monarch and what one lady-in-waiting called 'shawling and pinning duties',[156] remained politically important. Queen Victoria's closest female friend, the companion of her first days of widowhood, was her Whig Mistress of the Robes, the Duchess of Sutherland (who held office, during Whig ministries, in 1837–41, 1846–52, 1853–8 and 1859–61). In 1839 the Queen's refusal to dismiss the Duchess and other Whig ladies of the bedchamber led to a political crisis – 'the Bedchamber Question' – opposing the Queen and Robert Peel, leader of the more powerful party in the Commons, the Tories. After heated conversations with the Queen, in which she declared she could not consent to part with any of 'my ladies' and

45 Franz Winterhalter, The reception of King Louis-Philippe at Windsor Castle on 8 October 1844.
During a visit undertaken to strengthen the first *entente cordiale*, the Queen wears mourning. King Louis-Philippe and his suite wear military or civil uniform – the revolutionary origins of his monarchy are long forgotten. Prince Albert, the Duke of Wellington, Peel and Lords Exeter, Jersey and Liverpool (Groom of the Stole, Master of the Horse and Lord Steward of the Household respectively) are in Windsor uniform. Behind the Queen are the Tory ladies whom she had been so reluctant to appoint during the 'Bedchamber crisis' in 1839.

swore she 'never' talked politics with them, Peel declined to become Prime Minister, despite his Commons majority. The politician attributed more political importance to ladies-in-waiting than did the Queen herself.[157] He also considered appointments in the royal household a critical sign of the Queen's confidence in his government. Only in 1841, when Peel was assured that Prince Albert would arrange the resignations of the Duchess of Sutherland, the Duchess of Bedford and Lady Normanby, and that Peel would be allowed to help select new ladies himself, did he agree to take office as Prime Minister.[158]

As in Second Empire France, due to the wealth generated by the industrial revolution, to a desire to differentiate court dress from the elaborate dress which the middle classes could now afford, and to a female desire to compete with men's uniforms, in the nineteenth century female court dress attained a peak of elaboration comparable to the reign of Louis XIV. In order to help makers of Spitalfields silks, Irish poplin and Honiton lace, Queen Victoria gave three grandiose costume balls (medieval in 1842, Georgian in 1845, Stuart in 1851), to which guests were asked to wear dresses of British manufacture.[159] Queen Charlotte's court train had been nine feet long.[160] By the end of the century, like Russian and Prussian court trains, British court trains could be elaborate structures fifteen feet long, covered in gold and silver embroidery, trimmed with feathers and flowers of tulle or silk. They occupied so much space that they were compared to railway carriages or boa constrictors. Women were told in etiquette books: 'at the drawing room you cannot be too resplendent. The richer your brocade, the more fitting the occasion.'[161] Girls often added lace heirlooms to their presentation dresses, thereby linking their family history to their presentation to the monarch.[162]

Presentation at court was an outward demonstration of respectability and wealth: young girls were being branded as suitable for the marriage market; married women as respectable members of society. Until World War II, the Lord Chamberlain's office was proud that 'the most scrupulous supervision over the names of those who seek the honour is exercised'.[163] As Thackeray wrote in *Vanity Fair* (1848) of Becky Sharp, by then Mrs Rawdon Crawley: 'If she did not wish to lead a virtuous life, at least she wished to enjoy a character for virtue, and we know that no lady in the genteel world can possess this desideratum, until she has put on a train and feathers and has been presented to her Sovereign at Court.' *Vanity Fair* describes Mrs Rawdon Crawley's 'grand, self satisfied, deliberate and imposing' demeanour as, to the dismay of her female acquaintance, she attends a drawing-room of the Prince Regent, wearing 'the most elegant and brilliant costume de cour' with lace, diamonds, 'grand feathers' and a 'train of magnificent brocade'.[164]

Court dress continued to assert femininity. It was distinguished from ordinary dress not only by the obligation to wear a veil, feathers, gloves and a train, and to carry a fan and bouquet of flowers, but also by *décolleté*. Taking a passionate interest in court dress throughout her reign, Queen Victoria insisted that even old ladies must wear full *décolleté* to court, and bare shoulders. Until 1903 officials were posted at doors of the state apartments to remove any offending covers.[165]

The purchase of a court dress for presentation was followed by the further ordeals of fittings at the dress-makers' (sometimes, because they took so long, the dress and train were made by different firms); dressing at home, often in the presence of friends and relations; queuing both in the Mall and inside the palace with as many as 1,500 other débutantes; curtsying to the monarch and other members of the royal family; backing out of the royal presence, while holding your train over your left arm, in order to avoid falling over; perhaps then proceeding to a photographer's studio such as Lafayette or Vandyk, to be photographed in full array. The process required the expenditure of so much time, energy and money that it was compared to a military campaign.[166] Ladies' exhaustion was far exceeded by their dress-makers'. Seamstresses,

46 Balliol Salmon, Débutantes climbing the staircase of Buckingham Palace on their way to presentation in the Presence Chamber, 1904.
Dress as status symbol: wearing trains and feathers, ladies dressed for presentation at the British court looked so impressive that they were compared to battleships or moving barricades.

especially during the court season, were overworked and underpaid; in 1863 a young seamstress called Mary Anne Walkley died from exhaustion. Similar conditions prevailed among men. A workshop for a men's court tailor like Poole (see below, p. 141) employed twenty or more men to a room, working cross-legged on the floor from 6 a.m. to 7 p.m. – and, in the summer, later.[167] A strike in 1891 revealed that Poole's also farmed out work, even on clothes for the royal family, to men in disease-ridden 'evil, dark and dirty dens'.[168]

Under Queen Victoria, who first visited Scotland in 1842, the British monarchy continued to favour Scottish dress. Even in London, her young sons wore Scottish dress, both for the state opening of the 1851 exhibition and for the marriage of the Princess Royal in 1858.[169] In 1860 Prince Albert, who often designed his wife's dresses and jewellery, also created a tartan for exclusive use in Scotland by the royal household. There were three forms: Dress Stewart, Royal Stewart and Hunting Stewart, as well as Balmoral and Victoria tartans, designed by the Queen and the Prince around 1850 for the servants. Many Scottish neighbours remarked, like the future Edward VIII, on the unnatural length of the royal kilts, almost covering the knee: 'so very German'.[170]

Indeed the Queen encouraged the use of tartan not only among her British family and servants but also among her German relations. Perhaps already marking him as a husband for her eldest daughter, she sent Prince Frederick William of Prussia a kilt when he was fifteen.[171] In 1863 she sent her eldest grandson, Prince William of Prussia, a Scottish cloak, sporran, shoes and kilt in Royal Stewart tartan, for him to wear to the wedding of the Prince of Wales at Windsor. Her daughter wrote: 'I am so pleased we can bring Willy: he is very much preoccupied with his Scotch dress.' During the service he brandished his dirk and threw his sporran into the choir.[172] On his visit in 1878, the Queen gave him further tartan,[173] in green, grey and red, about which he wrote at some length fifty years later in his memoirs.[174] After his abdication the child's Royal Stewart outfit was among the costumes selected from his possessions in Berlin and sent to Huis Doorn, his residence in exile in the Netherlands. It is still there, on display with a selection of his military uniforms.[175]

If the Queen encouraged Scottish dress, some Lord-Lieutenants of Ireland favoured Irish. Supporters of Home Rule, the Earl and Countess of Aberdeen were barely prevented, by local officials, from dressing their children in green velvet for their state entry into Dublin in 1886: instead the children wore white Irish poplin. In the next twenty years there were many schemes for encouraging Irish poplin, lace and tweed, even Irish kilts and Irish evening dress in green.[176] The revival of national dress in Ireland was not an isolated phenomenon: it was paralleled, at the same time, in Scotland, Hungary, Russia, Romania (where the foreign-born Queens Carmen Sylva and Marie wore embroidered peasant blouses, kerchiefs and skirts and encouraged others to do so).[177] The revival of national dress was not only an affirmation of national pride, but also in an age of rapid industrialisation, when Europe was being covered with factories and railways, a form of psychological reassurance.

Despite Queen Victoria's passion for Scottish dress, the British monarchy remained a military monarchy. The Queen, who frequently proclaimed that she was a soldier's daughter,[178] designed her own red military tunic, 'the ornaments of the collar beautifully embroidered in gold and silver, the device the same as a Field Marshal's'.[179] In her widowhood, the only public duties she was eager to resume were military ones, even, as at Edinburgh in 1881, reviewing troops in the pouring rain.[180] The picture in the Royal Collection of Queen Victoria and her family at her Golden Jubilee in Windsor in 1887, by L. R. Tuxen, shows all her sons, sons-in-law and grandsons in uniform, with the exception of young princes in kilts.

The reign of Queen Victoria continued nationalisation of court mourning. In London in 1760, within half an hour of the death of George II, every shop had been hung with 'the appendages of mourning'.[181] Even on the death of

George III's youngest daughter Princess Amelia, who was barely known to the public, 'all tradespeople, workpeople, servants out of livery, every creature who can scrape up money to buy a black rag', according to Lady Lyttelton, had worn 'the deepest mourning', giving London in late 1810 'quite an odd look'.[182] Black again became 'universal' in the United Kingdom after the deaths of Princess Charlotte in 1817,[183] Queen Victoria in 1901, Edward VII in 1910 (when, to honour his memory, race-goers wore mourning dress to a 'Black Ascot').[184]

The practice of mourning reached a peak in the second half of the nineteenth century, with different nuances of deep mourning, second mourning, third mourning, ordinary mourning and half mourning: in England the city of Norwich dominated 'the black trade' in jet objects, crape, bombazine and cloth.[185] For Prince Albert in 1861, mourning was deeper and more extensive than in 1708 for the previous husband of a queen regnant, Prince George of Denmark.[186] On 16 December 1861 the deputy Earl Marshal issued the following order: 'In pursuance of Her Majesty's commands, this is to give public notice that upon the melancholy occasion of the death of His Royal Highness the Prince Consort, it is expected that all persons [a phrase repeated for George VI] do forthwith put themselves into decent mourning.'[187] Faced with 'almost incalculable demand for mourning', London shops, 'particularly in the West End, were crowded to inconvenience'.[188] Until her death forty years later, the Queen herself, almost demented with grief, and her immediate household never, even for her children's weddings or her own jubilees, came out of mourning dress.[189]

The morning after Queen Victoria's death in 1901, in the small English town of Wilton, 'every man and woman . . . from the highest to the lowest appeared in mourning'. This was reflected throughout the country: even ladies' underwear was black.[190] British factories proving unable to cope with demand, factories on the continent immediately began the production of mourning clothes.[191]

Like his great-uncle George IV and his nephew Wilhelm II, the new king Edward VII also suffered from clothes mania. In 1858 Prince Albert had lamented: 'unfortunately he takes no interest in anything but clothes and again clothes. Even when out shooting, he is more occupied with the cut of his trousers than with the game.'[192] He became an arbiter of elegance, closely watched by tailors, both English and foreign, in case he launched a new fashion. Under his patronage the lounge suit, the Homburg hat and the use of side creases in trousers, among other sartorial innovations, became fashionable.[193]

Some of the King's remarks on clothes became famous. 'Un costume un peu plus écossais demain', he told his Swiss valet, as the royal yacht approached Scotland one summer.[194] On another occasion: 'I thought everyone must know that a short jacket is always worn with a silk hat at a private view in the morning.'[195] 'I see you have come in the suite of the American ambassador,' he complained one evening to Lord Rosebery, who was wearing trousers instead of knee breeches.[196] In obedience to the Secretary of State's circular of 1853, instructing American ambassadors to show their 'devotion to republican institutions' by appearing at state functions abroad in 'the simple dress of an American citizen', most – but not all – American ambassadors, to the fury of the King, insisted on wearing trousers rather than knee breeches to court balls in London. The American ambassador in black tail coat stands out, in contrast to other ambassadors in embroidered civil uniforms, in Dickinson's picture of a levee of Edward VII in Saint James's Palace.[197]

The book *Dress and Insignia worn at His Majesty's Court* reveals a court dress code at once more precise, and more global, than those of Versailles and Vienna. It should be read by anyone who believes that the British were not fond of uniforms. The difference was that they wore uniforms on fewer occasions than other Europeans. First published with the authorisation of the Lord Chamberlain in 1883, it expanded continuously thereafter, with different editions in 1897, 1908, 1921 and 1929, until the final edition in 1937. Forty-five pages of advertisements at the front and back of the 1921 edition, 'issued with the authority of the Lord Chamberlain illustrated by coloured plates specially prepared', reveal the continued importance of dress as a commercial link between the court and London shops:

> Wilkinson and Son Tailors and Robe makers to His Majesty and the Royal Family. Court and Levee Dress. Household, Diplomatic, Civil and Consular Uniforms. Mantles and Ribands of the Orders of Knighthood. Peers' Parliamentary and Coronation Robes. Recognised as the Leading authorities upon Court Dress, attend Court Functions Under the direction of The Lord Chamberlain. 34 and 36 Maddox Street, Hanover Square London W1.

There were also advertisements for jewellers, hatters, makers of 'Flat Watches for Court Dress', court dress-makers, glove-makers, and 'Nutting and Kent Gold Lacemen and Embroiderers'.

Dress and Insignia worn at His Majesty's Court shows that, after World War I, there was a late-flowering militarisation of the British court. Military service

47 M. Dickinson, Levee of Edward VII in Saint James's Palace, 1903.
Uniforms and court dress surround the King, except for the tail coat and trousers of the
American ambassador, standing second from left with the other ambassadors in the
uniforms of their respective monarchies. On the right of the King are court officials
wearing the levee version of civil uniform. While insistent on others always wearing the
correct uniform, the King disregarded regulations concerning his own uniforms, for
example when visiting the Kaiser in Berlin.

was placed as high as at the French, Prussian and Austrian courts: 'The King
has commanded that officers of superior Naval and Military rank in His
Majesty's Household, should have the option of wearing Naval and Military
uniform.' As a sign of increasing simplicity and economy, 'Levee dress is
substituted for full dress when wanted.'[198] In 1921 feathers, veils and trains
were in theory abolished, on Queen Mary's initiative; in reality, more
conservative than Queen Mary, ladies continued wearing them – although
bouquets and fans had become optional – at the courts and presentations
which were held with traditional formality until 1939.[199] The rooms of
Buckingham Palace on court days continued to look like waving fields of
feathers.[200] As they had been since the late eighteenth century, ladies' costumes
at court were fully described in newspapers: at the first court in 1937, the
Queen's 'full court train was of gold lamé with Indian embroideries'; Mrs
Baldwin wore a gown of white cloth with 'gold lamé flowers round the neck, a
gold lamé court train and topaz and diamond tiara'.[201]

Men without official positions continued to wear 'cloth court dress
mulberry claret or green but not blue or black',[202] although Queen Victoria,
and many others, had already thought that men in traditional court dress

looked 'so odd'.[203] As an alternative, Poole's, one of the principal court tailors and one of the most famous firms on Savile Row (where at one time it occupied numbers 36–38, with a further building for liveries, and additional premises at 3–5 Old Burlington Street), had in 1839 helped devise a simpler court suit, of black velvet with steel buttons, for men without official positions. If the King was in London, Guards officers were expected to wear frock or morning coat in the street, and white tie and tails to dinner. Members of the royal household, into the 1950s (and in the Lord Chamberlain's office until today), wore stiff collars in the daytime.[204]

The rules reflected the variety of climates and cultures in the British Empire. More than most imperial powers, the British Empire, whose manpower was often overstretched, used uniforms and ceremonies to help instil confidence in its officials, respect in its subjects.[205] As the empire expanded, its uniforms became more elaborate. Thus there were special court uniforms for every official, from the Chief Clerk of the Supreme Court at Shanghai, to the Chief Commissioner of the Dublin Metropolitan Police.[206]

Such was British love of uniforms that by 1876, on their own initiative, British officials in the Indian Civil Service had, on formal occasions, begun to wear civil uniforms resembling third- and fifth-class levee dress in Britain.[207] When, at the end of the century, they finally acquired the right to wear British civil uniforms, rules were defined with manic precision: 'uniform is not obligatory in the case of Assistant Superintendents who are not Assistant Commissioners . . . Officers who are not on the permanent graded list of the Bombay Political Department and who are appointed as Special Political Agents in charge of 1st Class Native States in Bombay when under management, or during a minority, may wear the 3rd class uniform, and those so appointed in charge of 2nd Class States, 5th Class uniform.'[208] In order to reinforce barriers between races, and their own sense of racial supremacy, since 1830 British officials had been forbidden to wear Indian dress on public occasions.[209] By the twentieth century officials of the colonial Civil Service could wear 'the white undress tropical uniform', with the feathered solar topee devised by Poole's, which was one of the principal innovations in British court dress, 'at Court in this country' as well as in the tropics.[210]

As befitted the greatest sea power, British court dress had a naval element. Levee dress was worn by consuls not only at court but also 'on State Occasions abroad; on paying official visits to and receiving official visits from the commanders of His Majesty's ships of war; and at naval courts'. At the same time that Russian, German and Austrian uniforms were becoming more elaborate, the Royal Navy introduced ball dress and mess dress for officers in

1891. As late as the 1930s, 'Gieves's dress indicator,' published by the famous firm of military and naval tailors Gieves and Hawkes, which worked in collaboration with the military and naval authorities, was needed to tell naval officers which form of naval dress to wear on which occasion: ball dress, ceremonial blue undress, mess dress, frock coat dress with epaulettes, modified white dress alternative, tropical mess undress (in white rather than blue) – to name but a few.[211]

'Always', in his son's words, 'exceptionally conservative in his dress', George V restored traditional dress rules after the years in 'khaki' during World War I – perhaps, like Ottoman sultans before him, regarding them as a rampart against political unrest, and compensation for his own increasing powerlessness. Unable to punish his subjects with Ottoman severity, the King compensated by launching diatribes against those, in particular his eldest son, who dressed differently from himself.[212] The King's own clothes, according to his biographer Kenneth Rose, had 'an unobtrusive elegance of style that concealed nature's deficiencies'.[213] A levee under George V in 1923 was described by Chips Channon as 'a gorgeous male sight . . . much preening and red and plumes and pomp and tightly fitting tunics and splendid English faces'.[214]

Unable to decide his ministers' policies, the King could at least decide what they wore. In 1924 the first Labour government in British history adapted with relatively little difficulty to the court dress code. Clearly a believer in the influence of dress on politics, the King ensured that Labour ministers knew they could buy from Moss Bros cheap second-hand versions of levee dress, costing £30, instead of paying £73 15s. 6d. for new full dress versions. He noted: 'In no case do I expect anyone to get more than the Levee coat: full dress is not necessary on account of the expense.'[215] In the end some ministers were allowed to attend levees and other functions in evening dress with breeches.[216] Prevented by a late train from changing into a frock coat and top hat, the Conservative Lord Chancellor Lord Birkenhead once arrived at a cabinet meeting in country clothes. Rebuked by a letter from the King's private secretary, he reacted with fury, pointing out that, although he disliked the King's brown bowler hat, he did not write to the King to tell him so.[217]

At a state ball at Buckingham Palace in May 1924, Chips Channon admired the Labour Prime Minister Ramsay MacDonald, who looked 'very distinguished in his Privy Councillor's full dress uniform . . . green [*sic* for blue] and white and gold . . . giving his arm to the Duchess of Buccleuch, to whom, I hear, he made himself most affable'.[218] MacDonald's view was: 'These braids and uniforms are but part of the official pageantry and as my conscience is not on my back, a gold coat means nothing to me but a form of dress to be worn or rejected as that would be in relation to the rest of one's clothes.'[219] However, he would not have so frequently attended entertainments and official functions at Buckingham Palace if he had not enjoyed wearing the required dress. The people he met there, in particular Lady Londonderry, and the King himself, did help dilute his Labour principles. Outside the court and government, moreover, many were beginning to hate uniforms. Virginia Woolf wrote in *Three Guineas* (1938) that British male uniforms and dressing up with orders and medals were 'ridiculous . . . contemptible'.[220]

If the Labour cabinet adopted the dress code of the British court, India was beginning to defy it. The Indian officials of the British Empire, who were allowed to wear an Indian version of court dress – a blue cloth coat, 'trousers white or white pyjamas', and the 'distinctive national head dress worn on ceremonial occasions'[221] – were less numerous than hostile Indian national-ists. In order to challenge British, and help Indian, clothes industries, from 22 September 1921 Gandhi abandoned the western clothes he had worn in his youth and began to wear a dhoti cap, shirt and loincloth. They were made of Indian cloth, which he wove on his own spinning wheel. Like American nationalists at the end of the eighteenth century, he started a 'homespun movement' to encourage local industry and reduce imports of British cloth, which was sometimes symbolically burnt by his followers. 'Resembling the poorest peasants, he could more easily represent himself as the leader of poor peasants.' As he toured India speaking in favour of independence, non-violence and the homespun movement, he said: 'it is my certain conviction that with every thread that I draw I am spinning the destiny of India.' Dress was as important a political weapon for Gandhi as for Peter the Great. In the end Gandhi's loincloths defeated British uniforms. A chakhra spinning wheel spinning homespun Indian cloth appeared on the flag of the Indian National Congress, as it still does on that of India itself. Indian politicians and officials continue to prefer the tie-less, Indian-made 'Nehru jacket' or *achkan* to the western suit.[222]

If George V was a clothes traditionalist, Edward VIII was the third Prince of Wales, as he later remembered with pride, after the future kings George IV and Edward VII, to be a fashion leader: they were helped to play the part by the large independent income they enjoyed, free of government or parental control, from the revenues of the Duchy of Cornwall.[223] 'As worn by the Prince' became the boast of fortunate West End shops. He later explained his lifelong interest in dress by his circumstances and upbringing: 'My position as

Prince of Wales dictated that I should always be well and suitably dressed for every conceivable occasion . . . in the eye of certain sections of the Press I was . . . more of a clothes-peg than the heir-apparent.'[224] Reflecting the spirit of the age, he helped bring comfort and freedom back to dress.[225] 'All my life, hitherto,' he later remembered, 'I had been fretting against those constrictions of dress which reflected my family's world of rigid social convention. It was my impulse, whenever I found myself alone, to remove my coat, rip off my tie, loosen my collar and roll up my sleeves.' One of his first acts on his accession, as he himself recorded, was to abolish the frock coat, which he had never liked, 'for wear at Court'.[226]

His loss of rank after abdication, however, led to a reversal of principle, from reverse ostention back to ostentation. Winston Churchill wrote to his wife, after dining with the Duke of Windsor in the south of France: 'Red liveries and the little man himself dressed up to the nines in the Balmoral tartan with dagger and jabot etc. When you think that you could hardly get him to put on a black coat and tie when he was Prince of Wales, one sees the change in the point of view.'[227]

Tartan remained a link with his royal past. Moreover, it suited the Duke of Windsor's figure. Like the Kaiser, he had been given his first tartan by Queen Victoria, who wrote in 1898: 'dear little David appeared for the first time in a kilt I gave him, of which he is very proud, and in which he looked charming'.[228] After his abdication, he wore kilts in Balmoral and Royal Stewart tartan, both on his honeymoon in Austria and in the evening in the Moulin de la Tuilerie, his country residence outside Paris.[229] The one costume of his father that the Duke of Windsor kept and had altered (replacing the trouser buttons with a Freudian zip) for himself was a suit in Rothesay hunting tartan. Bought at the Windsor sale in 1987, it is now displayed by Jimmy's Bronx Café in New York as 'the suit of two kings'.[230] The royal passion for tartans continues: some of the Duke of Windsor's kilts were the only possessions chosen after his death, by the present Prince of Wales, as gifts for his sons.[231]

In the nineteenth and twentieth centuries London remained the capital of men's tailoring. The favourite tailor of the future Edward VII, Henry Poole, and his descendants were appointed tailors not only to Queen Victoria (1869) and all subsequent British monarchs (the firm still makes state liveries for Elizabeth II's footmen today),[232] but also to Napoleon III (1858);[233] the King of the Belgians (1869); the Khedive of Egypt (1870); the Emperor of Brazil (1874); the Emperor of Russia (1875); the King of the Hellenes (1877); the King of Italy (1879); the King of Denmark (1893); the Shah of Iran (1906;)[234] the King of Bulgaria (1936 – after making him a tail coat in a day so that he

48 Edward VIII at Windsor, 1936.
Dress as rebellion: in public as well as
private, Edward VIII challenged the court
system in his dress. He banned frockcoats
at court, and was seen without a hat.

could dine that evening at Buckingham Palace); and the Emperor of Ethiopia (1959).[235]

At the Paris Peace Conference in 1919 the Emir Faisal, leader of the Arab revolt, had worn white Hejazi dress in order to strengthen his public impact as an Arab leader.[236] Once he had become king of the newly independent country of Iraq, he adopted modern uniforms with a special head-dress called, after the King, the *faisaliye*. In 1933 he waited for several days at Ostend until his London tailor J. B. Johnson of Savile Row could deliver the embroidered uniform in which he arrived at Victoria Station on 20 June 1933 for his state visit to George V. The tunic of King Faisal resembled that of a British Field Marshal, in white instead of red: his son King Ghazi and grandson King Faisal II on ceremonial occasions wore similar tunics, and a feathered helmet resembling the solar topi of a British colonial governor.[237]

In 1941, in the darkest days of World War II, London tailoring received a tribute from an unexpected source. The Soviet government placed orders for gold braid for uniforms: like courtiers of Louis XIV and Napoleon I, Communists too derived reassurance from embroidery. In 1943, in the interests of 'order and discipline', Soviet uniforms acquired epaulettes and

49 Vandyk, King Faisal I of Iraq in Field-Marshal's uniform in London, June 1933. The King's uniform, embroidered with gold palm leaves, made him look no less regal than George V when he arrived in London for the state visit marking the declaration of full independence for Iraq.

gold braid, which had been discarded to cries of 'Down with the golden shoulder-boards!' after the 1917 revolution. The re-creation of a new officer class, almost as privileged as the Tsarist officer corps, was recorded by George Orwell in his parable on Soviet Communism, *Animal Farm* (written between November 1943 and February 1944). After their revolt against the old ruling class of farmers, the animals on *Animal Farm* at first reject clothes and ribbons. By the end the new ruling class of pigs has not only been given the privilege of wearing green ribbons on Sundays, but is wearing clothes once worn by the farmers themselves.[238]

In his attitude to dress, Stalin showed further elements of monarchical psychology. Hitherto he had often worn a traditional Communist Party tunic and shabby greatcoat. From 1943, newsreels show him in a smart marshal's uniform with a gilded collar. Like Peter the Great and Potemkin, however, he also, at times, wore clothes shabbier than those of his staff – to confirm that he was so powerful that he was above dress rules.[239]

The dress of Stalin's wartime ally Churchill also showed a monarchical mentality. Always dapper, with a preference for silk underwear,[240] like most British statesmen of his day, except A. J. Balfour, he paid considerable

50 Churchill, Truman and Stalin at Potsdam, 2 August 1945.
Churchill wears military uniform since he had been a professional soldier and was Prime
Minister in war-time. Stalin wears a white uniform with gold epaulettes, which had been
abolished in the Russian revolution but which he had recently reinstated.

attention to dress. Since he held so many different ranks and offices, during his
public career Churchill spent large sums at Poole's, on civil, naval and military
uniforms. On his promotion to the post of Home Secretary, his privy
councillor's suit was given 'first class Lace', at a cost of 13 guineas, on 5 July
1910; he wore it to administer the oath to the Prince of Wales at his investiture
at Caernarvon Castle in 1911.[241] However, Churchill's manner towards his
tailors, and dilatoriness in paying bills, were resented. In 1941, after an
especially firm reminder from Poole's, he took his custom to Turnbull and
Asser. The historian of Savile Row records: 'the only element of the trade to
really appreciate him were the repairers of cigar burns.'[242]

In keeping with the century in which he lived, he was the only British Prime
Minister to wear uniform. Formerly a professional soldier in, among other
units, the 4th (Queen's Own) Hussars (1895–9), the Royal Scots Fusiliers
(1915) and Grenadier Guards (1915–16), he no doubt felt justified in wearing
uniform when meeting his rival warlords Roosevelt and Stalin.[243] At Yalta, for
example, he sometimes wore the uniform of a colonel of the Hussars.[244] His
private secretary John Colville thought that Royal Air Force uniform (a
professional pilot, Churchill was honorary Air Commodore of a Hurricane

Squadron) 'suited him well'. He wore it when descending the Champs-Elysées with De Gaulle on 11 November 1944, and planned to do so again when receiving the Médaille militaire at the Invalides in 1947. However, his wife, always more Liberal, urged him not to: 'I would like to persuade you to wear civilian clothes when visiting Paris. To me, Air Force uniform except when worn by air crews is rather bogus. And it is not as an Air-Commodore that you conquered in the War but in your capacity and power as a statesman.' In the end, for this military ceremony, he wore the uniform of the 4th (Queen's Own) Hussars.[245]

Whereas court dress-makers for women have closed since 1939,[246] London today still contains a flourishing world of court tailors for men. Hand and Lock Ltd (www.handembroidery.com), founded in 1767, boasts that they are 'the oldest gold lacemen in the world'. Their laces, cords, wires, purls, filigree (sometimes sewn through rather than on the fabric), epaulettes, sashes and aiguillettes are often made in India, which has kept its traditional embroidery skills better than England. Their principal customers, both at home and abroad, are theatre and film companies, regiments and royal households, especially in two outposts of monarchical splendour, the sultanates of Oman and Brunei.[247]

Founded in 1689, Ede and Ravenscroft has been making coronation and parliament robes for monarchs, peers, knights of orders of chivalry and officers of the Houses of Parliament since the reign of George III. Its business in academic and legal robes is expanding, as colleges and law courts round the world assert their identity through dress. Like most formal tailors, it is looking forward to the next coronation: 'From the Savile Row point of view it can't come soon enough.'[248] Other Savile Row tailors like Gieves and Hawkes, Mortimer and Meyer and Henry Poole still make uniforms for the Household Division and liveries for the royal household.

In the United Kingdom today traditional court dress survives mainly outside the royal palaces: it is worn by some mayors and high sheriffs (who pay about £3,600 for a new velvet court suit and sword); by officials of the Houses of Parliament like the Speaker, clerks, sergeants at arms and ushers; and by judges and barristers.[249] An ominous portent for the future of legal robes, however, was that in 2003, for the first time, the Lord Chancellor did not wear them at the ceremonies marking the opening of the legal year.[250] The last politician to wear civil (privy councillor's) uniform may have been Jeremy Thorpe, in Brussels in 1973, at the signature of the United Kingdom's treaty of accession to the European Union.[251]

In London today court dress is most easily seen in a museum, the Royal Ceremonial Dress Collection, established in 1984 in rooms on the ground floor of Kensington Palace. It contains clothes formerly worn by members of the royal family, many collected by Queen Mary (who also presented historic royal costumes, such as the parliament robes of Queen Victoria, to the Museum of London), and uniforms, court suits and presentation dresses donated by private individuals. Particularly striking are the re-creations of dressing rooms, which show the lengthy preparations, and multiplicity of utensils, once necessary for dressing for court.[252]

The most popular attraction in the collection are the dresses of Diana, Princess of Wales – as much an international fashion leader and idol as Edward VIII had been when Prince of Wales. Between her wedding in 1981 and her death in 1997 she earned fortunes for the British fashion industry and British fashion magazines. Aware of the power of dress, trying to assert her own personality, she departed from royal tradition and wore fashionable and individual clothes. Especially after her divorce, she became victim as well as showcase of the fashion industry, inundated by unsolicited gifts. Versace and Valentino replaced Catherine Walker and Victor Edelstein as her favourite dress-makers. Her personality and style had such popular appeal that in June 1997 an auction for charity of seventy-nine of her dresses realised $5,600,000.[253]

In contrast, Elizabeth II is a traditionalist who, like her father George VI, misses 'no sartorial irregularity, no unusual detail of dress'.[254] Like Edward VII and George V, George VI had been an autocrat in dress. In 1932, as Duke of York, he had written a four-page letter to the Secretary of State for Air on the use of swords, on ceremonial occasions, by officers of the Royal Air Force. Just before his death in 1952, 'after much careful thought and trying out various ideas', George VI redesigned the shape of the trousers to be worn with the Order of the Garter in the evening, and devoted his last letter to the subject.[255]

Elizabeth II also, when possible, prefers formal dress on those around her. Her own clothes, frequently criticised, are intended to present a striking but comforting image. She sees preparatory drawings herself. Her dress-maker in the 1950s and 1960s, Norman Hartnell, said 'we do not dress the Queen; she orders clothes from us.'[256] Her principal dress blunder was caused by under-dressing. At the procession of the 'Honours of Scotland' in Saint Giles's Cathedral, Edinburgh, on 24 June 1953, while Scottish dignitaries wore splendid traditional robes, the Queen wore day dress with a handbag. Part of Establishment Scotland was outraged.[257]

Her preference for choosing military and naval officers as household officials solves the problem caused by the disappearance, since 1939, of civil uniform and court dress. On formal occasions most of her court officials –

unless they have inherited their father's civil uniform – wear military uniform – 'number I dress': full dress (except at State Openings of Parliament) seems 'rather incongruous'.[258] Full evening dress of white tie and tails is still worn by the Queen's guests, including Labour cabinet ministers, at state banquets. On formal occasions, such as the Queen Mother's funeral, the Queen's grandsons wear morning coats.

Only in June 2003, and only for reasons of economy, was there a relaxation of the rule requiring newly appointed heads of diplomatic missions to wear morning coats to their audience with the Queen in Buckingham Palace.[259] By then, however, morning coats at royal investitures and garden parties were becoming rarer. Today Lieutenant-Colonel Sir Malcolm Ross, an officer in the Scots Guards and Comptroller in the Lord Chamberlain's Office, advises both the royal family and members of the public on what to wear on formal occasions. Like members of the royal family, he believes both in the 'crucial importance' of dress and in the necessity of flexibility: 'We cannot dictate what people wear when they come to events here . . . they don't get instructions, just guidance . . . We are in a transitional stage. The Queen's feeling is that people should not go to unnecessary expense.' In London he usually wears a stiff collar to work.

Given the 'normalisation' of dress rules at Buckingham Palace, the principal impact of the court on the London dress trade comes from the money spent on buying or hiring formal clothes for the annual race meeting at Ascot near Windsor, founded by Queen Anne in 1711.[260] Introduced in 1968, the lounge suit was dropped two years later, since so few men wanted to wear it (a plan in 1919 to encourage officers to wear uniform at Ascot had been equally unsuccessful).[261] Rules for people who have bought tickets to the Royal Enclosure remain the following:

> Ladies are asked to wear formal day dress with a hat to cover the crown of the head. Trouser suits are permitted. Gentlemen are reminded that black or grey morning dress with top hat is required. Service dress may be worn. Overseas visitors are welcome to wear the national dress of their country. Those not complying with the dress code will be asked to leave the Royal Enclosure.

The rules make 'Royal Ascot' unlike any other occasion in the world. It is at once a race meeting, an occasion for status reassurance, and the last large-scale court function with strict dress rules. They are enforced on people entering the Royal Enclosure by eagle-eyed gentlemen at the gates, who oblige rule-breakers either to leave or to buy the missing items on the spot. As at French royal weddings before 1789, spectators in the adjoining grandstand often imitate the dress worn in the Royal Enclosure.[262] On 19 June 2002, during her Golden Jubilee year, the Queen ordered an Ascot official to ask a TV cameraman, who was not wearing a tail coat and a top hat, to leave the paddock where she was inspecting horses: the dress code enforced in the Royal Enclosure is automatically extended to the paddock when the Queen enters it.[263]

In the limited spheres available to modern royalty, valets can play a role as controversial as dressers in the days of Queen Anne and Lady Masham. In 1983 Michael Fawcett entered the Prince of Wales's service as one of his valets, handing him shirts and ties, with control of the Prince's dressing room (the Prince's uniforms are the domain of an orderly from the Welsh Guards). Never complaining if he had to get up early in the morning, he soon gained both the trust and intimacy of the Prince and the loathing of the rest of the Prince's household. With the title of 'The Personal Assistant to The Prince of Wales', he had a princely salary, special responsibility for organising royal entertainments through his own company Premier Mode Events, and a house in Hampton, bought for him by his master. Money, rather than politics, brought him to public notice. His personal tastes, and profits from purchases of clothes and jewels for the Prince, and disposal of the Prince's gifts, became the subject of intense criticism in the press and the royal household. In March 2003 he was forced to resign (his third offer of resignation). But the resignation is a facade. Michael Fawcett continues to see the Prince as before.[264]

If Britain is a bastion of formal dress, the Middle East is a stronghold of national dress. At first the British Empire had helped spread western dress in the region. Across barriers of race, religion and culture, monarchs spoke the same language of clothes. In Muscat, wrote a British consul, Sir Percy Sykes, 'My uniform delighted the Sultan so much that he asked how many of the officers of the Queen Empress wore such a uniform and on being told "many hundreds", said "What a happy sovereign she must be" with such feeling that we all laughed.'[265]

Other monarchies in Asia had already adopted western dress. As part of the reforms which would make Japan a great power, in 1871 the Emperor of Japan began to wear, and impose on officials, European-style tail coats or uniforms. Pride was the motive: to be accepted as an equal by, and win the respect of, European powers and the United States. Thus when one Japanese asked for the Emperor to wear traditional dress, the Minister of the Imperial Household shouted: 'Are you still ignorant of the world situation?'[266] Traditional Japanese court dress, in the Emperor's opinion, 'gave the impression of weakness'. Thenceforth, at public ceremonies, the Emperor and princes of Japan generally wore, and were painted or photographed in, military uniforms, like the European monarchs on whom they modelled themselves.[267]

The new dress code helped the Japanese Empire to modernise itself. In contrast, the Chinese Empire remained trapped in the past. Loyal to the elaborate dress regulations promulgated in 1759, which blended traditional Chinese dress with elements from Manchu culture, on formal occasions the Emperor of China, like his ancestors, wore bright yellow and blue silk robes embroidered with dragons and other symbols of imperial authority. The ceremonial dress of the nine ranks of court officials varied according to season and occasion.[268] There were five major categories: formal court dress, semi-formal festive dress, informal dress, travelling dress and wet weather dress.[269] The Chinese Empire was defeated by Japan in 1898 and overthrown by revolution in 1911.

Such was the power of the British Empire that, in addition to Japan, it influenced the dress of two other monarchies, Afghanistan and Persia. Emir Abdur Rahman of Afghanistan, who reigned from 1880 to 1901, saw dress westernisation as indispensable to his country's unification and modernisation. Perhaps because Afghanistan was never annexed or colonised, its rulers felt less reluctant than Indian rajahs to introduce western clothes and uniforms: as in Japan, western dress was a sign of power and modernity rather than servility. Abdur Rahman employed hundreds of Indian tailors to make tight trousers to replace baggy trousers, which he considered 'made people lazy and unable to move without dragging along yards and yards of stuff hanging behind them'. After a visit to the Viceroy of India in 1885, he also employed an English tailor called Mr Walter, who made modern uniforms for the court and army, and in Kabul in 1892–3 published a tailoring manual with cutting patterns. In the words of the Emir, it contained 'all the designs and drawings of the various ways of cutting and sewing the suits and uniforms used in England'. He wrote with delight: 'All the civil and military officials of my Government can easily be distinguished and the office or rank of each is indicated by his uniform . . . A book especially treating of the rules and regulations attaching to the various uniforms' was used to help seat the officials at the durbar.'[270]

His son Habibullah, who ascended the throne in 1901, also adopted western dress. His attitudes show how greatly public dress policy can differ from personal preferences. A traveller in 1906 wrote: 'While nothing affords

51 Khalillullah Enayat Seraj, Hajera ukht us-Seraj, daughter of the Emir Abdur Rahman, with her husband Mohammed Yunus, commander of the household troops, 1915.
Already members of the Afghan royal family are at ease wearing western dress.

Habibullah so much pleasure as showing himself in European costume in public, nothing will induce him to wear Western clothes once the doors of his palace have closed and he can recline at his ease amid well-placed cushions.' On state occasions he wore a splendid scarlet and gold military uniform, like that of British field marshals. He also had a regulation court costume for men consisting of a black cloth coat, vest and trousers, white shirt and black tie, all English-cut to a prescribed pattern. Afghan women of the élite wore the latest fashions from Europe in their homes: Afghan princes were photographed in Highland kilts or Napoleonic uniforms.[271]

One reason for this interest in western dress was to try to lessen differences between the many rival groups in Afghanistan – Sunni, Shiah, Uzbek, Tajik and others.[272] After 1919 the dress reforms of King Amanallah, Habibullah's son, were even more radical. In a manner reminiscent of Peter the Great, fines were levied on those who did not wear western dress, in the new court suburb of Paghman in the hills above Kabul and in certain sections of Kabul itself. In 1928 after a tour of Europe, King Amanullah and his wife Queen Soraya went further. The Queen appeared in public wearing only a short diaphanous veil tacked to the brim of her stylish cloche hat – and a raised hemline: senior

52 Deputies at the Loya Jirgah, Paghman, near Kabul, 2 September 1928.
Dress as failed transformation: King Amanallah and Queen Soraya, at the top of the race-
stand in western dress, are surrounded by Afghans who have just been compelled by the
King, for the first time in their lives, to wear western dress. Such compulsory
westernisation was one reason, with the Queen's daring modern dress, for the King's
overthrow the following year.

officials' wives were also compelled to unveil and wear western dress. The King
commanded that delegates to a 700-strong Great Parliamentary Council wear
black frock coats, western trousers and felt fedora hats instead of ethnic dress
and turbans. Three months later the first revolts broke out. Among the rebels'
demands were that insistence on western dress be dropped and bobbed hair
for women forbidden. By May 1929, in part because of their flouting of Afghan
dress traditions, King Amanallah and Queen Soraya had left the country. No
subsequent Afghan government attempted to make western dress compulsory. Indeed on his visit to Washington in January 2002, and on many
subsequent occasions, the Afghan Prime Minister Hamid Karzai wore a self-
designed Afghan cloak, to try to assert his Afghan identity.[273]

At the same time as King Amanallah, Reza Shah, the first of the Pahlavi
rulers of Persia, also imposed new dress rules. Persian monarchs and courtiers
had begun to wear modern uniforms in the reign of Mohammed Shah
(1834–48). In 1926 Lady Loraine, the wife of the British ambassador, helped
design new, lavishly embroidered, court uniforms in time for Reza Shah's
coronation as Shah of Iran: they were worn on formal occasions until the
revolution of 1978–9.[274] In March 1929 a law imposed western dress and the

53 The Crown Prince of Iran, later Mohammed Reza Shah, with ministers and court officials at Gulestan Palace in Tehran, 1936.
The civil uniform, devised in 1925, continued to be worn until the overthrow of the monarchy in 1979.

peaked 'Pahlavi hat' on all officials except religious clerics. Punishment for non-observance included fines and imprisonment. Article 1 stated: 'All Iranian subjects who are not required to wear special clothing in conformity with service in the government shall wear uniform clothing . . . and all government employees whether civil or judicial shall, when on government duty, wear civil or judicial clothing as officially prescribed and at other times they shall wear the uniform attire.'[275]

As in the case of Japan, pride was the principal motive: to use dress to make Iran look Europe's equal. When the Foreign Minister was about to receive foreign diplomats, the Shah said with approval: 'You look like one of them and their equal and not like a subordinate.' Reza Shah was also, like the Kings of Afghanistan, hoping to use dress to promote modernisation and national unification: 'I am determined to have all Iranians wearing the same clothes, since when Shirazis, Tabrizis and all others no longer wear different costumes there will be no reason for differences among them.'[276] Despite bitter opposition from religious authorities, and Iranian women themselves, from 1 February 1936 until Reza Shah's fall in September 1941 the chador or enveloping black cloak for women was also banned.[277]

Further westernisation of dress had also been imposed in Turkey. Through-out the war of 1919–22 with Greece in Anatolia, the fez had remained a symbol of Turkish nationalism. The progress of the war could be judged by the number of fezzes worn on the streets of Constantinople. When Greece seemed triumphant, Ottoman Christians discarded the fez and bought hats: some even stamped on their fez or tore the fez off others' heads.[278] When Turkish forces began to fight back, Christians put on the fez again. The run on hats was over.[279]

Ottoman uniforms disappeared after Mustafa Kemal's expulsion of the dynasty in 1924. The veil was discouraged, although not, as in Iran, explicitly forbidden, and headscarves were banned in public places. Within a few years, so strong was the pressure of the Turkish state, that it was hard to find one veiled woman in Istanbul.

Since his childhood in Salonica, Mustafa Kemal had aspired to look like a European officer, and had derived a feeling of strength and equality with the West from wearing smart western-style uniforms.[280] By the 'Law concerning the wearing of hats' of 25 November 1925, the fez, which Kemal would call 'an emblem of ignorance, negligence, fanaticism and hatred of progress', was outlawed, as the turban had been a hundred years earlier: to wear it is still in theory a criminal offence. Like the Emperors of Japan and Iran, Kemal believed that hats, which were made compulsory for civil servants, and 'civilised international dress' would make Turks 'civilised people from every point of view' and enable Turkey to take its 'rightful place in the family of nations'. Overnight Istanbul acquired thousands of black and brown hats.[281]

In the provinces, the hat was detested as a symbol of Christianity and, worse, apostasy. There were disturbances and executions.[282] Outside Turkey, however, the fez survived as part of the official dress of Egypt, under Kings Fouad [283] and Farouk, until shortly after the military coup of 1952. As the last item of dress not to be westernised, it remained a symbol of nationalism in Syria and Lebanon until the 1960s:[284] the last public figure to wear the fez was a Prime Minister of Lebanon, Tahieddine al-Solh, in 1972–5. To this day it continues to be worn by men of the older generation in former Ottoman provinces such as Bosnia, Kosovo and Lebanon: a symbol of the Ottoman Empire which has outlasted the empire itself. Thus Kemal's suppression of the fez had been an exercise in totalitarianism as well as modernisation. Wearing the fez did not make Bosnians or Lebanese more or less modern than hat-wearing Turks. Kemal was using the proscription of the fez, and the imposition of the hat, which made prostration in prayer more difficult, in order to signal his government's severance of modern Turkey from every aspect of its Ottoman heritage, including Islam.

Outside the Middle East national dress is disappearing in accordance with Osman Hamdy Bey's prophecy in 1873: 'Day by day clothing tends to become more uniform across the world and to efface not only all distinctions between diverse classes of society but also those between different nations which seemed otherwise to be permanently separated by natural and moral barriers.'[285] In most countries the use of national dress is restricted to special occasions like national days, election days, or the opening ceremony of the Olympic Games.[286]

In the Gulf and Saudi Arabia, however, perhaps because those countries feel their identities threatened by the speed of their modernisation, the power of their neighbours and the number of foreign immigrants in their midst, national dress of coloured keffiyeh and white dishdasha is almost universally worn by local men. In Saudi Arabia and Oman government officials are obliged to wear national dress to their offices. In these vulnerable countries it has become a symbol of identity and cohesion, and gives what Isak Dinesen called 'dignity and expressiveness' to figures who, in other dress, frequently lack both.[287] Moreover, it suits the local climate, and the demands of the Prophet Muhammad for Muslims to wear white. Some consider, however, that as well as strengthening cohesion in the states of the Arabian peninsula, national dress helps their inhabitants live in a comfortable and deferential cocoon, protected from contact and competition with foreigners. National dress also has a political function. Photographs of Saddam Hussein in Kurdish or Bedouin dress,[288] or Omar al-Bashir of Sudan, shown on billboards in July 2003 wearing the dress of southern Sudan over his military uniform (the only known example of a head of state simultaneously wearing military uniform and national dress), emphasised their control of, or desire to please, rebellious parts of their country.[289]

The fall of the Shah of Iran in 1979, and revulsion at his 'westoxication' and love of western dress, have led to one of the few cases of dress de-westernistion. Standard male dress in Iran is now the buttoned-down, tieless shirt: for all women over the age of twelve, despite initial protests in the cities, the *manto*, or buttoned-down coat, always in a neutral colour, and a headscarf covering most of the hair, are now compulsory. Rules continue to be enforced even more strictly than, in the opposite direction, they had been under Reza Shah. Non-compliance means a year in prison.[290] In other parts of the Muslim world, such as Egypt, Syria and Lebanon, influenced by their own and foreign Islamic movements, by a search for identity, and by resentment of western hegemony, there has been a de-westernisation of female dress. Pious 'Muslim' dress codes of headscarf and chador, or cloak, have spread since the early

54 The Emperor and Empress of Iran, *c.* 1975.
Their rulers' western-style dress dismayed some Iranians. The Empress's wardrobe is now on display in Niavaran palace, guarded by black-robed 'Daughters of the Revolution'.

1980s, even among women whose mothers, as old films on television daily remind them, wore the latest western fashions.[291] The modern chador is generally more unrelievedly black, and all-enveloping, than in the past: it is the product of a reinvented, rather than a continuous, tradition.

The power of dress to touch a nerve, as in Versailles in 1789 or Berlin in 1918, is confirmed by the emergence of the Islamic headscarf as a cutting edge of conflict between Muslim fundamentalists and secular governments in Turkey, France and Germany. A mirror image of the Islamic Republic of Iran, those governments try to ban it in the schoolroom – on teachers as well as pupils – on the grounds that it threatens 'national identity', 'the principles of the Turkish Republic stated in the constitution' or 'the concept of the [French] republic'. Students have been expelled from school, and deputies from the Turkish parliament, for wearing the offending item. On 29 October 2003 the President of Turkey refused to invite to his Republic Day reception ministers' and deputies' scarf-wearing wives. Renewing the anti-religious traditions of the First and Third Republics, President Chirac has called wearing headscarfs, and other religious signs like Jewish skull-caps and large crosses (eventually bandanas and beards as well), 'aggressive', a threat both to the future and to the soul of the French republic. In February 2004 the National Assembly voted by a crushing majority to reassert the ban in state schools on 'the wearing of signs or clothes which conspicuously display a a pupil's religious affiliations': scarves, large crosses, skull-caps, turbans.[292] Since Christians, if they wear religious signs, wear small crosses, their feelings are protected.

For some Muslims, however, the compulsory removal of the headscarf is more aggressive than its adoption. Many women say the headscarf is part of their identity as well as their religion: it is 'my arm, my foot', according to one Algerian in France. Perhaps 70 per cent of Turkish women and 90 per cent of Syrian women now wear a headscarf. One Muslim woman spoke for millions when she wrote:

> We do not wear scarves in order to proselytise our religion, nor do we wear them because we are forced to by our husbands, fathers, uncles, other relatives or religious leaders. We have been ordered, by none other than God, to cover our heads. This is a commandment. We the hundreds of millions of headscarf wearing Muslim women and girls in France and world wide would no more remove our scarves in public than we would worship any other than god, kill, commit adultery, steal, dishonour our father or mother or commit other sins.[293]

Outside the Islamic world, however, dress globalisation continues. The empire of global capitalism has replaced state service, status reassurance and national identity as the dominant ethos in dress. Uniforms for state employees such as postmen, and for schoolchildren, are being abandoned, while those for employees of international companies like McDonald's and Carrefour are spreading. Fashion comes from the company and the street, not the court or the couturier. Since most people dress alike, clothes mask, rather than advertise, disparities of wealth. The last private individual to have servants in livery on a regular basis, until 1990, was probably the Prince of Thurn und Taxis, in his palace in Regensburg.[294] The importance of dress as an expression of power and control, rather than status and wealth, is suggested by the reluctance of western politicians, on normal public occasions, to be seen wearing anything but a suit and tie.

Among the young, dress globalisation is growing stronger: even those who reject western food or music wear western clothes. Indians might have seemed likely to retain national dress, due to the example of Mahatma Gandhi, concern for the survival of traditional Indian textile manufacture employing around fifteen million people, and the rise of Hindu nationalism. In 2004, however, among the young and in cities, 90 per cent of Indian men and a growing proportion of young women, outside the home, wear western dress. At his funeral on 25 February 1997 the Chinese leader Deng Xiaoping lay in state wearing a modified form of the old Sun Yat-sen suit – still the preferred dress for Communist veterans. The new Communist élite, however, were all wearing western suits. For most Chinese, western dress is now 'The Way'.[295]

Despite government opposition to 'improper dress', western suits and American baseball caps are reappearing even in Tehran, capital of the Islamic Republic of Iran. Since the fall of the Taliban they have also reappeared in Kabul. Giving interviews in 2001, Osama bin Laden, the most anti-western of Muslims, wore a white robe and head-dress. Inspired by the teachings of the Prophet Muhammad, his dress is intended to recall the purity of the early years of Islam. However, Osama bin Laden has also worn, with Islamic dress, an American combat jacket and watch. Even in an 'ideal' Islamic emirate, the empire of global capitalism is inescapable.

55 Ossama bin Laden, Autumn 2001.
Seeking to create an Islamic emirate in Afghanistan, Ossama bin Laden wears the white Islamic dress of the Wahhabis of his native Saudi Arabia; over it he wears an American combat jacket, thereby suggesting both his determination to pursue a 'holy war', and the power of the empire he is fighting.

Notes

Unless otherwise stated all books in English are published in London, all books in French in Paris.

Epigraph

1 Alma Söderhjelm, ed., *Marie-Antoinette et Barnave. Correspondance secrète*, 1934, pp. 199, 195.
2 Richard Cobb, *Still Life. Scenes from a Tunbridge Wells Childhood*, 1983, p. 18.

Introduction: The Power of Clothes

1 I am grateful for this reference to Michael Voggenauer and Brigid Keenan.
2 Honoré de Balzac, *Traité de la vie élégante* (1830), 1998 edn, p. x.
3 Carole Collier Frick, *Dressing Renaissance Florence. Families, Fortunes and Fine Clothing*, Baltimore, 2002, p. 1.
4 Papendiek, Charlotte Louisa Henrietta, Mrs, *Court and Private Life in the Time of Queen Charlotte: Being the Journals of Mrs Papendiek, Assistant-keeper of the Wardrobe and Reader to Her Majesty*, ed. Mrs Vernon Delves Broughton, 2 vols, 1887, I, 219.
5 Giles Waterfield and Anne French, eds, *Below Stairs. 400 Years of Servants' Portraits*, 2003, p. 103.
6 Such as James Boswell: see Aileen Ribeiro, *The Art of Dress. Fashion in England and France 1750 to 1820*, New Haven and London, 1995, p. 29.
7 Daniel Roche, *The Culture of Clothing. Dress and Fashion in the Ancien Régime*, 1994, p. 186; for monarchs' concern with courtiers' dress, see e.g. R. O. Buchholz, *The Augustan Court, Queen Anne and the Decline of Court Culture*, Stanford, 1993, p. 203; and Queen Victoria's diary entry for 14 June 1838 recording her request to Lord Melbourne: 'if he did not dislike it, I should be so very happy if he would wear the Windsor uniform when he came down to Windsor'. It was a sign that she hoped he 'would often be at Windsor': Viscount Esher, ed., *The Girlhood of Queen Victoria*, 2 vols, 1912, I, 351, 14 June 1838, II, 65, 4 November 1838.
8 Lord Glenbervie, *Diaries*, 2 vols, 1928, I, 39, 15 January 1794.
9 Robert G. L. Waite, *Vanguard of Nazism. The Freecorps Movement in Postwar Germany 1918–1923*, Cambridge, Mass., 1952, pp. 8–9.
10 This letter was approvingly quoted, a hundred years later, by the recipient's grandson, the Duke of Windsor, in a work that analyses dress at some length: *A Family Album*, 1960, pp. 11–12.

11 See e.g. the references in Dudley Ryder's *Diary*, n. 17 below; and in Thomas Wentworth, *The Wentworth Papers 1705–1739*, ed. James J. Cartwright, 1883, pp. 522, 540, letters of Lady Strafford, May 1736, 'We are my dearest just come from Court where there was really a great deal of Finery'; 2 January 1739, 'There was a vast crowd at court yesterday and every body in their best cloths'.

12 Samuel Pepys, *Diary*, ed. Robert Latham and William Matthews, 11 vols, 2000–03, II, 81–2, 22 April 1661.

13 Jonathan Swift, *Journal to Stella*, 1923 edn, p. 425, 6 February 1713.

14 John M. Beattie, *The English Court in the Reign of George I*, 1967, p. 208.

15 John Evelyn, *Diary*, ed. John Bowle, 1985, p. 396, 20 January 1695, cf. 5 March 1695 re 'never so universal a mourning' at the Queen's funeral.

16 R. O. Buchholz, 'Going to Court in 1700', *The Court Historian*, V, 3 (December 2000), p. 193; Papendiek, *Court and Private Life*, I, 63.

17 Dudley Ryder, *Diary*, 1939, p. 66, 1 August 1715, cf. pp. 76, 356, 15 August 1715, 30 October 1716.

18 See e.g. Beattie, *English Court*, p. 206; Wentworth, *Wentworth Papers*, p. 262, Lady Strafford's letter of 8 February 1712, re Lady Arundell who 'could not be as fine as I and goe to Court on the Birth'.

19 Rosalind K. Marshall, *The Days of Duchess Anne*, 1973, p. 86.

20 Pepys, *Diary*, I, 299 n.

21 Ryder, *Diary*, pp. 299, 310, 18, 30 August 1716.

22 Duc de Croÿ, *Journal inédit*, 4 vols, 1906–7, II, 399, May 1770.

23 M. Georgi, *Description de la ville de Saint Petersbourg et de ses environs*, St Petersburg, 1793, p. 128.

24 Wentworth, *Wentworth Papers*, p. 262, Lady Strafford, 8 February 1712, 'the Queen told me I was very fine and my cloths was very handsom'; 12 February, 'the Duchess of Summerset told me a Sonday that noe Body was so fine of the Birthday as I'.

25 See e.g. Anne Hollander, *Seeing through Clothes*, New York, 1980 edn, pp. 257–8.

26 'Solomon in all his glory': a synonym for royal magnificence; Matthew 6: 28–9.

27 Thomas Patrick Hughes, *A Dictionary of Islam*, Lahore, 1885, p. 92.

28 Philippe de Commynes, *Mémoires*, 2001 edn, p. 192.

29 Baldassare Castiglione, *The Book of the Courtier*, 2000, pp. 97 and 99.

Chapter 1: Splendour

1 John Harvey, *Men in Black*, 1995, pp. 80–81.

2 Diana de Marly, *Louis XIV and Versailles*, 1987, p. 69; cf. for an example of this black costume the portrait of the Count-Duke of Olivares by Velázquez (*c.* 1625–6) at the Hispanic Society of America, New York. Mme de Motteville (*Mémoires . . . sur Anne d'Autriche et sa cour*, 4 vols, 1855), IV, 214, states that at the marriage Philip IV 'avait un habit noir et nulles pierreries'; but Mlle de Montpensier in her *Mémoires* (4 vols, 1859), III, 459, states: 'le roi avait un habit gris avec de la broderie d'argent, un diamant en table qui troussait son chapeau d'où pendait une perle en poire.'

3 De Marly, *Louis XIV*, p. 23.

4 Already the French nobles' embroidered clothes and hats, during the entry of the embassy of the maréchal de Gramont into Madrid in October 1659, had astonished Spanish spectators; Spanish nobles, in contrast, were dressed 'fort simplement': Motteville, *Mémoires*, IV, 169–72, letter from her brother, Madrid, 21 October 1659; for a similar style clash at the English court, see Malcolm Smuts,

Court Culture and the Origins of a Royalist Tradition in Early Stuart England, Philadelphia, 1987, p. 104.

5 Motteville, *Mémoires*, IV, 225–6; cf. John Evelyn on the King returning from the Paris Parlement in 1651, quoted in De Marly, *Louis XIV*, p. 21: 'in a suit so covered with rich embroidery that one could perceive nothing of the stuff under it'.

6 Roche, *Culture of Clothing*, p. 368.

7 Primi Visconti, *Mémoires sur la cour de Louis XIV 1673–1681*, 1988 edn, p. 12 and n.

8 Philippe Perrot, *Le Luxe. Une richesse vestimentaire entre faste et confort XVIII–XIX siècles*, 1995, pp. 54–5, 69.

9 Musée des Beaux-Arts, *À la gloire du roi. Van der Meulen*, Dijon, 1998, pp. 106–8; Daniel Roche, ed., *Voitures, chevaux et attelages du XVIe au XIXe siècle*, 2000, pp. 295–307.

10 De Marly, *Louis XIV*, pp. 36–7.

11 Madame de Sévigné, *Lettres*, 1891 edn, p. 447, 17 January 1680; duchesse d'Orléans, *Lettres de la Princesse Palatine 1672–1722*, 1985, p. 57, duchesse d'Orléans to duchesse de Hanovre, 1 November 1679; Visconti, *Mémoires*, p. 107.

12 Duc de Saint-Simon, *Mémoires*, Pléiade edn, 8 vols, 1959, II, 527, 566; III, 112; V, 570; Aileen Ribeiro, *Fashion in the French Revolution*, 1988, p. 27; idem, *Dress in Eighteenth-Century Europe*, 2000 edn, p. 186; de Marly, *Louis XIV*, pp. 67, 89; d'Orléans, *Lettres de la Princesse Palatine*, pp. 321, 522, letters to Raugrave Louise, 9 August 1702, 24 October 1715.

13 Roche, *Culture of Clothing*, p. 123.

14 Saint-Simon, *Mémoires*, III, 527.

15 De Marly, *Louis XIV*, p. 64.

16 Ribeiro, *Fashion in the French Revolution*, p. 27.

17 Roche, *Culture of Clothing*, pp. 95, 326.

18 Cf. E.-J.-F. Barbier, *Journal d'un avocat de Paris*, 4 vols, Clermont-Ferrand, 2002–4, I, 177, 8 March 1722: 'M. le Régent a trouvé le secret de faire endetter les gens de cour car toutes les femmes étaient superbes en robes de cour et pleines de diamants.'

19 Marquis d'Argenson, *Journal*, Clermont-Ferrand, 2002– , II, 72, 209, 211, 23 February, 27 August 1739; Barbier, *Journal d'un avocat de Paris*, III, 328, December 1751; cf. Papillon de La Ferté, *Journal des menus-plaisirs du roi*, 2002 edn, p. 41, 28 January 1763: 'le bal de lundi a été des plus magnifiques . . . J'ai vu, mardi, Madame de Pompadour qui m'a témoigné sa satisfaction sur les arrangements de la salle de bal et de la beauté des habits.' Madame de Pompadour herself supplied the cloth for the purple and gold *uniforme de Bellevue* for guests at her private château there: Duc de Luynes, *Mémoires . . . sur la cour de Louis XV*, 15 vols, 1860–65, X, 381, 25 November 1750.

20 Such as the chamberers, or keepers of the robes, who dressed the Queen of England; cf. Jeroen Duindam, *Vienna and Versailles. The Courts of Europe's Dynastic Rivals 1550–1780*, Cambridge, 2003, p. 157.

21 Waterfield and French, *Below Stairs*, p. 140. However, as late as the reign of George III, on 21 July 1761, 'Ld. Huntingdon, Groom of the Stole, and Ld. Ashburnham, Lord in Waiting to the King, had great altercation on the subject of giving the King his shirt': Elizabeth, Duchess of Northumberland, *The Diaries of a Duchess*, 1926, p. 27.

22 Quoted in Nicolas Le Roux, 'La Cour dans l'espace du palais: l'exemple de Henri

III', in Marie-France Auzepy and Joel Cornette, eds, *Palais et pouvoir. De Constantinople à Versailles*, 2003, p. 246; cf. p. 264 for similar rules promulgated by Henri III on 10 September 1574.

23 Monique Châtenet, *La Cour de France au XVIe siècle. Vie sociale et architecture*, 2002, pp. 113–15.

24 De Marly, *Louis XIV*, p. 38; abbé de Choisy, *Mémoires*, 1966 edn, p. 215; Jean-François Solnon, *La Cour de France*, 1987, pp. 321–7. For a recent description see Béatrix Saule, *Versailles triomphant. Une journée de Louis XIV*, 1996, pp. 32–45, 180–82.

25 Visconti, *Mémoires*, p. 61; cf. a letter of 1658 describing this ceremony in *The Court Historian*, VII, 2 (December 2002), p. 200.

26 Jean-Richard Pierrette, ed., *Graveurs français de la seconde moitié du XVIIIe siècle*, 1985, pp. 71–3, showing prints of *la petite toilette* and *la grande toilette*; re Choiseul, the author disagrees with F. J. Watson, 'The Choiseul Box', in A. Kenneth Snowman, ed., *Eighteenth Century Gold Boxes of Europe*, 1966, p. 151. The cardinal de Fleury also saw courtiers at his *petit lever*: D'Argenson, *Journal*, III, 47, 31 December 1739; Ribeiro, *Dress*, p. 180.

27 Emmanuel de Waresquiel, *Talleyrand ou le prince immobile*, 2003, pp. 287, 348, 367, 442, 450, 512–13, 591.

28 Leonhard Horowski, '"Such a Great Advantage for my Son": Office-holding and Career Mechanisms at the Court of France 1661–1789', *The Court Historian*, VIII, 2 (December 2003), p. 133.

29 De Marly, *Louis XIV*, pp. 136–7.

30 William R. Newton, *L'Espace du roi. La cour de France au château de Versailles*, 2000, pp. 140–41.

31 Daniel de Cosnac, *Mémoires*, 2 vols, 1852, II, 29.

32 Duc de La Rochefoucauld, *Oeuvres complètes*, 1964 edn, p. 606, letter to the Marquise de Sablé, n.d. (1660); for similar views a hundred years later, see Dr Johnson to Boswell: 'Fine clothes are good only as they supply the want of other means of procuring respect': James Boswell, *The Life of Dr Johnson*, 4 vols, 1964 edn, II, 475, 27 March 1776.

33 Wentworth, *Wentworth Papers*, p. 317, letter of 6 February 1713.

34 Duc de Saint-Simon, *Mémoires*, 22 vols, ed. MM. Cheruel and Regnier, X, 105, 119.

35 Choisy, *Mémoires*, p. 40.

36 Marquis de Dangeau, *Journal*, Clermont-Ferrand, 2002– , III, 39, 25 March 1688; Saint-Simon, *Mémoires*, Pléiade edn, I, 308, 425; V, 49.

37 J. D. de La Rochefoucauld, C. Wolikow and G. Ikni, *Le Duc de La Rochefoucauld-Liancourt 1747–1827*, 1980, p. 49; Saint-Simon, *Mémoires*, ed. Cheruel and Regnier, X, 120–21, 124.

38 Saint-Simon, *Mémoires*, Pléiade edn, I, 441.

39 D'Orléans, *Lettres de la Princesse Palatine*, pp. 216–17, letter of 8 December 1697.

40 N. B. Harte, 'State Control of Dress and Social Change in Pre-Industrial England', in D. C. Coleman and A. H. John, eds, *Trade, Government and Economy in Pre-Industrial England*, 1976, p. 134.

41 Alan Hunt, *Governance of the Consuming Passions. A History of Sumptuary Laws*, 1996, *passim* esp. pp. 29–33; Perrot, *Le Luxe*, p. 63; Roche, *Culture of Clothing*, pp. 91, 100; cf. Alison Lurie, *The Language of Clothes*, 1982, p. 116.

42 Musée de l'Histoire de France, Versailles (MV) 5638, reproduced in Saule,

Versailles triomphant, pp. 84–5; cf. the picture in the same museum by Michel-Barthélemy Ollivier of *Le Thé à l'anglaise* in the Paris residence of the prince de Conti in 1766, where among the courtiers in their finery, Président Hénault alone wears black. Both Colbert and Calonne wear a version of the Order of the Saint Esprit sewn on their cloak, which showed that they were merely officers, rather than knights, of the Order.

43　Chevalier d'Arvieux, *Mémoires*, 6 vols, 1735, IV, 244.

44　On Paris, see Roche, *Culture of Clothing*, pp. 279, 287; on France as a whole, Henriette Vanier, *La Mode et ses métiers: frivolités et luttes des classes*, 1960, p. 34.

45　Anne Kraatz, *Lace: History and Fashion*, 1989, pp. 45, 46, 50; Louis XIV, *Mémoires*, ed. Jean Longnon, 2001 edn, p. 185.

46　Madame de Sévigné, *Lettres*, p. 364, Sévigné to Madame de Grignan, 29 July 1676.

47　Dangeau, *Journal*, II, 225 and n., 18 November 1687.

48　E. Pariset, *Histoire de la fabrique lyonnaise. Étude sur le régime social et économique de l'industrie de la soie à Lyon depuis le XVIe siècle*, Lyon, 1901, *passim*.

49　De Marly, *Louis XIV*, pp. 51, 53–4.

50　Madeleine Delpierre, *Se vêtir au XVIIIe siècle*, 1996, p. 177; the phenomenon of the French fashion doll had begun in the Renaissance: see Sergio Bertelli, Franco Cardini and Elvira Garbeo Zorzi, *Italian Renaissance Courts*, 1986, p. 176. One miniature fashion doll dressed in French court dress of the mid-eighteenth century is in the Museum of Costume at Bath.

51　Musée des Tissus, *Soieries de Lyon. Commandes royales au XVIIIe siècle*, Lyon, 1988, p. 50.

52　Ribeiro, *Dress*, pp. 61–2.

53　Astrid Tyden Jordan, *Queen Christina's Coronation Coach*, Stockholm, 1988, p. 23.

54　Anne Marie Dahlberg, *Royal Splendour in the Royal Armoury*, Stockholm, 1996, p. 9.

55　A. Morel-Fatio, *Études sur l'Espagne*, 3 vols, 1888–1904, III, 241, 245. His predecessor Charles II, however, had worn French dress to please his foreign wives, in 1680 and 1697.

56　Yves Bottineau, *L'Art de cour dans l'Espagne de Philippe V 1700–1746*, 1993 edn, pp. 297–8.

57　Major William Dalrymple, *Travels through Spain and Portugal in 1774*, 1777, p. 46, 29 July 1774.

58　Benedetto Croce, *History of the Kingdom of Naples*, Chicago, 1970, p. 140; Harold Acton, *The Last Medici*, 1980 edn, p. 279.

59　Helen Watanabe O'Kelly, *Court Culture in Dresden from Renaissance to Baroque*, 2002, p. 205, letter of 25 December 1717.

60　Cf. Comte Gabriel Mareschal de Bièvre, *Le Marquis de Bièvre*, 1910, p. 208; Miss Knight, *Autobiography*, 1960, p. 44.

61　Joan Raymond, 'An Eye-witness to King Cromwell', *History Today*, 47, 7 (July 1997), p. 38, based on the diary of Reverend James Fraser.

62　Sir John Reresby, *Memoirs*, 1875, p. 37; even in the 1780s mud continued to be thrown at a man for wearing an *habit habillé* in London: Ribeiro, *Dress*, p. 116; James Boswell, *London Journal 1762–1763*, 1950, p. 94n.

63　Pepys, *Diary*, I, 141–3, 190, 194, 15–16 May, 1 July, 6 July 1660. For 3 February 1661, see II, 29.

64　Richard Ollard, *The Image of the King. Charles I and Charles II*, 1993 edn, pp. 86 and 159.

65 Pepys, *Diary*, II, 157–8, 19 August 1661.

66 Ibid., 226, 3 December 1661.

67 Ollard, *Image of the King*, p. 159, quoting Antony Wood.

68 De Marly, *Louis XIV*, p. 39.

69 J. C. Sainty and R. O. Buchholz, *Officials of the Royal Household 1660–1837*, 1997, I, 33–4, 78–9.

70 Patricia Wardle, *For Our Royal Person. Master of the Robes' Bills of King-Stadholder William III*, Apeldoorn, 2002, *passim*, and see pp. 24, 27, 33, 35, 38.

71 Comte Alexandre de Tilly, *Mémoires*, 1965, p. 192.

72 John Gwynn, *London and Westminster Improved, Illustrated by Plans, to which is Prefixed a Discourse on Publick Magnificence*, 1766, reprinted 1969, pp. 10–11. I am grateful to Dr Simon Thurley for this reference.

73 Buchholz, *Augustan Court*, p. 216, cf. pp. 218, 222; cf., Duchess of Northumberland, *Diaries of a Duchess*, pp. 31–2, 8, 9 September 1761, for detailed recording of the magnificence of royal and court dress at St James's – and at Versailles: ibid., p. 89, 4 April 1769.

74 Anne Somerset, *Ladies-in-Waiting*, 1984, p. 136.

75 Ophelia Field, *The Favourite. Sarah, Duchess of Marlborough*, 2003 edn, pp. 140, 159.

76 Ibid., pp. 224, 292; Edward Gregg, *Queen Anne*, 1980, pp. 276, 278–9; Buchholz, *Augustan Court*, pp. 50, 239.

77 Elizabeth Hamilton, *The Backstairs Dragon*, 1969, p. 68.

78 Buchholz, *Augustan Court*, pp. 123–4, 163–4, 169, 183; Hamilton, *Backstairs Dragon*, p. 129.

79 Gregg, *Queen Anne*, pp. 331 352; Buchholz, *Augustan Court*, pp. 80, 167; Wentworth, *Wentworth Papers*, pp. 244, 250, 258, 270, 408, letters of Lady Strafford, 8 January 1712; Peter Wentworth, 12 January 1712; Lord Berkeley, 25 January 1712; Lady Strafford, 25 February 1712; Peter Wentworth, 30 July 1714.

80 British Library Add. Ms 38503, f. 6, Horatio Walpole to Lord Townshend, 12 September 1725. Under the weight of her clothes, on her way to the chapel the King's bride was obliged 'frequently' to stop and rest.

81 Horace Walpole, *Correspondence*, 48 vols, New Haven and London, 1970–87, XXXVII, 116, Walpole to Conway, 31 October 1741: 'Lord Fitzwilliam and myself were the only two very fine. I was in a great taking about my clothes. They came from Paris and did not arrive until nine o'clock of the Birthday morning; I was obliged to send one of the King's Messengers for them.'

82 Fielding quoted in Ribeiro, *Dress*, pp. 64, 122.

83 Cf. the Gobelins tapestry showing him visiting the factory in 1673, wearing red heels, reproduced in André Chastel, *L'Art français. Ancien régime*, 1995, p. 173.

84 Madame de Genlis, *Mémoires*, 8 vols, 1825, II, 341: 'tous les hommes présentés avaient des talons rouges'. However, a man in a 1731 portrait of the family of the nurse of Louis XV, therefore not presented, also displays a red heel: Jacques Ruppert *et al.*, *Le Costume français*, 1996, p. 136.

85 The dwarfs were shown at the sale held by Sothebys at the château de Groussay, 2 June 1999, number 90; *Il neoclassicismo in Italia: da Tiepolo a Canova*, Milan, 2002, pp. 259, 346; John Adamson, ed., *The Princely Courts of Europe 1500–1750*, 1999, p. 203.

86 They are made by gluing red tape around heels, then varnishing them with nail varnish. Interview with Christopher Allen of Ede and Ravenscroft, 20 March 2003.

87 Olivia Bland, *The Royal Way of Death*, 1986, pp. 29, 47; Lou Taylor, *Mourning Dress*, 1983, pp. 101, 119.

88 Wardle, *Royal Person*, p. 85; Evelyn, *Diary*, p. 418, 11 March 1702.

89 Pepys, *Diary*, I, 248, 251 19, 23 September 1660.

90 Bland, *The Royal Way of Death*, p. 72; Taylor, *Mourning Dress*, pp. 104–5, 108.

91 Buchholz, *Augustan Court*, p. 241; Bland, *The Royal Way of Death*, pp. 95, 121.

92 Taylor, *Mourning Dress*, p. 200.

93 See for example the lists of periods for court mourning observed on the death of the King in Prussia, the Queen of Denmark, the Duke and Duchess of Holstein in Buchholz, *Augustan Court*, pp. 240–41.

94 Taylor, *Mourning Dress*, pp. 105, 200.

95 Paul S. Fritz, 'The Trade in Death: Royal Funerals in England 1685–1830', *Eighteenth-Century Studies*, 15, 3 (Spring 1982), pp. 306–8, 311–12; Taylor, *Mourning Dress*, p. 198.

96 Taylor, *Mourning Dress*, p. 200.

97 Ribeiro, *Dress*, pp. 202–3.

98 Delpierre, *Se vêtir au XVIIIe siècle*, p. 103; Sébastien Mercier, *Tableau de Paris, nouvelle édition corrigée et augmentée*, 8 vols, 1782–3, I, 144.

Chapter 2: Service

1 Ragnhild Hatton, *Charles XII of Sweden*, 1968, pp. 9, 12.

2 Ibid., pp. 5, 218; Robert Frost, 'Poles and Swedes', *The Court Historian*, VII, 2 (December 2002), p. 173

3 Roche, *Culture of Clothing*, pp. 229, 235, 239; cf. Gregory Hanlon, *The Twilight of a Military Tradition. Italian Aristocrats and European Conflicts 1560–1800*, 1998, p. 352; cf. Archives Nationales, AN F7 9875, correspondence of prefects with the Minister of Police 1815–16, proclamation of the Prefect of the Creuse, 15 November 1815, for recruiting posters for the new Garde royale, detailing the beauty of its uniforms.

4 Beverley Lemire, *Dress, Culture and Commerce. The English Clothing Trade before the Factory, 1660–1800*, 1997, p. 25.

5 Abigail Green, *Fatherlands*, 2001, p. 22.

6 Roche, *Culture of Clothing*, p. 244; John Mollo, *Military Fashion*, 1972, p. 45.

7 Dangeau, *Journal*, I, 52, 120, 1 October 1684, 24 March 1685.

8 Philip Longworth, *Alexis, Tsar of All the Russias*, 1984, pp. 120–21, 242.

9 Tamara Korshunova, *The Art of Costume in Russia, 18th to Early 20th Century*, Leningrad, 1979, p. 4; Isabel de Madariaga, 'The Russian Nobility in the Seventeenth and Eighteenth Centuries', in H. M. Scott, ed., *The European Nobilities in the Seventeenth and Eighteenth Centuries*, 2 vols, 1995, II, 240; for pictures of kaftaned Russian tsars and boyars, see Barry Shifman and Guy Walton, eds, *Gifts to the Tsars 1500–1700. Treasures from the Kremlin*, New York, 2001, pp. 82, 86–7, 308–9. Examples of boyars' robes survive in the Armoury Museum in the Kremlin.

10 Lindsey Hughes, *Russia in the Age of Peter the Great*, 1998, p. 280.

11 Lindsey Hughes, *Peter the Great*, 2002, pp. 54, 59; Korshunova, *Art of Costume*, p. 5.

12 Hughes, *Russia*, pp. 281–5; Ribeiro, *Dress*, pp. 101–2; Scott, *European Nobilities*, II, 240, 266.

13 Lindsey Hughes, 'From Caftans into Corsets: The Sartorial Transformation of

Women in the Reign of Peter the Great', in Peter I. Barta, ed., *Gender and Sexuality in Russian Civilization*, 2001, p. 18.

14 Hughes, 'From Caftans into Corsets', pp. 24, 26.

15 John L. H. Keep, *Soldiers of the Tsar. Army and Society in Russia 1462–1874*, Oxford, 1985, p. 98; Philip Mansel, *Pillars of Monarchy*, 1984, p. 20.

16 Reflecting the definition of a courtier by an early seventeenth-century print:
    Ainsi sont vêtus gents de cour,
    changeant d'habits de jour en jour.

17 D'Argenson, *Journal*, I, 19, 1716; Elena Moiseyenko, 'The Emperor's New Clothes', *Hermitage*, 1 (Summer 2003), pp. 42–7.

18 Nina Tarasova, 'The Cult of Peter the Great', *Hermitage*, 1 (Summer 2003), pp. 34–41; Moiseyenko, 'The Emperor's New Clothes', pp. 42–7.

19 Basil Dmytryshyn, *Imperial Russia: A Source-Book 1700–1917*, New York, 1967, p. 21; Keep, *Soldiers*, p. 124; Mansel, *Pillars of Monarchy*, p. 88; Isabel de Madariaga, *Russia in the Age of Catherine the Great*, 2002 edn, p. 80.

20 *Sbornik* (Recueil de la Société Impériale Russe d'Histoire), 1889, p. 549, dispatch of 3 February 1733.

21 William Coxe, AM, FRS, *Travels into Poland, Russia, Sweden, and Denmark*, 2 vols, 1784, I, 492. For pictures see e. g. the portrait of Alexander Kurakin, *c.* 1800 in Korshunova, *Art of Costume*, illus. 26. The gold, silver, diamond and amethyst dress ornaments of Catherine II's son the Grand Duke Paul, sewn along hems, cuffs and collar, and over buttons, now form part of the state diamond fund of the Russian Federation.

22 Simon Sebag Montefiore, *Prince of Princes. The Life of Potemkin*, 2000, pp. 333, 434, 467 and cover illustration.

23 Derek McKay, *The Great Elector*, 2001, pp. 174–5; Robert Ergang, *The Potsdam Führer. Frederick William I, Father of Prussian Militarism*, New York, 1941, pp. 42–3.

24 Ribeiro, *Dress*, p. 91; Albert Waddington, *Histoire de Prusse*, 2 vols, 1911–22, II, 518.

25 Ergang, *Potsdam Führer*, pp. 53–4.

26 Margrave de Bayreuth, *Mémoires*, 1967 edn, pp. 82–3. Count Brühl, chief minister of the court of Saxony-Poland, was said to own 500 suits: François Boucher, *A History of Costume in the West*, 1987 edn, p. 326.

27 Ergang, *Potsdam Führer*, p. 222; Giles MacDonogh, *Frederick the Great: A Life in Deed and Letters*, 1999, p. 47.

28 Bayreuth, *Mémoires*, p. 146.

29 Nevertheless he maintained the court office of *grand maître de la garde-robe* which had been established in 1701 by his grandfather, to mark his promotion to royal rank. Also see Ribeiro, *Dress*, pp. 20, 75, 77–8, 92.

30 David Fraser, *Frederick the Great*, 2000, p. 213, quoting the King's First Political Testament; Michael Roberts, *Essays in Swedish History*, 1967, p. 198.

31 MacDonogh, *Frederick the Great*, pp. 272, 333. For photographs of Frederick's uniforms see Deutsches Historisches Museum, *Bilder und Zeugnisse der deutschen Geschichte*, 2 vols, Berlin, 1997, I, 247.

32 Daniel L. Purdy, *The Tyranny of Elegance: Consumer Cosmopolitanism in the Age of Goethe*, Baltimore, 1998, p. 212.

33 Frederick A. Pottle, ed., *Boswell on the Grand Tour*, 1953, p. 23, 13 July 1764; Fraser, *Frederick the Great*, p. 126.

34 Peter H. Wilson, *German Armies. War and German Politics 1648–1806*, 1998, p. 277.

35 Purdy, *Tyranny*, p. 199.

36 Carol S. Leonard, *Reform and Regicide. The Reign of Peter III of Russia*, Bloomington, 1993, pp. 10, 139–40, 146–8.

37 Mikhail B. Pistrovski, ed., *Treasures of Catherine the Great*, 2000, pp. 31, 41 and n.; Nationalmuseum, *Catherine the Great and Gustav III*, Stockholm, 1999, pp. 98–100.

38 Mansel, *Pillars of Monarchy*, p. 89; Coxe, *Travels*, I, 193, 2 December 1777; Marquess of Londonderry, *Recollections of a Tour in the North of Europe in 1836–7*, 2 vols, 1838, I, 241.

39 Douglas Smith, ed. and tr., *Love and Conquest: Personal Correspondence of Catherine the Great and Prince Grygory Potemkin*, De Kalby, 2004, p. 175, Empress to Potemkin, 18 December 1786.

40 *Catherine the Great. Treasures of Imperial Russia from the State Hermitage Museum, Leningrad*, Dallas, 1990, pp. 48–9.

41 Smith, *Love and Conquest*, pp. 126–8, 344, Potemkin to Empress, March, April 1783, 29 May 1790.

42 Herbert Haupt, 'Die Aufhebung des Spanischen Mantelkleides durch Kaiser Joseph II. Ein Wendepunkt im hofischen Zeremoniell', *Österreich zur Zeit Kaiser Josephs II*, Melk Abbey, 1980, pp. 79–81; Morel-Fatio, *Études sur l'Espagne*, II, 256–7. There was a special black version for legal and government officials, like the black costume of the *noblesse de robe* in France.

43 Christopher Duffy, *The Army of Maria Theresa. The Armed Forces of Imperial Austria 1740–1780*, 1977, p. 18.

44 Robert Pick, *Empress Maria Theresa. The Earlier Years 1717–1757*, 1966, pp. 239, 303.

45 Christopher Duffy, *The Military Experience in the Age of Reason*, 1987, p. 43.

46 Alfred Ritter von Arneth, ed., *Maria Theresia und Joseph II: Ihre Correspondenz*, 3 vols, Vienna, 1867–68, I, 150, Joseph to Leopold, 31 October 1765; Haupt, 'Die Aufhebung des Spanischen Mantelkleides', pp. 79–81.

47 Comte de Guibert, *Journal d'un voyage en Allemagne fait en 1773*, 2 vols, 1803, I, 288, 2 July 1773.

48 Haupt, 'Die Aufhebung des Spanischen Mantelkleides', pp. 79–81.

49 *Oesterreich zur Zeit Kaiser Joseph II*, p. 341.

50 Lady Mary Coke, *Diary*, 4 vols, 1970, III, 324, 331, 17 November, 1 December 1770: 'I have never seen the Emperor and the Arch Dukes in anything but uniform'; comte de Pimodan, *Le Comte F. C. de Mercy-Argenteau*, 1911, p. 151, comte de Rosenberg to Mercy-Argenteau, 23 November 1774.

51 See e. g. Michael Roberts, 'The Military Revolution', in *Essays in Swedish History*, p. 198.

52 Quintin Colville, 'Jack Tar and the Gentleman Officer: The Role of Uniform in Shaping the Class- and Gender-related Identities of British Naval Personnel 1930–1939', *Transactions of the Royal Historical Society*, 6th series, 13 (2003), p. 106.

53 Anthony Powell, *Faces in my Time*, 1980, p. 98.

54 Lesley Blanch, *Romain, un regard particulier*, 1998, p. 38.

55 Croÿ, *Journal inédit*, IV, 45, May 1778.

56 Alma Söderhjelm, *Fersen et Marie-Antoinette*, 1934, p. 96, diary for 24 January 1784.

57 Marilyn Morris, *The British Monarchy and the French Revolution*, 1998, p. 148; cf. *Annual Register*, 1805, p. 369, for an account of a ball at Windsor on 25 February 1805: 'the gentlemen were dressed in the full Windsor uniform, except those who wore the military habit of their respective regiments. Some, however, appeared in magnificent court suits.'

58 M. de Bourgoing, *Nouveau voyage en Espagne*, 3 vols, 1789, II, 116.

59 Ibid., I, 89; Lord Auckland, *Journal and Correspondence*, 4 vols, 1860–62, II, 166, 9 April 1789; this uniform can be seen in a picture by Luis Paret of the oath-taking of the Prince of the Asturias in 1789 in the Prado. Another uniform was introduced in 1797: *Fasti della burocrazia: uniformi civili e di corte dei secoli XVIII–XIX*, Palazzo Ducale, Genoa, 1984, p. 21.

60 M. de Fortia-Piles, *Voyage de deux français en Allemagne, Danemark, Suède, Russie et Pologne fait en 1790–92*, 4 vols, 1796, IV, 19.

61 Pottle, *Boswell on the Grand Tour*, p. 133, 12 October 1764; cf., for a similar case in 1793, Ernest Taylor, ed., *The Taylor Papers*, 1913, p. 21 n. In 1810 the duc d'Orléans created his own uniform to wear to the court of Sardinia: Guy Antonetti, *Louis-Philippe*, 1994, p. 381.

62 Geoffrey Symcox, *Victor Amadeus II. Absolutism in the Savoyard State 1675–1730*, 1983, p. 169; cf. Hanlon, *Twilight of a Military Tradition*, p. 291.

63 Comte d'Espinchal, *Journal*, 1912, p. 55, 26 September 1789; S. Loriga, 'Continuité aristocratique et tradition militaire du Piémont de la dynastie de Savoie XVIe–XIXe siècles', *Revue d'histoire moderne*, XXXIV, 7–9 (1987), 400; cf. Thomas Watkins, *Travels through Swisserland, Italy, Sicily, the Greek Islands to Constantinople . . . in the Years 1787, 1788, 1789*, 2 vols, 1792, I, 203, re the birthday court of the Princess of Piedmont in 1787: 'All military officers as in England appear at it in their uniforms; at Versailles, you know it is quite the reverse.'

64 Nick Foulkes, *Last of the Dandies*, 2003, p. 58; cf. Marquess of Anglesey, *One-Leg*, 1961, p. 32, Lord Paget to Lavinia, Countess of Uxbridge, 6 June 1787: 'I feel much the want of an uniform and shall still more, as on all occasions where a frock is too negligee or a dress Coat too troublesome an uniform comes in between and is perfectly proper.'

65 E. and F. Anson, eds, *Mary Hamilton . . . at Court and at Home*, 1925, p. 87, letter of November 1779.

66 Steven Parissien, *George IV: The Grand Entertainment*, 2001, pp. 99, 108.

67 Presented to his equerry, a serving officer called Colonel Saint-Leger, the portrait now hangs at Waddesdon Manor. Miniatures by Prepiani of Byron in the self-invented red uniform which he wore for presentation to foreign dignitaries such as Ali Pasha in 1809 and Mahmud II in 1810 are now at Newstead Abbey and the Biblioteca Classense, Ravenna.

68 Christopher Hibbert, *George IV, Prince of Wales*, 1972, p. 121; cf., for a study of the Prince and the 10th Hussars, John Mollo, *The Prince's Dolls. Scandals, Skirmishes and Splendours of the First British Hussars 1793–1815*, 1997. See also the picture by George Stubbs of its soldiers in the Royal Collection.

69 Parissien, *George IV*, pp. 108, 254.

70 Luc Boisnard, *La Noblesse dans la tourmente 1774–1802*, 1992, p. 71; Roche, *Culture of Clothing*, p. 241.

71 D'Argenson, *Journal*, II, 72, 209, 211, 23 February, 27 August 1739; Barbier, *Journal*, III, 328, December 1751; Croÿ, *Journal inédit*, II, 373, May 1770.

72 Archives Nationales, AN 01 835: *État des dépenses de la Garde robe du Roi ordonnées par Monseigneur le Duc de Liancourt Grand maître pendant l'année 1786.*

73 Ribeiro, *Dress*, p. 124.

74 Croÿ, *Journal inédit*, II, 373, May 1770.

75 Archives Nationales, AN K 1715, 8 (1).

76 Louis Nicolardot, *Journal de Louis XVI*, 1873, pp. 55–7; Louis XIV, on the other hand, known as *le roi des revues*, had reviewed the *gardes du corps* every month: Visconti, *Mémoires*, p. 62. Louis XVI also wore this red and gold uniform on his visit to Cherbourg in 1786.

77 Baron de Tricornet, *Mémoires*, 2 vols, Besançon, 1894, I, 78, 1765; Daniel Roche, ed., *Le Cheval et la guerre*, 2002, p. 147, shows Louis XVI in uniform in April 1778; James St John, *Letters from . . . to a Gentleman in the South of Ireland*, 2 vols, Dublin, 1788, I, 46, letter of 10 May 1787; cf. Dangeau, *Journal*, I, 161, 27 May 1685.

78 Duc d'Escars, *Mémoires*, 2 vols, 1890, I, 115.

79 Archives du château de Mouchy: Prince de Poix, 'Note autobiographique', 1806.

80 Marquis de Bombelles, *Journal*, Geneva, 1977– , I, 246, 22 July 1783.

81 Mme de La Tour du Pin, *Journal d'une femme de cinquante ans*, 2 vols, 1913, I, 72–3.

82 Ibid., I, 114.

83 Comte d'Hézecques, *Souvenirs d'un page à la cour de Louis XVI*, 1873, p. 9.

84 Papillon de La Ferté, *Journal des menus-plaisirs du roi*, pp. 280, 288, 13, 24 December 1775, 19 November 1776.

85 *Les Atours de la reine. Art et commerce au service de Marie-Antoinette*, Archives Nationales 2001, p. 83; Musée des Tissus, *Soieries de Lyon*, p. 63.

86 Laurent Hugues, 'La Famille royale et ses portraitistes sous Louis XV et Louis XVI', in Xavier Salmon, ed., *De soie et de poudre. Portraits de cour dans l'Europe des lumières*, Arles, 2002, pp. 158–61.

87 Millia Davenport, *Book of Costume*, New York, 1950, pp. 535–47.

88 Roche, *Culture of Clothing*, pp. 471, 480.

89 Antonia Fraser, *Marie-Antoinette*, 2001, pp. 56–7. The abandoned Austrian clothes (in fact bought in France) were then given to the new Dauphine's *dames du palais*; cf. the views of the marquis de Bombelles in 1792: 'les français eussent adoré cette princesse si elle ne se fût pas trop abandonnée à un sentiment qui fait l'éloge de son coeur: celui d'une constante affection pour le pays et la famille où elle naquit', *Journal*, III, Geneva, 1993, 284, 5 February 1792.

90 Madame Campan, *Mémoires*, 1988 edn, p. 89.

91 Émile Langlade, *La Marchande de modes de Marie-Antoinette, Rose Bertin*, 1932, p. 54.

92 Davenport, *Book of Costume*, pp. 694–5; Langlade, *La Marchande de modes*, p. 66.

93 Thus the 'Prince of Wales's feathers' worn by débutantes were in fact the Queen of France's; Langlade, *La Marchande de modes*, pp. 59, 66; Amanda Foreman, *Georgiana, Duchess of Devonshire*, 1999 edn, p. 38. The future Empress Marie Feodorovna, who visited France in 1782, also adopted feathers (see her portrait in Grand Duke Nicholas Michailovich, *L'Empereur Alexandre Ier*, 2 vols, St Petersburg, 1912, I, 128), as did, despite her banishment from court, Madame du Barry (portrait by Madame Vigée-Lebrun, 1782, Corcoran Art Gallery, Washington).

94 Roche, *Culture of Clothing*, p. 303; Diana de Marly, *A History of Haute Couture 1850–1950*, 1980, p. 11; Michelle Sapori, *Rose Bertin, Ministre des modes de Marie-Antoinette*, 2003, p. 29.

95 Baronne d'Oberkirch, *Mémoires*, 1989, pp. 145, 478.

96 Langlade, *La Marchande de modes*, pp. 42, 111.

97 Mme Cradock, *Journal*, 1896, p. 64, 12 July 1784.

98 Pamela Pilbeam, *Madame Tussaud and the History of Waxworks*, 2003, pp. 23, 27, 29–30.

99 See description in d'Hézecques, *Souvenirs d'un page*, pp. 161–9.

100 Campan, *Mémoires*, p. 89; Prince de Ligne, *Mélanges militaires, littéraires et sentimentaires*, 35 vols, Dresden, 1795–1811, XXIX, 271–2.

101 Ribeiro, *Fashion in the French Revolution*, p. 27.

102 Vicomte de Reiset, *Louise d'Esparbès, comtesse de Polastron*, 1907, p. 52, M. de Rougeot to comte d'Esparbès, 25 November 1780; cf., for the pressure on the Queen, Musée des Tissus, *Soieries de Lyon*, p. 95, letter of 1778: 'si la Reine refuse de porter de l'étoffe brochée et continue de la dédaigner c'en est fait de cette branche de commerce et une ville des plus peuplées et des plus opulentes de la France va devenir un vaste désert.'

103 La Tour du Pin, *Journal*, I, 110–11.

104 *Les Atours de la Reine*, pp. 7–8, 10.

105 Delpierre, *Se vêtir*, p. 121.

106 Pierrette, *Graveurs français*, p. 54.

107 Ribeiro, *Dress*, pp. 226–8. She gave such dresses to her friend the Duchess of Devonshire, who helped make them fashionable in England.

108 Bombelles, *Journal*, II, 201, 3 June 1788.

109 Émile Léonard, *L'Armée et ses problèmes au XVIIIe siècle*, 1960, pp. 89–90, 183.

110 Prince de Ligne, *Mémoires et mélanges historiques et littéraires*, 5 vols, 1828, IV, 135.

111 Dieudonné Thiébault, *Souvenirs de vingt ans de séjour à Berlin*, 2 vols, 1860, II, 3.

112 Jérôme Zieseniss, *Berthier, frère d'armes de Napoléon*, 1985, p. 44 quoting Berthier's journal of his *Voyage en Prusse août–septembre 1783*.

113 Antonetti, *Louis-Philippe*, p. 348.

Chapter 3: Identity

1 Robin Nicholson, *Bonnie Prince Charlie and the Making of a Myth 1720–1892*, 2002, p. 62

2 A detailed picture of the different national costumes of Europe in the late eighteenth century is given in Ribeiro, *Dress*, p. 91; cf. John Gilbert, *National Costumes of the World*, 1972, *passim*; R. Turner Wilcox, *Folk and Festival Costume of the World*, 1989 edn, *passim*.

3 Soraya Antonius, *The Lord*, 1986, p. 93.

4 Whitworth Art Gallery, *Historic Hungarian Costume from Budapest*, Manchester, 1979, pp. 16–17; Margaret Fitzherbert, *The Man who was Greenmantle*, 1983, p. 118.

5 Personal information, Ossama el-Kaoukgi, 30 April 2002; *Beirut Daily Star*, 24 April 2002, 'Refugees' anger reaches boiling point'.

6 Madeline C. Zilfi, 'Whose Laws? Gendering the Ottoman Sumptuary Regime', in Suraiya Faroqhi and Christoph K. Neumann, eds, *Ottoman Costumes from Textile to Identity*, Istanbul, 2004, pp. 131–3.

7 Donald Quataert, 'Clothing Laws, State and Society in the Ottoman Empire 1720–1829', *International Journal of Middle Eastern Studies*, XXIX, 1997, p. 406.

8 Zilfi, 'Whose Laws?', p. 34; Yedida Kalfon Stillman, *Arab Dress. A Short History. From the Dawn of Islam to Modern Times*, Leiden, 2000, pp. 83–4, 102–3.

9 John Norton, 'Faith and Fashion in Turkey', in Nancy Lindisfarne-Tapper and Bruce Ingham, eds, *Languages of Dress in the Middle East*, Richmond, 1997, p. 153.

10 Guillaume Postel, *Des histoires orientales*, ed. Jacques Rollet, Istanbul, 1999, pp. xx, xxv.

11 Leslie Meral Schick, 'The Place of Dress in Pre-modern Costume Albums', in Suraiya Faroqhi and Christoph K. Neumann, eds, *Ottoman Costumes from Textile to Identity*, Istanbul, 2004, p. 99; Eveline Sint Nicolaas *et al.*, *An Eyewitness of the Tulip Era. Jean Baptiste Vanmour*, Istanbul, 2003, *passim*.

12 For a thorough discussion of these codes see Matthew Elliot, 'Dress Codes in the Ottoman Empire: The Case of the Franks', in Suraiya Faroqhi and Christoph K. Neumann, eds, *Ottoman Costumes from Textile to Identity*, Istanbul, 2004, pp. 103–23; Maréchal de Moltke, *Lettres sur l'orient*, 1872, p. 40, 9 February 1836.

13 J. M. Rogers, ed., *The Topkapi Saray Museum. Costumes, Embroideries and Other Textiles*, 1986, pp. 11–12, and illustrations, *passim*.

14 J. von Hammer-Purgstall, *Histoire de l'empire ottoman*, 16 vols, 1835–40, V, 24; Rogers, *Topkapi*, pp. 25, 37.

15 Rogers, *Topkapi*, pp. 11, 37 and *passim*; Esin Atil, *Turkish Art*, 1980, p. 350; J. M. Rogers and Rachel Ward, *Suleyman the Magnificent*, 1988, p. 166; Franz Babinger, *Mehmed the Conqueror and his Time*, 1978 edn, p. 441.

16 See the acounts by Ogier Ghislain de Busbecq in 1559 and Thomas Dallam in 1599, quoted in Philip Mansel, *Constantinople: City of the World's Desire*, 1995, pp. 57, 67; Philippe du Fresne-Canaye, *Le Voyage du Levant*, 1986 edn, p. 68; Watkins, *Tour through Swisserland . . . to Constantinople*, II, 218, 139, 214, 227; Domenico Sestini, *Lettres . . . écrites à ses amis en Toscane*, 3 vols, 1789, III, 350, letter of 31 August 1778; John Rodenbeck, 'Dressing Native', in Paul and Janet Starkey, eds, *Unfolding the Orient. Travellers in Egypt and the Near East*, Reading, 2001, p. 76.

17 Atil, *Turkish Art*, p. 349; Rogers, *Topkapi*, p. 160.

18 The late President Hafez al-Assad of Syria presented his cloak or *abaya* to his political client, Suleiman Franjieh of Lebanon.

19 Stewart Gordon, 'A World of Investiture', in Gordon, ed., *Robes and Honour. The Medieval World of Investiture*, 2001, p. 11, and 'Robes, Kings and Semiotic Ambiguity', ibid., p. 379; Carl F. Petry, 'Robing Ceremonials in Late Mamluk Egypt', ibid., pp. 354, 366.

20 Colin Imber, *The Ottoman Empire*, 2002, p. 122.

21 Nicolas Vatin and Gilles Veinstein, *Le Sérail ébranlé: essai sur les morts, dépositions et avènements des sultans ottomans XIVe–XIXe siècle*, 2003, pp. 272, 289.

22 Evliya Tchelebi, *La Guerre des Turcs*, Arles, 2000, p. 126.

23 Ibid., pp. 109, 205, 229.

24 Mansel, *Constantinople*, pp. 49, 154–5; M. Grelot, *Relation nouvelle d'un voyage de Constantinople*, 1680, p. 169; I. Mouradgea I. d'Ohsson, *Tableau général de l'Empire Ottoman*, 3 vols, 1787–1820, II, 458.

25 Maxime Rodinson, *Muhammad*, 2002 edn, p. 53.

26 Vatin and Veinstein, *Sérail ébranlé*, pp. 294–5.

27 Rodenbeck, 'Dressing Native', pp. 66–7, 75, 79, 81. Travelling near Baalbek in 1785, the painter Louis François Cassas attributed to his Arab clothes his survival of a robbers' attack: if he had been in European clothes, he would have been assumed to be rich and robbed and murdered: diary of Louis François Cassas, cited in Annie Gilet, 'Le voyageur dans l'Empire ottoman', in *Louis François Cassas 1756–1827*, Mainz, 1994, p. 104.

When travelling in especially dangerous districts, some merchants obtained special permission from the Ottoman government to wear Muslim dress. See Elliot, 'Dress Codes', pp. 113–15.

28 Léonce Pingaud, *Choiseul-Gouffier: la France en Orient sous Louis XVI*, 1887, p. 96.

29 François Charles-Roux, *Les Échelles de Syrie et de Palestine au XVIIIe siècle*, 1928, p. 16.

30 Mouradgea d'Ohsson, *Tableau général*, II, 458.

31 Pictures of this ceremony were frequently commissioned by ambassadors. See e.g. the pictures by the official *peintre ordinaire du roi en Levant*, J. B. Vanmour, in Sint Nicolaas *et al.*, *Eyewitness*, pp. 87, 195; Topkapi Palace, *The Sultan's Portrait. Picturing the House of Osman*, Istanbul, 2000, p. 414; and Semra Germaner and Eynep Inankur, *Constantinople and the Orientalists*, Istanbul, 2002, pp. 65–6.

32 Mouradgea d'Ohsson, *Tableau général*, III, 455–7.

33 *At the Sublime Porte: Ambassadors to the Ottoman Empire 1550–1800*, 1988, p. 53.

34 Mouradgea d'Ohsson, *Tableau général*, II, 457.

35 Rogers, *Topkapi*, p. 21; Norman Itzkowitz and Max Mote, *Mubadele: An Ottoman-Russian Exchange of Ambassadors*, Chicago, 1970, p. 167; Sestini, *Lettres*, II, 158, 20 April 1778.

36 Ritu Kumar, *Costumes and Textiles of Royal India*, 1999, pp. 39–40, 150–63; B. N. Goswamy, *Indian Costumes in the Collection of the Calico Museum of Textiles*, Ahmedabad, 1996, pp. 14, 21; for pictures of *khilats* see also Naveen Patnaik, *A Second Paradise: Indian Courtly Life 1590–1947*, New York, 1985, pp. 49, 53, 54.

37 Gordon, *Robes and Honour*, p. 2.

38 Abu'l-fazl Allami, *The A'ini Akbari*, 2nd rev. edn, 3 vols, New Delhi, 1977, I, 93, 94, 96; Nicola Manucci, *Mogul India or Storia do Mogor*, 4 vols, New Delhi, 1989, II, 39.

39 Bernard S. Cohn, 'Cloth, Clothes and Colonialism. India in the Nineteenth Century', in Annette B. Weiner and Jane Schneider, eds, *Cloth and Human Experience*, Washington, 1989, p. 314.

40 Gordon, *Robes and Honour*, p. 3.

41 Cf. Zilfi, 'Whose Laws?', p. 137.

42 Quataert, 'Clothing Laws', p. 410.

43 Louis Bonneville de Marsangy, *Le Chevalier de Vergennes. Son ambassade à Constantinople*, 2 vols, 1894, II, 53–4, Vergennes to duc de Choiseul, 1 June 1758; cf. Hammer-Purgstall, *Histoire*, XI, 129–30, for similar stories about the Sultan enforcing dress regulations in 1657.

44 Stanford J. Shaw, *Between Old and New: The Ottoman Empire under Sultan Selim III, 1789–1807*, Cambridge, Mass., 1971, p. 77; Zilfi, 'Whose Laws?', p. 136.

45 Quataert, 'Clothing Laws', p. 411.

46 Edhem Eldem, *French Trade in Istanbul in the Eighteenth Century*, Leiden, 1999, p. 63.

47 Ibid., p. 282; Norton, 'Faith and Fashion in Turkey', p. 151.

48 www.hobby-o.com: John Cam Hobhouse, diary, 1 December 1809.

49 See the reproductions of such portraits, by Liotard in 1740 and Antoine de Favray in 1768, in Mansel, *Constantinople*.

50 See the portraits of Kings Wladislaw IV and John II Casimir in, for example, Shifman and Walton, *Gifts to the Tsars*, p. 318; Musée des Tissus, *Ceintures polonaises. Quand la Pologne s'habillait à Lyon*, Lyon, 2001, p. 7.

51 Dulwich Picture Gallery, *Treasures of a Polish King*, 1997, p. 71.

52 I am grateful for this point to Dr Robert Frost. In the 1670s a similar desire not to look French led King Christian V to try to institute a national dress in Denmark: Sigrid Flamand Christensen, *Kongedragterne fra 17 og 18 Aarhundrede*, 2 vols, Copenhagen, 1940, II, 274.

53 Cf. Corina Nicolescu, *Le Costume de cour dans les pays roumains XIVe siècle–XVIIIe siècle*, Bucharest, 1970, *passim*.

54 De Marly, *Louis XIV*, p. 17.

55 Adam Zamoyski, *The Polish Way*, 1987, p. 197.

56 *Unter einer Krone. Kunst und Kultur der sächsisch-polnischen Union*, Leipzig, 1997, p. 294; Zamoyski, *The Polish Way*, p. 217.

57 Tadeusz Jeziorowski and Andrzej Jeziorkowski, *Mundury Wojewódzkie, Rzeczypospolitej Obojga Narodów*, Warsaw, 1992, pp. 37–9.

58 Memoir of 1788 in Prince de Ligne, *Oeuvres choisies*, 2 vols, 1809, II, 27.

59 Alfred Potocki, *Master of Lancut*, 1959, pp. 81, 91; Mari Taszycka and Manfred Holst, 'Symbols of Nationhood. History of the Polish Sash', *Hali*, 84 (2001), p. 77; Musée des Tissus, *Ceintures polonaises*, pp. 11, 13. In the second half of the nineteenth century many Polish nobles were painted in national dress: cf. the portraits by Jan Matejko of Piotra Moszynskiego (1873) and of Mikolaja Zyblikiewicza (1880) in the National Museum, Cracow.

60 Personal communication from Jaroslaw Dumanovski, 20 September 2004.

61 Cf. M. Bertrand de Molleville, *The Costume of the Hereditary States of the House of Austria*, 1804, *passim*.

62 Frances Trollope, *Vienna and the Austrians*, 2 vols, 1838, I, 317.

63 Ribeiro, *Dress*, p. 99; Metropolitan Museum, *The Imperial Style. Fashions of the Hapsburg Era*, New York, 1980, pp. 75–88; Whitworth Art Gallery, *Historic Hungarian Costume*, p. 30.

64 Cf. Sir Robert Murray Keith, *Memoirs and Correspondence*, 2 vols, 1849, II, 305, Keith to his sisters, Vienna, 15 November 1790.

65 *Oesterreich zur Zeit Kaiser Josephs II*, p. 327.

66 Mansel, *Pillars of Monarchy*, p. 160.

67 See Christian Hesketh, *Tartans*, 1961, *passim*; Fitzroy Maclean, *Highlanders. A History of the Highland Clans*, 1995, pp. 36–7, 185.

68 Hugh Trevor-Roper, 'The Highland Tradition of Scotland', in Eric Hobsbawm and Terence Ranger, eds, *The Invention of Tradition*, 1983, p. 21.

69 Hugh Cheape, *Tartan*, Edinburgh, 2nd edn, 1995, p. 25.

70 Ibid., p. 26.

71 Ibid., p. 31.

72 Nicholson, *Bonnie Prince Charlie*, p. 64.

73 National Army Museum, *1745. Charles Edward Stuart and the Jacobites*, ed. Robert C. Woosnam-Savage, 1995, pp. 83, 91.

74 Cheape, *Tartan*, p. 31; Maclean, *Highlanders*, p. 202.

75 Robin Eagles, *Francophilia in English Society 1748–1815*, 2000, p. 19; cf. Hesketh, *Tartans*, p. 17, for a picture of the future George III wearing tartan.

76 This picture was sold as part of the Bute collection by Christie's, London, 3 July 1996.

77 Cheape, *Tartan*, p. 32; Trevor-Roper, 'Highland Tradition', p. 24; cf. Maclean, *Highlanders*, p. 220, reproducing a warrant of 14 October 1751, for evidence that the proscription was enforced.

78 Cheape, *Tartan*, p. 44; W. A. Speck, *The Butcher*, Oxford, 1989, p. 174; Boswell, *London Journal*, p. 71, 8 December 1763.

79 Hesketh, *Tartans*, p. 55; see e.g. the following posters of 1915–30 in the National War Museum of Scotland: *Recruits wanted for the Scottish Regiments: This is the life for a Scotsman; Join the Scots Guards; Line up boys! Enlist today.*

80 See e.g. the portraits, painted during the period of proscription, in Maclean, *Highlanders*, pp. 73, 93, 226, 236.

81 Trevor-Roper, 'Highland Tradition', pp. 29–32; John Prebble, *The King's Jaunt. George IV in Scotland August 1822*, 1988, pp. 115–21.

82 Parissien, *George IV*, pp. 325–30. The portrait of the King in tartan, by David Wilkie, is in the Royal Collection. His outfit cost £1,354 18s: cf. Prebble, *King's Jaunt*, pp. 74–5, 306, 315, 321.

83 Prebble, *King's Jaunt*, pp. 268–9.

84 Watanabe O'Kelly, *Court Culture in Dresden*, p. 226.

85 Georg J. Kügler, 'Viennese Court Dress', in Metropolitan Museum, *The Imperial Style. Fashions of the Hapsburg Era*, New York, 1980, p. 109; cf. Friedrich Hottenroth, *Handbuch der deutschen Tracht*, Stuttgart, n.d., p. 873; Purdy, *Tyranny*, pp. 184–5.

86 Janis A. Tomlinson, *Goya in the Twilight of Enlightenment*, 1992, pp. 81–3. There had already been proposals for a revival of national dress in 1788. See Eleanor A. Sayer, *Goya and the Spirit of Enlightenment*, Boston, 1989, pp. 76–7. The Queen of Spain and the infantas still wear mantillas on formal occasions today.

87 Mike Cronin and Daryl Adair, *The Wearing of the Green. A History of St Patrick's Day*, 2002, pp. xiii, xxiii, 2. I am grateful for this reference to Roy Foster.

88 Mairead Dunlevy, *Dress in Ireland*, 1989, p. 80.

89 Sarah Foster, 'Buying Irish in Eighteenth Century Dublin: Consumer Nationalism in Eighteenth Century Dublin', *History Today* (June 1997), pp. 46–9; Dunlevy, *Dress*, p. 120; Joseph Robins, *Champagne and Silver Buckles: The Viceregal Court at Dublin Castle 1700–1922*, Dublin, 2001, pp. 14, 43, 54, 155.

90 De Marly, *Louis XIV*, pp. 40–42; James Laver, *A Concise History of Costume*, 1969, p. 114.

91 Evelyn, *Diary*, pp. 216–17, 18, 30 October 1666.

92 Hardy Amies, *The Englishman's Suit*, 1994, p. 3.

93 Esmond S. de Beer, 'King Charles II's Own Fashion. An Episode in English–French Relations 1666–1670', *Journal of the Warburg Institute*, 2 (2 October 1938), pp. 105–115

94 De Marly, *Louis XIV*, pp. 40, 56.

95 Ribeiro, *Dress*, p. 56; Spitalfields silk waistcoats are on display in the Museum of London.

96 Valerie Cumming, *Royal Dress. The Image and the Reality. 1580 to the Present Day*, 1989, pp. 53, 142; Wardle, *Royal Person*, pp. 60, 73.

97 Alan Mansfield, *Ceremonial Costume*, 1980, p. 103; Cumming, *Royal Dress*, p. 69. Flora Fraser, *Princesses*, 2004, p. 19.

98 Morris, *The British Monarchy*, p. 151.

99 Baron de Klinkowström, *Le Comte de Fersen et la cour de France*, 2 vols, 1877–8, I, xviii, diary of Fersen, 15 February 1774; Ribeiro, *Dress*, p. 276.

100 A. Geffroy, *Gustave III et la cour de France*, 2nd edn, 2 vols, 1867, I, 308, 319, dispatches from the Saxon minister and the Swedish ambassador to France, 19 January 1775; cf. Madame du Deffand, *Lettres de Madame du Deffand*, 2002 edn, p. 680, 28 January 1775 to Horace Walpole.

101 Papillon de La Ferté, *Journal*, p. 271, 8 February 1775.

102 Lena Rangström, *Kläder för tid och evighet*, Stockholm, 1997, pp. 124–35. This costume would also be adopted by his son Gustavus IV Adolphus until his deposition in 1809: Nationalmuseum, *Galenpannan*, Stockholm, 2000, *passim*.

103 A. D. Harvey, 'Gustav III of Sweden', *History Today*, December 2003, p. 10.

104 Nationalmuseum, *Catherine the Great and Gustav III*, Stockholm, 1998, pp. 123, 166.

105 Gunnar Jahlberg, ed., *Catherine II et Gustave III: une correspondance retrouvée*. Stockholm, 1998, p. 123 n.

106 Lena Rangström, ed., *Hovets dräkter*, Stockholm, 1994, pp. 14–15, 22, 45; Karl Lofström, 'Le Costume national de Gustave III, le costume de cour et la présentation à la cour', *Livrustkammaren*, 9, 7–8 (1962), pp. 142–5.

107 Nationalmuseum, *Catherine the Great and Gustav III*, pp. 145, 147, 164.

108 Rangström, *Hovets dräkter*, pp. 35, 136–50.

109 Coxe, *Travels*, II, 329; illustrations in Rangström, *Hovets dräkter*, pp. 48–9.

110 Söderhjelm, *Fersen*, p. 61, Fersen to his father Senator von Fersen, 11 December 1778, letter of Lindblom, 24 December 1778.

111 C. F. Ristell, *Characters and Anecdotes of the Court of Sweden*, 2 vols, 1790, II, 163–4, 167; cf. O. G. von Heidenstam, *La Fin d'une dynastie*, 1911, pp. 126–7: 'je trouve le nouveau costume si sérieux, si chaud, si léger, si commode, si durable, en un mot si suédois que je lui suis devoué corps et âme.'

112 Nationalmuseum, *Catherine the Great and Gustav III*, p. 161; Jahlberg, *Catherine II et Gustave III*, p. 181, quoting a letter of Catherine II to Joseph II, 2 August 1783; Smith, *Love and Conquest*, p. 141, Empress to Potemkin 29 June 1783.

113 Ribeiro, *Dress*, p. 104; Nationalmuseum, *Catherine the Great and Gustav III*, p. 629; Piotrovsky, *Treasures of Catherine the Great*, p. 45; cf. Comte Valentin Esterhazy, *Lettres à sa femme 1784–1792*, 1907, p. 301, letter of 9/20 September 1791.

114 De Madariaga, 'The Russian Nobility in the Seventeenth and Eighteenth Centuries', 271.

115 Rangström, *Hovets dräkter*, pp. 38–9.

116 Lena Rangström, *1766. Le Roi se marie*, 2001, pp. 1, 5.

117 Nationalmuseum, *Tournaments and the Dream of Chivalry*, Stockholm, 1992, *passim*.

118 Gardar Sahlberg, *Murder at the Masked Ball*, 1974, p. 17; the costume is preserved in the Livrustkammaren in the Royal Palace. Wearing orders could be fatal on other occasions. At the Battle of Trafalgar Admiral Nelson was easily 'picked off' by a French marksman, or marksmen, because his naval officer's coat, the epaulettes and braid on which already made him conspicuous, was a blaze of orders: of the Bath, of Saint Ferdinand of Naples, of Saint Joachim and the Ottoman Order of the Crescent. Not to wear his orders, the correct positioning

of which had much preoccupied him, was as unthinkable to the British Admiral as it was to the Swedish King. See Terry Coleman, *Nelson*, 2002 edn, pp. 239, 311, 320, and p. 404, Mr to Mrs Wells, from the *Thunderer*, 29 October 1805: 'I very much fear his honours were the cause of his death as he evidently was picked off from the rest wearing his stars in action which in my opinion was rather indiscreet.'

119 Stig Ramel, *Gustaf Mauritz Armfelt, fondateur de la Finlande*, 1999, p. 136.
120 R. K. Porter, *Travelling Sketches in Russia and Sweden*, 2 vols, 1809, II, 130–32.
121 H. Arnold Barton, *Count Hans Axel von Fersen*, Boston, 1975, p. 320, diary for January 1804.
122 See e.g. Ribeiro, *Dress*, p. 99.

Chapter 4: Revolutions

1 For example the small royal residence at Ekolsund in Sweden had its own coat: Ake Setterwall *et al.*, *The Chinese Pavilion at Drottningholm*, Malmo, 1974, p. 29.
2 Charles Jean Hallo, *Historique des tenues de vénerie*, 1999, p. 68.
3 The picture by Oudry of *Louis XV chassant le cerf dans la forêt de la Celle Saint-Cloud* is at Versailles, another is in the Musée des Augustins, Toulouse, another in Fontainebleau; Rangström, *Kläder*, pp. 84, 89. The habit of awarding the right to wear the uniform of the King's hunt to favoured foreigners continued until 1830. The *Livret des chasses du roi* (1822), sold on 25 May 1995 at Sotheby's, London, contained a *Liste des personnes à qui le roi a bien voulu accorder la permission de porter l'habit de ses chasses à courre*, which included the Duke of Wellington.
4 De Marly, *Louis XIV*, pp. 61–2; Palais Galliéra, *Uniformes civil français. Cérémonial, circonstances 1750–1980*, 1982, pp. 21–2; Lucy Norton, ed. and tr., *Saint-Simon at Versailles*, 1959, 254; Saule, *Versailles triomphant*, p. 115.
5 Dangeau, *Journal*, II, 81, 207, 15 June 1686, 8 June 1687; III, 38, 23 March 1688.
6 Philippe Salvadori, *La Chasse sous l'ancien régime*, 1996, p. 205; Luynes, *Mémoires* IX, 491 and n., 15 and 16 September 1749.
7 Gustave Desjardins, *Le Petit Trianon. Histoire et déscription*, Versailles, 1885, p. 259; Henry Swinburne, *Memoirs of the Courts of Europe*, 2 vols, 1895, II, 7, 24 and 25 October 1786. A portrait of the duc d'Enghien by Nanine Vallain in the coat of the Condé hunt, and two pictures of the last prince de Condé and his fellow huntsmen and women, also wearing the hunt coat, painted by A. Ladurner in 1828 and 1829, are now in the château de Chantilly.
8 They are also the colours of the King of Spain's guards' uniforms and liveries today. See d'Hézecques, *Souvenirs*, p. 130.
9 Cf. Bombelles, *Journal*, I, 117, 120, 10 June 1782, re *uniforme de Chantilly*.
10 Personal communication, Celestria Noel, March 2003.
11 Salvadori, *La Chasse*, p. 226; De Marly, *Louis XIV*, p. 44; Visconti, *Mémoires*, p. 14.
12 Cumming, *Royal Dress*, pp. 52, 62–3; A. E. Haswell Miller and N. P. Dawnay, *Military Drawings and Paintings in the Collection of Her Majesty the Queen*, 2 vols, 1966–70, I, numbers 23–93. A portrait by John Wootton of George II in a red and gold uniform is in the National Army Museum.
13 Quoted in Sasha Llewellyn, 'George III and the Windsor Uniform', *The Court Historian* (1996), p. 12.
14 A. M. W. Stirling, *Coke of Norfolk and his Friends*, 2 vols, 1907–11, I, 209–10.

Similarly in 1712, in order to show disrespect to the Queen, at the height of their power struggle with the Tories, Whig ladies had sat at windows 'all in an undress', jeering at Tory ladies proceeding to St James's Palace in their finery: Jonathan Swift, *Journal to Stella*, 1923 edn, p. 331, 5 January 1712.

15 Llewellyn, 'George III', pp. 12–13; cf. J. B. Hone, *The History of the Royal Buckhounds*, Newmarket, 1895, p. 272.

16 Cumming, *Royal Dress*, p. 72; Anson, *Mary Hamilton*, p. 106, Mary Hamilton to Lady Charlotte Finch, 3 September 1781.

17 Raymond Carr, *English Fox Hunting*, rev. edn, 1986, p. 50; personal communication, Celestria Noel, 18 June 2003.

18 See e.g. Richard Godfrey, *James Gillray: The Art of Caricature*, 2001, pp. 41, 71, 93, 136, 144, 166, 172–3. Cf. Gillray's cartoon of Charles James Fox, *A Right Honourable sans culotte* (Duckham collection, London), showing him dressed half as a French revolutionary, half in Windsor uniform.

19 Mollo, *Military Fashion*, 1972, pp. 72–3; Richard Ollard, 'The Brooks's of Charles James Fox', in Philip Ziegler and Desmond Seward, eds, *Brooks's. A Social History*, 1991, p. 35.

20 Godfrey, *Gillray*, pp. 65, 155, 177; Valerie Pakenham, *The Big House in Ireland*, 2000, p. 66.

21 Foreman, *Georgiana*, pp. 153–6, 206.

22 Papendiek, *Court and Private Life*, I, 196; Earl of Bessborough, *Georgiana*, 1955, p. 96, Duchess of Devonshire to Countess Spencer, 16 February 1785: 'the Dss of Gordon was drest in the Prince's uniform, blue and buff, and his buttons'.

23 Stanley Ayling, *Fox*, 1991, pp. 136–7.

24 Alexander Mackay-Smith, *Man and the Horse*, New York, 1984, p. 65; Foreman, *Georgiana*, p. 65.

25 Thus the feathers launched by Marie-Antoinette had, within fourteen years, become 'Prince of Wales's feathers'.

26 Lord Granville Leveson-Gower, *Private Correspondence 1781–1821*, 2 vols, 1916, I, 14, Lady Strafford to Lord Granville Leveson-Gower, 12 February 1789; Foreman, *Georgiana*, p. 210.

27 Countess of Portarlington, *Gleanings from an Old Portfolio*, 3 vols, Edinburgh, 1895–8, II, 119, 121, Lady Louisa Stuart to Miss Herbert, 30 March, 5 April 1789; Papendiek, *Court and Private Life*, II, 82.

28 Ribeiro, *Dress*, p. 190.

29 Somerset, *Ladies-in-Waiting*, pp. 216–17, 237.

30 Madame d'Arblay, *Diary and Letters*, 6 vols, 1904–5, II, 370, 396, 399, letters of 27 June 1786, 24 July 1786; IV, 106, 22 September 1788, 144, 5 November 1788; cf. Papendiek, *Court and Private Life*, II, 4.

31 D'Arblay, *Diary*, III, 56, 88, 251, 6 October, 3 November 1786, 4 June 1787.

32 Ibid., IV, 392, 28 May 1790.

33 Foreman, *Georgiana*, p. 38.

34 Cumming, *Royal Dress*, p. 80.

35 Fraser, *Princesses*, pp. 249 and 315. In September 1667 Charles II found himself with no handkerchiefs and only three neck-bands: at the end of every quarter the grooms of the bedchamber took his linen as their fees and 'let the King get more as he can': Pepys, *Diary*, VIII, 418, 2 September 1667; cf. for private houses Bridget Hill, *Servants. English Domestics in the Eighteenth Century*, Oxford, 1996, pp. 65–6.

36 Delpierre, *Se vêtir*, p. 139.

37 Earl of Bessborough, ed., *Lady Bessborough and her Family Circle*, 1940, pp. 48, 52, diary of Lady Duncannon, 12 April 1789; d'Arblay, *Diary*, IV, 279.

38 Percy Colson, *Whites 1693–1950*, 1951, p. 67.

39 Portarlington, *Gleanings*, p. 219, Lady Louisa to Lady Portarlington, 30 April 1789. For an illustration of the ladies' dress see Edward Maeder, ed., *An Elegant Art. Fashion and Fantasy in the Eighteenth Century*, Los Angeles, 1983, p. 18.

40 Portarlington, *Gleanings*, II, 117, 121, 132–3; Papendiek, *Court and Private Life*, II, 87. At Windsor ladies-in-waiting continued, at least until 1811, to wear a blue and red Windsor uniform: see Hon. Amelia Murray, *Recollections*, 1868, p. 19.

41 Private archives, Journal of Lady Elizabeth Foster, later Elizabeth Duchess of Devonshire, 1800–24, 29 May 1789.

42 Sophie Dupré, 'Wilton', *Manuscript catalogue No. 40*, item 37, letter of 21 April 1789.

43 A. Aspinall, ed., *Later Correspondence of George III*, 5 vols, Cambridge, 1962–70, II, 122, Lord Grenville to George III, 15 November 1793, George III to Lord Grenville, 16 November 1793.

44 Ibid., II, 229, letter of 6 August 1794.

45 Nigel Arch and Joanna Marschner, *Splendour at Court. Dressing for Royal Occasions since 1700*, 1987, p. 81.

46 Cumming, *Royal Dress*, p. 72; Thomas Macgill, *Travels in Turkey, Italy and Russia*, 2 vols, 1808, II, 15; Isabey's print of the Congress of Vienna in 1815 shows Lords Castlereagh and Clancartney in Windsor uniform; Moritz von Kotzebue, *Narrative of a Journey to Persia in the Suite of the Imperial Russian Embassy in the Year 1817*, 1819, pp. 305–6 n.

47 *Annual Register . . . for the Year 1805*, 1806, p. 369; ibid., *1811*, 1812, p. 70.

48 Boswell, *London Journal*, p. 305, 16 July 1763; Anne Buck, *Dress in Eighteenth-Century England*, 1979, p. 31; Mrs Philip Lybbe Powys, *Passages from the Diaries*, 1899, p. 161, 1776, re Mr Bamfield's coat, 'blue trimmed with Devonshire point and olives of fine pearl', costing £800, worn at Exeter races. In 1766 the Marquess of Kildare bought a velvet coat costing £60 to wear for the King of Naples's birthday celebrations. He complained: 'my coat was very handsome and cost me a great deal of money': Brian Fitzgerald, *Emily, Duchess of Leinster*, 1949, pp. 121, 125, to Duchess of Leinster, December 1766, January 1769.

49 Mansfield, *Ceremonial Costume*, p. 147.

50 Mark Girouard, *Life in the English Country-house*, 1974, p. 238. Laurence Stone, *The Family, Sex and Marriage in England 1500–1800*, rev. edn, 1978, pp. 175, 180, 276, 277.

51 Roche, *Culture of Clothing*, pp. 417–19.

52 Harvey, *Men in Black*, pp. 27–9.

53 César de Saussure, *A Foreign View of England in the Reigns of George I and George II*, 1902, p. 113, February 1726.

54 Ribeiro, *Dress*, pp. 125–6.

55 Letter quoted in Maeder, ed., *An Elegant Art*, p. 37.

56 Buck, *Dress*, pp. 31, 59; Diana de Marly, *Fashion for Men*, 1985, pp. 75–7; Duchess of Northumberland, *Diaries*, p. 196, 27 November 1772; Lord Glenbervie, *Diaries*, 2 vols, 1928, I, 39, 15 January 1794.

57 Président de Brosses, *Lettres d'Italie*, ed. Frédéric d'Agay, 2 vols, 1986, I, 397, letter of 24 November 1739; Henry Swinburne, *Travels through Spain in the Years*

1775 and 1776, 1779, p. 334. However, in state portraits, this king was represented in traditional *habit habillé*: Museo del Prado, *Carlos III en Italia 1731–1759*, Madrid, 1989, pp. 81, 95, 105.

58 Ribeiro, *Dress*, p. 115; cf. the portraits by Mengs and Goya of Charles IV, in the Prado, in hunting dress.

59 Constantia Maxwell, *The English Traveller in France 1698–1815*, 1932, p. 84. Tobias Smollett, in *Travels through France and Italy*, Oxford, 1981, p. 46, 12 October 1763; cf. Ribeiro, *Art of Dress*, p. 36 quoting John Andrews writing in 1770, that 'People of Fashion' were beginning to be seen 'walking in Undress on a morning in Paris who would have thought it beneath their Dignity'.

60 Delpierre, *Se vêtir*, p. 43; J. Andrews quoted in C. H. Lockitt, *The Relations of French and English Society 1765–1793*, 1920, p. 41.

61 M. de Lescure, *Correspondance secrète inédite sur Louis XVI, Marie-Antoinette, la cour et la ville*, 2 vols, 1866, II, 10, 29 January 1786; cf. comte de Vaublanc, *Mémoires*, 1857, p. 64.

62 Issue of 15 May 1786, quoted in Ribeiro, *Fashion*, p. 39.

63 M. Genty, *Discours sur le luxe*, 1783, p. 57.

64 Paul Lacroix, *XVIIIe siècle: institutions, usages et costumes*, 1875, p. 486.

65 Bombelles, *Journal*, III, 276, 23 January 1789.

66 Bernard Morel, *Les Joyaux de la couronne de France*, 1988, p. 228.

67 Ribeiro, *Fashion*, p. 45; François d'Ormesson and Jean-Pierre Thomas, *Jean-Joseph de Laborde banquier de Louis XV, mécène des lumières*, 2002, p. 103.

68 [J. M. Moreau], *Le Costume français, représentant les différents États du Royaume, avec les habillements propres à chaque État, et accompagné de Réflexions Critiques et Morales*, 1776, planche VI.

69 Richard Wrigley, *The Politics of Appearances. Representations of Dress in Revolutionary France*, Oxford, 2002, p. 62; Georges Lefebvre and Anne Terroine, eds, *Recueil de documents relatifs aux séances des États Généraux mai–juin 1789*, 1953, I, 73–82.

70 La Rochefoucauld, Wolikow and Ikni, *Le Duc de La Rochefoucauld-Liancourt* pp. 355–64.

71 Baron de Besenval, *Mémoires sur la cour de France*, 1987 edn, p. 468; Philip Mansel, *The Court of France, 1789–1830*, 1989, p. 15.

72 Ferdinand Dreyfus, *Un philanthrope d'autrefois. La Rochefoucauld-Liancourt 1747–1827*, 1903, pp. 65, 82.

73 The colours of the tricolour were also a variation on the livery colours of the King of France.

74 Wrigley, *Politics*, pp. 99, 124; Dreyfus, *Philanthrope*, pp. 84, 92, 120–21.

75 Pierre Narbonne, *Journal de police*, 2 vols, Clermont-Ferrand, 2002, I, 133, September 1725.

76 *Procédure criminelle instruite au Châtelet de Paris*, 3 vols, 1790, II, 13–15, 71, 83, 125–6, eyewitness accounts by MM de Frondeville, Brayer, de La Serre and Jobert.

77 Wrigley, *Politics*, pp. 101, 104, 112–13, 126.

78 Roche, *Culture of Clothing*, p. 254.

79 Ibid., p. 148. Former *gardes français* who had deserted to the National Guard, however, had theirs paid by the municipality of Paris.

80 Henry Paulin Panon Desbassyns, *Voyage à Paris pendant la Révolution 1790–1792*, 1985, pp. 39, 42, 12, 17 July 1790.

81 Archives Nationales, AN C 189: (papers of the Liste Civile of Louis XVI), 118 f. 59, La Fayette to Louis XVI, 17 July 1790.

82 Lescure, *Correspondance*, II, 425, 20 February 1790; for the Russian minister visiting in secret *en frac*, see Baron F. S. Feuillet de Conches, *Louis XVI, Marie-Antoinette et Madame Élizabeth*, 6 vols, 1864–73, V, 167, Baron de Simolin to Catherine II, 31 January/11 February 1792.

83 *Pièces imprimées d'après le Décret de la Convention Nationale du 5 décembre 1792*, 2 vols, Agen, 1793, I, 199; Philip Mansel, 'Monarchy, Uniform and the Rise of the *Frac* 1760–1830', *Past and Present*, 96 (August 1981), p. 130; but Henry Paulin Panon Desbassyns (*Voyage*, p. 38, 11 July 1790) states that at a review the King wore 'un habit rouge qui avait du service ainsi qu'un chapeau bordé d'un bord en or'. Evidence about Louis XVI's dress is as contradictory as evidence about his politics.

84 Archives du château de Mouchy: Prince de Poix, 'Note autobiographique', f. 8.

85 Duc de Choiseul, *Relation du départ de Louis XVI le 20 juin 1791 écrite en août 1791*, 1822, pp. 50, 56; cf. Klinkowström, *Fersen*, I 137, Fersen to Bouillé, 13 June 1791: 'le roi aura un habit rouge et se fera connaître, selon ce que le duc de Choiseul lui dira de la bonne disposition des troupes'. Naturally all accounts of the flight to Varennes, written to excuse the author's role in its outcome, should be treated with extreme caution.

86 Philip Mansel, *Louis XVIII*, 1981, p. 63.

87 Eugène Bimbenet, *Fuite de Louis XVI à Varennes*, 2 vols, 1868 edn, II, 96, 105, 107, interrogations of MM Maldent, Dumoustier, 7 July 1791.

88 Söderhjelm, *Fersen*, p. 178, Fersen to Taube, 4 April 1791.

89 C. Beaulieu, *Histoire du commerce de l'industrie et des fabriques de la soie*, Lyon, 1838, pp. 101–3, 107–8, 111.

90 Musée des Tissus, *Soieries de Lyon*, pp. 16–17.

91 Louis Trénard, *Lyon de l'Encyclopédie au romantisme*, 2 vols, 1958, I, 240–41.

92 Roche, *Culture of Clothing*, p. 315.

93 Langlade, *La Marchande de modes*, pp. 196–7, 213. The dress cost 1,218 livres and was never paid for.

94 Musée de la mode et du costume, *Modes et révolutions 1780–1804*, 1989, p. 76.

95 La Tour du Pin, *Journal*, I, 240.

96 Vicomte de Grouchy and Antoine Guillois, eds, *La Révolution française vue par un diplomate étranger*, 1903, Bailli de Virieu to Duke of Parma 2 October 1791; Madame de Staël, *Considérations sur la révolution française*, 1983 edn, p. 276; cf. the picture by Charles Thévenin of the Fête de la Fédération, 14 July 1790, in the Musée Carnavalet.

97 Espinchal, *Journal*, p. 57, 27 September 1789; Emmanuel Vingtrinier, *La Contre-révolution*, 2 vols, 1924–5, I, 68.

98 Vingtrinier, *Contre-révolution*, II 142 and n.

99 Madame de Falaiseau, *Dix ans de la vie d'une femme pendant l'émigration. Mémoires*, 1893, p. 73, journal May 1792.

100 Roche, *Culture of Clothing*, pp. 181–2.

101 Wrigley, *Politics*, pp. 187, 190, 196; Ribeiro, *Fashion*, pp. 85–6.

102 François de La Rochefoucauld, *Souvenirs du 10 août 1792 et de l'armée de Bourbon*, 1929, p. 33.

103 Wrigley, *Politics*, p. 155.

104 Archives Nationales, AN C222: *déposition* of M de Bourcet, 27 June 1792; duc de

Lévis-Mirepoix, *Aventures d'une famille française*, 1949, p. 279, duc to duchesse de Lévis, late June 1792.

105 *Le Postillon de la guerre*, 25 June 1792, quoted in *Découverte: Bulletin trimestriel du comité pour l'étude de Louis XVI et de son procès*, 4, 1982, 30–31; Hans Glagau, *Die Französische Legislative und der Ursprung der Revolutionskriege*, Berlin, 1908, p. 341, Abbé Louis to Mercy-Argenteau, 26 June 1792. A print of his son in National Guard uniform was engraved by Moitte: Jacques Charles, ed., *Louis XVII*, n.d., p. 110. The Prince Royal wore National Guard uniform, and his mother and her ladies had tricolour ribbons in their hair, at the celebrations on 14 July 1792: Rose Barral-Mazoyer, *Thomas-Augustin de Gasparin, officier de l'armée royale et conventionnelle*, Marseille, 1982, p. 212, letter of Adrien Gasparin, 16 July 1792.

106 Archives Nationales, AN C192: *déposition* of Larchey, n.d.

107 De Staël, *Considérations*, p. 278.

108 Archives Nationales, AN C192: *dépositions* of Calley, 16 August 1792, of Larchey, Toupet, Frenot, n.d.

109 'Je montai dans la chambre du Roi. J'y trouvai beaucoup de monde, peu de gens habillés; j'étais moi-même en frac', La Rochefoucauld, *Souvenirs*, p. 8.

110 Comte de Montmort, *Antoine Charles du Houx, Baron de Vioménil*, Baltimore, 1935, pp. 18–21, *déposition* of Toussaint, p. 25; Bombelles, *Journal*, III, 119, 29 August 1790; Baron Hue, *Souvenirs*, 1908, pp. 37, 47.

111 Philippe Godet, *Madame de Charrière et ses amis*, 2 vols, Geneva, 1906, II, 23, M. Montmollin to his father, 8 August 1792.

112 Rodney Allen, *Threshold of Terror: The Last Hours of the Monarchy in the French Revolution*, 1999, p. 234; royalist officers like the prince de Poix also discarded their uniforms: Archives de Mouchy: Prince de Poix, 'Note autobiographique', f. 9.

113 La Rochefoucauld, *Souvenirs*, p. 32.

114 Richard Twiss, *A Trip to Paris in July and August 1792*, 1793, p. 66.

115 Wrigley, *Politics*, pp. 63–4.

116 Ibid., pp. 22–3, 25–6.

117 Ribeiro, *Fashion*, p. 75.

118 Langlade, *La Marchande de modes*, pp. 226, 255. Thus no clothes of Marie-Antoinette can be seen in public collections in France today.

119 Kirsty Carpenter, *Refugees of the French Revolution. Émigrés in London 1789–1802*, 1999, pp. 69–70.

120 Ribeiro, *Fashion*, p. 21.

121 *Les Grandes Demeures d'Espagne*, 1998, pp. 106–8, 116, 120.

122 Alexandre Poidebard and Jacques Châtel, *Camille Pernon*, Lyon, 1912, pp. 10–12.

123 Katell Le Bourhis, ed., *The Age of Napoleon. Costume from Revolution to Empire*, Metropolitan Museum of New York, 1989, p. 152.

124 Wrigley, *Politics*, p. 107; Roche, *Culture of Clothing*, p. 149 n.

125 Ribeiro, *Fashion*, pp. 99–103.

126 Delpierre, *Se vêtir*, p. 154.

127 Thus coats made in 1779 for Prince Charles de Ligne and his father, to wear for the signature by the royal family at Versailles of the former's wedding contract, embroidered with diamonds on the cloth and the *garnitures de boutons* and costing 1,606 livres and 1,126 livres respectively, were sold in Paris by their descendants on 14 January 2004, for several thousand euros each: Viktor

Klarwill, ed., *Mémoires et lettres du prince de Ligne*, 1923, p. 17; *Beaux-Arts Magazine*, 238 (March 2004), p. 117. On 7 November 1996 the National Museum of Wales acquired a sequined and embroidered *habit habillé* of Sir Watkin Williams Wynn from his descendants for £15,291.

128 Marquise de Montcalm, *Journal*, 1934, p. 325, 1 February 1818; for pictures of parties, see, *inter alia*, Charlotte Augusta Sneyd, *Almacks 1819* (Keele University Collection); Eugène Lami, *Salon de famille, Eu*, 1843 (Royal Collection); Jean Béraud, *La Soirée c.* 1880 (Musée Carnavalet).

129 *Journal des dames et des modes*, 25 September 1824, p. 424: 'Le costume des hommes n'a guère changé que par le crêpe qu'ils ont ajouté à leur chapeau. Depuis longtemps le noir était pour eux la couleur dominante.'

130 Cf. Ilario Rinieri, ed., *Corrispondenza inedita dei Cardinali Consalvi e Pacca*, Turin, 1903, p. lxiii, 25 November 1814: 'l'effet que produit le fait que tous les souverains soient tous les jours en frac en société'; cf. M. N. Balisson de Rougemont, *Le Rôdeur français ou les moeurs du jour*, 6 vols, 1816–21, IV, 233, 27 January 1820: 'le frac est devenu l'habit de tout le monde'.

131 Baron Comeau, *Souvenirs des guerres d'Allemagne pendant la Révolution et l'Empire*, 1900, p. 326.

132 Mansel, 'Monarchy, Uniform and the Rise of the *Frac*', p. 206; Paul Morand, *Le Prince de Ligne*, 1964, p. 82: 'how can one show respect to names, ranks, classes and one's superiors in the army? Down to the shoe-maker everyone is dressed the same'; cf. for equal indignation, from a surgeon in Paris in 1815, Jane Vansittart, ed., *Surgeon James's Journal 1815*, 1964, pp. 80–81: 'It is not always easy to distinguish the middle classes from the upper as there is very little difference in the dress' – even between masters and servants.

133 Jonathan Dewald, *The European Nobility 1400–1800*, 1996, p. 197.

134 Comte Fédor Golovkine, *La Cour et le règne de Paul Ier*, 1905, pp. 131–2.

135 Harriette Wilson, *Harriette Wilson's Memoirs*, ed. Lesley Blanch, 2003 edn, p. 95. See illustrations in Ribeiro, *Art of Dress*, pp. 99–105.

136 Lewis Melville, *Beau Brummell, his Life and Letters*, 1904, p. 46; cf. the advice of the baronne de Gérando to her son in 1822 that 'la société aristocratique et de l'ancien ton' defined itself 'above all by this great simplicity of clothes and manners', in contrast to 'les commis de magasins, les garçons limonadiers, les jeunes provinciaux', who 'font jabot': baronne de Gérando, *Lettres de la baronne de Gérando*, 1880, p. 365, letter of August 1822.

137 Philippe Perrot, *Le Luxe. Une richesse entre faste et confort XVIIIe–XIXe siècle*, 1995, p. 113; Charles Baudelaire, 'Le Dandy', November–December 1863, in Jules Barbey d'Aurevilly, *Du Dandysme et de George Brummell*, 1997 edn, pp. 149–51; James Laver, *Dandies*, 1968, *passim*, with many illustrations.

138 For example 'on the cod' – gone drinking; 'whipping the cat' – travelling around and working in private houses.

139 Richard Walker, *The Savile Row Story*, 1988, pp. 21, 186–7.

140 Purdy, *Tyranny*, pp. 119–20, 141.

141 Giuseppe Tomasi di Lampedusa, *The Leopard*, 1973 edn, p. 65.

142 J.-P. Garnier, *Barras, roi du Directoire*, 1970, p. 153.

143 Wilhelm von Wolzogen, *Journal de voyage à Paris*, Lille, 1998, p. 206, 31 January 1793.

144 Michael Zakim, *Ready-Made Democracy: A History of Men's Dress in the American Republic 1760–1860*, Chicago, 2003, *passim*, and pp. 1, 22.

145 Letter of 13 January 1783, quoted in Colin McDowell, ed., *The Literary Companion to Fashion*, 1995, p. 10.

146 Catherine Allgor, *Parlor Politics. In which the Ladies of Washington help build a City and a Government*, Charlottesville, 2000, p. 32.

Chapter 5: The Age of Gold

1   Malcolm Vale, *The Princely Court: Medieval Courts and Culture in North-West Europe 1270–1380*, Oxford, 2001, pp. 94–5, 103; Waterfield and French, *Below Stairs*, p. 42.

2   Anne French, 'Stewards to Scullery-Maids', in Waterfield and French, *Below Stairs*, p. 41; Gwen Squire, *Livery Buttons. The Pitt Collection*, Pulborough, 1976, p. xx.

3   Papendiek, *Court and Private Life*, I, 196.

4   Mansel, 'Monarchy', p. 246; cf. the comte de Flahaut's fear of looking like a livery servant of Marshal Murat, grand duc de Berg, whose aide de camp he was: Frédéric Masson, *Napoléon et sa famille*, 15 vols, 1908–19, VI, 289.

5   Mrs Arbuthnot, *Journal*, 2 vols, 1950, I, 94, 11 May 1821.

6   William Roscoe Thayer, *The Life and Times of Cavour*, 2 vols, 1911, I, 7.

7   T. J. Binyon, *Pushkin*, 2003 edn, pp. 320, 437–9.

8   Charles Dickens, *The Pickwick Papers*, 1837, Chapter 37, 'The Gentleman in Blue'.

9   Lampedusa, *The Leopard*, p. 122.

10 The portrait, by Michele Gordigiani, is in the Museo Nazionale del Risorgimento, Turin. Cavour's successor Ricasoli, however, refused the King's request to wear the uniform, saying that his ancestors had never worn anyone's livery: Denis Mack-Smith, *Italy. A Modern History*, Ann Arbor, 1959, p. 62.

11 Madame de Beaulaincourt, *B. L. A. de Castellane*, 1901, p. 215, 14 February 1817, and p. 367.

12 Textilmuseum, *Nach Rang und Stand. Deutsche Ziviluniformen im 19. Jahrhundert*, Krefeld, 2002, pp. 66–70.

13 Baron G. Peyrusse, *Lettres inédites du Baron Guillaume Peyrusse écrites à son frère André*, 1894, pp. 4, 6, letters of 26 March, 9 April 1809; Baron G. Peyrusse, *Mémorial et archives*, Carcassonne, 1869, p. 8, 7 April 1809.

14 Archives Nationales, AN 03 222: 75, letter of 24 November 1818.

15 Wrigley, *Politics*, pp. 80–82.

16 Ibid., p. 202.

17 Palais Galliéra, *Uniformes civils français*, pp. 26–9; Ribeiro, *Fashion*, p. 105; Jean Duplessis-Bertaux, *Audience du directoire en costume*, 30 brumaire an IV, Louvre Dept des Estamps.

18 Jacques Grasset de Saint-Sauveur, *Costumes des représentants du peuple français*, 1795, p. 4.

19 M. Bonneville, *Costumes actuels des deux conseils législatifs et du directoire exécutif*, 1796, *passim*.

20 Stella Tillyard, *Citizen Lord*, 1997, p. 266.

21 Henry Lachouque, *The Anatomy of Glory*, 1997 edn, pp. 7–11.

22 Le Bourhis, *Napoleon*, pp. 35–6, 83–4; Palais Galliéra, *Uniformes civils français*, pp. 34, 38, 43.

23 See portraits of Champagny, Lebrun and Savary in the Musée de l'histoire de France, Versailles, MV 4721, 1808, 4731.

24 Waresquiel, *Talleyrand*, p. 290.

25 J. G. Lemaistre, *A Rough Sketch of Modern Paris*, 1803, pp. 159, 161; for examples of such costumes, see Le Bourhis, *Napoleon*, pp. 109–11.

26 Mansel, *Court of France*, p. 50.

27 See e.g. Comte Louis de Bentheim-Steinfurst, 'Journal de mon séjour à Paris', *Revue de Paris*, 25 October 1908, p. 332, 25 December 1803.

28 Madame de Rémusat, *Mémoires*, 3 vols, 1880, II, 333; Galeries nationales du Grand Palais, *Napoléon*, 1969, pp. 442–3; Colombe Samoyault-Verlet and Pierre Samoyault, *Château de Fontainebleau. Musée Napoléon Ier*, 1986, p. 59.

29 Le Bourhis, *Napoleon*, p. 209.

30 Galeries nationales du Grand Palais, *Napoléon*, pp. 442–3; cf. Rémusat, *Mémoires*, II, 333, 337.

31 Galeries nationales du Grand Palais, *Cinq années d'enrichissement du patrimoine national 1975–1980*, Grand Palais, 1980, p. 175; Anne Plumptre, *A Narrative of a Three Years Residence in France*, 3 vols, 1810, I, 124–5. Parisians were also said to be delighted by the reappearance of foreign diplomats' liveries: Comte Remacle, ed., *Relations secrètes des agents de Louis XVIII à Paris sous le consulat (1802–1803)*, 1899, p. 50, 27 June 1802.

32 Remacle, *Relations*, p. 233, 15 January 1803.

33 Comte d'Haussonville, *Madame de Staël et Monsieur Necker*, 1925, p. 279, Madame de Staël to Necker, 1 October 1803.

34 Comte Miot de Mélito, *Mémoires*, 3 vols, 1858, II, 61.

35 Remacle, *Relations*, p. 264, 28 February 1803.

36 Raoul Brunon, 'Uniformes de l'armée française', in Jean Tulard, ed., *Dictionnaire Napoléon*, 1989, pp. 1666–87; Le Bourhis, *Napoleon*, pp. 179–201.

37 Le Bourhis, *Napoleon*, p. 149.

38 Frédéric Masson, *Le Sacre et le couronnement de Napoléon*, 1978 edn, p. 122; Palais Galliéra, *Uniformes civils français*, pp. 19–20; the costumes can be seen in Thierry Lentz, ed., *Le Sacre de Napoléon*, 2003, pp. 96–7.

39 Lentz, *Le Sacre*, p. 54.

40 *Les Autographes* (45 rue de l'Abbé Grégoire, 75006 Paris), cat. 104, February 2003, item 265, Ségur to Joseph Bonaparte, 22 November 1804.

41 Lentz, *Le Sacre*, pp. 73, 78–9, 114.

42 Le Bourhis, *Napoleon*, pp. 92–3. The order book of the Maison Brocard (consulted in Paris on 27 June 1985) shows the amount Napoleon and his officials were prepared to spend on the embroidery for their uniforms: 15 *brumaire* an 13, 650 francs for the 'habit grand costume de Prefet du Palais' of Monsieur de Rémusat; 1,090 francs for Choiseul-Praslin's 'habit de velours bleu grand costume du sénat surdoré'; 10 *frimaire* an 13, 29,750 francs for embroideries for a *grand* and *petit costume* of the Emperor; 50,000 francs for the embroideries for the throne and *fauteuil* of the Tuileries Palace on the same day. Marshal Ney was said to spend more than 12,000 francs on each dress uniform.

43 Stendhal, *Oeuvres intimes*, 1955, p. 965, 12 August 1810.

44 Frank Lestringant, *Alfred de Musset*, 1999, p. 25.

45 Samoyault-Verlet and Samoyault, *Château de Fontainebleau*, pp. 11, 19–22; Le Bourhis, *Napoleon*, p. 214.

46 Balzac, *Traité de la vie élégante*, p. 34.

47 Archives Nationales, AN 400 AP 4: Registre du grand maréchal du palais, note by Duroc, 14 January 1811.

48 See e.g. Museo Nazionale di Palazzo Mansi, *Abiti alla corte di Elisa*, Lucca, 1995. The accounts of Napoleon's youngest brother Jerôme-Napoléon, King of Westphalia, show that he owned the cloaks and costumes of a French prince, of a grand dignitary of the French Empire and of Westphalia, uniforms of the army and the Order of the Crown, 'habits de cour et de fantaisie, fracs du matin, habits de chasse, habits bourgeois', ball and quadrille costumes: Bibliothèque Thiers, Paris, Fonds Masson, Ms. 41274, 'Garde-robe du roi, journal de sortie', 15 September 1812; cf. Samoyault-Verlet and Samoyault, *Château de Fontainebleau*, p. 104.

49 Anon., *Louis Bonaparte et sa cour*, 1820, pp. 17, 89. No doubt similar learning processes were occurring at the same time in the former republics of Venice, Genoa and Lucca.

50 Stanislas de Girardin, *Souvenirs*, 4 vols, 1828, III, 403, 3 May 1807.

51 Thomas Baring, *A Tour through Italy . . . and Austria*, 2nd edn, 1817, p. 263, 4 July 1814.

52 J. B. S. Morritt, *A Grand Tour*, 1985 edn, pp. 270–73, 18 December 1795; cf. for the popularity of the *frac* in Naples, Brian Connell, *Portrait of a Whig Peer*, 1957, p. 275, Lord Palmerston's diary, 10 January 1793.

53 Pictures of Neapolitan troop manoeuvres in 1787 and in 1794 by the court painter Jacob Philipp Hackert nevertheless hang in the royal palace of Caserta.

54 Comtesse Rasponi, *Souvenirs d'enfance*, 1929, pp. 69–73; for photographs of Murat's uniforms see Deutsches Historisches Museum, *Bilder und Zeugnisse*, I, 303.

55 Hippolyte d'Espinchal, *Souvenirs*, 2 vols, 1929, I, 324.

56 Paul Le Brethon, *Lettres et documents pour servir à l'histoire de Joachim Murat*, 8 vols, 1908–14, VI, 238.

57 Frédéric Masson, *Joséphine impératrice et reine*, 1899 illustrated edn, p. 37.

58 Rémusat, *Mémoires*, II, 343–6; Masson, *Joséphine*, pp. 31–4.

59 Henri Bouchot, *La Toilette à la cour de Napoléon. Chiffons et politique de grandes dames 1810–1815*, 1895, pp. 76, 201–13 for the account of the duchesse de Bassano *chez* Leroy.

60 Rémusat, *Mémoires*, II, 348, 349 n.

61 Ibid., III, 229.

62 D'Espinchal, *Souvenirs*, I, 103–7; cf. comte de Rambuteau, *Mémoires*, 1903, p. 16.

63 Henri Deherain, *La Vie de Pierre Ruffin*, 2 vols, 1929–30, II, 19, Magnytot to Ruffin, 20 January 1806.

64 Le Bourhis, *Napoleon*, p. 212.

65 Ibid., p. 162.

66 Frédéric Masson, *L'Impératrice Marie-Louise*, 1909, p. 277.

67 Napoléon I, *Correspondance générale*, 32 vols, 1858–70, XXI, 327, 19 December 1810.

68 Philippe Séguy, *Histoire des modes sous l'Empire*, 1988, pp. 176–8.

69 Maréchal de Castellane, *Journal*, 5 vols, 1896–7, I, 82, September 1810. The *habit* of Maréchal Lannes is in the Musée de l'Armée.

70 G. Pellissier, *Le Portefeuille de la comtesse d'Albany*, 1902, p. 91, letter of 18 January 1811.

71 L. Lanzac de Laborie, *Paris sous Napoléon*, 8 vols, 1905, III, 98.

72 Le Bourhis, *Napoleon*, p. 208.

73 *Talleyrand*, Bibliothèque Nationale, 1965, p. 93, Talleyrand to Bertin de Vaux, 11 August 1820.

74 Anticipated by Marguerite de Navarre's sentence, in the Heptameron, 'L'habit est si loin de faire le moine, que bien souvent, par orgueil, il le défait.'

75 Balisson de Rougemont, *Rôdeur français*, I, 87, 14 November 1814; cf. Castellane, *Journal*, III, 403, 31 December 1830: 'la chambre des députés à decidé en comité secret la suppression de son costume; elle a tort car cela influe plus qu'on ne croit sur la considération d'un corps, même souvent sur les actions de ses membres.'

76 Honoré de Balzac, *Les Illusions perdues*, 2000 edn, p. 145.

77 [Stephen Weston], *Two Sketches of France, Belgium and Spa during the Summers of 1771 and 1816*, 1817, p. 87.

78 Archives Nationales, AN 03 519: *Consigne générale des gardes du corps*, 1814; A. Galignani's, *Galignani's New Paris Guide*, Thirteenth Edition, 1825, p. 47.

79 Étienne de Jouy, *Guillaume le franc-parleur*, 2 vols, 1816, I, 64, 18 June 1814.

80 Mrs Henry-Simon et Maréchal, *Les Étrennes forcées, ou Ah! mon habit que je vous remercie!*, 1814 (first performed 30 December 1813), p. 40.

81 Édouard Gachot, *Marie-Louise intime*, 2 vols, 1911–12, I, 207, duc de Feltre to Marie-Louise, 23 October 1812; S. C. Gigon, *Le Général Malet*, 1913, p. 107; a servant had been sent to fetch the uniform from General Malet's apartment two weeks before he escaped from the *maison de santé* where he was detained: Max Billard, *La Conspiration de Malet*, 1907, p. 45 n.

82 Général de Caulaincourt, *Mémoires*, 3 vols, 1933, II, 349.

83 *Journal des dames et des modes*, 10 July 1814, p. 40.

84 Archives Nationales, AN 03 (papers of the Maison du roi 1814–30), 487: doss. Longueil, marquise de Sémonville, to marquis de Lauriston, 9 January 1821; cf. Comte d'Haussonville, *Ma jeunesse*, 1885, pp. 292–6.

85 Baron de Frénilly, *Souvenirs*, 1908, p. 440. When Thierry de Ville d'Avray, grandson of the *premier valet de chambre* who had visited Lyon for Louis XVI, danced in a *habit habillé* at a ball in 1817 he remembered years later 'que tous les yeux étaient braqués sur moi': Thierry de Ville d'Avray Archives, 'Mémoires of vicomte Thierry de Ville d'Avray', I f. 218. However, Victor Hugo, who had no official position, wore it to an audience with Charles X in 1829: Victor Hugo, *Correspondance familiale et écrits intimes*, 4 vols, 1988, I, 650.

86 Archives Nationales, AN 341 AP 25 (La Grange Papers), Mondenard to Marquis de La Grange, n.d.

87 British Library Add. Ms 41648 f. 4ᵛ account by Sir Thomas Clifford.

88 E. D. Pasquier, *Histoire de mon temps*, 6 vols, 1893–5, IV, 254.

89 Archives Nationales, AN 03 72, Baron d'Egvilly to prince de Condé, 8 March 1815.

90 Castellane, *Journal*, I, 261, 5 August 1814.

91 Louis-Philippe's uniform as a republican lieutenant-general, which he had kept, was useful for the painters he employed forty years later to celebrate the 1792 campaign: Daniel Halévy, *Le Courrier de Monsieur Thiers*, 1921, p. 54, letter of 1 August 1838 to Thiers.

92 Cf. Antonetti, *Louis-Philippe*, p. 436.

93 Alexandre de Laborde, *Quarante-huit heures de garde au château des Tuileries*, 1816, pp. 19–20.

94 Philip Mansel, *Paris between Empires*, 2001, p. 80; cf. the caricature of the Emperor on this occasion in the Andrew Edmunds collection, Lexington Street, London: *En habit d'Empereur il jure la liberté*.

95 [John Cam Hobhouse], *The Substance of some Letters written by an Englishman resident at Paris during the Last Reign of the Emperor Napoleon*, 2 vols, 1816, I, 415, 420, 424, 1 June 1815.

96 Lord Rosebery, *Napoleon: The Last Phase*, 1928 edn, pp. 169, 72, 275–6, quoting Lady Malcolm, 25 June 1816, and Mr Henry, 1 September 1817.

97 Frank Giles, *Napoleon Bonaparte: England's Prisoner*, 2001, p. 115.

98 Adolphe Maze-Sencier, *Les Fournisseurs de Napoléon Ier et des deux impératrices*, 1893, pp. 361–3.

99 The portrait is in the Museo Napoleonico, Rome.

100 Archives Nationales, AN 03 508, ordonnance of 12 September 1815.

101 A. Dayot, *Les Vernet*, 1898, p. 174, General Foy, diary of 14 March 1825; Anne Lister, diary for June 1825, private archive.

102 Archives Nationales, AN 885, 101, *règlement* of 10 December 1820.

103 Théodore Anne, *Mémoires, souvenirs et anecdotes sur l'intérieur de Palais de Charles X*, 2 vols, 1831, II, 153.

104 Archives Nationales, AN 03 194: La Châtre to Lauriston, 10 November 1820; 03 628 Correspondance 1820, Lauriston to La Châtre, 13 December 1820.

105 Archives Nationales, AN 03 360: (application for court office) doss. Jumilhac.

106 Richelieu to Decazes, 7 October 1818, in Emmanuel de Waresquiel and Benoît Yvert, 'Le duc de Richelieu et le comte Decazes d'après leur correspondance inédite', *Revue de la société d'histoire de la restauration*, II (1988), p. 91.

107 Général Marquis Alphonse d'Hautpoul, *Mémoires*, 1906, p. 159. Bordeaux continued to wear Restoration military uniform on formal occasions in exile: A. Cuvillier-Fleury, *Journal intime*, 2 vols, 1900–03, I, 191, 6 December 1843.

108 Marie-Amélie, *Journal*, 1988, p. 329, 21 December 1824; comte de Montbel, *Souvenirs*, 1913, p. 203, 12 April 1829.

109 Bibliothèque Administrative de la Ville de Paris, Ms. 387, duc de Lévis, 'Notes de cour', ff. 80–86, 21 December 1824.

110 Fiona Ffoulkes, 'Luxury Clothing in Nineteenth-century Paris', in Maxine Berg and Helen Clifford, eds, *Consumers and Luxury. Consumer Culture in Europe 1650–1850*, Manchester, 1999, pp. 191–3; Bouchot, *La Toilette, passim*, is a fine study of LeRoy, based on an order book.

111 *Journal des débats*, 30 May 1814.

112 Madame de Boigne, *Mémoires*, 2 vols, 1986 edn, I, 260.

113 *Journal des dames et des modes*, 25 June 1825, pp. 274, 280.

114 In all portraits, prints and busts of the Restoration, whatever her dress, the duchesse d'Angoulême wears feathers.

115 Mansel, *Paris between Empires*, p. 180.

116 General Foy, *Notes autobiographiques*, 3 vols, 1926, I, 201, 24 June 1821.

117 Jacqueline du Pasquier, 'La Duchesse de Berry arbitre de la mode et reine du style troubadour', in *Marie Caroline de Berry. Naples, Paris, Graz. Itinéraire d'une princesse romantique*, 2002, pp. 124–37.

118 Archives Nationales, AN 03 529, *Supplément au règlement arrêté par le Roi le 10 décembre*, 15 December 1820.

119 Ibid., 03 885, 101, *ordonnance* of 5 February 1830.

120 A. Dumesnil, *Moeurs politiques au XIXe siècle*, 2 vols, 1830, II, 194.

121 Marquis de Custine, *Mémoires et voyages*, 2nd edn, 2 vols, 1830, II, 95.

122 Comte Rodolphe Apponyi, *Journal*, 4 vols, 1913–26, I, 258, 260–62, 31 May, 2 June 1830; Cuvillier-Fleury, *Journal*, I, 186–9, 31 May 1830; N. A. de Salvandy,

'Une Fête au Palais-Royal', in *Paris, ou le Livre des cent et un*, 15 vols, 1831–5, I, 398.

123 Textilmuseum, *Nach Rang und Stand*, pp. 66–70; *Bildliche Darstellung der königlich preussische Civil-Uniformen*, Berlin, 1804.

124 Schloss Halbthurn, *Uniform und Mode am Kaiserhof*, Vienna, 1983, pp. 42, 43, 61–2; Palais Galliéra, *Costumes à la cour de Vienne, 1815–1918*, 1995, p. 79.

125 Palais Galliéra, *Costumes à la cour de Vienne*, p. 66.

126 Ibid., pp. 63–4.

127 Ibid., pp. 64–6.

128 Schloss Halbthurn, *Uniform und Mode am Kaiserhof*, pp. 50–51; Palais Galliéra, *Costumes à la cour de Vienne*, pp. 67–9, 74–7.

129 Palais Galliéra, *Costumes à la cour de Vienne*, p. 67.

130 Bibliothèque municipale de Genève, Ms. 1684, Mme Eynard, 'Journal'.

131 Palais Galliéra, *Costumes à la cour de Vienne*, pp. 70, 109.

132 Bianca M. du Mortier, *Aristocratic Attire. The Donation of the Six Family*, Amsterdam, 2000, p. 32, refers to King William I's promulgation of 'Regulations pertaining to court dress' on 17 March 1815, the day after his assumption of the royal title; Rangström, *Hovets dräkter*, p. 113; Carla Cavelli Traverso, 'Dall'uniforme sabauda a quella italiana', *Studi Piemontesi*, March 2000, xxix, fasc i, pp. 131–40 (I am grateful for this reference to Dr Robert Oresko). Already, in 1777, at their own request, the *gentilshommes de la chambre* of the King of Sardinia had been given a civil uniform to distinguish them from other courtiers: *Fasti della burocrazia*, p. 19.

133 Kirsten Schultz, *Tropical Versailles. Empire, Monarchy and the Portuguese Royal Court in Rio de Janeiro 1808–1821*, New York, 2002, p. 103; Roderick J. Barman, *Citizen Emperor Pedro II and the Making of Brazil 1825–91*, Stanford, 1999, pp. 11, 78–9, 260.

134 Cf. Mrs Arbuthnot, *Journal*, I, 94, 11 May 1821.

135 Mollo, *Prince's Dolls*, p. 99; Parissien, *George IV*, p. 255; cf. the pages of the surviving ledger of Meyer and Mortimer, 6 Sackville Street, London W1 (consulted 25 June 2003), Prince of Wales's account, 7 September 1810: 'altering the sleeves of a Field Marshal's uniform to open behind'; 9 March 1811: 'altering a Field Marshal's blue frock uniform'. Other items include 'a pair of rich gold epaulettes', 2 May 1814, £16 16s. There is also mention of fringes, braids, embroidery, gilt buttons, fur pelisses and scarlet plush. Some items were charged to the Prince's Privy Purse, others to the army's Board of Clothing.

136 Quoted in Valerie Cumming, 'Pantomime and Pageantry: The Coronation of George IV', in Celina Fox, ed., *London – World City 1800–1840*, 1992, pp. 39–50; p. 42.

137 Charles Greville, *Memoirs*, 8 vols, 1938, I, 337, 1 December 1829. His uniform as colonel of the 10th Dragoons and his and his successors' Field Marshals' batons are on show in the King's and Queen's Guard Rooms in Windsor Castle.

138 Lady Jackson, ed., *The Bath Archives*, 2 vols, 1873, I, 342–3, Lady Jackson to her mother, 14 March 1812.

139 Herbert Maxwell, ed., *The Creevey Papers*, 2 vols, 1903, I, 161, Creevey to Mrs Creevey, 1 June 1812.

140 Windsor Castle, Royal Archives 21478: Lord Conyngham to Colonel Macmahon, 9 July 1814; cf. John Cam Hobhouse who, despite his radical views, wrote, before

taking dispatches to the continent, to ask 'if I might apply without binding myself to parties for the G. P. R. [George Prince Regent] uniform': Lord Broughton, *Recollections of a Long Life*, 6 vols, 1909–11, I, 210, 14 March 1815.

141   *Annual Register . . . for the Year 1817*, 1818, p. 100; Valerie Cumming, *Royal Dress*, 1989, p. 88.

142   Cumming, 'Pantomime and Pageantry, p. 42.

143   Cumming, *Royal Dress*, p. 100; Greville, *Memoirs*, II, 24, 3 August 1830.

144   Kay Staniland, *In Royal Fashion*, 1997, pp. 13–14; Pilbeam, *Madame Tussaud*, p. 107.

145   Mansel, *Pillars of Monarchy*, p. 160.

146   Mansfield, *Ceremonial Costume*, pp. 172–3.

147   Esher, *The Girlhood of Queen Victoria*, II, 303, diary, 22 January 1840.

148   National Library of Scotland, Ms 6242 ff. 384–5, report of 30 July 1830 to Stuart de Rothesay: 'le bas peuple crie Vive Napoléon II!'

149   Countess of Blessington, *The Idler in France*, 2 vols, 1841, II, 185; Mary Berry, *Social Life in England and France, from the French Revolution in 1789 to that of July 1830*, 1831, p. 200 n.

150   Archives Nationales, AN 565 AP Flahaut Papers, FL 8 117, letter to comtesse de Flahaut, 7 August 1830.

151   Cf. Dangeau, *Journal*, II, 59, 29 April 1686, for discussion of whether or not the Venetian ambassador should visit Orléans 'en habits de cérémonie'.

152   Comte de Villèle, *Mémoires et correspondance*, 5 vols, 1888–96, V, 145, Orléans to Villèle, 17 December 1824.

153   Ferdinand de Bertier, *Souvenirs d'un ultra-royaliste (1815–1832)*, 1993, p. 561; Castellane, *Journal*, III, 493, 27 February 1832.

154   Vanier, *La Mode*, p. 93.

155   Ibid., p. 92.

156   Castellane, *Journal*, II, 407, 12 January 1831; duchesse de Dino, *Chronique de 1831 à 1862*, 4 vols, 1909, I, 313, 23 January 1835.

157   Dino, *Chronique*, I, 310, 31 December 1834.

158   Jacques Laffitte, *Mémoires*, 1932, p. 320.

159   Théophile Gautier, *Paris et les Parisiens*, 1996 edn, pp. 358–9, February 1837.

160   Eugène Delacroix, *Correspondance générale*, 5 vols, 1935–8, I, 436, letter to Feuillet, 7 June 1837; Boigne, *Mémoires*, II, 351; cf., for a full contemporary account, Jules Janin, *Fontainebleau, Versailles, Paris*, 1837, *passim*.

161   Vanier, *La Mode*, p. 96.

162   J. Lucas-Dubreton, *Louis-Philippe et la Machine infernale*, 1951, p.188; Cuvillier-Fleury, *Journal*, II, 111, 13 April 1834; duchesse de Maillé, *Mémoires*, 1989, p. 93, April 1834.

163   Hugh Collingham, *The July Monarchy*, 1988, p. 403; Captain Gronow, *Reminiscences and Recollections*, 2 vols, 1892 edn, I, 245; E. D. Pasquier, *Souvenirs sur la révolution de 1848*, 1948, p. 160; Alan Sked, *The Decline and Fall of the Habsburg Empire 1815–1918*, 1989, p. 82.

164   Philip Mansel, *Prince of Europe: The Life of Charles Joseph de Ligne 1735–1814*, 2003, p. 121, Ligne to comte de Ségur, 1 December 1788.

165   Jennifer Scarce, *Women's Costume of the Near and Middle East*, 1987, p. 105; William Macmichael, *Journey from Moscow to Constantinople*, 1819, p. 118.

166   Khaled Fahmy, *All the Pasha's Men. Mehmed Ali, his Army and the Making of Modern Egypt*, Cambridge, 1997, pp. 185–6.

167 Stanley Lane-Poole, *Life of Sir Stratford Canning*, 2 vols, 1888, I, 421, Stratford Canning to George Canning, 20 June 1826; for a contemporary picture of modern Ottoman troops on parade in the hippodrome, see Germaner and Inankur, *Constantinople*, p. 144.

168 Charles MacFarlane, *Constantinople in 1828*, 2nd edn, 2 vols, 1829, I, 499, 505.

169 MacFarlane, *Constantinople in 1828*, II, 164–5, 189.

170 I owe these points to conversations with Hakan Erdem and Caroline Finkel; Julia Pardoe, *The City of the Sultans*, 4th edn, 1854, p. 256.

171 Eldem, *French Trade*, pp. 63–5.

172 Tchelebi, *Guerre des Tures*, p. 220.

173 Quataert, 'Clothing Laws', pp. 412–13; Norton, 'Faith and Fashion', p. 153.

174 Revd R. Walsh, *A Residence at Constantinople*, 2 vols, 1836, I, 358.

175 Lane-Poole, *Stratford Canning*, I, 505, Canning to Lady Canning, 24 March 1832, Walsh, *Residence*, II, 297.

176 Lane-Poole, *Stratford Canning*, II, 75, Mellish to Stratford Canning, 28 June 1829.

177 Patricia L. Baker, 'The Fez in Turkey: A Symbol of Modernisation?', in *Costume*, 1986, pp. 72–85; Bernard Lewis, *The Emergence of Modern Turkey*, 1960, p. 100.

178 See the photographs in Philip Mansel, *Sultans in Splendour: The Last Years of the Ottoman World 1869–1939*, 1988, pp. 21, 113, 116–71. Pashas' uniforms can be seen in the Sadberk Hanim Müzesi, Buyukdere, Istanbul: see Hulya Tezcan, *A Late 19th Century Tailor's Order Book*, Istanbul, 1992, *passim*, and illus.

179 François Georgeon, *Abdulhamid II*, 2003, p. 139.

180 Charles Eliot, *Turkey in Europe*, 1900, p. 361; Engin Özendeş, *Abdullah Frères. Ottoman Court Photographers*, Istanbul, 1998, pp. 21, 99, 174.

181 Palmira Brummett, *Image and Imperialism in the Ottoman Revolutionary Press 1908–1911*, Albany, 2000, p. 226.

182 [Jean Brindesi], *Elbicei Attika: musée des anciens costumes turcs de Constantinople*, 1855, with 22 lithographs; Mahmud Salih Arif Pasha, *Les Anciens Costumes de l'Empire Ottoman depuis l'origine de la monarchie jusqu'à la réforme du Sultan Mahmoud*, 1863, *passim*.

183 Rodenbeck, 'Dressing Native', pp. 44, 46, 51.

184 Women in western dress, however, were still spat at in Damascus in 1870: see Mary A. Lovell, *A Rage to Live, A Biography of Richard and Isabel Burton*, 1999 edn, p. 511.

185 Henry Laurens, *L'Expédition d'Égypte 1798–1801*, 1997 edn, p. 229; for Muslim dismay see Hayyat el-Eid al-Buluan, 'The Image of the European in Niqula al-Turk's Mudhakkarat (Chronique d'Égypte)', in Bernard Heyberger and Carsten Halbiner, eds, *Les Européens vus par les Libanais à l'époque ottomane*, Beirut, 2002, pp. 77–8; for Egyptian women, Vivant Denon and Abdel Rahman el-Gabarti, *Sur l'expédition de Bonaparte en Egypte*, 1998 edn, p. 204.

186 Rodenbeck, 'Dressing Native', pp. 84–5 and 89. Richard Burton, however, adopted Indian Muslim dress to go on pilgrimage to Mecca in 1853: see Lovell, *A Rage to Live*, pp. 124–5.

187 Quataert, 'Clothing Laws', pp. 412–13.

188 Ibid., pp. 414, 421–6; Maha Kayal, 'Le Système socio-vestimentaire à Tripoli (Liban) entre 1885 et 1985', University of Neuchâtel thesis, 1989, pp. 72, 75.

189 Kayal, 'Le Système', p. 131.

190 Falih Rifki Atay, *The Atatürk I Knew*, Ankara, 1982, p. 155.

191 Charles MacFarlane, *Turkey and its Destiny*, 2 vols, 1850, II, 622–3; Aziz Nesin, *Istanbul Boy*, 3 vols, Austin, Texas, 1977–90, II, 12; Elias Kazan, *A Life*, 1988,

p. 14; cf. Ezra K. Zilkha with Ken Emerson, *From Baghdad to Boardroom*, New York, 1999, p. 8 and photographs, for use of the fez by Baghdad Jews.

192 Georgeon, *Abdulhamid II*, p. 209.

193 Bosnian officials at Sarajevo, in the last photographs of the Archduke Franz Ferdinand on his visit in July 1914, wear the fez.

194 Osman Hamdy Bey and Marie de Launay, *Les Costumes populaires de la Turquie en 1873*, Constantinople, 1873, *passim*; similar costumes can be seen in the collections of the Victoria and Albert Museum and the Sadberk Hanim Museum, Istanbul. The Ottoman government's pride in the empire's dress variety was also shown by the institution in 1864–76 of a multi-ethnic guard for the Sultan of chiefs' sons, wearing local dress, and by the photographs of chiefs' sons, in their local dress, attending the École des tribus nomades in Constantinople in 1893–1907.

195 Personal information, Antoine Courban and Hussein el-Mudarris, Beirut, 29 October 2002.

196 James M. Brophy, 'Mirth and Subversion: Carnival in Cologne', *History Today*, 47 (7 July 1997), pp. 45–6.

197 Grete Klingenstein, ed., *Erzherzog Johann von Österreich*, 2 vols, Graz, 1982, II:. *Beiträge sur Geschichte seiner Zeit*, pp. 393, 423–4; cf. Dieter A. Binder, 'Province versus Metropolis: The Instrumentalised Myth of Archduke John of Styria (1782–1859)', in Karin Friedrich, ed., *Festive Culture in Germany and Europe from the Twentieth Century*, New York, 2000, p. 234.

198 Christopher Hibbert, *Garibaldi and his Enemies*, 1987 edn, p. 22; a picture by Girolamo Induino of Garibaldi's visit to Victor Emmanuel II on 30 January 1875 is in the Museo del Risorgimento, Milan.

    Since he lived in Argentina in 1835–48 and 1850–57, Garibaldi's red shirt has traditionally been thought to be South American in origin, taken from the clothes worn by the butchers of Montevideo, in order to hide the blood of the animals they had slaughtered; but a red shirt was also the uniform of Garibaldi's predecessors in the fight for a united Italy, the Carbonari.

199 Adam Wandruszka, *The House of Habsburg*, 1964, p. 167.

200 Klingenstein, *Erzherzog Johann*, II, p. 422.

201 Klingenstein, *Erzherzog Johann*, I: *Landesaustellung. Katalog*, p. 450.

202 Franz Hubmann, *Dream of Empire. The World of Germany in Original Photographs 1840–1914*, 1973, pp. 70–71; Frank Eyck, *The Frankfurt Parliament 1848–1849*, 1968, illustrations between pages 66 and 67; p. 95.

Chapter 6: Empires

1 Sked, *Decline and Fall*, p. 121.

2 Prince de Joinville, ed., *Vieux souvenirs*, 1970, p. 271.

3 Lampedusa, *The Leopard*, pp. 48, 123.

4 Jean-Paul Bled, *Histoire de Vienne*, 1998, pp. 208–9.

5 Alan Palmer, *Twilight of the Habsburgs. The Life and Times of the Emperor Francis Joseph*, 2001 edn, pp. 293–4.

6 Palais Galliéra, *Costumes à la cour de Vienne*, p. 89. Thus at a ball in Lemberg in 1908 Count Andreas Potocki wore Austrian civil uniform rather than Polish magnate's dress, 'to demonstrate to all the guests that he regarded himself as simply an Austrian official': Prince Clary, *A European Past*, 1978, p. 132.

7 Vilmos Heiszler, *Photo Habsburg. The Private Life of an Archduke*, Budapest, 1989, pp. 87–8.

8 Miklos Banffy, *The Phoenix Land,* 2003, p. 48.

9 Ibid., pp. 48, 394.

10 Palais Galliéra, *Costumes à la cour de Vienne,* pp. 89, 90–91, 93, 95.

11 Ibid., p. 97; cf. Bled, *Histoire de Vienne,* p. 479.

12 Richard A. Wortman, *Scenarios of Power: Myth and Ceremony in Russian Monarchy,* 2 vols, 1995–2000, I, 311–12.

13 Atalanta Clifford, *The Guards Museum,* 1997 edn, pp. 20–21. The Duke repeated the tradition for his son, Prince Arthur of Connaught, in 1885.

14 Palmer, *Twilight,* pp. 13, 128.

15 Jean-Paul Bled, *François Joseph,* 1987, p. 18.

16 Palmer *Twilight,* p. 194.

17 Friedrich Ferdinand, Count von Beust, *Memoirs,* 2 vols, 1887, II, 41.

18 Baron von Margutti, *The Emperor Francis Joseph and his Times,* 1921, pp. 36–7; Eugen Ketterl, *The Emperor Francis Joseph. An Intimate Study,* 1929, pp. 27–9, 47.

19 Hugo Vickers, *Alice, Princess Andrew of Greece,* 2001 edn, pp. 85, 87, 91.

20 However, he had learnt the lesson of Nelson's death at Trafalgar, and on the battlefield, probably in order to be inconspicuous, he preferred to wear a plain dark *frac,* rather than military uniform.

21 Duke of Windsor, *A Family Album,* p. 33; cf., for pictures, Michael Sturmer, *The German Century,* 1999, pp. 53, 55.

22 Palmer, *Twilight,* p. 186, cf. p. 259 for a similar reaction by Crown Prince Rudolf in 1889.

23 Ibid., pp. 276, 306.

24 Letter of 14 June 1889 quoted in R. R. McLean, *Royalty and Diplomacy in Europe 1890–1914,* 2001, p. 78; for photographs of monarchs wearing the uniforms of each other's forces see ibid., Figures 5, 10, 15.

25 John Lukács, *Budapest 1900,* 1988, p. 99; Palais Galliéra, *Costumes à la cour de Vienne,* p. 86; Gyongi Eri and Zsuzsa Jobbagyi, eds, *A Golden Age: Art and Society in Hungary 1896–1914,* Budapest, 1990, pp. 48–9, 50.

26 Tom Barczay, 'The 1896 Millennial Festivities in Hungary', in Friedrich, *Festive Culture,* p. 202.

27 Ibid., p. 207.

28 Banffy, *Phoenix Land,* p. 20.

29 See, for example, photographs in Baje Etleha *et al., Kastelyok es magnarsok,* Budapest, 1994, pp. 45, 61–2, 73, 88; personal information, Tom Barczay, 14 April 2002.

30 *Sigismund III – Sobieski-Stanislaus,* Schlosshof, 1990, p. 50; Ketterl, *Emperor,* p. 117.

31 Palmer, *Twilight,* pp. 61, 244, 270.

32 For a well-illustrated survey of the use of local dress by the Austrian and Bavarian dynasties, with an English summary, see Christian Brandstater and Franz Hubmann, *Die Lederhose,* Vienna, 1978, pp. 109–118; Palmer, *Twilight,* p. 234.

33 Hilde Spiel, *Vienna's Golden Autumn,* 1987, p. 147.

34 William M. Johnston, *The Austrian Mind: An Intellectual and Social History,* Berkeley, 1972, p. 27; cf. Geoffrey Wheatcroft, *The Controversy of Zion,* 1996, p. 92, for Karl Kraus's dislike of these clothes.

35 Wortman, *Scenarios,* I, 311–12.

36 Viscount Esher, ed., *Letters of Queen Victoria 1837–1861,* 3 vols, 1907, II, 14 to Leopold I, 4 June 1844.

37 Geraldine Norman, *The Hermitage: The Biography of a Great Museum*, 1999 edn, pp. 81–3.

38 N. V. Riasanovsky, *Nicholas I and Official Nationality in Russia, 1825–1855*, Cambridge, 1959, p. 106.

39 Binyon, *Pushkin*, pp. 320, 437–9.

40 Ibid., p. 631.

41 Henri Mérimée, *Une année en Russie*, 1847, p. 130.

42 Edward Dicey, *A Month in Russia during the Marriage of the Czarevitch*, 1867, p. 214.

43 Laurence Kelly, *Diplomacy and Murder in Tehran*, 2002, illus. 21, shows K. K. Rodofnikin, the Under-Secretary for Asian Affairs in the Foreign Ministry in the 1820s, at his desk in uniform; cf. King Frederick William IV in his 1846 portrait by Franz Krueger in Gert Streidt and Peter Feierabend, eds, *Prussia. Art and Architecture*, 1999, p. 270.

44 Scott, *European Nobilities*, II, 271; Kelly, *Diplomacy*, p. 11.

45 Chloe Obolensky, *The Russian Empire. A Portrait in Photographs*, New York, 1979, pp. 75, 83, 126, 131.

46 Angelica Capifava, *Splendore della corte degli Zar*, Lugano, 1999, pp. 267, 280–81, 299.

47 Tamara Korshunova, *The Art of Costume in Russia 18th to Early 20th Century*, rev. edn, Leningrad, 1983, p. 21; Jacqueline Kennedy Onassis, *In the Russian Style*, New York, 1977, pp. 32 34, 93, 126–7.

48 Laurence Kelly, *Moscow*, 1983, p. 294.

49 Wortman, *Scenarios*, II, 204, 274, 380, 402, 412; A. A. Mossolov, *At the Court of the Last Tsar*, 1935, pp. 20, 139.

50 Wortman, *Scenarios*, II, 320, 413, 425.

51 McLean, *Royalty and Diplomacy*, p. 36.

52 Mossolov, *At the Court*, pp. 183, 191; cf. *Costumes des tsars de Pierre le Grand à Nicolas II, collection du Musée de l'Ermitage, Saint Petersbourg*, Moscow, 1999, p. 103.

53 Patrick de Gmeline and Gérard Gorokhoff, *La Garde impériale russe 1896–1914*, 1986, pp. 18, 51, 93, 277.

54 Ibid., p. 112.

55 Robert K. Massie, ed., *The Romanov Family Album*, 1982, pp. 78, 104, 125; Peter Kurth, *Tsar: The Lost World of Nicholas and Alexandra*, 1995, pp. 91, 96, 103, 104, 157–62, 170.

56 Mary Margaret Potocka, 'Memoirs' (manuscript consulted by kind permission of Adam Zamoyski), ff. 150, 147; Abraham Ascher, *The Search for Stability in Late Imperial Russia*, Stanford, 2001, p. 372.

57 Helju Anlik Bennet, 'Evolution of the Meanings of Chin: An Introduction to the Russian Institution of Rank Ordering and Noble Assignment from the Time of Peter the Great to the Bolshevik Revolution', *Canadian Slavic Studies*, 10 (1977), p. 8 n.

58 Capifava, *Splendore*, passim.

59 Vanier, *La Mode*, pp. 157–63; cf. E. Kerckoff, *Le Costume à la cour et à la ville*, 1865, p. 139.

60 Sophie Dosne, *Mémoires de Madame Dosne*, 2 vols, II, 64–5, 25 November 1848.

61 Mathew Truesdell, *Spectacular Politics: Louis-Napoleon Bonaparte and the Fête Impériale, 1849–1870*, New York, 1997, p. 94 cf. the picture *Rendez-vous de la vénerie impériale* by Gustave Parquet now in the château de Compiègne.

62 Castellane, *Journal*, V, 28, 8 December 1853.

63 Madame Carette, *Souvenirs intimes de la cour des Tuileries*, 13th edn, 1889, pp. 165–70, 261; 3rd series 1891, pp. 136–41; Jean Philippe Worth, *A Century of Fashion*, Boston, 1928, p. 42; Harold Kurtz, *The Empress Eugénie*, 1964, p. 181. Descriptions of the Empress's wardrobes and dresses, by the officer who in the autumn of 1870 helped send some of their contents to England, via the Austrian embassy, can be found in comte d'Hérisson, *Journal d'un officier d'ordonnance*, 1885, pp. 125–39.

64 Nassau William Senior, *Conversations with M. Thiers, M. Guizot, and Other Distinguished Persons, During the Second Empire*, 2 vols, 1878, I, 175, 242, 19 May 1853, 14 February 1854; II, 114, 20 April 1857.

65 Similarly, for four days at Windsor Castle during Ascot week, Elizabeth II's female guests are expected to bring at least eight different sets of clothes.

66 Princesse Pauline Metternich, *Souvenirs*, 1922, pp. 79, 94, 98.

67 Ibid., pp. 134–8, 145.

68 Diana de Marly, *Worth: Father of Haute Couture*, 1980, p. 28.

69 Ibid., pp. 125–6; idem, *History of Haute Couture*, p. 28.

70 Lurie, *The Language of Clothes*, p. 145.

71 Patrice Higonnet, *Paris, Capital of the World*, Cambridge, Mass., 2002, p. 117; cf. Metternich, *Souvenirs*, p. 79.

72 Frederick John Gorst, *Of Carriages and Kings*, 1956, p. 129.

73 De Marly, *Worth*, p. 101.

74 Ibid., pp. 152–6; idem, *History of Haute Couture*, p. 44.

75 Edmond and Jules de Goncourt, *Journal*, 4 vols, 1989 edn, II, 491, 15 January 1872.

76 Elizabeth Anne Coleman, *The Opulent Era. Fashions of Worth, Doucet and Pingat*, 1989, p. 90.

77 De Marly, *History of Haute Couture*, p. 206.

78 Information derived from the Bismarck Museum Friederichsruh, permanent exhibition.

79 See the 1855 portrait by Jakob Becker in Lothar Gall and Karl-Heinz Jürgens, *Bismarck Lebensbilder*, Berlin, 1990, no. 72.

80 Gretel Wagner, *Der bunte Rock in Preussen*, Berlin, 1989, pp. 34–3, 350.

81 Alan Palmer, *Bismarck*, 1976, pp. 126–7; Dr Alfred Funke, *Das Bismarck-Buch des Deutschen Volkes*, 2 vols, Berlin, 1921, I, 761, 769–70; II, 295; see Bismarck Stiftung, Friedrichsruh, permanent exhibition, for an illustration of the opening of the north German Reichstag.

82 Moritz Busch, *Bismarck. Some Secret Pages of his History*, 3 vols, 1898, I, 71.

83 Karina Urbach, *Bismarck's Favourite Englishman. Lord Odo Russell's Mission to Berlin*, 1999, p. 69, letter of 2 December 1870; Textilmuseum, *Nach Rang und Stand*, pp. 74–5.

84 Ibid., pp. 208, 252.

85 Gall and Jürgens, *Bismarck*, numbers 159, 187; Andreas Biefang, *Bismarcks Reichstag. Das Parlament in der Leipziger Strasse*, Düsseldorf, 2002, pp. 83, 85, 86 143, 147–8.

86 Funke, *Bismarck-Buch*, II, 407, 425, 429. The Burgermeister of Hamburg is the only figure in civilian dress (sixteenth-century ruff and tunic like that of papal chamberlains until 1969) in the picture of German princes congratulating Franz Josef in 1908, on the sixtieth anniversary of his accession.

87 Hugh and Mirabel Cecil, *Imperial Marriage*, 2002, p. 24; the picture, by Konrad Siemenroth (1887), is in the Bismarck Museum, Friedrichsruh.

88 Giles MacDonogh, *Wilhelm the Impetuous: The Last Kaiser*, 2000, p. 139; Otto-Ernst Schisddekopf, *Herrliche Kaiserzeit. Deutschland 1871–1914*, Frankfurt, 1973, pp. 33, 40, 90; Hubmann, *Dream of Empire*, p. 252; for pictures of ministers' uniforms see Wagner, *Der bunte Rock*, pp. 340–43, 351.

89 Matila Ghyka, *The World Mine Oyster*, 1961, p. 119.

90 Lovell, *A Rage to Live*, p. 598.

91 Wilhelm II, *My Early Life*, 1973 edn, p. 329, letter to Wilhelm I, 21 May 1884.

92 Count Robert Zedlitz-Trützschler, *Twelve Years at the Imperial German Court*, 1924, p. 95, 3 November 1904, cf. pp. 51, 59.

93 However, as Friedrich Reck-Malleczewen pointed out, 'this master of military nicety and the theatrical effect in uniforms was himself never quite able to appear correctly dressed'; *Diary of a Man in Despair*, 2000, p. 143, September 1943.

94 Karl Demeter, *The German Officer Corps in Society and State 1650–1945*, 1965, p. 242; cf., for the Kaiser's sketches of uniforms, Arthur Brehmer, *Am Hofe Kaiser Wilhelm II*, Berlin, 1898, p. 111; Joseph Kurchner, *Kaiser Wilhelm II als Soldat und Seemann*, Berlin, 1902, pp. 145, 160–61, 173–4. I am grateful to Professor John Röhl for the opportunity to consult these works.

95 John C. G. Röhl, *Wilhelm II. The Kaiser's Personal Monarchy 1888–1900*, Cambridge, 2004.

96 James W. Gerard, *My Four Years in Germany*, 1917, p. 38.

97 Leo von Pfannenberg, *Geschichte der Schlossgarde Kompagnie*, Berlin, 1909, *passim*. Major-General Sir Leopold V. Swaine, *Camp and Chancery in a Soldier's Life*, 1926, p. 217.

98 Wagner, *Der bunte Rock*, pp. 446–7; Georg Riedel, *Die deutschen Reichs und königlichen Preussische Staats- und Hofbeamten Uniformen*, Berlin, 1974 reprint of the 1897 edn.

99 Brehmer, *Am Hofe*, pp. 252, 294–5, 297, 306; Duke of Windsor, *Family Album*, p. 33.

100 Hubmann, *Dream of Empire*, p. 255; Lamar Cecil, *Wilhelm II: Prince and Emperor*, 1996, p. 274; Anne Topham, *Memories of the Kaiser's Court*, 1914, pp. 121, 209; letter of Nicholas II, 1/14 August 1897, quoted in McLean, *Royalty and Diplomacy*, p. 35.

101 Pless, Daisy, Princess of, *The Private Diaries*, ed. D. Chapman-Huston, 1950, p. 25.

102 Textilmuseum, *Nach Rang und Stand*, pp. 185, 191, 199–200, 203–5.

103 See the display in the Berlin City Museum.

104 *Majestät brauchen Sonne*, film made in 1999; Gerhard Masur, *Imperial Berlin*, 1971, p. 146.

105 Lord Hardinge of Penshurst, *Old Diplomacy*, 1947, p. 25.

106 John C. G. Röhl, 'The Emperor's New Clothes', in John C. G. Röhl, ed., *Kaiser Wilhelm II: New Interpretations*, 1982, p. 22; cf. Hochberg, *Private Diaries*, p. 35, 7 September 1896; Winston Churchill, *Thoughts and Adventures*, 1990 edn, p. 49.

107 James Timothy Voorhies, ed., *My Dear Stieglitz. Letters of Marsden Hartley and Alfred Stieglitz 1912–1915*, Columbia, South Carolina, 2002, p. 76.

108 Michael Geyer, 'The German Officer Corps as a Profession', in Geoffrey Cocks, ed., *German Professions 1800–1950*, New York, 1990, p. 195.

109 Nicholas Stargadt, *The German Idea of Militarism*, Cambridge, 1994, p. 3; Alexandra Richie, *Faust's Metropolis*, 1998, p. 205.

110 Translation by Giles MacDonogh, 15 May 2002.
111 Zedlitz-Trützschler, *Twelve Years*, p. 7.
112 Personal information, Martin Kohlrausch, 8 November 2003.
113 Personal information, Giles MacDonogh, 15 May 2002; Textilmuseum, *Nach Rang und Stand*, p. 39.
114 Laird M. Easton, *The Red Count: the Life and Times of Harry Kessler*, Berkeley, 2002, p. 52.
115 Masur, *Imperial Berlin*, p. 95; Gordon A. Craig, *The Politics of the Prussian Army*, 1955, pp. 217, 237.
116 *Unser Kaiser. Fünf und zwanzig Jahre der Regierung Kaiser Wilhelms II 1888–1913*, Berlin, 1913 pp. 64–7; Willibald Gutsche, *Aufstieg und Fall eines kaiserlichen Reichskanzlers*, Berlin, 1973, pp. 49, 113; Gerard, *Four Years*, p. 45.
117 Jost Rebentisch, *Die viele Gesichte des Kaisers Wilhelm II in der deutschen und britischen Karicatur*, Berlin, 2000, p. 346.
118 Textilmuseum, *Nach Rang und Stand*, pp. 33–7.
119 Personal communication, Martin Kohlrausch, Berlin, 8 November 2003.
120 Deutsches Historisches Museum, *Bismarck – Prussia, Germany and Europe*, Berlin, 1990, pp. 196, 200–01.
121 Zedlitz-Trützschler, *Twelve Years*, p. 220, 20 March 1908.
122 Dominic Lieven, *Nicholas II, Emperor of all the Russias*, 1993, p. 233.
123 Evelyn, Princess Blücher, *An English Wife in Berlin*, 1920, p. 233, July 1918.
124 Cecil, *Wilhelm II*, II, 291–3; Isobel V. Hull, *The Entourage of Kaiser Wilhelm II 1888–1918*, 1982, p. 291.
125 Sir John Wheeler-Bennett, *Three Episodes in the Life of Kaiser Wilhelm II*, 1955, p. 16.
126 Count Harry Kessler, *Diaries of a Cosmopolitan 1918–1937*, 1971, pp. 6, 36, 8 November, 17 December 1918; Evelyn, Princess Blücher, *English Wife*, p. 281, 9 November 1918; Admiral Müller, *The Kaiser and his Court*, 1961, pp. 422–3, 9 November 1918. The same ripping-off of emblems of rank also took place in Budapest in 1918: see Banffy, *Phoenix Land*, p. 44.
127 Nigel Jones, *A Brief History of the Rise of the Nazis*, 2004 edn, p. 40.
128 Ibid., pp. 55, 167, 257.
129 Metropolitan Museum, *Imperial Style*, p. 122; Onassis, *Russian Style*, p. 13.
130 Personal communication, Professor Paolo Nello, 3 October 2003.
131 Simonetta Falasca-Zamponi, *Fascist Spectacle: The Aesthetics of Power in Mussolini's Italy*, Berkeley, 1997, pp. 101, 103, 241. For illustrations see Ugo Pericoli, *Le divise del Duce*, Milan, 1983, *passim*.
132 *International Herald Tribune*, 21 April 2003.
133 Falasca-Zamponi, *Fascist Spectacle*, pp. 103–4; Mack-Smith, *Italy*, p. 434.
134 F. W. Deakin, *The Brutal Friendship: Mussolini, Hitler and the Fall of Italian Fascism*, 1962, p. 696.
135 Robert Lewis Koehl, *The Black Corps. The Structure and Power Struggles of the Nazi SS*, Madison, Wisc., 1983, p. 19 n.
136 Christina Entner and Friedemann Bedurfting, *Encyclopedia of the Third Reich*, 2 vols, New York, 1991, I, 93, 116; Henry Ashby Turner Jr., *Hitler's Thirty Days to Power*, 1996, pp. 23, 56.
137 Koehl, *Black Corps*, pp. 22, 40.
138 See e.g. Sturmer, *German Century*, p. 140, for illustrations of Communists in uniform.

139 Ian Kershaw, *Hitler 1889–1936: Hubris*, 1998, pp. 365–8; William Sheridan Allen, *The Nazi Seizure of Power*, rev. edn, 1989, pp. 36, 114; Andreas Dorpalen, *Hindenburg and the Weimar Republic*, Princeton, 1964, p. 340; Richard W. Rolfs, *The Sorcerer's Apprentice: The Life of Franz von Papen*, 1996, pp. 97, 103.

140 Sebastian Haffner, *Defying Hitler*, 2002, pp. 104, 186, 195.

141 Ibid., pp. 31, 107, 116, 175.

142 There would be a similar juxtaposition of Nazi and imperial uniforms in the ex-Kaiser's funeral procession at Doorn on 9 June 1941; See *Majestät brauchen Sonne* (1999 film); Sir John Wheeler-Bennett, *Hindenburg: Wooden Titan*, 1967 edn, p. 443.

143 James J. Sheehan, *German History 1770–1866*, Oxford, 1989, p. 405.

144 Brian L. Davis, *German Army Uniforms and Insignia 1933–1945*, rev. edn, 1992, pp. 7, 122.

145 Howard R. Smith, *Last Train from Berlin*, 2000 edn, pp. 6–7.

146 Heinz Höhne, *The Order of the Death's Head*, 1972 edn, p. 122.

147 Michael Bloch, *Ribbentrop*, 1992, p. 159; Smith, *Last Train*, p. 50.

148 Paul Preston, *Franco*, 1993, pp. 329, 437 n; personal communication, Miguel Carriedo, 10 December 2003.

149 Robert Skidelsky, *Oswald Mosley*, 1990 edn, pp. 292–3, 329.

150 M. Scott, 'The New China', pp. 129, 132; Claire Roberts, ed., *Evolution and Revolution. Chinese Dress 1700s–1990s*, Sydney, 1997, pp. 18, 22.

151 Public Record Office, Kew [Lord Chamberlain's Papers], LC5/220, schedules of civil uniforms.

152 Ibid., Schedule of officials' full and levee dress; Mansfield, *Ceremonial Costume*, p. 175.

153 Cf. photographs of Lords Bledisloe and Curzon in David Cannadine, *Ornamentalism. How the British saw their Empire*, 2001, pp. 37, 91.

154 On some occasions outside London, George IV and his household had worn Windsor uniform: Prebble, *King's Jaunt*, pp. 329, 348.

155 A picture by James Gunn of Lords Halifax and Salisbury and George VI, in Windsor uniform, hangs in the equerries' room at Windsor Castle; personal communication, Sir John Johnstone, September 2003. When hunting, the Prince of Wales wears his own version of Windsor uniform, a dark blue coat with scarlet collar and cuffs, and Garter buttons – to avoid changing buttons according to the hunt he is with: Michael Clayton, *Prince Charles, Horseman*, 1987, pp. 82–3.

156 Lady Sarah Lyttelton, *Correspondence of Sarah Spencer, Lady Lyttelton, 1787–1870*, ed. Hon. Mrs H. Wyndham, 1912, p. 304, letter of 13 October 1840.

157 Norman Gash, *Sir Robert Peel*, 2nd edn, 1986, pp. 221–7; Esher, *Girlhood of Queen Victoria*, II, 171, 5 May 1839.

158 Gash, *Sir Robert Peel*, pp. 259–60, 273, 275.

159 Cumming, *Royal Dress*, pp. 111, 113, 120. The balls were recorded in drawings by Louis Haghe and Eugène Lami, in the Royal Collection.

160 Cumming, *Royal Dress*, p. 76.

161 Hon. Katharine Villiers, *Memoirs of a Maid of Honour*, 1931, p. 35; Mansfield, *Ceremonial Costumes*, pp. 122, 124–5, 132; cf. Jacqueline Ansell, 'The Seal of Social Approval', *The Court Historian*, IV, 2 (August 1999), p. 155.

162 Papendiek, *Court and Private Life*, I, 247.

163   Frank Burlington Fawcett, *Court Ceremonial and Book of the Court of King George the Sixth*, 1937, p. 35.

164   W. M. Thackeray, *Vanity Fair*, 1933 edn, pp. 476–483 (chapter 48).

165   Benita Stoney and Heinrich Weltzien, eds, *My Mistress the Queen: The Letters of Frieda Arnold, Dresser to Queen Victoria 1854–9*, 1994, pp. 15, 41; Ansell, 'Seal', p. 156.

166   Lillie Langtry, *The Days I Knew*, n.d., pp. 105–9; Caresse Crosby, *The Passionate Years*, 1955, pp. 61–3. The process is best evoked, and understood, in the displays of clothes, dressing rooms and shops in the rooms of the Royal Ceremonial Dress Collection on the ground floor of Kensington Palace.

167   Walker, *Savile Row*, pp. 69, 71.

168   Stephen Howarth, *Henry Poole of Savile Row: The Making of a Legend*, Honiton, 2003, pp. 2, 35, 51, 73, 151; Walker, *Savile Row*, pp. 70, 77–9.

169   Helmut and Alison Gernsheim, *Queen Victoria. A Biography in Word and Picture*, 1959, pp. 97, 121.

170   Delia Millar, *Queen Victoria's Life in the Scottish Highlands depicted by her Watercolour Artists*, 1985, p. 75; Cheape, *Tartan*, p. 63; Cumming, *Royal Dress*, pp. 119, 132; Duke of Windsor, *Family Album*, p. 128.

171   Millar, *Queen Victoria's Life*, pp. 70, 73, 75. Hannah Pakula, *An Uncommon Woman: The Empress Frederick*, 1996, p. 48.

172   Roger Fulford, ed., *Your Dear Letter, Private Correspondence of Queen Victoria and the Crown Prince of Prussia 1865–1875*, 1971, pp. 213, 233, 320.

173   Macdonogh, *Wilhelm the Impetuous*, p. 65.

174   Wilhelm II, *My Early Life*, pp. 156–7, 247.

175   *Huis Doorn*, Amsterdam, 1992, p. 30.

176   Jeanne Sheehy, *The Rediscovery of Ireland's Past: The Celtic Revival 1830–1930*, 1980, pp. 103, 148–9. I am grateful for this reference to Roy Foster.

177   I am grateful for this information to Russell Harris.

178   Walter L. Arnstein, 'The Warrior Queen: Reflections on Queen Victoria and her World', *Albion*, 30, 1 (Spring 1998), p. 5.

179   Staniland, *In Royal Fashion* pp. 151–2; Stoney and Weltzien, *My Mistress*, p. 19; cf. Elizabeth Ewing, *Women in Uniform through the Centuries*, 1975, pp. 62–3.

180   Arnstein, 'Warrior Queen', p. 6.

181   Fritz, 'The Trade in Death', pp. 306–8, 311–12.

182   Lyttelton, *Correspondence*, p. 114, letter of 8 November 1810.

183   Stephen C. Behrendt, *Royal Mourning and Regency Culture*, 1997, pp. 199–203; even the postboys and turnpike men on the road wore mourning: Taylor, *Mourning Dress*, p. 127.

184   Bland, *Royal Way of Death*, p. 159; Taylor, *Mourning Dress*, p. 273; Sir John Wheeler-Bennett, *Friends, Enemies and Sovereigns*, 1976, p. 133.

185   Taylor, *Mourning Dress*, pp. 184, 202, 233, 303.

186   Wentworth, *Wentworth Papers*, p. 82, letter of Peter Wentworth to Lord Strafford, 5 April 1709.

187   Hon. Mrs Armytage, *Old Court Customs and Modern Court Rule*, 1883, p. 182; Bland, *Royal Way of Death*, p. 242.

188   Taylor, *Mourning Dress*, p. 156.

189   Bland, *Royal Way of Death*, p. 174; Taylor, *Mourning Dress*, pp. 122, 155–6, 159–160.

190 Edith Olivier, *Without Knowing Mr Walkley*, 1938, p. 285; Taylor, *Mourning Dress*, p. 252.

191 Staniland, *In Royal Fashion*, p. 76; Tony Rennell, *The Death of Queen Victoria: Last Days of Glory*, 2001, p. 163; for illustrations of court mourning see Taylor, *Mourning Dress*, pp. 149, 155–6, 162–3.

192 Cumming, *Royal Dress*, p. 123.

193 Duke of Windsor, *Family Album*, pp. 35, 40; Pauline Stevenson, *Edwardian Fashion*, 1980, pp. 5–11; Gorst, *Carriages and Kings*, p. 153.

194 Frederick Ponsonby, *Recollections of Three Reigns*, 1957 edn, p. 150; cf. pp. 202, 213, 221, 273, 275 for similar stories and attitudes.

195 Quoted in Amies, *Englishman's Suit*, p. 18.

196 Sir Philip Magnus, *King Edward VII*, 1964, pp. 364–5.

197 Christopher Hibbert, *The Court of St James's*, 1979, pp. 195–7; Kenneth Rose, *King George V*, 1983 edn, p. 282; cf. Zakim, *Ready-Made Democracy*, pp. 213–14.

198 Herbert A. P. Trendell, *Dress and Insignia worn at His Majesty's Court*, 1921, pp. 3, 36.

199 Trendell, *Dress and Insignia*, p. 149; Fawcett, *Court Ceremonial*, p. 70.

200 Richard Rush, *A Residence at the Court of London*, 1987, pp. 114, 117.

201 Richard Buckle, *The Prettiest Girl in England*, 1958, p. 60; Frank Burlington Fawcett, ed., *Their Majesties' Courts holden at Buckingham Palace and at the Palace of Holyroodhouse, 1937*, 1938, pp. 27, 42–81.

202 Fawcett, *Their Majesties' Courts*, p. 78.

203 Esher, *Girlhood of Queen Victoria*, II, 20, I, 15 June 1839; cf. Buckle, *Prettiest Girl*, pp. 48, 75, for similar disdain expressed by Louisa and Georgina Smythe.

204 Duke of Windsor, *Family Album*, p. 56; cf. Anne de Courcy, *1939: The Last Season*, 2003 p. 89.

205 Cf. Harriet Sergeant, *Shanghai*, 1991, pp. 118–19.

206 Trendell, *Dress and Insignia*, pp. 47, 99.

207 Cohn, 'Cloth', p. 328; Trendell, *Dress and Insignia*, pp. 36, 169–78.

208 Trendell, *Dress and Insignia*, p. 174 n.

209 Cohn, 'Cloth', p. 310.

210 Cf. Charles Belgrave, *Personal Column*, 1960, p. 277.

211 Colville, 'Jack Tar', p. 110; Walker, *Savile Row*, p. 160.

212 Duke of Windsor, *Family Album*, p. 13; Rose, *George V*, p. 306.

213 Rose, *George V*, pp. 79–80.

214 Chips Channon, diary for June 1923 quoted in Rose, *George V*, p. 282.

215 Hibbert, *Court of St James's*, p. 197.

216 Rose, *George V*, p. 551.

217 Personal communication, Kenneth Rose, 13 February 2004. Another Conservative, the Prime Minister Lord Salisbury, when rebuked for wearing at a levee a civil uniform coat and the trousers of an Elder Brother of Trinity House, replied: 'It was a dark morning and my mind must have been occupied by a subject of lesser importance.'

218 Rose, *George V*, p. 332.

219 Hibbert, *Court of St James's*, p. 196.

220 Virginia Woolf, *Three Guineas*, 1938, pp. 19, 21. I am grateful for this reference to Linda Kelly.

221 Trendell, *Dress and Insignia*, pp. 46, 48, 53.

222 Kumar, *Costumes and Textiles*, pp. 8, 16, 59, 81; Cohn, 'Cloth', pp. 333, 343; Robert Payne, *The Life and Death of Mahatma Gandhi*, 1969, pp. 321, 355, 376.

223 Cumming, *Royal Dress,* p. 164.

224 Duke of Windsor, *Family Album,* p. 12.

225 Walker, *Savile Row,* p. 94.

226 Duke of Windsor, *Family Album,* p. 25.

227 Mary Soames, ed., *Speaking for Themselves: The Personal Letters of Winston and Clementine Churchill,* 1999 edn, p. 448, letter of 18 January 1939. For a dissection of the Windsors' clothes see Suzy Menkes, *The Windsor Style,* 1987, p. 127. The Duke of Windsor kept the same tailor, Scholte, from 1919 to 1959.

228 Millar, *Queen Victoria's Life,* p. 73.

229 *The Windsor Sale,* 2 vols, New York, 1998, items 2843, 2886, 2890, 2893.

230 Robert Lacey, *Sothebys: Bidding for Class,* 1999 edn, pp. 312–16; Duke of Windsor, *Family Album* p. 129.

231 Menkes, *Windsor Style,* p. 126.

232 Howarth, *Henry Poole,* pp. 2, 35, 51, 73, 151.

233 Napoleon III had been ordering clothes, such as a new frock coat for St Napoleon's Day, 15 August 1846, from Poole's since his second exile in London.

234 The Ottoman Sultan Abdulhamid II (1876–1909), however, despite his determination to revive his country's industries, had his suits made in Paris, *chez* Doucet.

235 Howarth, *Henry Poole,* pp. 50, 103, 151.

236 Margaret MacMillan, *Peacemakers. The Peace Conference of 1919 and its Attempt to End War,* 2002 edn, p. 402. T. E. Lawrence's use of Arab dress in the West shows both his love of publicity and his divided loyalties.

237 Interview with J. B. Johnson, 7 February 1983; for pictures see Cannadine, *Ornamentalism,* pp. 60, 81.

238 Simon Sebag Montefiore, *Stalin: The Court of the Red Tsar,* 2003, p. 393. George Orwell, *Animal Farm,* 2003 edn, pp. 14, 98.

239 Sebag Montefiore, *Prince of Princes,* p. 333; idem, *Stalin,* pp. 393, 409, 425 n, 439.

240 Mary Soames, *Clementine Churchill,* rev. edn, 2003, p. 58.

241 Ledgers consulted during a visit to Henry Poole, 25 June 2003. In 1938, long out of office, he was still being charged five guineas a year for 'preserving' a minister's uniform.

242 Walker, *Savile Row,* p. 99.

243 Roy Jenkins, *Churchill,* 2002, p. 50 n. He also served in the 31st Punjab Infantry, the 21st Lancers (1898), the Lancashire Hussars and the South African Light Horse.

244 Ibid., pp. 52 n, 742.

245 John Colville, *The Fringes of Power,* 1986 edn, I, 224, 12 July 1940; cf. p. 323, 23 October 1940, for the 'yachting cap and navy-blue brass-buttoned suit' he wore to address the crew of a new battleship; Martin Gilbert, *In Search of Churchill,* 1995 edn, p. 203.

246 De Courcy, *1939,* p. 29 lists some of the court dress-makers.

247 Interview with Carne Griffiths, Hand and Lock, 28 March 2003.

248 Interview with Christopher Allen, Ede and Ravenscroft, 20 March 2003; Walker, *Savile Row,* p. 162.

249 Mansfield, *Ceremonial Costume,* pp. 32, 40, 166; Una Campbell, *Robes of the Realm,* 1989, passim.

250 *The Times,* 2 October 2003.

251 Personal information, Kenneth Rose, 13 February 2004.

252 Interview with Joanna Marschner, 27 March 2003; there are also collections of court

dress in the Victoria and Albert Museum and the Museum of London; also in the Galleria del Costume, Palazzo Pitti, Florence, and the Lateran Museum, Rome.

253 Georgina Howell, *Diana: Her Life in Fashion*, 1998, pp. 14, 30, 184, 189, 200.

254 Sir John Wheeler-Bennett, *King George VI*, 1958, p. 736.

255 Sarah Bradford, *George VI*, 1991 edn, p. 535, George VI to Lord Halifax, 4 February 1952.

256 Anne Edwards, *The Queen's Clothes*, 1977, pp. 17, 72.

257 Jean Goodman with Sir Iain Moncrieffe, *Debrett's Royal Scotland*, 1983, p. 11.

258 Personal communication, Sir John Johnson, former Comptroller Lord Chamberlain's Office, September 2003.

259 *Daily Telegraph*, 25 June 2003.

260 Dorothy Laird, *Royal Ascot*, 1976, pp. 15–16.

261 Ibid., pp. 89, 40.

262 Personal information, Elizabeth Crofton, former official in the Ascot Office, 21 November 2003.

263 *Daily Telegraph*, 20 June 2002.

264 *Daily Telegraph*, 14 March 2003; personal information from a former member of the Prince of Wales's household, March–December 2003.

265 Sir Percy Sykes, *Ten Thousand Miles in Persia*, 1902, p. 292.

266 Donald Keene, *Meiji and his World, 1852–1912*, New York, 2002, pp. 194, 213, 237.

267 See T. Fujitani, *Splendid Monarchy. Power and Pageantry in Modern Japan*, Berkeley, 1996, *passim*; esp. p. 174.

268 Gary Dickinson and Linda Wrigglesworth, *Imperial Wardrobe*, 1990, pp. 54, 63.

269 Roberts, *Evolution and Revolution*, p. 27.

270 Emir Abdur Rahman, *Autobiography*, 2 vols, 1900, II, 44, 97; Vartan Gregorian, *The Emergence of Modern Afghanistan*, Stanford, 1969, p. 151.

271 Angus Hamilton, *Afghanistan*, 1906, p. 382; Mansel, *Sultans in Splendour*, pp. 89–93.

272 Nancy Hatch Dupree, 'Behind the Veil in Afghanistan', *Asia*, July 1978, pp. 10–12.

273 Leon B. Poullada, *Reform and Rebellion in Afghanistan 1919–1929*, 1973, p. 82; Mansel, *Sultans in Splendour*, pp. 158–61; *International Herald Tribune*, 31 January 2002.

274 Gordon Waterfield, *Professional Diplomat*, 1973, p. 127; Mansel, *Sultans in Splendour*, p. 151.

275 Donald N. Wilber, *Riza Shah Pahlavi*, Hicksville, 1975, pp. 138, 233.

276 Ibid., p. 275. See also Houchang E. Chehabi, 'Staging the Emperor's New Clothes: Dress Codes and Nation Building under Reza Shah', *Iranian Studies*, 26, 3–4 (Summer 1993), pp. 209–29.

277 Patricia L. Baker, 'Politics of Dress: The Dress Reform Laws of 1920s/1930s Iran', in Lindisfarne-Tapper and Ingham, *Languages of Dress in the Middle East*, Richmond, 1997, p. 186.

278 Nesin, *Istanbul Boy*, II, 57; Harold Armstrong, *Turkey in Travail*, 1925, p. 97.

279 Arnaud d'Andurain, *Souvenirs plaisants de la vie sérieuse*, 1985, p. 33.

280 Andrew Mango, *Atatürk*, 1999, p. 33.

281 Lord Kinross, *Atatürk: The Rebirth of a Nation*, 1969 edn, p. 415; Norton, 'Faith and Fashion', pp. 159–61; Mango, *Atatürk*, p. 435.

282 Norton, 'Faith and Fashion', pp. 160–61; Mango, *Atatürk*, p. 436.

283 At a ball at Ankara on 29 October 1932 Kemal ordered the Egyptian ambassador to remove his fez. After protests from King Fouad, the ambassador was allowed to keep his fez.

284 Kayal, 'Le Système', p. 183.

285 Quoted in Usama Makdisi, 'Rethinking Ottoman Imperialism: Modernity, Violence and the Cultural Logic of Ottoman Reform', in Jens Hansen, Thomas Philipp and Stefan Weber, eds, *The Empire in the City: Arab Provincial Capitals in the Late Ottoman Empire*, Beirut, 2002, p. 44.

286 See e.g. Nancy Lindisfarne-Tapper and Bruce Ingham, 'Approaches to the Study of Dress in the Middle East', in Lindisifarne-Tapper and Ingham, *Languages of Dress in the Middle East*, Richmond, 1997, p. 30; for Bavarians voting in *tracht*, see *Daily Telegraph*, 23 September 2002.

287 Isak Dinesen, *Daguerreotypes and Other Essays*, 1979, p. 25.

288 Saddam Hussein was also represented on murals as Ashburnipal and Nebuchadnezzar.

289 *Beirut Daily Star*, 2 July 2003.

290 Baker, 'Politics of Dress', pp. 187–8.

291 The old headscarf and veil had almost disappeared from Lebanon between the two civil wars of 1958 and 1975–91: Kayal, 'Le Système', pp. 186, 219.

292 *International Herald Tribune*, 12 December 2003, letter of Susan Akyurt; ibid., 18 December, 'Chirac Backs a "Pillar" of France'; ibid., 11 February 2004, 'French Vote to Ban School Religious Symbols'.

293 *Beirut Daily Star*, 17 October, 2003, 'Muslim Headscarves Force France to Grapple with its Identity'; *International Herald Tribune*, 21 October 2003, 'Expulsions over Veil Intensify French Debate on Secularity'; *Beirut Daily Star*, 30 October, 1 November, 6 December 2003, 'Turkey Celebrates 80th Birthday amid Headscarf Tensions', 'Entire Turkish Ruling Party Boycotts President's Reception'; cf. Elizabeth Ozdalga, *The Veiling Issue: Official Secularism and Popular Islam in Modern Turkey*, 1998, *passim*.

294 It is said that in 1945, since he had forgotten his tail coat, Count Kinsky, a refugee cousin from Bohemia, was allowed to stay, but not to dine, with the prince.

295 Roberts, *Evolution and Revolution*, p. 25. An early and startling sign of China's evolution had been the appearance on television, in 1984, of the Secretary-General of the Communist Party wearing a western, rather than Sun Yat-sen, suit.

Bibliography

I Manuscript Sources

Archives du château de Mouchy: Prince de Poix, 'Note autobiographique', 1806
Archives Nationales, Paris
   O1 835, K1715 papers of the pre-1789 Maison du roi
   C 189, 192, 222 papers of the Liste Civile of Louis XVI, 1790–92
   O3 papers of the Maison du roi 1814–30: 72, 75, 194, 222, 360, 508, 519, 529, 885
   Archives privées
      341 AP 25 (La Grange Papers)
      400 AP 4 Registre du grand maréchal du palais 1808-14
      565 AP Flahaut Papers, FL 8 Correspondence of Comte de Flahaut, 1830
Bibliothèque Administrative de la Ville de Paris, Ms. 387 Duc de Lévis, 'Notes de cour'
Bibliothèque municipale de Genève, Ms. 1684, Mme Eynard, 'Journal'
Bibliothèque Thiers, Paris, Fonds Masson, Ms. 41274, 'Garde-robe du roi, journal de sortie'
British Library Department of Manuscripts
   Add. Ms. 38503, despatches of Horatio Walpole to Lord Townshend, 1725
   Add. Ms. 41648 account of his relations with Louis XVIII by Sir Thomas Clifford
Private archives, Journal of Lady Elizabeth Foster, later Elizabeth Duchess of Devonshire, 1788–1824
Public Record Office, Kew [Lord Chamberlain's Papers], LC5/220, schedules of civil uniforms
Thierry de Ville d'Avray Archives, 'Mémoires of vicomte Thierry de Ville d'Avray'
Windsor Castle, Royal Archives 21478, letter of Lord Conyngham to Colonel Macmahon, 9 July 1814

II Published Works

Acton, Harold, *The Last Medici*, 1980 edn
Adamson, John, ed., *The Princely Courts of Europe 1500–1750*, 1999
Allami, Abu'l-fazl, *The A'ini Akbari*, 2nd rev. edn, 3 vols, New Delhi, 1977
Allen, Rodney, *Threshold of Terror: The Last Hours of the Monarchy in the French Revolution*, 1999

Allgor, Catherine, *Parlor Politics. In which the Ladies of Washington help build a City and a Government*, Charlottesville, 2000

Amies, Hardy, *The Englishman's Suit*, 1994

Andurain, Arnaud d', *Souvenirs plaisants de la vie sérieuse*, 1985

Anglesey, Marquess of, *One-Leg*, 1961

Anlik Bennet, Helju, 'Evolution of the Meanings of Chin: An Introduction to the Russian Institution of Rank Ordering and Noble Assignment from the Time of Peter the Great to the Bolshevik Revolution', *Canadian Slavic Studies*, 10, 1977

Anne, Théodore, *Mémoires, souvenirs et anecdotes sur l'intérieur du Palais de Charles X*, 2 vols, 1831

Anon., *Louis Bonaparte et sa cour*, 1820

Ansell, Jacqueline, 'The Seal of Social Approval', *The Court Historian*, IV, 2, August 1999

Anson, E. and F., eds, *Mary Hamilton...at Court and at Home*, 1925

Antonetti, Guy, *Louis-Philippe*, 1994

Antonius, Soraya, *The Lord*, 1986

Apponyi, Comte Rodolphe, *Journal*, 4 vols, 1913–26

Arblay, Madame d', *Diary and Letters*, 6 vols, 1904–5

Arbuthnot, Harriet, *The Journal of Mrs Arbuthnot, 1820–1832*, 2 vols, 1950

Arch, Nigel, and Joanna Marschner, *Splendour at Court. Dressing for Royal Occasions since 1700*, 1987

Armstrong, Harold, *Turkey in Travail*, 1925

Armytage, Hon. Mrs, *Old Court Customs and Modern Court Rule*, 1883

Arneth, Alfred Ritter von, ed., *Maria Theresia und Joseph II: Ihre Correspondenz*, 3 vols, Vienna, 1867–68

Arnstein, Walter L., 'The Warrior Queen: Reflections on Queen Victoria and her World', *Albion*, 30, 1, Spring 1998

Arvieux, Chevalier d', *Mémoires*, 6 vols, 1735

Ascher, Abraham, *The Search for Stability in Late Imperial Russia*, Stanford, 2001

Ashby Turner Jr., Henry, *Hitler's Thirty Days to Power*, 1996

Aspinall, A., *Later Correspondence of George III*, 5 vols, Cambridge, 1962–70

At the Sublime Porte: Ambassadors to the Ottoman Empire 1550–1800, Hazlitt, Gooden and Fox, 1988

Atil, Esin, *Turkish Art*, 1980

Auckland, Lord, *Journal and Correspondence*, 4 vols, 1860–62

Ayling, Stanley, *Fox*, 1991

Babinger, Franz, *Mehmed the Conqueror and his Time*, 1978 edn

Baker, Patricia L., 'The Fez in Turkey: A Symbol of Modernisation', in *Costume*, 1986

——, 'Politics of Dress: The Dress Reform Laws of 1920s/1930s Iran', in Nancy Lindisfarne-Tapper and Bruce Ingham, eds, *Languages of Dress in the Middle East*, Richmond, 1997

Balisson de Rougemont, M. N., *Le Rôdeur français ou les moeurs du jour*, 6 vols, 1816–21

Balzac, Honoré de, *Traité de la vie élégante*, 1998 edn

——, *Les Illusions perdues*, 2000 edn

Banffy, Miklos, *The Phoenix Land*, 2003

Barbey d' Aurevilly, Jules, *Du Dandysme et de George Brummell*, 1997 edn

Barbier, E. J. F., *Journal d'un avocat de Paris*, 4 vols, Clermont-Ferrand, 2002–4

Barczay, Tom, 'The 1896 Millennial Festivities in Hungary', in Karin Friedrich, ed.,

Festive Culture in Germany and Europe from the Twentieth Century, New York, 2000

Baring, Thomas, *A Tour through Italy…and Austria*, 2nd edn, 1817

Barman, Roderick J., *Citizen Emperor: Pedro II and the Making of Brazil 1825–91*, Stanford, 1999

Barral-Mazoyer, Rose, *Thomas-Augustin de Gasparin, officier de l'armée royale et conventionnelle*, Marseille, 1982

Barton, H. Arnold, *Count Hans Axel von Fersen*, Boston, 1975

Bayreuth, Margrave de, *Mémoires*, 1967 edn

Beattie, John M., *The English Court in the Reign of George I*, 1967

Beaulaincourt, Madame de, *B. L. A. de Castellane*, 1901

Beaulieu, C., *Histoire du commerce de l'industrie et des fabriques de la soie*, Lyon, 1838

Beer, Esmond S. de, 'King Charles II's Own Fashion. An Episode in English–French Relations 1666–1670', *Journal of the Warburg Institute*, 2, 2 October 1938

Behrendt, Stephen C., *Royal Mourning and Regency Culture*, 1997

Belgrave, Charles, *Personal Column*, 1960

Bentheim-Steinfurst, Comte Louis de, 'Journal de mon séjour à Paris', *Revue de Paris*, 25 October 1908

Bergman, Eva, *Nationella Dräkten. En studie kring Gustaf III's dräkt-reform, 1778*, Stockholm, 1938

Berry, Mary, *Social Life in England and France, from the French Revolution in 1789 to that of July 1830*, 1831

Bertelli, Sergio, Franco Cardini and Elvira Garveo Zorzi, *Italian Renaissance Courts*, 1986

Bertier, Ferdinand de, *Souvenirs d'un ultra-royaliste (1815–1832)*, 1993

Besenval, Baron de, *Mémoires sur la cour de France*, 1987 edn

Bessborough, Earl of, *Lady Bessborough and her Family Circle*, 1940

——, *Georgiana*, 1955

Beust, Friedrich Ferdinand, count von, *Memoirs*, 2 vols, 1887

Biefang, Andreas, *Bismarcks Reichstag. Das Parlament in der Leipziger Strasse*, Düsseldorf, 2002

Bildliche Darstellung der königlich preussischen Civil-Uniformen, Berlin, 1804

Billard, Max, *La Conspiration de Malet*, 1907

Bimbenet, Eugène, *Fuite de Louis XVI à Varennes*, 2 vols, 1868 edn

Binder, Dieter A., 'Province versus Metropolis: The Instrumentalised Myth of Archduke John of Styria (1782–1859)', in Karin Friedrich, ed., *Festive Culture in Germany and Europe from the Twentieth Century*, New York, 2000

Binyon, T. J., *Pushkin*, 2003 edn

Blanch, Lesley, *Romain, un regard particulier*, 1998

Bland, Olivia, *The Royal Way of Death*, 1986

Bled, Jean-Paul, *François Joseph*, 1987

——, *Histoire de Vienne*, 1998

Blessington, Countess of, *The Idler in France*, 2 vols, 1841

Bloch, Michael, *Ribbentrop*, 1992

Blücher, Princess Evelyn, *An English Wife in Berlin*, 1920

Boigne, Madame de, *Mémoires*, 2 vols, 1986 edn

Boisnard, Luc, *La Noblesse dans la tourmente 1774–1802*, 1992

Bombelles, Marquis de, *Journal*, Geneva, 1977–

Bonneville de Marsangy, Louis, *Le Chevalier de Vergennes. Son ambassade à Constantinople*, 2 vols, 1894

Bonneville, M., *Costumes actuels des deux conseils législatifs et du directoire exécutif*, 1796
Boswell, James, *London Journal 1762–1763*, 1950
——, *The Life of Dr Johnson*, 4 vols, 1964 edn
Bottineau, Yves, *L'Art de cour dans L'Espagne de Philippe V 1700–1746*, 1993 edn
Boucher, François, *A History of Costume in the West*, 1987 edn
Bouchot, Henri, *La Toilette à la cour de Napoléon. Chiffons et politique des grandes dames 1810–1815*, 1895
Bourgoing, M. de, *Nouveau voyage en Espagne*, 3 vols, 1789
Bradford, Sarah, *George VI*, 1991 edn
Brandstätter, Christian, and Franz Hubmann, *Die Lederhose*, Vienna, 1978
Brehmer, Arthur, *Am Hofe Kaiser Wilhelm II*, Berlin, 1898
Brethon, Paul Le, *Lettres et documents pour servir à l'histoire de Joachim Murat*, 8 vols, 1908–14
[Brindesi, Jean], *Elbicei Attika: musée des anciens costumes turcs de Constantinople*, 1855
Brophy, James M., 'Mirth and Subversion: Carnival in Cologne', *History Today*, 47, July 1997
Brosses, Président de, *Lettres d'Italie*, ed. Frédéric d'Agay, 2 vols, 1986
Broughton, Lord, *Recollections of a Long Life*, 6 vols, 1909–11
Brummett, Palmira, *Image and Imperialism in the Ottoman Revolutionary Press 1908–1911*, Albany, 2000
Brunon, Raoul, 'Uniformes de l'armée française', in Jean Tulard, ed., *Dictionnaire Napoléon*, 1989, pp. 1666–87.
Buchholz, R. O., *The Augustan Court, Queen Anne and the Decline of Court Culture*, Stanford, 1993
——, 'Going to Court in 1700', *The Court Historian*, V, 3, December 2000
Buck, Anne, *Dress in Eighteenth-Century England*, 1979
Buckle, Richard, *The Prettiest Girl in England*, 1958
Busch, Moritz, *Bismarck. Some Secret Pages of his History*, 3 vols, 1898
Campan, Madame, *Mémoires*, 1988 edn
Campbell, Una, *Robes of the Realm*, 1989
Cannadine, David, *Ornamentalism. How the British saw their Empire*, 2001
Capifava, Angelica, *Splendore della corte degli Zar*, Lugano, 1999
Carette, Madame, *Souvenirs intimes de la cour des Tuileries*, 13th edn, 1889
Carpenter, Kirsty, *Refugees of the French Revolution. Émigrés in London 1789-1802*, 1999
Carr, Raymond, *English Fox Hunting*, rev. edn, 1986
Castellane, Maréchal de, *Journal*, 5 vols, 1896–7
Castiglione, Baldassare, *The Book of the Courtier*, 2000
Catherine the Great. Treasures of Imperial Russia from the State Hermitage Museum, Leningrad, Dallas, 1990
Caulaincourt, Général de, *Mémoires*, 3 vols, 1933
Cavelli Traverso, Carla, 'Dall'uniforme sabauda a quella italiana', *Studi Piemontesi*, March 2000
Cecil, Hugh and Mirabel, *Imperial Marriage*, 2002
Cecil, Lamar, *Wilhelm II: Prince and Emperor*, 1996
Charles, Jacques, ed., *Louis XVII*, n.d.
Charles-Roux, François, *Les Echelles de Syrie et de Palestine au XVIIIe siècle*, 1928
Chastel, André, *L'Art français. Ancien régime*, 1995

Châtenet, Monique, *La Cour de France au XVIe siècle. Vie sociale et architecture*, 2002

Cheape, Hugh, *Tartan*, Edinburgh, 2nd edn, 1995

Chehabi, Houchang E., 'Staging the Emperor's New Clothes: Dress Codes and Nation Building under Rezi Shah', *Iranian Studies*, 26, 3–4, Summer 1993

Choiseul, Duc de, *Relation du départ de Louis XVI le 20 juin 1791 écrite en août 1791*, 1822

Choisy, Abbé de, *Mémoires*, 1966 edn

Churchill, Winston, *Thoughts and Adventures*, 1990 edn

Clary, Prince, *A European Past*, 1978

Clayton, Michael, *Prince Charles, Horseman*, 1987

Clifford, Atalanta, *The Guards Museum*, 1997 edn

Cobb, Richard, *Still Life. Scenes from a Tunbridge Wells Childhood*, 1983

Cohn, Bernard S., 'Cloth, Clothes and Colonialism. India in the Nineteenth Century', in Annette B. Weiner and Jane Schneider, eds, *Cloth and Human Experience*, Washington, 1989, pp. 303–53

Coke, Lady Mary, *Diary*, 4 vols, 1970

Coleman, Elizabeth Anne, *The Opulent Era. Fashions of Worth, Doucet and Pingat*, 1989

Coleman, Terry, *Nelson*, 2002 edn

Collingham, Hugh, *The July Monarchy*, 1988

Colson, Percy, *Whites 1693–1950*, 1951

Colville, John, *The Fringes of Power*, 1986 edn

Colville, Quintin, 'Jack Tar and the Gentleman Officer: The Role of the Uniform in Shaping the Class- and Gender-related Identities of British Naval Personnel 1930–1939', *Transactions of the Royal Historical Society*, 6th series, 13, 2003, pp. 105–29

Comeau, Baron, *Souvenirs des guerres d'Allemagne pendant la Révolution et l'Empire*, 1900

Commynes, Philippe de, *Mémoires*, 2001 edn

Connell, Brian, *Portrait of a Whig Peer*, 1957

Cosnac, Daniel de, *Mémoires*, 2 vols, 1852

Costumes des tsars de Pierre le Grand à Nicolas II, collection du Musée de l'Ermitage, Saint Petersbourg, Moscow, 1999

Courcy, Anne de, *1939: The Last Season*, 2003

Coxe, William, AM, FRS, *Travels into Poland, Russia, Sweden, and Denmark*, 2 vols, 1784

Cradock, Mme, *Journal*, 1896

Craig, Gordon A., *The Politics of the Prussian Army*, 1955

Croce, Benedetto, *History of the Kingdom of Naples*, Chicago, 1970

Cronin, Mike, and Daryl Adair, *The Wearing of the Green. A History of St Patrick's Day*, 2002

Crosby, Caresse, *The Passionate Years*, 1955

Croÿ, Duc de, *Journal inédit*, 4 vols, 1906–7

Cumming, Valerie, *Royal Dress. The Image and the Reality. 1580 to the Present Day*, 1989

——, 'Pantomime and Pageantry: The Coronation of Geroge IV', in Celina Fox, ed., *London – World City 1800–1840*, 1992

Custine, Marquis de, *Mémoires et voyages*, 2nd edn, 2 vols, 1830

Cuvillier-Fleury, A., *Journal intime*, 2 vols, 1900–03

Dahlberg, Anne Marie, *Royal Splendour in the Royal Armoury*, Stockholm, 1996

Dalrymple, Major William, *Travels through Spain and Portugal in 1774*, 1777

Dangeau, Marquis de, *Journal*, Clermont-Ferrand, 2002–

D'Argenson, Marquis, *Journal*, Clermont-Ferrand, 2002–

Davenport, Millia, *Book of Costume*, New York, 1950

Davis, Brian L., *German Army Uniforms and Insignia 1933–1945*, rev. edn, 1992

Dayot, A., *Les Vernet*, 1898

Deakin, F. W., *The Brutal Friendship: Mussolini, Hitler and the Fall of Italian Fascism*, 1962

Deffand, Madame du, *Lettres de Madame du Deffand*, 2002 edn

Deherain, Henri, *La Vie de Pierre Ruffin*, 2 vols, 1929–30

Delacroix, Eugène, *Correspondance générale*, 5 vols, 1935–8

Delpierre, Madeleine, *Se vêtir au XVIIIe siècle*, 1996

Demeter, Karl, *The German Officer Corps in Society and State 1650–1945*, 1965

Denon, Vivant, and Abdel Rahman el-Gabarti, *Sur l'expedition de Bonaparte en Egypte*, 1998 edn

Desjardins, Gustave, *Le Petit Trianon. Histoire et déscription*, Versailles, 1885

Deutsches Historisches Museum, *Bismarck – Prussia, Germany and Europe*, Berlin, 1990

——, *Bilder und Zeugnisse der deutschen Geschichte*, 2 vols, Berlin, 1997

Dewald, Jonathan, *The European Nobility 1400-1800*, 1996

Dicey, Edward, *A Month in Russia during the Marriage of the Czarevitch*, 1867

Dickens, Charles, *The Pickwick Papers*, 1837

Dickinson, Gary, and Linda Wrigglesworth, *Imperial Wardrobe*, 1990

Dinesen, Isak, *Daguerreotypes and Other Essays*, 1979

Dino, Duchesse de, *Chronique de 1831 à 1862*, 4 vols, 1909

Dmytryshyn, Basil, *Imperial Russia: A Source-Book 1700–1917*, New York, 1967

Dorpalen, Andreas, *Hindenburg and the Weimar Republic*, Princeton, 1964

Dosne, Sophie, *Mémoires de Madame Dosne*, 2 vols, 1928

Dreyfus, Ferdinand, *Un philanthrope d'autrefois. La Rochfoucauld-Liancourt 1747–1827*, 1903

Duffy, Christopher, *The Army of Maria Theresa. The Armed Forces of Imperial Austria 1740–1780*, 1977

——, *The Military Experience in the Age of Reason*, 1987

Du Fresne-Canaye, Philippe, *Le voyage du Levant*, 1986 edn

Duindam, Jeroen, *Vienna and Versailles. The Courts of Europe's Dynastic Rivals 1550-1780*, Cambridge, 2003

Dulwich Picture Gallery, *Treasures of a Polish King*, 1997

Dumesnil, A., *Moeurs politiques au XIXe siècle*, 2 vols, 1830

Dunlevy, Mairead, *Dress in Ireland*, 1989

Eagles, Robin, *Francophilia in English Society 1748–1815*, 2000

Easton, Laird M., *The Red Count: The Life and Times of Harry Kessler*, Berkley, 2002

Edwards, Anne, *The Queen's Clothes*, 1977

Eldem, Edhem, *French Trade in Istanbul in the Eighteenth Century*, Leiden, 1999

El-Eid al-Buluan, Hayyat, 'The Image of the European in Niqula al-Turk's Mudhakkarat (Chronique d'Egypte)', in Bernard Heyberger and Carsten Halbiner, eds, *Les Européens vus par les Libanais à l'époque ottomane*, Beirut, 2002

Eliot, Charles, *Turkey in Europe*, 1900

Elliot, Matthew, 'Dress Codes in the Ottoman Empire: The case of the Franks', in

Suraiya Faroqhi and Christoph K. Neumann, eds, *Ottoman Costumes from Textile to Identity*, Istanbul, 2004

Entner, Christina, and Friedemann Bedurfting, *Encyclopedia of the Third Reich*, 2 vols, New York, 1991

Ergang, Robert, *The Potsdam Führer. Frederick William I, Father of Prussian Militarism*, New York, 1941

Eri, Gyongi, and Zsuzsa Jobbagyi, eds, *A Golden Age: Art and Society in Hungary 1896–1914*, Budapest, 1990

Escars, Duc d', *Mémoires*, 2 vols, 1890

Esher, Viscount, ed., *Letters of Queen Victoria 1837–1861*, 3 vols, 1907

——, ed., *The Girlhood of Queen Victoria*, 2 vols, 1912

Espinchal, Comte d', *Journal*, 1912

Espinchal, Hippolyte d', *Souvenirs*, 2 vols, 1929

Esterhazy, Comte Valentin, *Lettres à sa femme 1784–1792*, 1907

Etleha, Baje *et al.*, *Kastelyok es magnarsok*, Budapest, 1994

Evelyn, John, *Diary*, ed. John Bowle, 1985

Ewing, Elizabeth, *Women in Uniform through the Centuries*, 1975

Eyck, Frank, *The Frankfurt Parliament 1848–1849*, 1968

Fahmy, Khaled, *All the Pasha's Men. Mehmed Ali, his Army and the Making of Modern Egypt*, Cambridge, 1997

Falaiseau, Madame de, *Dix ans de la vie d'une femme pendant l'émigration. Mémoires*, 1893

Falasca-Zamponi, Simonetta, *Fascist Spectacle: The Aesthetics of Power in Mussolini's Italy*, Berkeley, 1997

Faroqhi, Suraiya, and Christoph K. Neumann, eds, *Ottoman Costumes from Textile to Identity*, Istanbul, 2004

Fasti della burocrazia: uniformi civili e di corte dei secoli XVIII–XIX, Palazzo Ducale, Genoa, 1984

Fawcett, Frank Burlington, *Court Ceremonial and Book of the Court of King George the Sixth*, 1937

——, ed., *Their Majesties Courts holden at Buckingham Palace and at the Palace of Holyroodhouse*, 1938

Feuillet de Conches, Baron F. S., *Louis XVI, Marie Antoinette et Madame Elizabeth*, 6 vols, 1864–73

Ffoulkes, Fiona, 'Luxury Clothing in Nineteenth-century Paris', in Maxine Berg and Helen Clifford, eds, *Consumers and Luxury. Consumer Culture in Europe 1650–1850*, Manchester, 1999

Field, Ophelia, *The Favourite. Sarah, Duchess of Malborough*, 2003 edn

Fitzgerald, Brian, *Emily, Duchess of Leinster*, 1949

Fitzherbert, Margaret, *The Man who was Greenmantle*, 1983

Flamand Christensen, Sigrid, *Kongedragterne fra 17 og 18 Aarhundrede*, 2 vols, Copenhagen, 1940

Foreman, Amanda, *Georgiana, Duchess of Devonshire*, 1999 edn

Fortia-Piles, M. de, *Voyage de deux français en Allemagne, Danemark, Suède, Russie et Pologne fait en 1790–92*, 4 vols, 1796

Foster, Sarah, 'Buying Irish in Eighteenth Century Dublin: Consumer Nationalism in Eighteenth Century Dublin', *History Today*, June 1997

Foulkes, Nick, *Last of the Dandies*, 2003

Fox, Robert, and Anthony Turner, eds, *Luxury Trades and Consumerism in Ancien Regime Paris: Studies in the History of the Skilled Workforce*, Aldershot, 1998

Foy, General, *Notes autobiographiques*, 3 vols, 1926

Fraser, Antonia, *Marie Antoinette*, 2001

Fraser, David, *Frederick the Great*, 2000

Fraser, Flora, *Princessses*, 2004

Frénilly, Baron de, *Souvenirs*, 1908

Frick, Carole Collier, *Dressing Renaisssance Florence. Families, Fortunes and Fine Clothing*, Baltimore, 2002

Fritz, Paul S., 'The Trade in Death: Royal Funerals in England 1685–1830', *Eighteenth Century Studies*, 15, 3, Spring 1982

Frost, Robert, 'Poles and Swedes', *The Court Historian*, VII, 2, December 2002

Fujitani, T., *Splendid Monarchy. Power and Pageantry in Modern Japan*, Berkeley, 1996

Fulford, Roger, *Your Dear Letter, Private Correspondence of Queen Victoria and the Crown Prince of Prussia 1865–1875*, 1971

Funke, Dr Alfred, *Das Bismarck-Buch des Deutschen Volkes*, 2 vols, Berlin, 1921

Gachot, Édouard, *Marie-Louise intime*, 2 vols, 1911–12

Galeries nationales du Grand Palais, *Cinq années d'enrichissement du patrimoine national 1975–1980*, 1980

Galignani, A., *Galignani's New Paris Guide*, Thirteenth Edition, 1825

Gall, Lothar, and Karl-Heinz Jürgens, *Bismarck. Lebensbilder*, Berlin, 1976

Garnier, J.-P., *Barras, roi du Directoire*, 1970

Gash, Norman, *Sir Robert Peel*, 2nd edn, 1986

Gautier, Théophile, *Paris et les Parisiens*, 1996 edn

Geffroy, A., *Gustave III et la cour de France*, 2nd edn, 2 vols, 1867

Genlis, Madame de, *Mémoires*, 8 vols, 1825

Genty, M., *Discours sur le luxe*, 1783

Georgeon, François, *Abdulhamid II*, 2003

Georgi, M., *Description de la ville de Saint Petersbourg et de ses environs*, St Petersburg, 1793

Gérando, baronne de, *Lettres de la baronne de Gérando*, 1880

Gerard, James W., *My Four Years in Germany*, 1917

Germaner, Semra, and Eynep Inankur, *Constantinople and the Orientalists*, Istanbul, 2002

Gernsheim, Helmut and Alison, *Queen Victoria. A Biography in Word and Picture*, 1959

Geyer, Michael, 'The German Officer Corps as a Profession', in Geoffrey Cocks, ed., *German Professions 1800–1950*, New York, 1990

Ghyka, Matila, *The World Mine Oyster*, 1961

Gigon, S. C., *Le Général Malet*, 1913

Gilbert, John, *National Costumes of the World*, 1972

Gilbert, Martin, *In Search of Churchill*, 1995 edn

Giles, Frank, *Napoleon Bonaparte: England's Prisoner*, 2001

Gilet, Annie, 'Le voyageur dans l'Empire ottoman', in *Louis François Cassas 1756–1827*, Mainz, 1994

Girardin, Stanislas de, *Souvenirs*, 4 vols, 1828

Girouard, Mark, *Life in the English Country-house*, 1974

Glagau, Hans, *Die französische Legislative und der Ursprung der Revolutionskriege*, Berlin, 1908

Glenbervie, Lord, *Diaries*, 2 vols, 1928

Gmeline, Patrick de, and Gerard Gorokhoff, *La Garde impériale russe 1896–1914*, 1986

Godet, Philippe, *Madame de Charrière et ses amis*, 2 vols, Geneva, 1906

Godfrey, Richard, *James Gillray: The Art of Caricature*, 2001

Golovkine, Fédor, Comte, *La Cour et le règne de Paul 1er*, 1905

Goncourt, Edmond and Jules de, *Journal*, 4 vols, 1989 edn

Goodman, Jean, with Sir Iain Moncrieffe, *Debrett's Royal Scotland*, 1983

Gordon, Stewart, 'A World of Investiture', in Stewart Gordon, ed., *Robes and Honour. The Medieval World of Investiture*, 2001

——, 'Robes, Kings and Semiotic Ambiguity', in Stewart Gordon, ed., *Robes and Honour. The Medieval World of Investiture*, 2001

Gorst, Frederick John, *Of Carriages and Kings*, 1956

Goswamy, B. N., *Indian Costumes in the Collection of the Calico Museum of Textiles*, Ahmedabad, 1996

Grasset de Saint-Sauveur, Jacques, *Costumes des représentants du peuple français*, 1795

Green, Abigail, *Fatherlands*, 2001

Gregg, Edward, *Queen Anne*, 1980

Gregorian, Vartan, *The Emergence of Modern Afghanistan*, Stanford, 1969

Grelot, M., *Relation nouvelle d'un voyage de Constantinople*, 1680

Greville, Charles, *Memoirs*, 8 vols, 1938

Gronow, Captain, *Reminiscences and Recollections*, 2 vols, 1892 edn

Grouchy, Vicomte de, and Antoine Guillois, *La Révolution française vue par un diplomate étranger*, 1903

Guibert, Comte de, *Journal d'un voyage en Allemagne fait en 1773*, 2 vols, 1803

Gutsche, Willibald, *Aufstieg und Fall eines kaiserlichen Reichskanzlers*, Berlin, 1973

Gwynn, John, *London and Westminster Improved, Illustrated by Plans, to which is Prefixed a Discourse on Publick Magnificence*, 1766, reprinted 1969

Haffner, Sebastian, *Defying Hitler*, 2002

Halévy, Daniel, *Le Courrier de Monsieur Thiers*, 1921

Hallo, Charles Jean, *Historique des tenues de vénerie*, 1999

Hamdy Bey, Osman, and Marie de Launay, *Les Costumes populaires de la Turquie en 1873*, Constantinople, 1873

Hamilton, Angus, *Afghanistan*, 1906

Hamilton, Elizabeth, *The Backstairs Dragon*, 1969

Hammer-Purgstall, J. von, *Histoire de l'empire ottoman*, 16 vols, 1835–40

Hanlon, Gregory, *The Twilight of a Military Tradition. Italian Aristocrats and European Conflicts 1560–1800*, 1998

Hardinge of Penshurst, Lord, *Old Diplomacy*, 1947

Harte, N. B., 'State Control of Dress and Social Change in Pre-Industrial England', in D. C. Coleman and A. H. John, eds, *Trade, Government and Economy in Pre-Industrial England*, 1976, pp. 132–65

Harvey, A. D., 'Gustav III of Sweden', *History Today*, December 2003

Harvey, John, *Men in Black*, 1995

Haswell Miller, A. E., and N. P. Dawnay, *Military Drawings and Paintings in the Collection of Her Majesty the Queen*, 2 vols, 1966–70

Hatch Dupree, Nancy, 'Behind the Veil in Afghanistan', *Asia*, July 1978

Hatton, Ragnhild, *Charles XII of Sweden*, 1968

Haupt, Herbert, 'Die Aufhebung des spanischen Mantelkleides durch Kaiser Joseph II. Ein Wendepunkt im höfischen Zeremoniell', *Österreich zur Zeit Kaiser Josephs II*, Melk Abbey, 1980, pp. 79–81

Haussonville, Comte d', *Ma jeunesse*, 1885

——, *Madame de Staël et Monsieur Necker*, 1925
Hautpoul, Général Marquis d', *Mémoires*, 1908
Heidenstam, O. G. von, *La Fin d'une dynastie*, 1911
Heiszler, Vilmos, *Photo Habsburg. The Private Life of an Archduke*, Budapest, 1989
Henry-Simon and Maréchal, Mrs, *Les Étrennes forcées, ou Ah! Mon habit que je vous remercie!*, 1814
Hérisson, comte d', *Journal d'un officier d'ordonnance*, 1885
Hesketh, Christian, *Tartans*, 1961
Hézecques, Comte d', *Souvenirs d'un page à la cour de Louis XVI*, 1873
Hibbert, Christopher, *George IV, Prince of Wales*, 1972
——, *The Court of St James's*, 1979
——, *Garibaldi and his Enemies*, 1987 edn
Higonnet, Patrice, *Paris, Capital of the World*, Cambridge, Mass., 2002
Hill, Bridget, *Servants. English Domestics in the Eighteenth Century*, Oxford, 1996
[Hobhouse, John Cam], *The Substance of some Letters written by an Englishman resident at Paris during the Last Reign of the Emperor Napoleon*, 2 vols, 1816
Höhne, Heinz, *The Order of the Death's Head*, 1972 edn
Hollander, Anne, *Seeing through Clothes*, New York, 1980
Hone, J. B., *The History of the Royal Buckhounds*, Newmarket, 1895
Horowski, Leonhard, '"Such a great advantage for my Son": Office-holding and Career Mechanisms at the Court of France 1661–1789', *The Court Historian*, VIII, 2, December 2003
Hottenroth, Friedrich, *Handbuch der deutschen Tracht*, Stuttgart, n.d.
Howarth, Stephen, *Henry Poole of Savile Row: The Making of a Legend*, Honiton, 2003
Howell, Georgina, *Diana: Her Life in Fashion*, 1998
Hubmann, Franz, *Dream of Empire. The World of Germany in Original Photographs 1840–1914*, 1973
Hue, Baron, *Souvenirs*, 1908
Hughes, Daniel J., *The King's Finest*, New York, 1987
Hughes, Lindsey, *Russia in the Age of Peter the Great*, 1998
——, 'From Caftans into Corsets: The Sartorial Transformation of Women in the Reign of Peter the Great', in Peter I. Barta, ed., *Gender and Sexuality in Russian Civilization*, 2001, pp. 17–32
——, *Peter the Great*, 2002
Hughes, Thomas Patrick, *A Dictionary of Islam*, Lahore, 1885
Hugo, Victor, *Correspondance familiale et écrits intimes*, 4 vols, 1988
Hugues, Laurent, 'La Famille royale et ses portraitistes sous Louis XV et Louis XVI', in Xavier Salmon, ed., *De soie et de poudre. Portraits de cour dans l'Europe des lumières*, Arles, 2002, pp. 158–61
Huis Doorn, Amsterdam, 1992
Hull, Isobel V., *The Entourage of Kaiser Wilhelm II 1888–1918*, 1982
Hunt, Alan, *Governance of the Consuming Passions. A History of Sumptuary Laws*, 1996
Il Neoclassicismo in Italia: da Tiepolo a Canova, Milan, 2002
Imber, Colin, *The Ottoman Empire*, 2002
Itzkowitz, Norman, and Max Mote, *Mubadele: An Ottoman-Russian Exchange of Ambassadors*, Chicago, 1970
Jackson, Lady, ed., *The Bath Archives*, 2 vols, 1873
Jahlberg, Gunnar, ed., *Catherine II et Gustave III: une correspondance retrouvée*, Stockholm, 1998

Janin, Jules, *Fontainebleau, Versailles, Paris,* 1837

Jenkins, Roy, *Churchill,* 2002

Jeziorowski, Tadeusz, and Andrzej Jeziorkwski, *Mundury Wojewódzkie, Rzeczypospolitej Obojga Narodów,* Warsaw, 1992

Johnston, William M., *The Austrian Mind: An Intellectual and Social History,* Berkeley, 1972

Joinville, Prince de, ed., *Vieux souvenirs,* 1970

Jones, Nigel, *A Brief History of the Rise of the Nazis,* 2004 edn

Jouy, Étienne de, *Guillaume le franc-parleur,* 2 vols, 1816

Kalfon Stillman, Yedida, *Arab Dress. A Short History. From the Dawn of Islam to Modern Times,* Leiden, 2000

Kayal, Maha, 'Le Système socio-vestimentaire à Tripoli (Liban) entre 1885 et 1985', University of Neuchâtel thesis, 1989

Kazan, Elias, *A Life,* 1988

Keene, Donald, *Meiji and his World, 1852–1912,* New York, 2002

Keep, John L. H., *Soldiers of the Tsar. Army and Society in Russia 1462–1874,* Oxford, 1985

Kelly, Laurence, *Moscow,* 1983

——, *Diplomacy and Murder in Tehran,* 2002

Kerckoff, E., *Le Costume à la cour et à la ville,* 1865

Kershaw, Ian, *Hitler 1889–1936: Hubris,* 1998

Kessler, Count Harry, *Diaries of a Cosmopolitan 1918–1937,* 1971

Ketterl, Eugen, *The Emperor Francis Joseph. An Intimate Study,* 1929

Kinross, Lord, *Atatürk: The rebirth of a Nation,* 1969 edn

Klarwill, Viktor, ed., *Mémoires et lettres du prince de Ligne,* 1923

Klingenstein, Grete, ed., *Erzherzog Johann von Österreich,* 2 vols, Graz, 1982

Klinkowström, Baron de, *Le Comte de Fersen et la cour de France,* 2 vols, 1877–8

Knight, Miss, *Autobiography,* 1960

Koehl, Robert Lewis, *The Black Corps. The Structure and Power Struggles of the Nazi SS,* Madison, Wisc., 1983

Korshunova, Tamara, *The Art of Costume in Russia, 18th to Early 20th Century,* Leningrad, 1979

——, *The Art of Costume in Russia, 18ᵗʰ to Early 20ᵗʰ Century,* rev. edn, Leningrad, 1983

Kotzebue, Moritz von, *Narrative of a Journey to Persia in the Suite of the Imperial Russian Embassy in the Year 1817,* 1819

Kraatze, Anne, ed., *Lace: History and Fashion,* 1989

Kügler, Georg J., 'Viennese Court Dress', in *The Imperial Style. Fashions of the Hapsburg Era,* Metropolitan Museum, New York, 1980

Kumar, Ritu, *Costumes and Textiles of Royal India,* 1999

Kurchner, Joseph, *Kaiser Wilhelm II als Soldat und Seemann,* Berlin, 1902

Kurth, Peter, *Tsar: The Lost World of Nicholas and Alexandra,* 1995

Kurtz, Harold, *The Empress Eugénie,* 1964

La Ferté, Papillon de, *Journal des menus-plaisirs du roi,* 2002 edn

La Rochefoucauld, Duc de, *Oeuvres complètes,* 1964 edn

La Rochefoucauld, François de, *Souvenirs du 10 août 1792 et de l'armée de Bourbon,* 1929

La Rochefoucauld, J. D. de, C. Wolikow and G. Ikni, *Le Duc de La Rochefoucauld-Liancourt 1747–1827,* 1980

La Tour du Pin, Mme de, *Journal d'une femme de cinquante ans*, 2 vols, 1913

Laborde, Alexandre de, *Quarante-huit heures de garde au château des Tuileries*, 1816

Lacey, Robert, *Sothebys: Bidding for Class*, 1999 edn

——, *Royal: Her Majesty Queen Elizabeth II*, 2002

Lachouque, Henry, *The Anatomy of Glory*, 1997 edn

Lacroix, Paul, *XVIIIe siècle: institutions, usages et costumes*, 1875

Laffitte, Jacques, *Mémoires*, 1932

Laird, Dorothy, *Royal Ascot*, 1976

Lampedusa, Giuseppe Tomasi di, *The Leopard*, 1973 edn

Lane-Poole, Stanley, *Life of Sir Stratford Canning*, 2 vols, 1888

Langlade, Émile, *La Marchande de modes de Marie-Antoinette Rose Bertin*, 1932

Langtry, Lillie, *The Days I Knew*, n.d.

Lanzac de Laborie, L., *Paris sous Napoléon*, 8 vols, 1905

Laurens, Henry, *L'Expédition d'Égypte 1798–1801*, 1997 edn

Laver, James, *Dandies*, 1968

——, *A Concise History of Costume*, 1969

Le Bourhis, Katell, ed., *The Age of Napoleon. Costume from Revolution to Empire*, Metropolitan Museum of New York, 1989

Le Roux, Nicolas, 'La Cour dans l'espace du palais: l'exemple de Henri III', in Marie-France Auzepy and Joel Cornette, eds, *Palais et pouvoir. De Constantinople à Versailles*, 2003, p. 246

Lefebvre, Georges, and Anne Terroine, eds., *Receuil de documents relatifs aux séances des États Généraux mai–juin, 1789*, 1953

Lemaistre, J. G., *A Rough Sketch of Modern Paris*, 1803

Lemire, Beverley, *Dress, Culture and Commerce. The English Clothing Trade before the Factory, 1660–1800*, 1997

Lentz, Thierry, ed., *Le Sacre de Napoléon*, 2003

Leonard, Carol S., *Reform and Regicide. The Reign of Peter III of Russia*, Bloomington, 1993

Léonard, Émile, *L'Armée et ses problèmes au XVIIIe siècle*, 1960

Les Grandes Demeures d'Espagne, 1998

Lescure, M. de, *Correspondance secrète inédite sur Louis XVI, Marie-Antoinette, la cour et la ville*, 2 vols, 1866

Lestringant, Frank, *Alfred de Musset*, 1999

Leveson-Gower, Lord Granville, *Private Correspondence 1781–1821*, 2 vols, 1916

Lévis-Mirepoix, Duc de, *Aventures d'une famille française*, 1949

Lewis, Bernard, *The Emergence of Modern Turkey*, 1960

Lieven, Dominic, *Nicholas II, Emperor of all the Russias*, 1993

Ligne, Prince de, *Mélanges militaires, littéraires et sentimentaires*, 35 vols, Dresden, 1795–1811

——, *Oeuvres choisies*, 2 vols, 1809

——, *Mémoires et mélanges historique et littéraires*, 5 vols, 1828

Lindisfarne-Tapper, Nancy, and Bruce Ingham, 'Approaches to the Study of Dress in the Middle East', in Nancy Lindisfarne-Tapper and Bruce Ingham, eds., *Languages of Dress in the Middle East*, Richmond, 1997

Llewellyn, Sasha, 'George III and the Windsor Uniform', *The Court Historian*, 1996

Lo Splendore di una regia corte. Uniformi e livree del Granducato di Toscana 1765–1799, Florence, 1983

Lockitt, C. H., *The Relations of French and English Society 1765–1793*, 1920

Lofström, Karl, 'Le Costume national de Gustave III, le costume de cour et la présentation à la cour', *Livrustkammaren*, 9, 7–8, 1962

Londonderry, Marquess of, *Recollections of a Tour in the North of Europe in 1836–7*, 2 vols, 1838

Longworth, Philip, *Alexis, Tsar of All the Russias*, 1984

Loriga, S., 'Continuité aristocratique et tradition militaire du Piémont de la dynastie de Savoie XVIe–XIXe siècles', *Revue d'histoire moderne*, XXXIV, 7–9, 1987

Louis XIV, *Mémoires*, ed. Jean Longnon, 2001

Lovell, Mary A., *A Rage to Live, A Biography of Richard and Isabel Burton*, 1999 edn

Lucas-Dubreton, J., *Louis-Philippe et la Machine infernale*, 1951

Lukács, John, *Budapest 1900*, 1988

Lurie, Alison, *The Language of Clothes*, 1982

Luynes, Duc de, *Mémoires . . . sur la cour de Louis XV*, 15 vols, 1860–65

Lybbe Powys, Mrs Philip, *Passages from the Diaries*, 1899

Lyttelton, Sarah, Lady, *Correspondence of Sarah Spencer, Lady Lyttelton, 1787–1840*, ed. Hon. Mrs H. Wyndham, 1912

MacDonogh, Giles, *Frederick the Great: A Life in Deed and Letters*, 1999

——, *Wilhelm the Impetuous: The Last Kaiser*, 2000

MacFarlane, Charles, *Constantinople in 1828*, 2nd edn, 2 vols, 1829

——, *Turkey and its Destiny*, 2 vols, 1850

Macgill, Thomas, *Travels in Turkey, Italy and Russia*, 2 vols, 1808

Mack-Smith, Denis, *Italy. A Modern History*, Ann Arbor, 1959

Mackay-Smith, Alexander, *Man and Horse*, New York, 1984

Maclean, Fitzroy, *Highlanders. A History of the Highland Clans*, 1995

Macmichael, William, *Journey from Moscow to Constantinople*, 1819

MacMillan, Margaret, *Peacemakers. The Peace Conference of 1919 and its Attempt to End War*, 2002 edn

Madariaga, Isabel de, 'The Russian Nobility in the Seventeenth and Eighteenth Centuries', in H. M. Scott, ed., *The European Nobilities in the Seventeenth and Eighteenth Centuries*, 2 vols, 1995

——, *Russia in the Age of Catherine the Great*, 2002 edn

Magnus, Sir Philip, *King Edward VII*, 1964

Maillé, Duchesse de, *Mémoires*, 1989

Makdisi, Usama, 'Rethinking Ottoman Imperialism: Modernity, Violence and the Culture Logic of Ottoman Reform', in Jens Hansen, Thomas Philip and Stefan Weber, eds, *The Empire in the City: Arab Provincial Capitals in the Late Ottoman Empire*, Beirut, 2002

Mango, Andrew, *Atatürk*, 1999

Mansel, Philip, *Louis XVIII*, 1981

——, 'Monarchy, Uniform and the Rise of the *Frac* 1760–1830', *Past and Present*, 96, August 1981

——, *Pillars of Monarchy*, 1984

——, *Sultans in Splendour: The Last Years of the Ottoman World 1896–1939*, 1988

——, *The Court of France, 1789–1830*, 1989

——, *Constantinople: City of the World's Desire*, 1995

——, *Paris between Empires*, 2001

——, *Prince of Europe: The Life of Charles Joseph de Ligne 1735–1814*, 2003

Mansfield, Alan, *Ceremonial Costume*, 1980

Manucci, Nicola, *Mogul India or Storia do Mogor*, 4 vols, New Dehli, 1989

Mareschal de Bièvre, Comte Gabriel, *Le Marquis de Bièvre*, 1910
Marie-Amélie, *Journal*, 1988 edn
Margutti, Baron von, *The Emperor Francis Joseph and his Times*, 1921
Marly, Diana de, *A History of Haute Couture 1850–1950*, 1980
——, *Worth: Father of Haute Couture*, 1980
——, *Fashion for Men*, 1985
——, *Louis XIV and Versailles*, 1987
Marshall, Rosalind, *The Days of Duchess Anne*, 1973
Massie, Robert K., ed., *The Romanov Family Album*, 1982
Masson, Frédéric, *Joséphine impératrice et reine*, 1899 illustrated edn
——, *Napoléon et sa famille*, 15 vols, 1908–19
——, *L'impératrice Marie-Louise*, 1909
——, *Le Sacre et le couronnement de Napoléon*, 1978 edn
Masur, Gerhard, *Imperial Berlin*, 1971
Maxwell, Constantia, *The English Traveller in France 1680–1815*, 1932
Maxwell, Herbert, ed., *The Creevey Papers*, 2 vols, 1903
Maze-Sencier, Adolphe, *Les Fournisseurs de Napoléon Ier et des deux impératrices*, 1893
McDowell, Colin, *The Literary Companion to Fashion*, 1995
McKay, Derek, *The Great Elector*, 2001
McLean, R. R., *Royalty and Diplomacy in Europe 1890–1914*, 2001
Melville, Lewis, *Beau Brummell, his Life and Letters*, 1904
Menkes, Suzy, *The Windsor Style*, 1987
Meral Schick, Leslie, 'The Place of Dress in Pre-modern Costume Albums', in Suraiya Faroqhi and Christoph K. Neumann, eds, *Ottoman Costumes from Textile to Identity*, Istanbul, 2004
Mercier, Sébastien, *Tableau de Paris, nouvelle édition corrigée et augmentée*, 8 vols, 1782–3
Mérimée, Henri, *Une année en Russie*, 1847
Metropolitan Museum, *The Imperial Style. Fashions of the Hapsburg Era*, New York, 1980
Metternich, Princesse Pauline, *Souvenirs*, 1922
Michailovich, Grand Duke Nicholas, *L'Empereur Alexandre Ier*, 2 vols, St Petersburg, 1912
Millar, Delia, *Queen Victoria's Life in the Scottish Highlands depicted by her Watercolour Artists*, 1985
Miot de Mélito, Comte, *Mémoires*, 3 vols, 1858
Moiseyenko, Elena, 'The Emperor's New Clothes', *Hermitage*, 1, Summer 2003
Molleville, Bertrand de, *The Costume of the Hereditary States of the House of Austria*, 1804
Mollo, John, *Military Fashion*, 1972
——, *The Prince's Dolls. Scandals, Skirmishes and Splendours of the First British Hussars 1793–1815*, 1997
Moltke, Maréchal de, *Lettres sur l'orient*, 1872
Montbel, Comte de, *Souvenirs*, 1913
Montcalm, Marquise de, *Journal*, 1934
Montmort, Comte de, *Antoine Charles du Houx, Baron de Vioménil*, Baltimore, 1935
Montpensier, Mlle de, *Mémoires*, 4 vols, 1859
Morand, Paul, *Le Prince de Ligne*, 1964
Moreau, J. M., *Le Costume français représentant les différents États du Royaume, avec les*

habillements propres à chaque État, et accompagné de Réflexions Critiques et Morales, 1776

Morel, Bernard, *Les Joyaux de la couronne de France,* 1988

Morel-Fatio, A., *Études sur l'Espagne,* 3 vols, 1888–1904

Morris, Marilyn, *The British Monarchy and the French Revolution,* 1998

Morritt, J. B. S., *A Grand Tour,* 1985 edn

Mortier, Bianca M. du, *Aristocratic Attire. The Donation of the Six Family,* Amsterdam, 2000

Mossolov, A. A., *At the Court of the Last Tsar,* 1935

Motteville, Madame de, *Mémoires . . . sur Anne d'Autriche et sa cour,* 4 vols, 1855

Müller, Admiral, *The Kaiser and his Court,* 1961

Murray, Hon. Amelia, *Recollections,* 1868

Murray Keith, Sir Robert, *Memoirs and Correspondence,* 2 vols, 1849

Musée de la mode et du costume, *Modes et révolutions 1780–1804,* 1989

Musée des Beaux-Arts, *À la gloire du roi. Van der Meulen,* Dijon, 1998

Musée des Tissus, *Soieries de Lyon. Commandes royales au XVIIIe siècle,* Lyon, 1988

———, *Ceintures polonaises. Quand la Pologne s'habillait à Lyon,* Lyon, 2001

Museo del Prado, *Carlos III en Italia 1731–1759,* Madrid, 1989

Museo Nazionale di Palazzo Mansi, *Abiti alla corte di Elisa,* Lucca, 1995

Napoléon I, *Correspondance générale,* 32 vols, 1858–70

Narbonne, Pierre, *Journal de police,* 2 vols, Clermont-Ferrand, 2002

National Army Museum, *1745. Charles Edward Stuart and the Jacobites,* ed. Robert C. Woosnam-Savage,1995

Nationalmuseum, *Tournaments and the Dream of Chivalry,* Stockholm, 1992

———, *Catherine the Great and Gustav III,* Stockholm, 1999

———, *Galenpannan,* Stockholm, 2000

Nesin, Aziz, *Istanbul Boy,* 3 vols, Austin, Texas, 1977–90

Newton, William R., *L'Espace du roi. La cour de France au château de Versailles,* 2000

Nicholson, Robin, *Bonnie Prince Charlie and the Making of a Myth 1720–1892,* 2002

Nicolardot, Louis, *Journal de Louis XVI,* 1873

Nicolescu, Corina, *Le Costume de cour dans les pays roumains XIVe siècle–XVIIIe siècle,* Bucharest, 1970

Norman, Geraldine, *The Hermitage: The Biography of a Great Museum,* 1999 edn

Northumberland, Elizabeth, Duchess of, *The Diaries of a Duchess,* 1926

Norton, John, 'Faith and Fashion in Turkey', in Nancy Lindisfarne-Tapper and Bruce Ingham, eds., *Languages of Dress in the Middle East,* Richmond, 1997

Norton, Lucy, ed. and tr., *Saint-Simon at Versaille,* 1959

Oberkirch, Baronne d', *Mémoires,* 1989

Obolensky, Chloe, *The Russian Empire. A Portrait in Photographs,* New York, 1979

Österreich zur Zeit Kaiser Joseph II, Melk Abbey, 1980

Ohsson, I. Mouradgea d', *Tableau général de l'Empire Ottoman,* 3 vols, 1787–1820

Olivier, Edith, *Without Knowing Mr Walkley,* 1938

Ollard, Richard, 'The Brooks's of Charles James Fox', in Philip Ziegler and Desmond Seward, eds, *Brooks's. A Social History,* 1991

———, *The Image of the King. Charles I and Charles II,* 1993 edn

Onassis, Jacqueline Kennedy, *In the Russian Style,* New York, 1977

Orléans, Duchesse d', *Lettres de la Princess Palatine 1672–1722,* 1985

Ormesson, François d', and Jean-Pierre Thomas, *Jean-Joseph de Laborde banquier de Louis XV, mécène des lumières,* 2002

Orwell, George, *Animal Farm*, 2003 edn

Ozdalga, Elizabeth, *The Veiling Issue: Official Secularism and Popular Islam in Modern Turkey*, 1998

Özendeş, Engin, *Abdullah Frères. Ottoman Court Photographers*, Istanbul, 1998

Pakenham, Valerie, *The Big House in Ireland*, 2000

Pakula, Hannah, *An Uncommon Woman: The Empress Frederick*, 1996

Palais Galliéra, *Uniformes civil français. Cérémonial, circonstances 1750–1980*, 1982–3

——, *Costumes à la cour de Vienne, 1815–1918*, 1995

Palmer, Alan, *Bismarck*, 1976

——, *Twilight of the Habsburgs. The Life and Times of the Emperor Francis Joseph*, 2001 edn

Papendiek, Charlotte Louisa Henrietta, Mrs, *Court and Private Life: Being the Journals of Mrs Papendiek, Assistant-keeper of the Wardrobe and Reader to Her Majesty*, ed. Mrs Vernon Delves Broughton, 2 vols, 1887

Pardoe, Julia, *The City of the Sultans*, 4th edn, 1854

Pariset, E., *Histoire de la fabrique lyonnaise. Étude sur le régime social et économique de l'industrie de la soie à Lyon depuis le XVIe siècle*, Lyon, 1901

Parissien, Steven, *George IV: The Grand Entertainment*, 2001

Pasquier, E. D., *Souvenirs sur la révolution de 1848*, 1948

——, *Histoire de mon temps*, 6 vols, 1893–5

Pasquier, Jacqueline du, 'La Duchesse de Berry arbitre de la mode et reine du style troubadour', in *Marie Caroline de Berry. Naples, Paris, Graz. Itinéraire d'une princesse romantique*, 2002, pp. 124–37

Patnaik, Naveen, *A Second Paradise: Indian Courtly Life 1590–1947*, New York, 1985

Paulin Panon Desbassyns, Henry, *Voyage à Paris pendant la Révolution 1790–1792*, 1985

Payne, Robert, *The Life and Death of Mahatma Gandhi*, 1969

Pellissier, G., *Le Portefeuille de la comtesse d'Albany*, 1902

Pepys, Samuel, *Diary*, ed. Robert Latham and Willam Matthews, 11 vols, 2000–03

Pericoli, Ugo, *Le divise del Duce*, Milan, 1983

Perrot, Philippe, *Le Luxe. Une richesse entre faste et confort XVIIIe-XIXe siècle*, 1995

Petry, Carl F., 'Robing Ceremonials in Late Mamluk Egypt', in Stewart Gordon, ed., *Robes and Honour. The Medival World of Investiture*, 2001

Peyrusse, Baron G., *Mémorial et archives*, Carcassonne, 1869

——, *Lettres inédites du Baron Guillame Peyrusse écrites à son frère André*, 1894

Pfannenberg, Leo von, *Geschichte der Schlossgarde Kompagnie*, Berlin, 1909

Pick, Robert, *Empress Maria Theresa. The Earlier Years 1717–1757*, 1966

Pièces imprimées d'après le Décret de la Convention Nationale du 5 décembre 1792, 2 vols, Agen, 1793

Pierrette, Jean-Richard, ed., *Graveurs français de la seconde moitié du XVIIIe siècle*, 1985

Pilbeam, Pamela, *Madame Tussaud and the History of Waxworks*, 2003

Pimodan, comte de, *Le comte F. C. de Mercy-Argenteau*, 1911

Pingaud, Léonce, *Choiseul-Gouffier: la France en Orient sous Louis XVI*, 1887

Piotrovsky, Mikhail B., ed., *Treasures of Catherine the Great*, 2000

Pless, Daisy Princess of, *The Private Diaries*, ed. D. Chapman-Huston, 1950

Plumptre, Anne, *A Narrative of a Three Years Residence in France*, 3 vols, 1810

Poidebard, Alexandre, and Jacques Châtel, *Camille Pernon*, Lyon, 1912

Ponsonby, Frederick, *Recollections of Three Reigns*, 1957 edn

Portarlington, Countess of, *Gleanings from an Old Portfolio*, 3 vols, Edinburgh, 1895–8

Porter, R. K., *Travelling Sketches in Russia and Sweden*, 2 vols, 1809

Postel, Guillaume, *Des histoires orientales*, ed. Jacques Rollet, Istanbul, 1999

Potocka, Mary Margaret, 'Memoirs', unpublished manuscript

Potocki, Alfred, *Master of Lancut*, 1959

Pottle, Frederick A., ed., *Boswell on the Grand Tour*, 1953

Poullada, Leon B., *Reform and Rebellion in Afghanistan 1919–1929*, 1973

Powell, Anthony, *Faces in my Time*, 1980

Prebble, John, *The King's Jaunt. George IV in Scotland August 1822*, 1988

Preston, Paul, *Franco*, 1993

Procédure criminelle instruite au Châtelet de Paris, 2 vols, 1790

Purdy, Daniel L., *The Tyranny of Elegance: Consumer Cosmopolitanism in the Age of Goethe*, Baltimore, 1998

Quataert, Donald, 'Clothing Laws, State and Society in the Ottoman Empire 1720–1829', *International Journal of Midlle Eastern Sudies*, XXIX, 1997

Rahman, Abdur, Emir, *Autobiography*, 2 vols, 1900

Rambuteau, Comte de, *Mémoires*, 1903

Ramel, Stig, *Gustaf Mauritz Armfelt, fondateur de la Finlande*, 1999

Rangström, Lena, ed., *Hovets dräkter*, Stockholm, 1994

——, *Kläder för tid och ewighet*, Stockholm, 1997

——, *1766. Le Roi se marie*, 2001

Rasponi, Comtesse, *Souvenirs d'enfance*, 1929

Raymond, Joan, 'An Eye-witness to Cromwell', *History Today*, 47, 7, July 1997

Rebentisch, Jost, *Die viele Gesichte des Kaisers Willhelm II in der deutschen und britischen Karicatur*, Berlin, 2000

Reck-Malleczewen, Friedrich, *Diary of a Man in Despair*, 2000

Reiset, Viscomte de, *Louise d'Esparbès, comtesse de Polastron*, 1907

Remacle, Comte, ed., *Relations secrètes des agents de Louis XVIII à Paris sous le consulat (1802–1803)*, 1899

Rémusat, Madame de, *Mémoires*, 3 vols, 1880

Rennell, Tony, *The Death of Queen Victoria: Last Days of Glory*, 2001

Reresby, Sir John, *Memoirs*, 1875

Riasanovsky, N. V., *Nicholas I and Official Nationality in Russia, 1825–1855*, Cambridge, 1959

Ribeiro, Aileen, *The Art of Dress. Fashion in England and France 1750 to 1820*, 1995

——, *Fashion in the French Revolution*, 1998

——, *Dress in Eighteenth-Century Europe*, 2000 edn

Richie, Alexandra, *Faust's Metropolis*, 1998

Riedel, Georg, *Die deutschen Reichs- und königlichen preussischen Staats- und Hofbeamten-Uniformen*, Berlin, 1974

Rifki Atay, Falïh, *The Atatürk I Knew*, Ankara, 1982

Rinieri, Ilario, ed., *Corrispondenza inedita dei Cardinali Consalvi e Pacca*, Turin, 1903

Ristell, C. F., *Characters and Anecdotes of the Court of Sweden*, 2 vols, 1790

Roberts, Claire, ed., *Evolution and Revolution. Chinese Dress 1700s–1900s*, Sydney, 1997

Roberts, Michael, *Essays in Swedish History*, 1967

Robins, Joseph, *Champagne and Silver Buckles: The Viceregal Court at Dublin Castle 1700–1922*, Dublin, 2001

Roche, Daniel, *The Culture of Clothing. Dress and Fashion in the Ancien Régime*, 1994

——, ed., *Voitures, chevaux et attelages de XVIe au XIXe siècle*, 2000

——, ed., *Le Cheval et la guerre*, 2002

Rodenbeck, John, 'Dressing Native', in Paul and Janet Starkey, eds, *Unfolding the Orient. Travellers in Egypt and the Near East*, Reading, 2001

Rodinson, Maxime, *Muhammad*, 2002 edn

Rogers, J. M., ed., *The Topkapi Saray Museum. Costumes, Embroideries and Other Textiles*, 1986

——, and Rachel Ward, *Suleyman the Magnificent*, 1988

Röhl, John C. G., 'The Emperor's New Clothes', in John C. G. Röhl, ed., *Kaiser Wilhelm II: New Interpretations*, 1982

——, *Wilhelm II, the Kaiser's Personal Monarchy 1888–1900*, Cambridge, 2004

Rolfs, Richard W., *The Sorcerer's Apprentice: The Life of Franz von Papen*, 1996

Rose, Kenneth, *King George V*, 1983 edn

Rosebery, Lord, *Napoleon: The Last Phase*, 1928 edn

Ruppert, Jacques, *et al.*, *Le Costume français*, 1996

Rush, Richard, *A Residence at the Court of London*, 1987

Ryder, Dudley, *Diary*, 1939

Sahlberg, Gardar, *Murder at the Masked Ball*, 1974

Saint-Simon, Duc de, *Mémoires*, Pléiade edn, 8 vols, 1959

Sainty, J. C. and R. O. Buchholz, *Officials of the Royal Household 1660–1837*, 1997

Salih Arif Pasha, Mahmud, *Les Anciens Costumes de l'Empire Ottoman depuis l'origine de la monarchie jusqu'à la réforme du Sultan Mahmoud*, 1863

Salmon, Xavier, ed., *De soie et de poudre. Portraits de cour dans l'Europe des lumières*, Arles, 2002

Salvadori, Philippe, *La Chasse sous l'ancien régime*, 1996

Salvandy, N. A. de, 'Une Fête au Palais-Royal', in *Paris, ou le Livre des cent et un*, 15 vols, 1831–5

Samoyault-Verlet, Colombe, and Pierre Samoyault, *Château de Fontainebleau. Musée Napoléon 1er*, 1986

Sapori, Michelle, *Rose Bertin, Ministre des modes de Marie-Antoinette*, 2003

Saule, Béatrix, *Versailles triomphant. Une journée de Louis XIV*, 1996

Saussure, César de, *A Foreign View of England in the Reigns of George I and George II*, 1902

Sayer, Eleanor A., *Goya and the Spirit of Enlightenment*, Boston, 1989

Scarce, Jennifer, *Women's Costume of the Near and Middle East*, 1987

Scarisbrick, Diana, *Ancestral Jewels*, 1989

Schloss Halbthurn, *Uniform und Mode am Kaiserhof*, Vienna, 1983

Schüddekopf, Otto-Ernst, *Herrliche Kaiserzeit. Deutschland 1871–1914*, Frankfurt, 1973

Schultz, Kirsten, *Tropical Versailles. Empire, Monarchy and the Portuguese Royal Court in Rio de Janeiro 1808–1821*, New York, 2002

Scott, M., 'The New China', in Annette B. Weiner and Jane Schneider, eds, *Cloth and Human Experience*, Washington, 1989

Sebag Montefiore, Simon, *Prince of Princes. The Life of Potemkin*, 2000

——, *Stalin. The Court of the Red Tsar*, 2003

Séguy, Philippe, *Histoire des modes sous l'Empire*, 1998

Senior, Nassau William, *Conversations with M. Thiers, M. Guizot, and Other Distinguished Persons, during the Second Empire*, 2 vols, 1878

Sergeant, Harriet, *Shanghai*, 1991

Sestini, Domenico, *Lettres…écrites à ses amis en Toscane*, 3 vols, 1789

Setterwall, Ake *et al.*, *The Chinese Pavilion at Drottningholm*, Malmo, 1974

Sévigné, Madame de, *Lettres*, 1891 edn

Shaw, Stanford J., *Between Old and New: The Ottoman Empire under Sultan Selim III, 1789–1807*, Cambridge, Mass., 1971

Sheehy, Jeanne, *The Rediscovery of Ireland's Past: The Celitc Revival 1830–1930*, 1980

Sheridan Allen, William, *The Nazi Seizure of Power*, rev. edn, 1989

Shifman, Barry, and Guy Walton, eds, *Gifts to the Tsars 1500–1700. Treasures from the Kremlin*, New York, 2001

Sigismund III – Sobieski-Stanislaus, Schlosshof, 1990

Sint Nicolaas, Eveline *et al.*, *An Eyewitness of the Tulip Era. Jean Baptiste Vanmour*, Istanbul, 2003

Sked, Alan, *The Decline and Fall of the Habsburg Empire 1815–1918*, 1989

Skidelsky, Robert, *Oswald Mosley*, 1990 edn

Smith, Douglas, ed. and tr., *Love and Conquest: Personal Correspondence of Catherine the Great and Prince Grygory Potemkin*, De Kalby, 2004

Smith, Howard R., *The Last Train from Berlin*, 2000 edn

Smollet, Tobias, *Travels through France and Italy*, Oxford, 1981

Smuts, Malcolm, *Court Culture and the Origins of a Royalist Tradition in Early Stuart England*, Philadelphia, 1987

Snowman, A. Kenneth, *Eighteenth Century Gold Boxes of Europe*, 1966

Soames, Mary, ed., *Speaking for Themselves: The Personal Letters of Winston and Clementine Churchill*, 1999 edn

——, *Clementine Churchill*, rev. edn, 2003

Söderhjelm, Alma, *Fersen et Marie-Antoinette*, 1934

——, ed., *Marie-Antoinette et Barnave. Correspondance secrète*, 1934

Solnon, Jean-François, *La Cour de France*, 1987

Somerset, Anne, *Ladies-in-Waiting*, 1984

Speck, W.A., *The Butcher*, Oxford, 1989

Spiel, Hilde, *Vienna's Golden Autumn*, 1987

Squire, Gwen, *Livery Buttons. The Pitt Collection*, Pullborough, 1976

St John, James, *Letters from…to a Gentleman in the South of Ireland*, 2 vols, Dublin, 1788

Staël, Madame de, *Considérations sur la révolution française*, 1983 edn

Staniland, Kay, *In Royal Fashion*, 1997

Stargadt, Nicholas, *The German Idea of Militarism*, Cambridge, 1994

Stendhal, *Oeuvres intimes*, 1955

Stevenson, Pauline, *Edwardian Fashion*, 1980

Stirling, A. M., *Coke of Norfolk and his Friends*, 2 vols, 1907–11

Stone, Laurence, *The Family, Sex and Marriage in England 1500–1800*, rev. edn, 1978

Stoney, Benita, and Heinrich Weltzien, eds, *My Mistress the Queen: The Letters of Frieda Arnold, Dresser to Queen Victoria 1854–9*, 1994

Streidt, Gert, and Peter Feierabend, eds, *Prussia. Art and Architecture*, 1999

Sturmer, Michael, *The German Century*, 1999

Swaine, Major General Sir Leopold V., *Camp and Chancery in a Soldier's Life*, 1926

Swift, Jonathan, *Journal to Stella*, 1923 edn

Swinburne, Henry, *Travels through Spain in the Years 1775 and 1776*, 1779

——, *Memoirs of the Courts of Europe*, 2 vols, 1895

Sykes, Sir Percy, *Ten Thousand Miles in Persia*, 1902

Symcox, Geoffrey, *Victor Amadeus II. Absolutism in the Savoyard State 1675–1730*, 1983

Talleyrand, Bibliothèque Nationale, 1965

Tarasova, Nina, 'The Cult of Peter the Great', *Hermitage*, 1, Summer 2004

Taszycka, Mari, and Manfred Holst, 'Symbols of Nationhood. History of the Polish Sash', *Hali*, 84, 2001

Taylor, Ernest, ed., *The Taylor Papers*, 1913

Taylor, Lou, *Mourning Dress*, 1983

Tchelebi, Evliya, *La Guerre des Turcs*, Arles, 2000

Textilmuseum, *Nach Rang und Stand. Deutsche Ziviluniformen im 19. Jahrhundert*, Krefeld, 2002

Tezcan, Hulya, *A Late 19th Century Tailor's Order Book*, Istanbul, 1992

Thackeray, W. M., *Vanity Fair*, 1933 edn

Thayer, William Roscoe, *The Life and Times of Cavour*, 2 vols, 1911

Thiébault, Dieudonné, *Souvenirs de vingt ans de séjour à Berlin*, 2 vols, 1860

Tilly, Comte Alexandre de, *Mémoires*, 1965

Tillyard, Stella, *Citizen Lord*, 1997

Tomlinson, Janis A., *Goya in the Twilight of Enlightenment*, 1992

Topham, Anne, *Memories of the Kaiser's Court*, 1914

Topkapi Palace, *The Sultan's Portrait. Picturing the House of Osman*, Istanbul, 2000

Trénard, Louis, *Lyon de l'Encyclopédie au romantisme*, 1958

Trendell, Herbert A. P., *Dress and Insignia worn at His Majesty's Court*, 1921

Trevor-Roper, Hugh, 'The Highland Tradition of Scotland', in Eric Hobsbawm and Terence Ranger, eds, *The Invention of Tradition*, 1983

Tricornet, Baron de, *Mémoires*, 2 vols, Besançon, 1894

Trollope, Frances, *Vienna and the Austrians*, 2 vols, 1838

Truedsell, Mathew, *Spectacular Politics: Louis-Napoleon Bonaparte and the Fête Impériale, 1849–1870*, New York, 1997

Twiss, Richard, *A Trip to Paris in July and August 1792*, 1793

Tyden Jordan, Astrid, *Queen Christina's Coronation Coach*, Stockholm, 1988

Unser Kaiser. Fünf und zwanzig Jahre der Regierung Kaiser Wilhelms II 1888–1913, Berlin, 1913

Unter einer Krone. Kunst und Kultur der sächsisch-polnischen Union, Leipzig, 1997

Urbach, Karina, *Bismarck's Favourite Englishman. Lord Odo Russell's Mission to Berlin*, 1999

Vale, Malcolm, *The Princely Court: Medieval Courts and Culture in North-West Europe 1270–1380*, Oxford, 2001

Vanier, Henriette, *La Mode et ses métiers: frivolités et luttes des classes*, 1960

Vansittart, Jane, *Surgeon James's Journal 1815*, 1964

Vatin, Nicholas, and Gilles Veinstein, *Le Sérail ébranlé: essai sur les morts, dépositions et avènements des sultans ottomans XIV–XIXe siècle*, 2003

Vaublanc, Comte de, *Mémoires*, 1857

Vickers, Hugo, *Alice, Princess Andrew of Greece*, 2001 edn

Villèle, Comte de, *Mémoires et correspondance*, 5 vols, 1888–96

Villiers, Hon. Katharine, *Memoirs of a Maid of Honour*, 1931

Vingtrinier, Emmanuel, *La Contre-révolution*, 2 vols, 1924–5

Visconti, Primi, *Mémoires sur la cour de Louis XIV 1673–1681*, 1998 edn

Voorhies, James Timothy, ed., *My Dear Stieglitz. Letters of Marsden Hartley and Alfred Stieglitz 1912–1915*, South Carolina, 2002

Waddington, Albert, *Histoire de Prusse*, 2 vols, 1911–22

Wagner, Gretel, *Der bunte Rock in Preussen*, Berlin, 1989

Waite, Robert G. L., *Vanguard of Nazism. The Freecorps Movement in Postwar Germany 1918–1923*, Cambridge, Mass., 1952

Walker, Richard, *The Savile Row Story*, 1988

Walpole, Horace, *Correspondence*, 48 vols, New Haven and London, 1970–87

Walsh, Revd R., *A Residence at Constantinople*, 2 vols, 1836

Wandruszka, Adam, *The House of Habsburg*, 1964

Wardle, Patricia, *For Our Royal Person. Master of the Robes' Bills of King-Stadholder William III*, Apeldoorn, 2002

Waresquiel, Emmanuel de, and Benoît Yvert, 'Le duc de Richelieu et le comte Decazes d'après leur correspondance inédite', *Revue de la société d'histoire de la restauration*, II, 1988

——, *Talleyrand ou le prince immobile*, 2003

Watanabe O'Kelly, Helen, *Court Culture in Dresden from Renaissance to Baroque*, 2002

Waterfield, Giles, and Anne French, *Below Stairs. 400 Years of Servants' Portraits*, 2003

Waterfield, Gordon, *Professional Diplomat*, 1973

Watkins, Thomas, *Travels through Swisserland, Italy, Sicily, the Greek Islands to Constantinople . . . in the Years 1787, 1788, 1789*, 2 vols, 1792

Watson, F. J., 'The Choiseul Box', in A. Kenneth Snowman, ed., *Eighteenth Century Gold Boxes in Europe*, 1966

Wentworth, Thomas, *The Wentworth Papers 1705–1739*, ed. James J. Cartwright,1883

[Weston, Stephen], *Two Sketches of France, Belgium and Spa during the Summers of 1771 and 1816*, 1817

Wheatcroft, Geoffrey, *The Controversy of Zion*, 1996

Wheeler-Bennett, Sir John, *Three Episodes in the Life of Kaiser Wilhelm II*, 1955

——, *King George VI*, 1958

——, *Hindenburg: Wooden Titan*, 1967 edn

——, *Friends, Enemies and Sovereigns*, 1976

Whitworth Art Gallery, *Historic Hungarian Costume from Budapest*, Manchester, 1979

Wilber, Donald N., *Riza Shah Pahlavi*, Hicksville, 1975

Wilcox, R. Turner, *Folk and Festival Costume of the World*, 1989 edn

Wilhelm II, *My Early Life*, 1973 edn

Wilson, Harriette, *Harriet Wilson's Memoirs*, ed. Lesley Blanch, 2003 edn

Wilson, Peter H., *German Armies. War and German Politics 1648–1806*, 1998

Windsor, Duke of, *A Family Album*, 1960

Windsor Sale, The, 2 vols, New York, 1998

Wolzogen, Wilhelm von, *Journal de voyage à Paris*, Lille, 1998

Woolf, Virginia, *Three Guineas*, 1938

Worth, Jean Philippe, *A Century of Fashion*, Boston, 1928

Wortman, Richard A., *Scenarios of Power: Myth and Ceremony in Russian Monarchy*, 2 vols, 1995–2000

Wrigley, Richard, *The Politics of Appearances. Representations of Dress in Revolutionary France*, Oxford, 2002

Zakim, Michael, *Ready-made Democracy: A History of Men's Dress in the American Republic 1760–1860*, Chicago, 2003

Zamoyski, Adam, *The Polish Way*, 1987

Zedlitz-Trützschler, Count Robert, *Twelve Years at the Imperial German Court*, 1924

Zieseniss, Jérôme, *Berthier, frère d'armes de Napoléon*, 1985

Zilfi, Madeleine C., 'Whose Laws? Gendering the Ottoman Sumptuary Regime', in Suraiya Faroqhi and Christoph K. Newmann, eds, *Ottoman Costumes from Textile to Identity*, Istanbul, 2004

Zilkha, Ezra K., with Ken Emerson, *From Baghdad to Boardroom*, New York, 1999

Index